The Eugene

Register-Guard

A Citizen of Its Community

The Eugene Register-Guard

A Citizen of Its Community

Volume I

by

Warren C. Price

Binford & Mort

Thomas Binford, Publisher

2536 S.E. Eleventh • Portland, Oregon 97202

The Eugene Register-Guard

Printed in the United States of America

First Edition 1976

Library of Congress Cataloging in Publication Data
Price, Warren C. 1908-1967
The Eugene Register-Guard

Bibliography: p.
Includes index.
1. Eugene Register-Guard. I. Title.
Pn4899.E85E87 071'.95'31 76-15203
ISBN 0-8323-0271-6 (v. 1)

To Lillian

FOREWORD

A newspaper, like the news in its columns, is unbalanced, uneven, inconsistent. It would be fine if we could record the story of any single newspaper as a simple chronological account, weigh its influence according to the accomplishments of its publishers and editors, or look up in catalogued records the important events that marked its past.

It doesn't work that way. Whether it be the New York *Times* or Eugene *Register-Guard,* information that is vital is often difficult to come by. This is particularly so for the frontier, Pacific slope Oregon newspaper that is the subject of this book. The Eugene City *Guard,* now *Register-Guard,* passed age 100 as this record was in preparation. And it may be accurate to say that almost everything known about it is a product of memory of its staff members, of what its files contain, of scattered entries that mention the newspaper in accounts of Eugene and Lane County, and, frankly, of chance.

The history of a newspaper like the *Guard,* which started on nothing—and but for chance remained almost nothing—"is where you find it."

Yet this ragged sheet of 1867 is regarded in 1967 as one of the status newspapers of the Pacific Coast, most certainly of Oregon. Some call it "Oregon's best newspaper," even though it is not a metropolitan newspaper and lacks Portland's potential. It has won no Pulitzer awards, but the *Register-Guard* is the only non-metropolitan newspaper outside Missouri ever to receive the University of Missouri School of Journalism's distinguished service award. It has received many more moderate honors, and in recent years its staff members have been recognized individually by numerous state and national organizations.

Nearly 50 years ago a little magazine called *Oregon Exchanges* was started by the University of Oregon School of Journalism as a means of broadening and strengthening the state's press by interchange of information. *Oregon Exchanges* was the predecessor of the present *Oregon Publisher.* In the first issue an anonymous writer, possibly the late Dean Eric W. Allen, wrote:

> A JOURNALIST'S HISTORY— There is a great opening for some man who can take the history of the newspapers of the Northwest and write a short snappy chronicle of events. . . .What is needed is a book giving the important events in the workings of the press, something giving the dates and places, together with the men who were instrumental in making the newspaper business what it is today. (*Oregon Exchanges*, Vol. 1, No. 5, p. 10, March 1918.)

George S. Turnbull, professor of journalism, took up this challenge in 1939 with his *History of Oregon Newspapers.* A fiftieth anniversary history of Portland's *Oregon Journal* was written by Marshall N. Dana in 1952, but no full-length history of any of the state's few centennial newspapers has heretofore been published, including the Portland *Oregonian.* A doctoral thesis has been done on Harvey W. Scott but no published biography of the distinguished *Oregonian* editor has appeared.

This book, then, is the first in Oregon recounting 100 years of a single newspaper—really of two papers, since the Eugene *Register* was consolidated with the parent *Guard* in 1930. The book isn't "short," and it isn't "snappy," though it may have snappy spots. Yet it chronicles events that include what in Eugene and Western Oregon made headlines in their time: suppression of *Guard* predecessors in the Civil War, the disputed presidential election of 1876, University of Oregon struggles for survival, battles to build a finer City of Eugene, and changes in *Guard* and *Register* ownerships.

Names in the story range from Eugene's Copperhead Joaquin Miller of the 1860s to her obstreperous Wayne Morse of the 1960s; from the paper's incompetent founder John B. Alexander in 1867 to her dedicated Alton F. Baker, Jr., in 1967, the son of the senior Alton Baker who after 1927 made the modern *Register-Guard* possible. And then there is the late William M. Tugman, the metropolitan reporter-turned-small-city-editor who came to Eugene a few weeks after Alton Baker, Sr. The two had their hands in almost everything that would benefit the town for nearly 30 years.

Information for this history came from scattered sources, mostly the files, and from interviews with staff members and old residents of Eugene. General histories of the city put the newspapers into a general context, and often that is not much. Almost nothing substantial is listed in card catalogs, for the *Guard* editors and publishers were not writers, except as they wrote for the paper. Only one publisher ever wrote a book. He was William Thompson, an Indian-fighter friend of Joaquin Miller who edited the *Guard* for a year in 1869 and wrote a nostalgic autobiography in 1912. Much of the interpretation that follows is based on my own insight, such as it is, on the basis of a quarter century of my own in Eugene.

I owe much to Alton Baker, Jr., and Edwin M. Baker, both of whom opened *Guard* records and correspondence to me. And I appreciate the help of William L. Wasmann, Robert B. Frazier, and Albert H. Currey, all of whom were my students a score of years ago and who today are carrying on the news and editorial policies where William M. Tugman left off. I wish to thank the rest of the *Register-Guard's* staff, too, collectively and singly. So, also, did newspaper men of Oregon help in their views of the newspaper and former residents of Eugene who, years after departure, remember the paper's contributions.

The University of Oregon made possible the block of time necessary for this work, particularly John L. Hulteng, dean of the School of Journalism, who supported a sabbatical leave for me. As it has done many times in my Oregon service, the University of Oregon Library opened many paths. Among those who helped were Martin Schmitt, curator of special collections; Eugene Barnes, acquisitions librarian, who listened to all of this as it grew; Elizabeth Findly, reference librarian; and Frances Schoen, newspaper collections librarian. Without Mrs. Schoen's sharp eye we might still not know the exact date on which the *Guard* was born in 1867—an elusive matter never specifically tracked down until this history was well under way.

WARREN C. PRICE
School of Journalism
University of Oregon, Eugene

CONTENTS

Credit: Insert photo, Page 271, courtesy Therkelsen Collection, University of Oregon Library.

INTRODUCTION

This history of the first hundred years of the Eugene *Register-Guard* was interrupted by the death of Warren C. Price on May 8, 1967.

The entire work was to have been completed and published by the autumn of that year, in time for the centennial of the *Register-Guard.* Price had written all but the final 15 years of the paper's history. He had completed his fact-gathering and had in mind a title appropriate for a 100-year history. The final chapters would be an account of the "new *Guard*", its new people, new printing plant on High Street, its new place of prominence in the journalism of the Northwest.

In the years between 1967 and the present, several attempts were made to fill in the blank chapters of those 15 years. University of Oregon Journalism School faculty members who qualified for the task because of their knowledge of the *Register-Guard* had commitments too demanding to permit the additional burden of finishing the work. Two attempts by a staff writer to complete the history were ultimately rejected, despite their obvious worth, because the best-respected newspaper histories have always been compiled by impartial observers. Price gained much of his extensive knowledge of the *Register-Guard* while a staff member, but for a respectable period of years before he wrote his history he had had no direct affiliation with the paper.

Long deliberation led finally to the conclusion that the Price manuscript, although not the hundred-year history originally envisioned, was nevertheless, a complete book that ended logically with the final days of Alton Baker, Sr., and William M. Tugman. The editing of the manuscript entailed a minimum number of changes, in the main the addition of a date or a few lines to include details which came to light after his death. Otherwise, it is HIS book from start to finish.

Some day in the future, the personalities and events of the "modern-day *Register-Guard*" will be given their place—in a Volume II—after those personalities and those events have proved themselves as worthy of historic notice as the personalities and occurrences of the first 85 years.

Finally, Price credited in the Foreword those who assisted him in his research and in the preparation of his manuscript. Many more persons—librarians, museum personnel, *Register-Guard* staff members past and present, and others too numerous to mention assisted, after Price's death, with the details of getting the book into print. A deep debt of gratitude is owed them.

William L. Wasmann
Eugene, Oregon
May 1976

The Eugene

Register-Guard

A Citizen of Its Community

Part One

CHAPTER 1

—1867—A Newspaper

"The first number of a paper called *The Guard*, published at Eugene City, has made its appearance. It is intensely Confederate, and we can see little use for such political papers since the surrender of Mr. Lee. *The Guard* may, however, be useful in other respects, and our hope is that it may be successful according to its deserts."

—*The Daily Oregonian*, Portland
Tuesday, June 4, 1867

The *Oregonian*, of course, was firmly Republican and it was not moved to cheer this journalistic development in Eugene City on Saturday, June 1, 1867. It put no headline on its item, which it sandwiched between two other six-line squibs: one on an Idaho judge who was passing through en route to a council with the Nez Perce Indians, the other on a different Democratic paper, the *Dispatch*, just started in Port Townsend, Washington Territory. The *Oregonian* couldn't have approved of the *Dispatch* any more than the *Guard*, but it made no snide remarks about how little the *Dispatch* would be of use.[1]

The name of the *Guard's* founder was John B. Alexander. The *Oregonian* must have known that, for Alexander had had previous experience—none of it successful—with Democratic newspapers in Eugene City. Yet the Portland paper didn't deign to mention Alexander's name. The strong-minded Harvey W. Scott was not one to recognize a pro-Confederate political editor who was starting up another opposition newspaper only two years after the fate of the Democratic Party had been settled on the battlefield.

For that matter, the other paper in Eugene City at the time, Harrison R. Kincaid's Republican *Oregon State Journal*, didn't mention the new *Guard* at all, although Kincaid did make some remarks about Democratic editors having "rump on the brain." [2]

A hundred years later the *Guard*—as does the *Oregonian*—still publishes. It thereby has fulfilled the Portland paper's shrug that it succeed "according to its deserts." Only four other Oregon newspapers dating back to June 1, 1867, have completed the full century with *Guard* and *Oregonian.* All the rest have died, been liquidated, or been so buried through consolidation with competitor sheets as to be no longer recognizable.

This cursory *Oregonian* announcement, however, did accomplish one thing of moment in Oregon's newspaper history. The *Oregonian's* long dormant file in the winter of 1967 verified the true birth date of the Eugene City *Guard.* No copies of any *Guards* published in 1867 have been located in the State of Oregon. The oldest *Guard* in any Oregon library is that of November 21, 1868: Volume 2, No. 5. But, fortuitously, a scattered set of 12 copies of Volume 1 were located in the Bancroft Library of the University of California. The earliest of these, Volume 1, Number 7, was dated Saturday, July 13, 1867, which would logically date the first issue back to June 1. But even this was uncertain, for frontier publishers were grievously erratic in their sequence of issues.

Then came the search of the *Oregonian* and the finding of those buried lines in the issue of June 4. The *Guard* therefore now knows when it was delivered. Nevertheless, finding this straggling fact is not as important to Oregon as the circumstance that the *Guard* survived at all. The *Oregonian* had frontier history and logic on its side when it put out the news about the *Guard* with a dim prospectus.

For the moment let us pass up the details of the *Guard's* birth and publisher Alexander and pursue them later in the due course of our story.

1967—A FLASHBACK

The Eugene *Register-Guard* as a backdrop to its conservative Old English logotype has carried for nearly 40 years a line-etching of the peaks of the Oregon Cascades. Represented here are The Three Sisters mountains, which occasionally can be seen from the Willamette Valley, 60 to 75 miles to the west and 10,000 feet below.

The *R-G's* nameplate is a matter of sentiment and pride with its centennial year publishers. Typographically it is dignified and beautiful, but dignity and beauty do not always mesh with heavy Cheltenham news headlines that too often report world tragedy. The clash in tone, however, is minor and the *Register-Guard*, today "Lane County's Home Newspaper," seldom subordinates its name beneath banner headlines—unless the news is monumental. What the Three Sisters do is to add a fitting geographical touch. One could argue of course that, Lane County being almost the size of Connecticut and the *Guard* [3] serving the whole of it, some artistic concession should be made to Oregon's Pacific Coast. After all, the paper circulates "from lava beds to ocean sand dunes."

The mountain background is nevertheless the proper one, since Cascades and Coast could hardly be joined in a single logotype. And however the newspaper's present owners might have decided upon this view to depict Eugene's setting—which first appeared May 17, 1928—there is history wrapped in the mountain view. Joaquin Miller, "Poet of the Sierras," who wrote for Eugene City newspapers five years before the *Guard* was born, set the literary stage for the paper's tribute to Eugene's and Oregon's grandeur. Miller as a boy of 13 had come to Oregon from Indiana in 1852 and was deeply impressed, although he gilded things when he wrote, "My cradle was a covered wagon, pointed west." [4] When the Miller family reached The Dalles on the Columbia River, the poet wrote many years later a description of what he saw.

> ". . . Papa went to see the officer in command of this military post, the first one we had found, to ask about the possibility of crossing the Cascade Mountains, or rather, the *Sierra Grande del Nord*, at that late season of the year.

> "This kind officer sent a yoke of strong fat oxen and two soldiers to see us to the summit. His name, we were told, was Grant—Capt. U.S. Grant, afterward President Grant. By taking this route papa landed his little family far up the Willamette River almost in the heart of the wonderful valley.[5] This is the most poetic, gorgeous, and glorious valley in flowers and girdle of snow-crowned mountains on the globe, and it is as fertile as it is beautiful." [6]

Miller's words were written years before the *Register-Guard's* nameplate was designed, but his emotions have been felt by thousands in the 115 years since his arrival. No Oregon editor ever fails to make the most of his setting journalistically, even though he knows geographical wonders cannot make great newspapers. It took decades for the Eugene *Guard*, later the Eugene *Register*, and finally the consolidated Eugene *Register-Guard* to combine location, population growth, social and economic development, political changes, and journalistic talent so that Joaquin Miller's "wonderful valley" would have one of the outstanding middle-sized newspapers in the Pacific Northwest.

The *Guard* is now 100 years old, its *Register* counterpart is 83 years old, and the consolidation 40 years old.[7] It is only the sixth Oregon newspaper to observe a centennial. This fact in itself indicates what the struggle to survive through the early years must have been. Between 1846, when the *Spectator* of Oregon City became the first newspaper on the Pacific Coast, and 1870, some 111 newspapers were established in Oregon.[8] By 1876 only 44 of the 111 were left. And of these 44 it appears that 14 were founded between 1870 and 1876. No more than 30 could be said accurately to have been still in existence after Oregon's first quarter-century.

Of those newspapers launched in the early years and that managed to survive to 1876 and to continue to today, the five that preceded the *Guard* are: the *Oregonian* of Portland (as a weekly in 1850 and daily in 1861), *Oregon Statesman* of Salem

(1851), *Democrat-Herald* of Albany (1859 as the *States Rights Democrat*), *Gazette-Times* of Corvallis (1862 as the *Gazette*), and *Enterprise-Courier* of Oregon City (1866 as the *Enterprise*).[9] Except for the history of the *Guard* presented here, accounts of the other 100-year-old newspapers have not yet been put into book form.

The record that follows represents an effort to put down as accurately as possible, using sources that for early years are frequently unreliable, the chronology of how the *Guard* got to 1967; the many troubles it faced, particularly in the frequency with which it changed hands; what its Eugene community was like, then and now; and the personalities, major and minor, who wrote for it and edited it. Much must be truncated and in many cases we can portray only a series of vignettes. Much also will be handled in extensive detail, for there were distinctive high points. The composite gives an overview of a living enterprise.

But first we should say something about the present-day *Register-Guard.*

1967—The '*R-G*': CITIZEN

On February 12, 1929, the then Eugene *Guard* adopted an editorial-page statement of purpose that it still carries on its masthead, "A Newspaper Is a Citizen of Its Community." At the time the personification was not explained, it being only a boxed insertion along with the names of Alton F. Baker, publisher, and William M. Tugman, managing editor. Alton Baker in early 1929 had owned the *Guard* less than two years, and it would be another 21 months before he would purchase the *Register.* The *Register-Guard* in 1967 spells out its "Citizen" concept formally:

"The *Register-Guard's* policy is the complete and impartial publication in its news pages of all news and statements on news. On this page, the editors of the *Register-*

> *Guard* offer their opinions on events of the day and matters of importance to the community, endeavoring to be candid but fair and helpful in the development of constructive community policy. A NEWSPAPER IS A CITIZEN OF ITS COMMUNITY."[10]

This is a commitment to independence, objectivity in news and attention to the home environment, an ideal we will not find in the pioneer *Guard* or *Register* for many years after each had been founded; and certainly the principle was never thought of in the short-lived sheets that were begun before 1867. The "citizen-of-its community" declaration is a modern-day one that grew out of many years of journalistic experience. The *Register-Guard* is only one of numerous fair-minded, well-balanced newspapers of 1967 that started out in the days of the personal and political press and slowly—sometimes too slowly—developed a sense of responsibility. In the Eugene *Guard* and the Eugene *Register* we shall notice a strong direction toward Alton Baker's principle in the *Register's* ownership that started in 1899 and the *Guard's* ownership that started in 1906, although the publishers then did not express themselves so explicitly.

A community-minded purpose presumes, too, a city and county concerned with its own growth and development and appreciative of a forward-looking newspaper. The two, newspaper and city, go together. Not all American cities with long-established newspapers have been as fortunate as Eugene, Oregon, in growth potential; nor, among those that have been favored, has a newspaper of the *Register-Guard's* stature grown in parallel. When city or city and county don't exist in some sort of balance with the press we have conditions in which the newspaper is of better quality than the community deserves—and perhaps is unappreciated; or conditions in which the community suffers because of poor local journalism. Vocal critics of the press are inclined to say the second condition more often holds. When the first exists, however, and it frequently does, it exists because the newspaper has a fair-minded and strong-minded publisher.

As the *Guard's* century unfolded the combination of city and county and newspaper worked out remarkably well: growing Oregon, especially Western Oregon; ideal conditions of climate, except for those few who refused to adjust to heavy winter rainfall; highly literate population; unlimited economic potential; magnificent natural surroundings; basically liberal political institutions; and, for Eugene, the site of what has become a major West Coast university. Further, the *Guard* and the *Register*, for more than a third of the *Guard's* century and 25 of the *Register's* first years, were not even the most distinguished of Eugene's newspapers.[11] They were the ones that survived, and when consolidation forces in 1930 brought them together the combined paper quickly dominated the scene. In Eugene's journalistic history, totaling 109 years from 1858 to 1967, more than 25 newspapers competed at one time or another and played a part in making the city what it is today.[12] Those who enjoy clichés like to call the Eugene of today the center of Oregon's *Emerald Empire*, an expression that, hearsay has it, Joaquin Miller first used. As part of its recognition of its favored region, the *Register-Guard* now publishes a Sunday magazine section under the title *Emerald Empire*. It is staff-produced, a rarity for magazine sections among newspapers of the *R-G's* size; in a way it reveals affluence put to use in an excellent way.

1867—EUGENE CITY

What was the town like in the years before the *Guard* was founded?

Eugene City,[13] established in 1846 by Eugene Skinner, one of hundreds of settlers looking for homes in the Oregon Country, lay originally within what became known as Skinner's Donation Claim. This was a triangular site bounded by the present-day Monroe Street on the west, Eighth Avenue on the south, and the Willamette River as a hypotenuse on the east and north. Skinner's Butte Park abuts the river in the north-central portion of the plat. Skinner when he arrived was 37 years old and had come to Oregon from New York and Illinois. When the town itself was laid out within his claim, grandiously named Eugene City, and chosen as the county seat of Lane County—all between 1851 and 1853—it covered only 20 to 24 square blocks: south along the present Pearl Street from the river to Seventh Avenue and then east to the river and the diagonal. The designation given it by those who saw no future for the place was "Skinner's Mud Hole." Decades later, when Eugene's most prominent editor of the early days, Harrison R. Kincaid, told how newspapers were distributed in winter, he made a point of mentioning that delivery had to be on horseback if carriers were to get through the sloughs.[14]

Whatever the rush of settlers to the Upper Willamette Valley was like in the 1850s, Eugene City seems from the vantage point of more than 100 years to have offered little promise of anything. It took some time, even, to get a crossing over the river near the location of the present Ferry Street Bridge. Skinner operated a ferry service himself for a time.

By 1858 (date of the first newspaper), the place had 500 to 600 inhabitants, and at the same time Eugene City's stronger boosters were saying, "The town is estimated to have a population of about two thousand souls, [and] they are a quiet, easygoing class."[15] The people were portrayed also as highly "moral," since Eugene City already had six evangelical churches valued at about $50,000.

Whatever the nature of its population, one has to agree that the young city was well located for agriculture, offered majestic scenery, provided water power in the foothills of the Willamette River, and—at the head of navigation—had the advantage of operating river steamers for freight to and from Portland. The steamers did manage to be in service "at least during the seasons of high water."[16]

Lumbering was also a part of the city's economic scene from the beginning, although Eugene City was not a lumbering center this early; the industry is not mentioned extensively in the history of this period.[17] A.G. Walling pays more attention to the desire to get a railroad, which arrived in the 1870s; to hotels (1855); flour mills (1856); a sash and door factory (1870); a tannery (1880); a bank and a woolen mill (1882); and, to a limited extent, the first newspapers (1858 on). Overall, the town was built on hope.

But hope was something a number of the pioneers did not have. Talk of incorporation didn't come until 1862, with sentiment in favor of it scanty, so that the Oregon Legislature delayed passage of a Eugene City act of incorporation until 1864. This the voters—with only a negligible turnout of strong advocates—did approve. The vote was 27-1 and the date October 22, 1864. At that moment Eugene City had already seen the births and deaths of six newspapers, including the one that had opposed incorporation.[18]

One of the arguments against formalizing Eugene City's government was this:

> "As to the maintaining a city government, merely to get rid of a few old sows that might perambulate the streets, that would be a very expensive way of accomplishing a small amount of good. . . .
>
> "There are always persons in every little village anxious to have it a city, and they are usually successful in getting the towns incorporated before they have enough population or wealth to maintain a city government."[19]

Such discouraging talk did not prevail. The newspaper that sounded this negative approach was gone by 1864. Within three more years the Eugene City *Guard* was under way. It survived.

---

1. The competing news: "PERSONAL—Judge Hough, of Idaho, who came passenger by the *Orifanne*, called on us yesterday. The judge will leave to-morrow for Ft. Lapwal, where he goes as special Indian agent to hold a council with the Nez Perce Indians, to induce them, if possible, to accept the treaty of 1863 as ratified by the Senate. The council will be held on the 10th inst."

"A NEW DEMOCRATIC NEWSPAPER—We have been shown the first issue of a new paper started at Port Townsend, W.T., under the proprietorship of Mr. Martin Cannavan, late a compositor in the *Farmer* job office, Portland. It is entitled *The Dispatch*, and is devoted to the interests of the Democratic ticket of Washington Territory."

2. *Oregon State Journal*, Eugene City, Saturday, June 8, 1867.

3. *The Register-Guard* in Eugene idiom is most frequently called the *Guard*. While the *Guard* was first to be established, *Register-Guard* may be more euphonious than *Guard-Register*. It is more probable that Alton F. Baker, Sr., in buying the *Register* in 1930 was showing a courtesy to a seller in putting his paper's name in the hyphenation ahead of the purchasing paper's name. The paper of 1967 bears only slight resemblance to the early *Register* but considerable resemblance to the more aggressive *Guard*.

4. Joaquin Miller, *Overland in a Covered Wagon: An Autobiography*, ed. by Sidney G. Firman. New York: D. Appleton & Company, 1930, p. 79.

5. Near Coburg, Oregon, about seven miles north of Eugene.

6. Miller, *op. cit.*, p. 78-79. (Miller was wrong about Grant; the future general was in the West at the time, but not at The Dalles.)

7. The *Register* of *Register-Guard* was actually the second Eugene City newspaper of that name; a *Democratic Register*, started in 1862 and soon suppressed, had no ownership connection with the later one. See p. 16.

8. Flora Belle Ludington, *The Newspapers of Oregon, 1846-1870*. Eugene, Oregon: Koke-Tiffany Company, 1925.

9. *Ayer Directory of Publications*, Philadelphia: Ayer Press, 1880-date. Ayer lists additionally as more than a century old the *Oregon Churchman* (Portland, 1861). This study, however, concerns general newspapers.

Ludington, *op. cit.*, p. 21. Numerous listings of founding dates in *Ayer*, further, are erroneous. At one time it carried the *Guard's* date as 1859.

10. Eugene *Guard*, February 12, 1929, editorial page; *Register-Guard*, editorial pages, 1967.

11. Eugene's most highly regarded newspaper from 1864 to 1909 was the weekly *Oregon State Journal*, edited by Harrison R. Kincaid. See pp. 29-36.

12. See Appendix for a longevity table for all newspapers published in Eugene.

13. Skinner's wife, Mary, named the city. Historical lore includes some stories that she chose her husband's first name because of possible *double entendre* over the surname. The "City" part was dropped in 1889. For the early years this history will use the Eugene City style insofar as possible.

14. "Beginnings of Oregon, an interview with Harrison R. Kincaid," *Oregon Exchanges*, School of Journalism, University of Oregon, Vol. 2, (April 1919), p. 13.

15. Albert G. Walling, *Illustrated History of Lane County Oregon*. Portland, Oregon: Walling Printing and Lithographing House, 1884. p. 392.

16. *Ibid.*, p. 393.

17. *Ibid.*, pp. 393-4.

18. *Ibid.*

19. *Ibid.*, quoting *Oregon State Republican* (1862); see pp. 26-28 for an account of this short-lived newspaper.

CHAPTER 2

Before The Guard: Nine Years, Ten Starts, Nine Stops

Pacific Journal

The newspaper mentioned most often as Eugene City's first was the *Pacific Journal*. Volume 1, issue No. 1 is dated June 26, 1858. Its editor was J.H. Rodgers and its publishers were Rodgers, Alexander Seavey and J.F. Wilson. Some sources indicate that a Eugene City *News* had been established as early as 1856 by John B. Alexander, who 11 years later founded the *Guard*.[1] The *Journal's* 19th issue of Volume 1, dated Oct. 30, 1858 still lists Rodgers as editor but the publisher is J.F. Wilson & Co.

There was a *News*, of which only one copy is on file in the University of Oregon Library, and the *News* was published by Alexander; but its date is June 9, 1866, Volume 1, Number 14. Unless Alexander made a false start in 1856 that cannot be verified, a 10-year error was made in listing the date of the *News'* founding. That Alexander made an error in listing his starting date seems to be substantiated by other sources and materials indicating the 1856 date—someplace between March and November—is correct.

Of the *Pacific Journal*, as of so many pioneer sheets, we know little. Walling's *Illustrated History of Lane County*, the only early record giving any substantial newspaper details, mentions that the *Journal* lived but a few months and that no files remained. Walling dates to 1884. However, the Lane County Pioneer Museum has microfilm copies of seven issues of the *Journal*.

Another source on the *Pacific Journal* notes that Professor Rodgers edited it as a "neutral paper." If this is accurate, the *Journal* was a newspaper oddity.[2] Even the politically supported ones had short enough lives. A third source, which may be the best, says the *Pacific Journal* was "devoted to Physical, Intellectual and Moral Improvement" and existed only a few months.[3] Then, after the paper had become Eugene City's first journalistic mortality, its plant went to the Eugene City *People's Press.* This fact seems to be substantiated.

Fred Lockley, a writer on Oregon history for the *Oregon Journal* of Portland in the 1920s, omits the *Pacific Journal* and the *People's Press* in discussing Eugene City's newspaper history and starts directly with the third paper, the *Democratic Herald.* Lockley, however, gave no rank position to the papers in the order of establishment.[4] Still another source on the early Eugene City press appears to make a double error, first by putting the can't-be-proved founding of the *News* of 1856 down as 1858, and second by stating that the "*Pacific Journal* became the *People's Press.*"[5] The transfer of a plant from one paper to another, common in pioneer days, does not make the second a lineal descendant of the first. Too many searchers for journalistic continuity have made this mistake. The *Guard* itself, as we shall see, was as recently as 1935 hitched back to the *Democratic Herald.*

The *Pacific Journal* simply began—and quickly died. Perhaps Hubert Howe Bancroft, the California entrepreneur, collector of Pacific Coast Americana, and historian, expressed the problem of the frontier press best when he wrote: "Many of them [the first newspapers in Oregon] had a brief existence, or so frequently changed their titles that it is difficult to follow them."[6]

The People's Press

What followed the *Pacific Journal*—and it was historically unfortunate for Eugene City that the second paper lived only two to three years—was a creditable newspaper. The *People's Press*[7] was the paper associated with Oregon's statehood period, Oregon being admitted to the Union as the thirty-third state February 14, 1859. The *People's Press* evidently was started sometime in January, 1859. It was strongly Republican, a necessity at the time to counteract strong Democratic, pro-Southern influences in pioneer Oregon. The editor was B.J. Pengra, while the owners were Hilyard Shaw and two associates named William and Hiram Smith.[8] Pengra and his brother, W.B. Pengra (not associated with the newspaper), became prominent residents of Lane County. B.J., through the *People's Press* and later through engineering and railroad activities, played a leading part in the young state; W.B. was active in saw mills, flour mills, and mining. The Pengra name more than a century later still carries entries in the Eugene telephone directory.

Pengra left the paper in 1860 to canvass Oregon as one of the Republican nominees for elector on the Lincoln presidential ticket; he turned the *People's Press* over to Joel Ware.[9] Ware in turn had a small part in the early days of the *Oregon State Journal*, to be founded in 1864. He is of little consequence in the *People's Press* account.[10]

In its Volume 1, Number 22, of June 22, 1859, the *People's Press* offered as its motto, "The Constitution as Expounded by the Fathers of the Republic," a statement broad enough to satisfy anyone. It was a standard-size paper of the time, four pages of five columns. It was issued on Tuesdays and carried in prominent position its subscription rates: "$3 per year in advance, $3.50 at six months, $4 at close, $1 additional for neglected payment." Warnings to subscribers against arrearages run through newspaper history from colonial times, with little effect. Many of the Oregon newspapers upon closing down blamed at least part of their failures upon the unwillingness of customers to pay up; or, if the papers didn't close, the publishers blamed subscribers for forcing changes in ownership. The *People's Press* charged $3 for one square of advertising (10 lines of body type).[11]

In his twenty-second issue Pengra had some fruitful sources of news. The tone of the paper was more moderate than that of the violent rhetoric of Oregon's outspoken political newspapers of the Civil War era.[12]

The *People's Press* carried a reasonable complement of foreign news, including accounts of politics in Austria and France and a report from Cochin China (the present-day embattled South Vietnam) dating back to January, 1859. National news in the form of reports by mail and lifts from other papers included a column reporting resolutions of the Pennsylvania Democratic Convention in Harrisburg opposing "Southern treason." There was also a letter from Schuyler Colfax (later vice president under Ulysses S. Grant) to an Oregon resident arguing that the Democrats—particularly Oregon's pro-Southern Joseph Lane—deserved no credit for Oregon's admission to the Union. It was not an achievement of the Buchanan administration, the writer said, that the Oregon bill had passed, since the Republicans had given the new state strong support. The *People's Press* published also an account from the Knoxville (Tenn.) *Whig*, most powerful anti-Buchanan newspaper in the South. The *Whig*, edited by the pro-Union William Gannaway Brownlow (Parson Brownlow), made a prognostication: "The Democratic Party Dead." History was not to bear this out.

Pengra seemed to be doing a good job on regional and local news, too. In "The Indian Massacre in the South," we learn of five white men being killed on their way to the Klamath Lake Country in southern Oregon by Klamath and Rogue River Indians near the mining town of Jacksonville. And close to Eugene City we have, as of May 31, 1859, a story on transportation that explains itself in revealing travel problems of the time:

> "The purser of the Steamer Elk writes, 'If there is water enough, we expect to start for Eugene City next week on Friday, which will be June 10.' "

The boat was to have started May 26. Meanwhile, freight service to Eugene by boat was to continue for more than another decade, or until Oregon and California railroad was completed across the state.

Pengra published about seven columns of advertising out of 20 total, most of the ads being what we would today call classified or "classified-display." One, interestingly, was an ad for the

New York *Evening Post* (W.C. Bryant & Company), a staunch anti-slavery paper at the time and today as the New York *Post* the longest-lived daily newspaper in the United States.[13]

Considering the nature of Oregon at the time, the Eugene City newspaper deserves good words. It was of higher quality than the three which followed it. Pengra was interested in transportation, and he soon turned his paper over to Ware, who abandoned it sometime after Abraham Lincoln's election, but no later than 1862. Pengra in 1862 became surveyor-general of Oregon. In 1865 he was superintendent of construction of a military wagon road leading up the middle fork of the Willamette River. He became a strong advocate of the Humboldt (or Winnemucca) route for a railroad to Eugene City.[14] Pengra lost that campaign, for a direct Sacramento-Portland route was surveyed, constructed and finally opened in 1887. In the 1870s Pengra was a director of the Oregon Central Pacific Railroad.[15]

The Eugene City *Guard* didn't have a man of Pengra's talents when it was established. Further, it was Democratic, and the *Guard* was published for its first 11 years by politically motivated printers not concerned with industrializing a state.

Democratic Herald-Democratic Register-Eugene City Review

Eugene City's next three newspapers were either three—or one with three names. In them (*it*, if we use hyphens) we find journalism in turmoil as a result of the Civil War, with *Herald*, *Register* and *Review* violently upholding the secessionist cause. All three offer a fascinating study that if it were expanded to the whole state would provide useful footnotes to Copperhead journalism in general.

The sequence itself is a confused story.

The Eugene City *Democratic Herald* was founded in March, 1859, in opposition to Pengra's *People's Press.* It might have survived two years, after which its publisher, an Alexander Blakely, was unable to continue it.[16] Or it might have been purchased before it died by an Anthony Noltner. Or Noltner might have resurrected it after Blakely had given it up.[17] The *Herald* came into Noltner's possession somehow, and after the Civil War started the publisher promptly got into trouble with the Union government and found the *Herald* barred from the mails. In March, 1862, therefore, he changed the name from *Herald* to *Democratic Register* and started up again.[18]

The *Democratic Register* continued for six months, to September 27, 1862, although an order for its suppression had been issued September 20. It said in its last issue, "Subscribers to the *Register* will be furnished the *Review* in its place, as the circulation is prohibited by Gen. [George] Wright, military ruler of this coast." One researcher says that for a time the *Register* was delivered by private conveyance, despite military coercion.[19]

On November 1, 1862, Noltner had the paper in operation again as the Eugene City *Review*, and this time it managed to get through the war. It left Eugene City September 16, 1865, when Noltner moved to Salem and combined it with the Salem *Arena* as the Salem *Weekly Democratic Review*.[20] Because of the common name, the fact that staff members in pioneer days moved freely from one paper to another—as did the presses after the demise of a particular sheet—and because of historical inaccuracies, the new Eugene City *Register* of 1884 is often regarded as a continuation of Noltner's *Democratic Register*. If this were so, the Eugene *Register-Guard* could be dated back to 1859 or at least to 1862. The facts, however, are otherwise. The *Guard* of 1867 had no secessionist predecessor, whatever Harvey Scott thought. And cross-listings of the *Guard* to the *Herald-Register-Review* by at least two directories of newspapers were erroneous.[21]

The suppressions of the *Democratic Herald* and the *Democratic Register* would not mean much historically if the military activities against the papers had been only regional matters of coercion caused by war conditions and emotional upsets. These Oregon "flaps" over liberty of the press became important because one of the editors of the *Democratic Register* and the *Review* was the Joaquin Miller whose fame was to spread so far in the following half-century. For that matter, Blakely and Noltner

THE EUGENE CITY REVIEW.

A DEMOCRATIC NEWSPAPER—DEVOTED TO THE POLITICAL AGRICULTURAL AND DOMESTIC INTERESTS OF THE PEOPLE OF OREGON.

$3 00 PER ANNUM. EUGENE CITY, OREGON, SATURDAY, JANUARY 31, 1863. VOL. I, NO. 14.

EUGENE CITY REVIEW.

PUBLISHED EVERY SATURDAY,

BY

A. NOLTNER & CO.

TERMS OF SUBSCRIPTION:

RATES OF ADVERTISING:

JOB WORK.

Letter from Orpheus C. Kerr.

To Mrs. E. F. Skinner,

On the Death of her Daughter, Leonora.

Letter from the Boise Mines.

T. J. Hendricks, merchant of this place has kindly furnished us with the following extract from a letter concerning the Boise Mines from his partner, E. L. Bristow, dated Jan. 8th, 1863:

I arrived here (Auburn) on the 6th inst.

Yours, comprisingly,
ORPHEUS C. KERR.

COFFEE SYRUP.—This confection is exceedingly handy to travelers when proceeding on a long journey.

ABOUT 2,000 people are already in the Boise mines.

THE DRAFT.—The Reading (Pa.) Times has the following amusing anecdote of the draft:

"I'm drafted?"

"The dare you are; it must have been a strong man that drafted you."

"Well, I'm drafted, and I want to get out. Can't march. I'll pay well."

"Very well."

"Here," said the lawyer, "Commissioner, I have got a substitute."

"He won't do; can't march."

"But he must do," blustered out the lawyer; "and I know he will."

"He can't march; he won't do; and I can't take him."

This was what our smart friend wanted.

"He won't do, eh?"

"No; he won't do."

"Well, then, scratch his name off the list; he *is drafted and wants to be exempted!*"

The Commissioner looked at the lawyer for about a minute; then regarded the fat draft, and, without speaking a word, scratched off his name.

RESOLUTIONS endorsing the emancipation proclamation of President Lincoln, passed the California Legislature. Six months hence any member that voted for the resolution will deny that he ever belonged to a California Legislature.

The Eugene City Review for Jan. 31, 1863 with insert photo (undated) of C.H. "Joaquin" Miller.

themselves had some journalistic prominence beyond Eugene City, while still another party—William Thompson—who was to become the third publisher of the *Guard*, was a printer's devil for the *Review*.

Blakely, years before starting the ill-fated Eugene City *Democratic Herald*, had been a partner with William G. T'Vault in the founding of a more famous Oregon newspaper in the mining town of Jacksonville, the *Table Rock Sentinel*. T'Vault had been the editor of Oregon's first newspaper, the *Oregon Spectator* of Oregon City. Why Blakely left Jacksonville to enter the Eugene City field is not recorded.[22]

Noltner had a much longer career, although there is some question as to his success in any of the many places he frequented. Bancroft mentions Noltner, one of the few individual Oregon editors he names.[23] A native of Germany, Noltner came to Oregon via Wisconsin and the California mining towns. He was for a time a printer in Corvallis, where he was a partner of James H. Slater, who from 1879 to 1885 was a Democratic senator from Oregon; Noltner and Slater ran the Corvallis *Weekly Union*, a secessionist newspaper with a Union name. Then he was in Eugene City for six years with his three pro-Southern sheets. He moved to Salem and then on to Oregon City, where he bought the *Enterprise* and ran it until 1875. In 1876 he founded the Portland *Daily and Weekly Standard*.[24] Even in frontier Oregon few editors had such a rambling career. He died October 9, 1907.[25]

By all measurements, though, it was Joaquin Miller who gained the most fame (his enemies would call it notoriety) in Eugene City's early press history. Joaquin did not work for the *Democratic Herald*, although some sources state that he did; but he contributed to and became a partner with Noltner in the *Democratic Register*. On June 22, 1862, Miller's name appeared as editor of the *Register*, and later that year and for six weeks in 1863 he was editor of the *Review*.[26] His Eugene City experiences always appear in the numerous biographical studies of Miller and, added to occasional free-lancing he engaged in for metropolitan newspapers after he had become famous as a poet, these experiences entitle him to at least a minor niche in journalistic history.

Joaquin in his days as a Eugene City editor was C.H. Miller. The "C.H." stood for Cincinnatus Hiner—a pretentious name his father, Hulings Miller, had bestowed on him before the family left the Ohio-Indiana region to cross the plains. Young Miller's later assumption of "Joaquin," after a Mexican brigand named Joaquin Murietta, who had caused consternation from time to time, suited him better. But all that lay in the future. In Oregon and elsewhere Miller was a youth growing up on a Coburg farm, an adventurer in California in the 1850s, a student for a while in Eugene City's first college,[27] a frequenter of Idaho mining camps, and an express rider from Oro Fino in Idaho to Washington Territory and on as far as Florence, Oregon.[28] While he was still in his early twenties and working in Eugene City he was a Copperhead newspaperman. Miller's pro-Southern sympathies have been attributed to his Quaker upbringing, a basically gentle nature, his sympathy for underdogs, and to the fact that Oregon from 1860 to at least 1863 was a center of Confederate ferment.

Miller himself told the story of these days:

> "I felt the need of more education and acting on Papa's advice went to the best school I could find in our new country, then went to college, taught school, studied law at home, but ever and ever the lure of the mountains called and called, and I could not keep my mind on my books. . . . Then came the discovery of gold in Idaho, Montana, and so on, and I was off like a rocket, with the rest. I came back to my gentle parents with gold enough to build a beautiful new home [in Eugene City] and had money to buy a newspaper besides.
>
> ". . . I plead for peace in my paper, believing in Papa's Quaker creed, and it was suppressed. I went into the mountains of Oregon, where hosts of my California friends

had opened mines, and after leading them against the hostile savages, was elected their judge." [29]

In the spring of 1862 Miller began writing for the *Democratic Register,* and he was almost certainly one of the causes of its suppression. For after becoming a part owner with Noltner in July Joaquin took on the distinguished Rev. Thomas Starr King of the First Unitarian Church of San Francisco, who was traveling in Oregon and Washington Territory in support of the Union cause. King was the minister who had delivered the funeral oration for Senator Edward D. Baker of Oregon, close friend of Abraham Lincoln, after Baker had been killed at the Battle of Ball's Bluff in October, 1861. There was some talk for a time of sending King to the Senate from California. King is credited by some historians with doing as much as any single person in keeping California loyal during the secessionist crisis of 1860 and 1861.

The clergyman appeared in the Willamette Valley and in the Columbia River area in July and August of 1862. Miller ran a lecture notice lifted from the Red Bluff (Calif.) *Independent* and then appended his own comment. This was it:

> "LECTURE. T. Starr King will deliver his guest lecture on 'The New Nation to Issue from the War' on Monday evening next in the Methodist Church. The price of admission will be fifty cents. He is a patriotic and elequent [sic] lecturer and will undoubtedly attract a large audience. [Miller's quoted matter.]
>
> * * *
>
> "This T. Starr King is another of the many patriots of the modern days. Noble, self-denying patriotic T. Starr King! He is going about the country lecturing on 'The New Nation to Issue from the War,' charging fifty cents a head for firing men's hearts by his finished addresses and well-turned falsehoods against their brothers and neighbors, who may differ with them in politics. If all such imposters

as Starr King had been banished from the country at the commencement of the present trouble, we would now have no Manassas, Pittsburg Landing or Fair Oaks to weep over, but peace and plenty would fill our country instead. But the Rev. T. Starr King is coming, and we suppose with the other of the journalists of Oregon, when he arrives, must rise up and do homage to the great expounder of abolitionism or be denounced as traitors." [30]

The Unionist press, of course, praised King, among those supporting his tour being the *Oregonian* on July 29, 1862. The clergyman's trip continued to make news, and some weeks later Miller attacked King again. Commenting on a piece in The Dalles *Enquirer*, Miller wrote:

> "T. Starr King, this human parody of a minister, was at The Dalles on the 30th ult. [August], dressed in a gray shirt. Sackcloth and ashes wouldn't be bad dress for him." [31]

Within a few days of this publication, Gen. George Wright's order of suppression had been received and the *Democratic Register* was out of circulation. But as the Eugene City *Review* the paper was soon back, with Joaquin Miller's name on the masthead as editor.

The last issue of the *Register* illustrates the violence of Miller's language. On September 8 the *Oregon Statesman* of Salem had attacked Miller personally as a "traitor" and had said, "As soon as his one-horse paper is busted up he will be found skedadling [sic] to the Southern Confederacy." [32]

Miller responded:

> "The Statesman of Sept. 8th, after quoting a few sentences from the *Register* in such a mutilated shape as to give them almost a different meaning comments and profoundly reasons as follows: 'The name of the miscreant and traitor who uttered the above quotations is C.H.

> Miller. As soon as his one-horse paper is busted up he will be found skedadling to the Southern Confederacy.'
>
> "Traitor do you say? You cowardly, perjured lantern-jawed green-eyed Yankee—traitor to what? You talk of traitor—you who have for ten years been a traitor to our infant state for the sake of filling your own greedy pockets. You who today stand a perjured traitor to the party that makes you what you are. . . . Scream 'traitor' because a man dares hope for the return of the peace and prosperity of our country. Go humble your diminished head in a gunny sack and ashes. . . . We dislike to enter the list of billingsgate against a man whose bravest act is to stab a friend in the back; . . . but when we are continually assailed with the charge of 'traitor' (a name no man dare apply in our hearing) by cowardly, pampered pets of the Abolitionists . . . we will sometimes turn and remind them of their rottenness of heart."[33]

On January 23, 1863, two days after Lincoln's Emancipation Proclamation had become effective, Miller came out with an editorial on "Freedom of the Press." He attacked "usurpations of power" and declared that the "administration has seen its error in interfering with the newspapers, though it has not the moral courage to acknowledge its fault." Miller was right about there being no further interference with the *Review*. Whether the Lincoln Administration was always unwilling to admit fault was another matter; outside of Oregon there were instances in which the press was victorious in battles with the military.[34]

Miller raised what he called a Democratic banner of freedom: "freedom of speech, freedom of the press, and freedom of the white man before the negro." He added:

> "A child cannot but hate the plea of freeing the negro to save the Union, and enslaving the press to liberate the negroes. . . . Slavery and servitude must and will be in some form in all time and among all people. Hewers of

wood and drawers of water were made by the Almighty to serve their superiors, and the insane attempt to change this inevitable decree is today enslaving the noblest nation that ever existed."[35]

Miller might have been gentle as a person, but he didn't use gentle words. Historically the young Eugene City editor was wrong about the Negro, but his racial bias continued in the Democratic Eugene City *Guard* more than four years later. In fact, one of Joaquin's printer's devils, a great admirer of Miller, became an early publisher of the *Guard.*

Miller's pro-slavery attitude didn't go unchallenged. The Portland *Oregonian* had strong words to say about Eugene City's Copperhead press. The *Oregonian* regarded the *Review* as a sheet engaging in a "suppression dodge." It said:

> "Start a newspaper, with the understanding that it is to be a Union Democratic paper, or a *neutral* [italics in original]; run it awhile; get all the advance subscriptions that you can; pocket them and get your paper suppressed. After this, abuse the tyrant Lincoln and his foul minions, ask your subscribers to take the circumstances into consideration and say no more about it. Go and play this over three or four times, and you will make more money. In this way we have the *Herald, Register,* and *Review,* published at Eugene City; the *Gazette,* and now the *Intelligencer,* at Jacksonville, besides some other instances. . . . All these have taken just such a course as would be sure to prevent the proprietors from furnishing their papers to their subscribers."[36]

Once again Miller was quick to answer. The *Oregonian* writer was a "wilful slanderer" and "villainous puppy seeking a quarrel." Joaquin denied having any connection with the suppressed *Herald,* since he was not even in Oregon when it was suspended.[37] Then when the *Democratic Register* was in turn suppressed, he said, the proprietor (Anthony Noltner) started a neutral paper, since none could be printed "other than a servile abolition sheet." The *Review*, Miller continued, was sent to subscribers of the *Register*, and the books and subscription lists of the *Register* and the *Review* were the same. He concluded:

> "Nobody but the proprietors lost money by the suppression, and it is the last thing in the world to be desired. No subscriber to the *Register* or *Review* has ever yet lost a penny or lost a paper by it, unless stolen by some Black Republican postmaster."[38]

Within two more weeks Miller had resigned from the *Review* (February 14, 1863), and we have no sources pin-pointing an authentic reason for his departure. One of Joaquin's biographers in an unattributed statement says Miller's reputation in Eugene City was severely tarnished and that "he was left with many enemies, and he barely escaped imprisonment."[39] This might or might not have been so. Miller is also said to have blamed his secessionist views on the fact that he was only 19 and too young to enlist. However, in 1863 he was at least 24.

How difficult it is to piece the story together is shown further by an inaccurate statement that "soon thereafter [following Miller's resignation] the paper closed down. In the meantime there was danger that he and other rebel sympathizers might be lynched. There was talk of running the *Review* editor out of town on a rail."[40] The rail story makes good anecdote, but all that happened was that Joaquin left Eugene City. As we have seen, the *Review* continued for another two and a half years before Noltner moved it to Salem.

After Joaquin Miller's departure the significance of Eugene City's pro-Southern press fades. There were no other suppressions locally, although Miller's successor on the *Review*, a James O'Meara, had had one of his papers suppressed.[41] The total of suppressed newspapers in Oregon during the Civil War was at least seven: Albany *Democrat, Southern Oregon Gazette* in Jacksonville, Eugene City's *Democratic Herald* and *Democratic Register*, Albany *Inquirer*, Portland *Advertiser*, and Corvallis

Union. William G. T'Vault of the pioneer *Oregon Spectator* edited a secession journal in Jacksonville, the *Oregon Intelligencer*, but there is no evidence that it was suppressed.[42]

As to disloyal newspapers in general, Harvey W. Scott of the *Oregonian* wrote an editorial about the Copperhead press in 1885, twenty years after Appomattox. Scott pointed out that Oregon editors had to please Missouri settlers and others from the Southwest who were strong advocates of Confederate policies. Oregon's newspapers therefore were in part as intensely pro-slavery as any in the cotton states; and it must be remembered that an Oregonian, Joseph Lane (after whom Eugene's county was named), had been the vice-presidential candidate on the secessionist ticket in 1860 with John C. Breckinridge. Scott continued:

> "During the Civil War the Democratic papers of Oregon were so entirely devoted to the Southern Confederacy, and so bitter in their denunciation of the national cause, that most of them were suppressed by the Government, through denial to them of the use of the mails." [43]

Moreover, after the war and during Reconstruction, when the Eugene City *Guard* appeared, these pro-Southern feelings did not die. The *Guard* started as a rabid anti-Reconstruction, anti-Radical sheet.

In the long run Joaquin Miller was not hurt by his disloyal attitude. His half-century career as a poet made his Oregon beginnings dim. After a few years as a resident of Canyon City (he was a judge there and even hoped to go to the Oregon Supreme Court), Joaquin left Oregon at the start of the 1870s. He achieved applause and scorn, world renown and notoriety, and the sobriquet "Poet of the Sierras." How one reacts to Joaquin Miller depends upon a literary and not a journalistic interpretation. There are some who say Joaquin was one of American literature's most delightful frauds.

One Oregonian who gave Miller the benefit of the doubt in these days, despite his anti-Union views, was Harrison R. Kincaid of the *Oregon State Journal,* established after Miller had left the *Review.* In 1870, Joaquin, a failure in Oregon, passed through Eugene City on his way to Europe. He offered Kincaid a poem he had written and Kincaid published it. More than 40 years later Kincaid recalled the meeting:

> "An intelligent man and prominent politician who then held an important office asked me why I had published the writings of that 'crazy man.' He went to Europe and had it printed in England and they said it was good poetry, and he got quite a reputation for writing what was in Oregon 'crazy stuff.' "[44]

Eugene and Oregon never have forgotten the young man who wrote for a newspaper called the *Register.* A full-length portrait of Joaquin Miller today hangs on the wall of the library of the Lane County Pioneer-Historical Society at 740 West Thirteenth Avenue, and it is the largest picture in the room. That it hangs there, however, is more likely in recognition of later fame than for Joaquin's editing of the *Register* and the *Review.*

Bancroft's tribute to Miller in 1888 is more objective as a contemporary one:

> "C.H. Miller became the most widely famous of all Oregon writers, and has said some good things in verse of the mountains and woods of his state. It is a pity he had not evolved from his inner consciousness some loftier human ideals than his fictitious characters. . . . Of all his pictures of life, none is so fine as his tribute to the Oregon pioneers, under the title of Pioneers of the Pacific, which fits California as well."[45]

The State Republican:
Plus Union Character and Herald of Reform

B.J. Pengra's short venture in journalism and Joel Ware's giving up the *People's Press* would have left Eugene City without a pro-Union newspaper had it not been for the concern of one of the pioneers of the 1840s that the town must not continue without an anti-slavery journal. He was Hilyard Shaw. Shaw was not a printer but a landowner, builder of Eugene City's first house and one of the operators of the first sawmill.[46] He got hold of Pengra's equipment and on January 1, 1862, under the name of H. Shaw and Company, started the *State Republican*. The paper had to have printers and Shaw, in hiring them, gave a start in journalism to two men who became successful publishers. These were James Newton Gale and Harrison R. Kincaid, husband of Gale's sister Elizabeth. Gale and Kincaid both had come across the plains with the pioneers in the early 1850s, from Indiana. Gale had been operating one of Eugene City's first bookstores, had had printing experience, and was a "sound Republican"; Kincaid had written for the *People's Press* and had more formal education than most of the printer-editors of the day.[47] Since the *State Republican* was not an immediate financial success, Kincaid took his pay from Shaw in land, choosing a site that became part of the University of Oregon; Kincaid owned his property for many years after the University was opened in 1876.[48]

The *State Republican* ran as its motto, "The Struggle for Today is Not Altogether for Today, It Is for the Vast Future Also."[49] One of the few existing files of the paper, however, carried under the nameplate the principle, "Devoted to the Political and General Interests of the People."[50] It was the second that appears in retrospect to have dominated. The first implied support of the Union cause in the war, but the paper's expression of editorial opinion had a strong business overtone:

> "There is money enough sent out of Oregon every year for goods that might be produced here, to establish manufactories that would supply the country with as good articles as are now imported."[51]

The paper was campaigning at the same time for establishment of a woolen factory and a tannery. It also ran the usual number of locals: about an excessively cold winter in 1862 and about a steamer making a five-mile run from Eugene City to Springfield in 26 minutes while carrying 13 tons of freight.[52]

Hilyard Shaw, who was 62 years old, died September 6, 1862, whereupon Gale took over the business side of the paper and young Kincaid (them 26) assumed editorial control. Then in May, 1863, Gale consolidated the *State Republican* with the *Oregon Argus* of Oregon City and Kincaid went prospecting in the John Day area of Central Oregon, more than 250 miles east. Luckily the departure of another Eugene City newspaper after less than a year and a half was not to mean Kincaid's leaving. Gale, however, did not return.

Earlier, in January of 1863, a Universalist preacher named A.C. Edmunds started a short-lived sheet called the *Herald of Reform*. Around November 1 of the same year, Edmunds announced a new paper, the *Union Crusader*, a "secular paper, devoted to the interests of the American people, and the perpetuity of our National Union. Our motto is 'Peace, when we can have it honorably, and war until then.' "

When Kincaid came back from the mines late in 1863 he wrote political editorials for the *Crusader* and on March 7, 1864, Kincaid bought Edmunds' interest in the *Crusader* with a personal note. Kincaid and Edmunds had disagreed with other Republicans over the formation of the Union Party, whereby loyal Democrats would join Republicans in supporting Lincoln in 1864.[53] Then on March 12, 1864, Kincaid started his own paper, the *Oregon State Journal*.

As to Gale, his merger of the *State Republican* with the Oregon City *Argus* resulted within a few months in another consolidation, this time the *Argus* joining with the *Oregon Statesman* in Salem. Gale then went on to found the Portland *Daily Union* and stayed a year; then established the *Marine Gazette* in Astoria and stayed about two years; and finally went to Olympia (Washington Territory) to begin the Olympia *Transcript*.

Amid all this shuffling, part of Gale's *Argus-Republican-Statesman* equipment came into the hands of Kincaid (circa

1868), the brother-in-law in Eugene City. This was the old Washington hand-press that had been used to print the *Oregon Spectator* in Oregon City in 1846. The pioneer press remained in the possession of the *Oregon State Journal* during Kincaid's lifetime. It eventually was given to the University of Oregon School of Journalism. The press stands today in the school's main lobby, a memento of pioneer times, with warning signs on it telling one not to pull the loosened lever that once forced down the platen onto the type. The press before 1846 had come around Cape Horn and had been used for a time in the Sandwich Islands before reaching Oregon.[54]

The Oregon State Journal

With the *Oregon State Journal* Eugene City finally gained a newspaper of some permanence—for 45 years. It had only one publisher, for Harrison Kincaid himself closed the paper in 1909. Three years after the *Journal* started the *Guard* became its competition; and until 1884, when the second *Register* was founded, the *Oregon State Journal* and the *Guard* had the field mostly to themselves. From 1884 to 1909 the competition was divided among the three newspapers, since sporadic interventions by other sheets never lasted long. The *Journal* was Republican, the *Guard* became Democratic, and the *Register* became Republican. All three developed into papers with a better sense of news and business responsibility than their predecessors, although there was some doubt about that for the *Guard* during its first 11 years.[55]

The *Oregon State Journal* in these 45 years was Eugene City's "status" newspaper. Several factors gave the *State Journal* its reputation: continuity of ownership, the ability and devotion of Kincaid, and the fact that the *Guard* and *Register* went into daily competition with each other before Eugene was big enough to support two daily newspapers. The burden on Kincaid with a weekly undoubtedly was less than on his competitors after 1891 and 1895, the years they entered the daily field. So, even though the Eugene *Register-Guard* is the principal of this history we cannot by-pass a biographical sketch of Harrison Kincaid and his newspaper. Except for currents of journalistic chance, Alton Baker, Sr., purchaser of the *Guard* in 1927 and *Register* in 1930, might have been buying the *Oregon State Journal* instead.

The Eugene *Daily Guard* itself more than a third of a century after its own founding testified to its competitor's achievements. On December 8, 1906, the *Guard* ran a four-section special edition to portray Eugene's and Lane County's economic achievements. For the lead article, relating to the growth of Oregon, the assignment went to "the great journalist of Oregon," Harrison Rittenhouse Kincaid.[56] In addition, the *Guard* ran a long feature on Kincaid's career. The *Journal* editor was then 70 years old and was to give up his paper in less than three years. He died in 1920.

Another third of a century later the then consolidated *Register-Guard* once more praised the old pioneer. This time the story was attached to the *Guard's* impending 75th anniversary. After outlining the many failures of Eugene City's newspapers before the *Journal* started in 1864, the *Register-Guard* said:

> "Kincaid ranks as Eugene's pioneer editor. Although the *Journal* did not survive into the present, its 45 years in the field here were a continuous record that is noteworthy in the state."[57]

What sort of man, then, was this unusual Eugenean who could win such laudatory treatment from his opposition in his own lifetime and so many years thereafter?

After the young Kincaid had reached Eugene City in 1853 (he was 17 years old and had driven an ox team all the way across the plains), he became a day laborer, helped to construct the mill race that for years ran from Springfield to Eugene, and worked in the southern Oregon and northern California mines. He went to Eugene City's Columbia College and then gained newspaper experience on the *People's Press* and *State Republican*.

Joining Kincaid in forming the *Oregon State Journal* were his brother John S. Kincaid and the Joel Ware of the old *People's Press*. Ware left the *Journal* within a year, while John Kincaid died in 1874. Then another brother, George Kincaid, became Harrison's partner (1878-1882). For the most part, however, the newspaper was a one-man operation. Since Harrison Kincaid was gone from Eugene City for long stretches of time, hired employes did the routine work. The owner wrote for the paper from afar and used it to help the Republican Party locally and nationally.

Kincaid, though more a gentleman than most early editors, was not a bashful man. In an interview given in 1919, when 83, he said that after he founded the *Journal* in 1864 he gave it "a leading place among the Republican papers in the state and held that place for many years." [58]

For extended intervals, however, Kincaid was chiefly a leader in the Republican Party, a reporter from Washington, D.C. (we might call him Eugene's first Washington correspondent), a traveler, and perhaps even a scholar. His long absences gave the *Journal* coverage advantages over the fledgling *Guard* and an enhanced reputation to Kincaid historically.

Kincaid made much of the fact that "no early files of the *Guard* were kept," whereas he always had three bound copies of the *Oregon State Journal* on hand in his home. He kept each file in a far corner of the house, each removed as far as possible from the other as a protection against fire. Kincaid's residence was on East Ninth (now Broadway) between Pearl and Willamette Streets. [59]

In his autobiographical *Sunshine and Shadow*, which was never published in full, Kincaid said that in 1867 he visited Harvard College and arranged with the librarian there to have the *Journal* bound and kept in Cambridge. "As long as the paper was continued after that date, for more than 40 years, I had every copy of the paper sent to that library," he said. [60] Kincaid also sent the *Journal* to the Library of Congress and to the public libraries of Portland, San Francisco, and New York, as well as to other places. But these files, he feared were not bound and were destroyed.[61]

Kincaid's care in editing and concern for the future were unusual among newspaper editors of his day, as the disappearance of the early Eugene City *Guards* shows. Furthermore, his activities, if the *Journal* were the subject of this book, would make it easier to unravel its history than that of the *Guard*. The *Journal* is the only Eugene newspaper for which the University of Oregon file is complete.

Kincaid was in the East at the time the United States House of Representatives voted to impeach President Andrew Johnson in February 1868, by a 126-47 vote. The editor covered this for his paper and was proud that he could get a two-column report to the *State Journal* by April.[62] "The great crowd," he wrote, "had witnessed, by the House the impeachment of the first American President, one of the most important acts ever performed by any legislative body in the history of the world."[63] Kincaid was in the anti-Johnson camp with the Radical Republicans at the time, but years later he changed his views. Of the Senate's trial of Johnson in May, in which the President was saved from removal from office by one vote (19 against removal to 35 for, with a two-thirds majority needed), Kincaid wrote nearly a half-century later:

> ". . .The trial was caused by anger and jealousy and by Johnson's foolish words rather than by any necessity of turning Johnson out of office. The seven [Republicans among the 19 in minority] who voted to save Johnson were right."[64]

Remaining in the East, Kincaid became one of six Oregon delegates to the Republican National Convention of 1868, which in Chicago nominated Ulysses S. Grant and Schuyler Colfax. Kincaid was on the platform committee. Likewise, he was an Oregon delegate in 1872 in Philadelphia, when Grant was renominated.

When the Grant Administration went into office in 1869, Harrison Kincaid became one of the clerks of the Senate and served until the Democrats discharged him upon taking control of that body during the Hayes Administration in 1879. In all these years the Eugene City editor wrote weekly letters home; in addition, he contributed material to the Portland *Oregonian*, the Oregon *Sentinel* in Jacksonville, and other newspapers in the West.[65]

Kincaid's discharge from the Senate clerkship offended him, and he sought a new government job before returning to Oregon. Thomas H. Brents, the delegate to the House from Washington Territory, on June 17, 1879, wrote a to-whom-it-may-concern letter of support for Kincaid:

> ". . . A few days ago . . . he was discharged [as clerk of the Senate] for the sole reason that his political opinions are not in accord with the dominant party in the Senate."[66]

Brent asked for fair and equitable employment for Kincaid elsewhere in government. The letter bore Brent's signature and the names of scores of others, among them Republicans Levi P. Morton of New York and William McKinley of Ohio, as well as John Whiteaker, a Democrat and Oregon's first governor under statehood in 1859.[67] Then, in 1870, Kincaid was nominated for state printer by Oregon Republicans but was defeated by Henry L. Pittock, manager of the *Oregonian*. A Democrat later got the job.[68]

These long absences, despite frequent returns home, did not always set well with Kincaid's political opponents in Eugene City.[69] By 1876 the *Guard*, now more than eight years under way, took note of Kincaid's Washington activities. The then publisher of the *Guard*, George J. Buys, wrote:

> "NEEDS A HEAD
>
> "If the owner of the State Journal cares anything for that property he should either return from Washington

> and take charge of it, or procure some responsible person of mature years to take such charge. It has been run by drunkards, gamblers and boys until it has come to be known as the 'hoodlum organ,' and has lost all the respectability it ever possessed. The youth now in control of it does not mean to do harm, but has not judgment enough to distinguish right from wrong."[70]

Such criticisms could be expected considering the strength of political divergencies in those days, for the early *Guard*, which had a difficult time getting started, could hardly have enjoyed the distinction of its absentee competitor. By the 1880s, in any event, with Democrats frequently in control of at least one branch of the government and of the Presidency after Grover Cleveland's election in 1884, Kincaid did return to Oregon. He remained active in politics and was secretary of state for Oregon from 1895 to 1899.

On major issues of the 1890s Kincaid went contrary to Republican Party doctrine by becoming a free-silverite. When he left the secretaryship of state he was among four nominees for a position on the University of Oregon Board of Regents, a post he deeply wanted. Enemies within the party prevented confirmation of the appointment by charging that Kincaid had deserted on the money issue. Kincaid, who was a great supporter of the university, felt that the money question had no relation to his qualifications for a regent's post and, further, that the Republicans themselves had deserted their principles. He emphasized that before 1896 Republican leaders (William McKinley among them) had been silver advocates. Kincaid also put some of the blame for losing the regent appointment on reports carried in Harvey W. Scott's *Oregonian*, a paper adamantly for the gold standard.[71]

By the turn of the Twentieth Century Harrison R. Kincaid was 65 years old. Though he was to continue his newspaper until 1909, he was no longer as active as before. For a time in the early 1900s he was a Lane County judge. When he did liquidate the *Oregon State Journal*, on May 29, 1909, he did so for purely personal reasons. He had hoped to round out 50 years for his paper—or to continue to 1914—but he stepped out early. Since 1909 was a peak year historically for American newspapers in number in existence and a highly prosperous year in Eugene, economic pressures were not a direct factor. Kincaid was old—and he was an individualist. When his printers wanted more wages than he thought they were worth, when he felt they were unwilling to do a day's job for a day's pay, he stopped. And if the wage issue was not a motivating factor then the closure could have been impelled by a fire in the Kincaid home at 85 East Ninth adjacent to the *State Journal* at 81 East Ninth.

In a valedictory editorial the old editor dwelled on his accomplishments, particularly the impressiveness of his conducting the paper for "45 years and 22 weeks." He was proud that the *State Journal* had never missed a number and had never failed to be mailed to subscribers on time; that he had never sought to carry it on as a "money-making business" but had always been willing to make up deficits out of his own pocket; and that he hoped to revive the paper in the future. But the competition for the advertising dollar—to use a modern-day term—was more than Kincaid cared to indulge in.[72]

Perhaps the most incisive tribute to Kincaid had come nearly two years earlier, from Harvey Scott, the hard-money editor who had opposed Kincaid for the University of Oregon regency. In a sketch of Kincaid the *Oregonian* said:

> "HARRISON R. KINCAID, EDITOR
>
> "The *Oregon State Journal* has been published at Eugene by Harrison R. Kincaid, forty-four years. He started the paper and, during the whole period, has been proprietor and editor. And he has done conscientious work. On certain economic matters of high importance, the *Oregonian* has not been able to agree with him. . . . But the *Oregonian* most willingly bears testimony to the

> character of sincerity and earnestness which always has been manifest in the work and bearing of Mr. Kincaid. In all his work he has shown himself a high-minded man." [73]

No other ownership of a newspaper in Eugene quite equals Harrison R. Kincaid's of the *State Journal.* The publishers of the *Register-Guard* will reach 45 years in 1972, when the Alton Baker family will have been in Eugene that long, through Alton F. Baker, Sr., and Alton F. Baker, Jr. The *Register-Guard,* aided by 40 years of the city's economic growth since 1927 and by the work of sub-editors far more professional than pioneer newspapermen, has had advantages Kincaid did not enjoy. In Kincaid's 45 years, only one of nine publishers and co-publishers of the *Guard* could match him in steadfastness to the paper; none until Charles H. Fisher, who bought the *Guard* three years before Kincaid retired, was his equal in ability. Nor could the Eugene City *Register,* founded in 1884, produce publishers of Kincaid's competence, at least to 1899.

The opposition, with a weekly, won the first round in the first third of the *Guard's* century, even though it did not lead in circulation. Harrison R. Kincaid came to Oregon journalism a generation, and maybe two generations, too soon. [74]

The Eugene City News

The *News* probably was the shortest-lived newspaper of all Eugene City's ill-fated pioneer journals, unless the uncertain life of the *Pacific Journal* was briefer. The *News* is also a paper about which sources differ, some placing it ahead of the *Pacific Journal.*

Only one copy of the *News* is available in the University of Oregon. This issue is dated Saturday, June 9, 1866, as Volume 1, Number 14. It was a two-page sheet, five columns by sixteen inches. The publisher's announcement read:

> "Published every Saturday by J.B. Alexander. . . . The *News* will be published till the 30th of June next, at $1.50 a copy, invariably in advance."

The June 9 date would put the first issue of the *News* on March 10, 1866. This March beginning and Alexander's part in it agrees with the suppositions that the Eugene City *Guard* had been founded in March the next year. Until this centennial history was prepared all *Guard* dates had been given erroneously as March or October, 1867, instead of June 1. But back to the *News:* The lone-preserved issue of it does bear Alexander's name and the contents bear out that he intended it to be a campaign paper. Why else would he ask $1.50 a copy for a two-page sheet?

The issue of June 9 turned out to be the final one. On page 2 Alexander controverted his statement on page 1 that he would go to June 30. He said he had been hoping to keep the paper going until all results of the spring election in Oregon were received from the whole state; unfortunately, those who owned the printing equipment he was using needed it and "we will be compelled to close with the present number." He gave no further details.

Alexander promised to make arrangements for new material —perhaps an indication that the Eugene City *Guard* was on its way.

Then Alexander launched into a typical lament of editors of the day. He had expected patronage from the Democrats of Lane County sufficient to insure against loss, "but our expectations have not been realized." The *News* had not brought in enough to meet expenses, "besides the loss of our own time."

Alexander found the death of his paper hard to take. The Democrats in 1866 had won control of Lane County "after long years of oppression." He gave his party some biting advice:

> "Now that the Democrats of the county have so nobly triumphed after enduring for five years all the indignities and insults that the tools and pimps of a fanatical and malignant mob could heap upon them, it behooves them to take immediate steps to establish and *sustain* [italics in original] a paper of their own. . . . And the Democrats of

> Lane County cannot, without the surrender of every vestage [sic] of independence, manhood and self-respect, bestow public patronage upon the shameless, apologists of mobs, incendiaries, and assassins, who, but a few days ago, were lauding the 'friends of the murdered Lincoln' for mobbing Democratic printing offices and assassinating Democrats. . . . We are satisfied that the Democracy of Lane County *can* and *will* [italics in original] permanently establish and sustain a paper in their county."[75]

Within a year John Alexander did establish that Democratic paper in the *Guard.* Unless others had taken the *Guard* over, however, after Alexander let it lapse in the spring of 1868—as he had the *News*—the *Guard* too would never have been *sustained.*

With the death of the *News* Eugene City's first years of journalism ended. Half were spent in civil war and all covered nearly a decade of passion. The papers had been run by printers of questionable ability, political agitators and hot-heads, a poet of the future, Eugene City's first bookseller, and in one case a builder of houses. Of all the pioneer founders, Rodgers of *Pacific Journal* to Alexander of the *News,* Alexander might have been the least capable. His *Guard* proved to be luckier than the other papers in that it alone was to be resurrected after a lapse.

As to Kincaid's *Oregon State Journal,* it is not surprising that it alone of the papers before 1867 lived to 1909. Only he had dedication enough and hope enough in Eugene's future.

As 1867 dawned, new issues were coming up—Reconstruction dominating them all—and the little town was bound to grow. As the last third of the Nineteenth Century opened few could realize how slow that growth was to be. The Twentieth Century had begun before Eugene, its named simplified, had even 5,000 people.

Then the *Guard* filled a vacuum. Despite Alexander and subsequent near-collapses, despite multiple ownership changes, despite one receivership forced by failure to pay rent, despite incompetence from time to time, and despite abortive threats from rivals (one even was called *Broad Axe*), the Eugene City *Guard* scraped through.

---

1. George S. Turnbull, *History of Oregon Newspapers.* Portland, Oregon: Binford & Mort, 1939. p. 103.

2. Flora Belle Ludington, *Newspapers of Oregon, 1846-1870.* Eugene, Oregon: Koke-Tiffany Company, 1925, p. 10.

3. Harrison R. Kincaid, "Pioneer Press Toast," *Lane County Historian.* Vol. 6, (September, 1961), p. 57.

4. Fred Lockley, *Oregon's Yesterdays.* New York: Knickerbocker Press, 1928.

5. Lucia W. Moore, Nina W. McCornack, and Gladys W. McCready, *The Story of Eugene.* New York: Stratford House, 1949, p. 103.

6. Hubert Howe Bancroft, *The Works of Hubert Howe Bancroft.* San Francisco: The History Company, 1888, Vol. 30, p. 448.

7. An interesting newspaper name to illustrate today how connotations of words will change. *People's Press* in the Twentieth Century would connote a Communist hue.

8. Kincaid, *op. cit.*, p. 57.

9. *Ibid.* Ware was active in Lane County politics until the 1900s. He became county clerk and at one time was United States commissioner.

10. Turnbull, *op. cit.*, p. 279.

11. *People's Press*, June 22, 1859.

12. The term used to describe West Coast news writing in Civil War days was "The Oregon Style." This was a "species of storm-and-stress journalism, strong in invective and availing itself of the disturbances of the times—in communities in which everyone's private affairs and personal name were known to every inhabitant—to coin amusing and even offensive titles for opponents." Two artists of "The Oregon Style" were Asahel Bush of the *Oregon Statesman* (Salem) and Thomas J. Dryer of the *Oregonian.* Eugene City's newspapers were relatively moderate, although not moderate enough to save Pengra from once being wounded because of an editorial he did not write, nor of the *People's Press* pro-secessionist opposition from being suppressed. The early Eugene City *Guard*, while often intemperate, was not a good enough newspaper to gain attention with its stylistic excesses.

Turnbull, *op. cit.*, p. 81.

Roy W. Adams, *The Oregon Style.* Eugene: unpublished M.A. thesis, University of Oregon School of Journalism, 1958.

13. All the preceding detail is from the *People's Press*, June 22, 1859.

14. Humboldt River in Nevada to Goose Lake in California (near the Oregon state line at Lakeview) to Eugene City.

15. Harvey W. Scott, *History of the Oregon Country*, compiled by Leslie Scott. Cambridge, Mass.: Riverside Press, 1924, Vol. 3, pp. 349-352.

16. Ludington, *op. cit.*, p. 9.

Bancroft, *op. cit.*, p. 448.

Albert G. Walling, *Illustrated History of Lane County, Oregon.* Portland, Oregon: Walling Printing and Lithographing House, 1884, p. 434.

None of these sources agrees with another.

17. Ludington, *op. cit.*, p. 9.
18. Lockley, *op. cit.*, p. 324.
19. Ludington, *op. cit.*, p. 9. It is quite likely that the military order did not reach Eugene City in time to stop the September 27 issue. The last *Democratic Register* carried under the nameplate a quotation from Washington's Farewell Address: "Every attempt to exercise powers beyond these limits (the Constitution) should be promptly and firmly opposed." The Oregon Historical Society, Portland, has a file of the *Register*, with only a few missing issues, from March 22 to September 27, 1862. Only two issues of the *Democratic Herald* are known to be extant, June 5, 1860, and February 5, 1861. Both are in the University of Oregon.
20. Ludington, *op. cit.*, p. 9.
Turnbull, *op. cit.*, p. 275.
Eugene City *Review*, Vol. 1, No. 1, to Vol. 3, No. 49, November 1, 1862, to September 16, 1865.
Salem *Weekly Democratic Review*, Vol. 3, No. 49, October 16, 1865 ff.
The Oregon Historical Society has extensive files up to 1872, although there are unfortunate gaps.
21. Winifred Gregory, *American Newspapers, 1921-1936*. New York: H.W. Wilson Company, 1937. Gregory cross-refers the Eugene City *Herald-Register-Review* to the *Eugene Register-Guard* and gives founding dates of the three as 1859, 1862, and 1863. Possibly working from Gregory, *Ayer Directory, op. cit.*, gave in its 1937 issue the *Register-Guard* founding date as 1859. This has long since been corrected.
22. Turnbull, *op. cit.*, p. 96.
Ludington, *op. cit.*, pp. 12, 13.
23. Bancroft, *op. cit.*, p. 448.
24. Lockley, *op. cit.*, p. 324.
25. Scott, *op. cit.*, Vol. 5, p. 34.
Portland *Oregonian*. Obituary, October 10, 1907.
26. Eugene City *Democratic Register*, June 28, 1862, *et seq.*
Review, November 1, 1862, and February 14, 1863.
27. This was Columbia College, which was hardly more than a high school. A number of Eugeneans who later gained distinction attended it, among them being Harrison R. Kincaid (see pp. 30-36 in text). The college closed down shortly after one of the presidents, a man listed only as Ryan, shot at B.J. Pengra because of personal attacks against Ryan in the *People's Press*. The professor was an ardent secessionist. He left Eugene, apparently for Virginia, and the college shortly closed down.
Harrison R. Kincaid, *Sunshine and Shadow: The Autobiography of H.R. Kincaid*. Microfilm, Oregon State Historical Society, Portland, 1917, pp. 25 ff.
28. Florence is a small port city in Lane County at the mouth of the Siuslaw River, about 65 miles west of Eugene. It was platted by Miller's younger brother, George Melvin Miller.
29. Joaquin Miller, *Overland in a Covered Wagon, An Autobiography*, ed. by Sidney G. Firman. New York: D. Appleton & Company, 1930, pp. 117-118. The record does not bear out Miller on buying a newspaper. At best he was co-proprietor of the *Register* with Noltner.
30. Eugene City *Democrat Register*, July 26, 1862, p. 2.
William G. Eliot, Jr., "Thomas Starr King in Oregon, 1862." *Oregon Historical Quarterly*, Vol. 32, (June 1931), pp. 105-113.

31. *Democratic Register*, September 20, 1862.
32. *Ibid.*
33. *Democratic Register*, September 27, 1862.
34. J. Cutler Andrews, *The North Reports the Civil War.* Pittsburgh: University of Pittsburgh Press, 1955. Particularly Chapter 2, pp. 6-35, covering General Ambrose Burnside's suppression of the Chicago *Times* and Lincoln's countermanding the order.
35. Eugene City *Review*, January 3, 1863.
36. Eugene City *Review*, January 31, 1863, quoting the *Oregonian.*
37. *Ibid.*
38. *Ibid.* Miller's own words clear up the misunderstanding of some biographers that he had been on the *Democratic Herald.* He was in Idaho in 1859 and 1860.
39. M. Marion Marberry, *Splendid Poseur: Joaquin Miller, American Poet.* New York: Crowell, 1953, p. 45.
40. *Ibid.*, p. 49.
41. O'Meara, whom Turnbull calls a "stormy petrel," did not spend enough time in Eugene City to add much to its story. He had come west from New York City, where he had been a typesetter for newspapers, went to California during the Gold Rush and worked for newspapers there until 1857, and then went to Portland to edit the *Democratic Standard.* He was defeated for the Oregon state printer's job in 1858. Then he bought the secessionist *Oregon Sentinel* in Jacksonville, edited it until May, 1861, when he took over the *Southern Oregon Gazette*, which was suppressed. It is not clear how long he remained in Eugene City after succeeding Miller. When he left the *Review* he went to Idaho City to edit the Idaho *World.* Turnbull, *op. cit.*, pp. 97 ff.
42. Bancroft, *op. cit.*, p. 492.
43. Harvey W. Scott, *History of the Oregon Country*, compiled by Leslie Scott. Cambridge, Mass.: Riverside Press, 1924, Vol. 2, p. 492.
Portland *Oregonian*, "Disunion Journalism in Oregon," April 7, 1885.
44. Kincaid, *Sunshine and Shadow, op. cit.*, p. 61.
45. Bancroft, *op. cit.*, p. 692. The literature of Miller is enormous, much of it negatively critical, See:
Marberry, *op. cit.*
Martin Severin Peterson, *Joaquin Miller: Literary Frontiersman.* Stanford University, California: Stanford University Press, 1937.
Harr Wagner, *Joaquin Miller and His Other Self.* San Francisco: Harr Wagner, 1929.
46. Moore, McCornack, and McCready, *op. cit.*, p. 17.
47. Turnbull, *op. cit.*, p. 274.
48. Kincaid, *Sunshine and Shadow, op. cit.*, p. 28.
49. Walling, *op. cit.*, quoting *State Republican* of July 12, 1862.
50. *State Republican*, January 31, 1863.
51. *Ibid.*
52. Walling, *op. cit.*, p. 399.
53. *Ibid.*, pp. 28 ff. Apparently no files of the *Union Crusader* or *Herald of Reform* remain. Neither is listed in holdings of Oregon research libraries, nor is either cited in Gregory's *Union List.*
54. This account of Gale has been pieced together from several sources: Turnbull, *op. cit.*, pp. 279 and 301.
Walling, *op. cit.*, pp. 478-479.

Ludington, *op. cit.*, p. 10.

Scott, *op. cit.*, Vol. 5, p. 169.

Interviews with George S. Turnbull, professor emeritus of journalism, University of Oregon.

Kincaid in an interview given in 1919 said only that the *Spectator* press came to him in a trade. "The Beginnings of Oregon Journalism: an Interview with Harrison R. Kincaid." *Oregon Exchanges*, Vol. 2, (April, 1919), p. 11.

Mrs. E.A. Barette, Gale's daughter, returned to Eugene; she lives at 1346 Willamette Street, now in downtown Eugene.

55. The *Oregon State Journal* of Eugene is not to be confused with the *Oregon Journal* of Portland. The *Oregon Journal*, founded in 1902 by C.S. Jackson as opposition to the *Oregonian* is today Portland's afternoon newspaper. Both Portland papers are now under the ownership of S.I. Newhouse.

56. *Daily Guard*, December 8, 1906.

57. *Register-Guard*, "Newspapers Came and Went in Days of Eugene City Pioneer Journalism," January 4, 1942, p. 32.

58. "The Beginnings of Oregon Journalism," *op. cit.*, p. 11.

59. *Ibid.*

60. Kincaid, *Sunshine and Shadow*, *op. cit.*, p. 129. Kincaid wrote much of his autobiography in 1915, but the typescript, taken from a manuscript owned by his daughter-in-law, Dorothy Kincaid, is dated January 31, 1917, the date carried by the Oregon Historical Society when the microfilm was made in 1957. Part of *Sunshine and Shadow* is carried in the *Quarterly of the Oregon Historical Society* as "Excerpts from the Autobiography of Harrison R. Kincaid," Vol. 17, (June, 1916), p. 8 ff.

61. The Library of Congress does carry an extensive file of the *State Journal* in its newspaper collection.

62. *Oregon State Journal*, April 11, 1868.

63. Kincaid, *Sunshine and Shadow*, *op. cit.*, pp. 34 ff.

64. *Ibid.*

65. Walling, *op. cit.*, p. 478.

In *Sunshine and Shadow* Kincaid said, "The Journal contains in full many of the speeches of Senators and Representatives from Oregon during the 45 years it existed. There is not room in this book for any of them." *Op. cit.*, pp. 34 ff.

66. Kincaid. *Ibid.*

67. *Ibid.* Before returning to Oregon, Kincaid said he traveled in the East and South looking for another place to live, but he decided that no place in the country could surpass Oregon.

68. *Ibid.*

69. Kincaid is reported to have returned to Oregon overland (the means of travel is not indicated) in 1869, 1870, 1872, 1874, 1877, and 1878. With the completion of the Pacific Railroad he could have come by train in these years. Walling, *op. cit.*, p. 478.

70. *Guard*, January 1, 1876, p. 2.

71. Kincaid, "Excerpts from the Autobiography," *op. cit.*, p. 104. Kincaid Street, western boundary of the University of Oregon, is named for the editor. At one time he owned land from East 13th to East 15th Avenues and from Kincaid to Alder Streets, a portion of which is now occupied by the University. *Map of Eugene City, Lane County Oregon.* Eugene, Oregon: W.G. Obenauer Company, 1892.

72. Kincaid was wrong about "22 weeks"; the *Journal* published only 45 years, 12 weeks, so Kincaid might have allowed a typographical error to slip through. *Oregon State Journal*, May 29, 1909. Kincaid's son, Webster Kincaid, never entered newspaper work but became a Eugene real estate man.

73. Portland *Oregonian*, December 29, 1909, section 3, page 8.

Also carried in Scott, *op. cit.*, Vol. 5, p. 119.

74. See pp. 80-88 ff. for discussion of Ira L. Campbell of the *Guard*, who did share Kincaid's devotion to journalism.

75. Eugene City *News*, June 9, 1866.

CHAPTER 3

Years To 1900: Journalism Expands—A Tiny City Grows

A newspaper can usually survive in a community whether the city grows much or not, for general communication needs will provide enough advertising and circulation to keep at least a single publication alive. Witness the hundreds of small cities in the United States with weeklies and dailies providing a news, advertising, reader-service, and entertainment need. With few exceptions these newspapers grow, languish, or die depending upon how their local communities develop, what kinds of publishers and editors operate them, and how their readers respond—socially, politically, economically, and intellectually. Involved, too, is the nature of the press at any given period.

The above paragraph merely sets forth truisms that anyone knowledgeable as to newspapers understands. Today the economic structure of the press is such that most cities in America have and will support only one newspaper of general circulation. Critics moan about this—about a community having only one press voice. It is not to the point here to go into the perils, if any, involved in this fact.

In the Oregon and the Eugene City about which we are writing, immediately after the Civil War, these same generalities held, though in different specific situations. The Eugene *Register-Guard* of 1967 is merely the survivor of a century-long "shakedown" that saw numerous newspapers developing in parallel. The *Register-Guard* could not have reached 100 years if, through many combinations of circumstances, *Guard* and *Register* years ago had not been able somehow to make things go; if the City of Eugene had not grown eventually to more than small-town size (become moderately *metropolitan* if we will); and if, in 1927, a new management had not bought the

Guard and given it the drive, idealism, competence, and continuity the paper needed. A right combination was called for. One cannot simplify the story. There are many *ifs* in the history, one of which has been noted already. What if Harrison R. Kincaid, with his great abilities, had been the founder of the *Guard*, had devoted himself to journalism alone and not been half-time or more in politics, had had a son who wanted to continue the *Oregon State Journal*, or had gone into daily competition with *Guard* and *Register*?

The pattern, however, unfolded otherwise.

Eugene City After the Civil War

Eugene City after the Civil War still had fewer than 1,000 people. Depending upon what figures we use, we could put the Eugene "area" at 1,852, though the city proper had only 861. [1] In 1860, before incorporation, the area population had been 1,183, giving the region in the decade of the *Guard's* birth a satisfactory increase of 57 per cent. But with so small a base on which to start the increase was miniscule. The whole of Oregon in the 1860s had done better than Eugene City, the state jumping from 52,465 to 90,923, or 73.3 per cent. Lane County, up from 4,780 to 6,426 by 1870, gained only 35 per cent. [2]

The fact is that although Lane County ranked fourth in Oregon in 1870, after Multnomah (Portland), Marion (Salem), and Linn (Albany), its total growth from 1860 to 1870 was less than that of the three leaders. Lane in addition had less than a 400 lead in population over Douglas (Roseburg).[3] There was no indication that the sprawling County of Lane and its little county seat had any advantages over competing sections of Oregon.

Actually for more than a quarter of a century to come (1870-1900) Lane County and Eugene City gave little promise of passing other places. By 1880 Lane had dropped to seventh in Oregon out of 22 counties, with its population still only 9,411; Eugene City proper, gaining only from 861 to 1,117 in ten years, ranked tenth in the state. To have Portland and Salem ahead of Eugene City is not surprising historically, but in these days the city trailed even Corvallis, Baker City in Eastern Oregon, and Oregon City just south of Portland. [4]

By 1890 Lane County and Eugene had begun to climb, Lane reaching fifth place with 15,198 and Eugene (now the corporate name) also jumping to fifth with 4,111.[5] Portland, East Portland (later annexed), Salem, and Astoria led Eugene in 1890. The city's relative state position in population was by then assured. Portland with East Portland became the state metropolis; Eugene was unable to pass Astoria until 1930, and it trailed Salem in third place until the 1950s. Finally, in 1960, Eugene passed Salem too to take second.

So Eugene's growth to 1900 was only a "steady slow" case of plodding ahead. Nothing distinguished it from any of a half dozen or more Oregon towns. One should not be disturbed, then, in looking back, that its journalism offered little that was different from the journalism of competing cities. Too many idealists tend to imagine the past to have been different from what it was. It is significant enough that Eugene City did support two weekly newspapers for 17 years (1867 to 1884) and three from 1884 to 1891. The *Guard* became a daily in 1891 and the *Register*, after two abortive efforts, in 1899. At the same time *Guard* and *Register* (which had been founded in 1884) were to continue weekly and semi-weekly editions into the teens of the Twentieth Century. [6] The Eugene picture was being duplicated in numerous other cities of Oregon.

This multi-paper competition could exist in tiny communities because journalism before 1900 was not too expensive to engage in; because political points of view were still expected among newspapers, making several sheets a necessity; because press industrialization had not yet become a consolidating force; and, perhaps as much as anything else, because the future appeared optimistic.

We must understand also that the *Guard* and the *Register* in their formative years never enjoyed the prestige of "big-name" editors who could gain them a place in national journalism. Eugene never had an Ed Howe of an Atchison (Kan.) *Globe*, or a William Allen White of an Emporia (Kan.) *Gazette*, or an Edgar Wilson (Bill) Nye of a Laramie (Wyo.) *Boomerang*, or a Mark Twain of Virginia City (Nev.) *Territorial Enterprise.* Only editors like these could put small Western towns on a national stage quickly, almost always because of a combination of news talent, writing ability, and showmanship.

Eugene's newspapers suffered considerably from a succession of changes in ownership—and this was particularly true of the *Guard.* Yet grow they did. What the story adds up to is that the history of the *Guard* and the *Register* turns out to be journalistic history in reverse: prominence and achievement toward the end of the papers' century, last third instead of first third.

Meanwhile, let us look first into the newspaper and the Oregon and Eugene picture as a whole in these two first generations after the Civil War.

The Oregon Journalistic Scene

Reliable comparative statistics began to be compiled in the same years in which the Eugene City *Guard* was starting. It was in 1869 that George P. Rowell, a New York advertising agent, put out his first *American Newspaper Directory.* This was the first relatively accurate list of all newspapers and periodicals published in the country, with circulations obtained from audited lists, along with descriptions of the communities in which newspapers were published. Rowell planned his directory as a service to advertisers so they would know what kind of circulation they were buying. When the Rowell directories were discontinued after 1908, a Rowell competitor, N.W. Ayer of Philadelphia, took over and combined Rowell with its directory. Today the N.W. Ayer *Directory of Newspapers and Periodicals* carries on the Rowell volume sequence. We now have 98 years of national figures available with which to make newspaper comparisons for Oregon and its cities.

A most useful report by Rowell, issued in 1876 as a newspaper exhibition in connection with the United States Centennial observance in Philadelphia, gives a view of Oregon journalism when the *Guard* was in its first decade.[7] Oregon's population was estimated at 101,882, less than that of any state except Nevada. Its 44 newspapers included 37 weeklies, five dailies, and two monthlies. The average daily circulation per paper was 1,739 and the average weekly circulation 888. Oregon's daily newspapers exceeded in circulation average the totals of papers in 17 states; the weekly averages exceeded those of 10 other states. What this indicates is that Oregon's infant press, in Eugene City and elsewhere, was—despite geographical limitations—circulating more widely than many people might have realized.

Newspaper readers in the Far West were a literate and articulate group. And the Eugene City *Guard's* circulation, which Rowell in the Seventies was estimating as "exceeding 500 and probably up to 1,000" was already as high as the average weekly newspaper circulating in Nebraska and only slightly less than the circulation average of Kansas weeklies. New York papers, of course, led in circulation then as now.[8]

We must also note that Oregon in area in 1870 was the fourth largest state—after Texas, California, and Nevada. Its few newspapers circulated on the average across 2,165 square miles each, second only to Nevada in area covered if a reader was to get hold of a newspaper at all. At the time, there were already enough newspapers in Texas so that, on average, each Texas journal circulated across only 1,475 square miles. The concentrated New York State press had one paper for every 43 square miles.

In frequency of delivery each Oregon newspaper did quite well. An average resident of Oregon, despite transportation difficulties and other frontier problems more demanding than news-reading interests, was able to get hold of 26 newspapers a year. This was at least one every other week, most of the 44 papers being weeklies. An Iowan in the 1870s was getting to see a copy of a newspaper only once in three weeks, and a prostrate Southerner (Alabaman, for example) would average seeing a newspaper only once in 10 weeks.

Oregon's 44 newspapers in 1876 were printing more than two and a half million copies annually (2,634,836). While this total represented one of the lower press-runs in the United States, it must be remembered that Oregon's population barely exceeded 100,000. A 26-to-1 ratio of press-runs to population exceeded that of 23 of the then 37 states and was the same as that of populous Connecticut and Illinois. Even literate Wisconsin, with more than 1,000,000 population—ten times that of Oregon —had newspaper press-runs only six times greater.[9]

Figures like these are deceptive and are subject to misinterpretation. They do indicate, however, the Oregon citizen's concern for information. It is easy a century later to take for granted one or more newspapers per inhabitant per day as against waiting a week or more. And while the Eugene City *Guard* in its first days did not shine particularly brightly among other struggling Oregon newspapers, the lot of these—all 44—were doing jobs equal to newspapers elsewhere. This is a bright side of Oregon's journalistic history not heavily emphasized.

Oregon's Burgeoning Newspapers

The 1870s and 1880s were 20 great years for the establishing of newspapers in Oregon. By 1890 the 44 of 1876 had jumped to 142, but the increase was actually 115 instead of 98, since 17 of the newspapers listed for the state by Rowell in 1876 were not among the 142 given by Ayer in 1890. As a pre-1870 paper, the *Guard* was already one of the 18 oldest in the state by 1890. About 30 papers were founded in Oregon in the 1870s and nearly 50 more in the 1880s. Of course, newspaper growth after the Civil War was tremendous throughout the country, with the Pacific Northwest illustrating this in particular.[10]

The fact that the Eugene City *Register* in 1884 was the only permanent newspaper established in this city in these booming press years is further evidence of how the Eugene area tended to mark time while the rest of Oregon temporarily passed it. Before the newspapers of Eugene could gain any leadership over others in Oregon, they had to wait until the journalistic boom elsewhere had ended. Other than the successful *Register* in the quarter century from 1867 to 1892, only one other Eugene newspaper is listed in the files of Oregon libraries as having a founding date in these years. This was the Eugene City *Hawk-Eye* in the mid-Seventies.[11] A *Hawk-Eye* was not included in Rowell's tabulations, nor in Ayer's, for it survived less than 13 months.

Eugene City's press aside, journalism's surge in Oregon was a fascinating phenomenon. With the eventual coming of the railroads, great masses of settlers reached Oregon, mostly from across the Northern Plains. The Northern Pacific Railroad of Henry Villard (himself a journalist in Civil War days and the owner of the New York *Evening Post* in the 1880s) reached the Pacific Coast in 1883. Those who came along the "NP" from its starting place in St. Paul changed the whole Oregon population picture. These new Oregonians were people with high standards of literacy and education, who needed public schools, who became business men and industrial leaders, and who started commercially minded newspapers. Most of them were Republicans.

The pioneer editors of the Civil War era had been equally divided between Republicans and Democrats, as the Eugene City press story shows, with the pro-Southern Democrats having come mostly from the Missouri region.[12]

Ayer's Directory in 1890 listed 41 Republican newspapers in Oregon and 27 Democratic. Fifteen by then reported themselves as having "no politics," while 38 called themselves "Independent." Twenty-one were special-interest papers.[13] All the state's 31 counties that year had one or more newspapers; 70 different towns shared the 142 total; weeklies led with 114, and there were already 16 dailies. Eugene, although not having a daily in Ayer's 1890 listing, saw the *Guard* go daily the next

The Guard office about 1871

year. Nine additional Oregon papers of 1890 were monthlies, two semi-monthly, and one semi-weekly.[14]

Every town in Oregon in these 25 years thought of itself as "a future metropolis," every property owner considered himself a "future millionaire," and every weekly was sure it was a "potential daily."[15] In fact, of the 16 dailies in the state 12 retained their weekly editions to serve outlying readers and counted themselves as two newspapers; one daily had a weekly and a semi-weekly and counted itself as three. The Portland *Oregonian* had a daily, weekly, and a Sunday—total three. Only the Portland *Telegram* and the Portland *Examiner* were dailies wholly.[16]

Claims of circulation in these years were utterly unrealistic. There was no Audit Bureau of Circulations in 1890, and Ayer shows only nine of Oregon's 142 newspapers as having sworn circulations. The remainder had circulations based on publisher's reports or Ayer Agency estimates. Not one Portland paper issued a sworn statement, nor did the three in Eugene. Ayer estimated the Eugene City *Guard* of 1890 at 1,082 circulation, the *Register* at 750, and the *Oregon State Journal* at 850 (Harrison Kincaid's own figure). The Eugene newspapers at least appeared to show reasonably accurate figures. The *Guard's* 1,082 circulation was for a city of 3,086 population in 1890. In Dallas (Polk County) one newspaper was claiming 1,056 circulation in a town of 800; a paper in Union (Union County) said it had 1,100 in a place of 1,169; a paper in Coquille on the coast (Coos County) claimed 880 in a hamlet of 350. So it ran throughout the state.

Hubert Howe Bancroft's contemporary history of Oregon commented on the Oregon press in 1888:

> "A few only of these [state newspapers] had any particular significance. The *Astorian*, founded in 1872 by D.C. Ireland as a marine journal should be excepted."

Bancroft also commented on the *Inland Empire* of The Dalles as a paper excellent in disseminating information on all topics.

He regarded the *West Shore* of Portland, established in 1875 by L. Samuels, as a worthy paper ranging from eight to 20 to 30 pages, local in character, illustrated, and interested in architectural improvements. The *West Shore* served Oregon, Washington, Idaho, Montana, and British Columbia.[17]

Of course this newspaper boom couldn't last. The mortality rate in ensuing years took care of the bulk of these hopeful sheets of the 1880s. Fifty years later the survival rate was 36 per cent.[18] Eugene City's newspapers, not a part of the boom, fared better.

The Seventies and Eighties saw also the beginnings of journalism in Lane County outside Eugene. Ayer in 1890 listed a paper in Junction City, 14 miles north. The Junction City *Pilot* was published by J.B. Morin; it had been established in 1888 and had a circulation estimated at 430. For Cottage Grove, 21 miles south of Eugene City, Ayer listed the *Leader*, published by F.W. Chausse and also established in 1888, with a sworn circulation of 300. Turnbull, who gives a more detailed account of Lane County newspapers outside Eugene,[19] says Junction City had a newspaper as early as 1878. Springfield, Eugene's sister city four miles east, had no newspaper until 1892—the *Messenger*. It was founded by W. Frank Gilstrap, who in 1899 became a co-publisher of the Eugene *Register*.[20]

Slow Pace in Eugene City

Meanwhile, Eugene City plugged ahead, with town and press showing none of the gleaming spurts taking place elsewhere in Oregon. The history of the city has been told in one full-length book and included in various histories of Oregon, but the Eugene newspaper story has been unreported heretofore. So some tie-in is needed to indicate the surroundings in which *Guard* and *Register* were operating.

"City" disappeared from Eugene's name in 1889. Lewis A. McArthur, once president of the Oregon Historical Society, who was an authority on Oregon place-names, notes that from Skinner's Post Office, January 8, 1850, the town changed to Eugene

City September 2, 1853, by choice of Mrs. Mary Skinner, and finally to Eugene May 29, 1889.[21] City ordinances indicate that Eugene City somewhat earlier had decided to drop the "City." An ordinance passed by the Council February 11, 1889, bears the imprint Eugene City. (It dealt with control of prostitution.) The next ordinance, passed March 11, 1889, indicated council action only as Eugene. (It dealt with control of smoking and the sale of tobacco to juveniles.)[22]

In its first issue in April, 1889, the Eugene City *Register* changed its logotype to Eugene *Register*, but its only editorial note was that the new form was leaving "City" out. The paper gave no reason.[23] The *Guard*, however, stuck with Eugene City *Guard* until the paper became the Eugene *Daily Guard* and Eugene *Weekly Guard* (two newspapers) two years later.[24] The *Oregon State Journal* had no problem in its name, but it did not drop "City" from its datelines until summer.[25]

This merely shows lack of interest in coverage of official news. Any formal change in a city's name would warrant specific attention in the news columns, but reporting practice was yet undeveloped in 1889. Unlike an Oregon City or Kansas City or New York City, Eugene did not need further identification to avoid confusion with the state.

In area, too, there was change by the 1890s, although not much by today's standards of size. From the 20-odd square blocks at the time of incorporation, Eugene by 1892 reached from the Willamette River at the foot of North Monroe Street south to Fifteenth, east (with a two-block jog) on Fifteenth and Seventeenth to University Street, north to a mill-pond at Ninth, and then diagonally northwest across open space back to the river. About 150 square blocks of this had been platted, but there were wide stretches of unimproved land. The University of Oregon, however, had come within the city limits—six to eight square blocks at the extreme eastern edge.[26]

Several "suburbs" (or, more accurately, real estate promotions) had sprung up to augment the 3,000-odd population. These were College Hill Park, the area of the ill-fated Columbia

College of pre-Civil War days, south and west; Fairmount, University Addition to Fairmount, and Glenwood, south and east; and the separate city of Springfield, four miles east. The first three are today part of Eugene; Glenwood has never been annexed; and Springfield, with different interests, has now 22,000 population in its own right. But as of 1892 Eugene's geography had assumed the general outlines of what it became in the 1960s.[27]

The W.G. Obenauer Company was the publisher of Eugene's first city directory, in 1892. Obenauer forecast, with only some inaccuracy: "Springfield, Eugene and Fairmount are fast growing into one city with Fairmount in the center."[28] Within another decade another Eugene directory publisher was even more optimistic: "Eugene will, if the rate of increase in population for the past two years is maintained, become a city of 10,000 inhabitants in five or six years. . . . [Eugene] has plenty of resources with which to support a population of 25,000 if the tillable lands were properly inhabited on the outside."[29] This forecast was more than a decade too hopeful on the 10,000 inhabitants, for Eugene did not reach that figure until 1920; on the 25,000 estimate the second directory far underestimated potential. But this was the way things looked in 1892 and 1902.

What had to develop in Eugene before 1900, quite apart from her small newspapers, was the building of essential services of a town. By 1869 the Eugene Water Ditch Company had been formed in order to bring a water supply from the hills two and a half miles above Eugene City. In the same year the Eugene City Distilling Company (70 gallons a day) was the biggest taxpayer. By 1871, October 8, the first Oregon and California train reached Eugene City, but it was to take another 16 years before this line crossed the mountains southward and was connected with the route coming north from San Francisco.

By 1872 the Oregon State Legislature passed an act providing that the state university be located permanently in Eugene City, subject to certain fulfillments by the city in land and money. It was long uncertain whether the University of Oregon would get under way; no students enrolled until 1876, and it wasn't until 1878 that the University graduated its first class of five. The tie-in between city and university was later to prove a vital one for both, with the University proving a boon to the community and in time gaining courageous and enduring support from Eugene's newspapers. In the Seventies, however, education was one of the least of the city's concerns.[30]

Plans for a bridge across the Willamette River were under way in 1873, and in 1879 residents of the Siuslaw area petitioned the Lane County Court for a road to the Oregon Coast. In the 1880s this road got as far as Mapleton along the general line of what is now the locally famous Route F (Eugene-Elmira-Noti-Walton-Mapleton). This is now Oregon State Highway 126.

Harrison Kincaid tells in his autobiography how in the 1860s he had to travel to the coast by a devious route through Corvallis. By two-horse wagon Kincaid could reach Corvallis and continue west across the Coast Range to tidewater on the Yaquina River east of the present Newport. From there, Kincaid says, a steamer operated.[31]

The struggle to get transportation across the Cascades was one to continue through the rest of the Nineteenth Century and into the paved-road developments up toward mid-Twentieth—from the McKenzie River Wagon Road Company (formed January 14, 1871) to completion of a highway across the McKenzie Pass in the 1920s and across the Willamette Pass as late as 1940. The *Guard*, the *Register*, and the *Register-Guard* are filled for decades with transportation news, much of it tied to modern-day Eugene's industrial and recreational growth. The full impact of press attention to this phase of Lane County's progress was not realized until the *Register-Guard* became the county's single journalistic force.

Schools, of course, were a continuing story before 1900, and in 1885 the Eugene City schools had to close down because the school board lacked funds.

The first bank came in 1883, the first electric lights in 1887, and the first Lane County Fair in 1884, when the City Council gave the Lane County Agricultural Society permission to use public streets for displays. The electric lights were not always satisfactory, for in 1892 they were out of commission for six weeks because of a fire in the plant of the Eugene Electric Light Company.

In 1890 and 1891, along with the *Guard* becoming the county's first daily, a street railway was started and $5,000 was raised to open a cannery. By 1894 there were 35 telephones, but that new invention wasn't taking hold; in 1900 only 46 telephones were in service.

Logging, always a major industry in Eugene, went back to the earliest days, but not until R.A. Booth, J.H. Booth, and John F. Kelly and George A. Kelly started the Booth-Kelly firm in 1896 did logging become large-scale.

By 1898, under the guidance of Dr. William Kuykendall and a group of physicians, Eugene opened its first hospital (Eugene Hospital) and early in 1902 the city had a Commercial Club, later the Eugene Chamber of Commerce.

Despite all these marks of progress, hogs for many years continued to be a nuisance. B.F. Dorris, mayor of Eugene City from 1875 to 1877 and from 1879 to 1881, said in his annual report to the City Council in 1876:

> "Within the last month complaints have been made to me against the marshal for non-performance of duty in permitting the hogs belonging to the Mill Company to run at large. I have suggested a pond near the jail to intern the hogs and other livestock."[32]

At the turn of the century there were 389 business establishments in Eugene under 54 different listings, from "Attorneys" to "Wood Saws." Carpenters led with 54; next came lawyers with 21; "manufactories," 20; dressmakers and physicians, tied at 19 each; and 11 saloons. There was still only one cannery, along with one ice-house.[33]

This truncated account of a gradually growing community far out in the Pacific Northwest gives perspective to the story of Eugene's newspapers. With local variations, the same kind of developments took place in community after community. Only personal names, specific kinds of business, and speed of success or failure changed much from one place to another. For Lane County, a regional history was compiled as far back as 1884, by A.G. Walling. The University of Oregon has had one history written, by Professor Henry D. Sheldon. Harvey W. Scott of the *Oregonian* compiled a history of the Oregon Country, this being filled with his own multitudinous comments in editorials from 1865 to 1910, many of which dealt with Lane County and Eugene. George S. Turnbull has written a 560-page *History of Oregon Newspapers.* Eugene has its own history in *The Story of Eugene,* by Lucia Moore, Nina W. McCormack, and Gladys W. McCready.[34]

Before we pick up again the newspaper story, let us quote from Walling, writing in the year the *Guard* was 17 and the *Register* was born:

> "Another potent sign of progress which is second to none, is the establishment and publication of newspapers in a settlement. Through their columns does the world without learn of the unknown land within; by their means information from abroad is disseminated through the home community; and through them are immigrants influenced."[35]

The files of the Eugene *Guard* and the Eugene *Register* and, since November 18, 1930, their successor Eugene *Register-Guard* tell Eugene's story in their own way.

---

1. U.S. Census Office, *Ninth Census, 1870.* Washington: G.P.O., 1872.
2. U.S. Census Office, *Eighth Census, 1860.* Washington: G.P.O., 1862. Oregon's first census, in 1850, showed 13,294 for the Territory; Lane County breakdowns were not given.

3. *Ibid.*, 1870. Multnomah, 11,510; Marion, 9,965; Linn, 8,717; Lane, 6,426; Douglas, 6,066.

4. U.S. Census Office, *Tenth Census, 1880.* Washington: G.P.O., 1883-1888. Portland, 17,577; Salem, 3,390; Astoria, 2,803; The Dalles, 2,232; Albany, 1,867; East Portland, 1,405; Oregon City, 1,263; Baker City, 1,258; Corvallis, 1,128; Eugene City, 1,117.

5. U.S. Census Office, *Eleventh Census, 1890.* Washington: G.P.O., 1892-1897. Eugene's population was given as the sum of two census districts. The inside-city-limits population appears to have been 3,086. Portland in 1890 had 46,385; East Portland, 10,532; Salem, 6,894, and Astoria, 6,184. Albany had dropped behind Eugene to 3,079; Oregon City to 3,062, and The Dalles to 3,029. After 1890 only Albany kept relatively close to Eugene for some years.

6. A weekly *Guard* continued to September 29, 1910, and a twice-a-week *Guard* to March, 1914. The *Register* dropped its weekly in 1904.

7. George P. Rowell, *Centennial Newspaper Exhibition, 1876.* New York, 1876. Exhibition displayed at Fairmount Park, Philadelphia.

8. *Rowell's American Newspaper Directory.* New York: G.P. Rowell, 1879.

Rowell, *Centennial, op. cit.*, p. xi. Rowell listed the Eugene City *Guard* and the *Oregon State Journal* as the 6,246th and 6,247th newspapers in alphabetized sequence by states, both as weeklies. He described Eugene City: "Court house, Lane County, 1,600 pop., on Willamette r., head of Willamette Valley, on Oregon & California Rd., 125 mi. S. of Portland and 72 S. of Salem. Grain producing the principal branch of industry." p. 135.

9. Rowell, *Centennial, op. cit.*, pp. xi-xii.

10. *Directory of Newspapers and Periodicals.* Philadelphia: N.W. Ayer & Son, 1890.

11. See pp. 77-78 ff. for discussion of the *Hawk-Eye.*

12. Eric W. Allen, "Oregon Journalism in 1887" *Oregon Historical Quarterly.* Vol. 38, (September, 1937), p. 252.

13. Special interests: religion, 6; "local," 5; labor 2; and real estate, prohibition, commercial, farm pharmacy, education, family, and college (Willamette University), all 1 each. Ayer, *op. cit.*, p. 595.

14. *Ibid.*, pp. 595-601.

15. Allen, *op. cit.*, pp. 255-264.

16. Ayer, *op. cit.*, p. 595-601.

17. Hubert Howe Bancroft, *The Works of Hubert Howe Bancroft.* San Francisco: The History Company, 1888, Vol. 30, p. 692.

18. Allen, *op. cit.*, pp. 595-601.

19. George S. Turnbull, *History of Oregon Newspapers.* Portland, Oregon: Binfords & Mort, 1939, pp. 268-274, 281-283.

20. *Ibid.*, pp. 281-283.

Ayer, *op. cit.*

21. Lewis A. McArthur, *Oregon Geographic Names*, 3rd ed. Portland, Oregon: Binfords & Mort, 1952, p. 218.

22. *Council Records*, Eugene City (Ordinance No. 64) 1889.

Council Records, City of Eugene (Ordinance No. 65), 1889.

23. Eugene *Register*, April 3, 1889.

24. Eugene City *Guard*, April 6, 1889.

25. *Oregon State Journal*, July 27, 1889.

26. University boundaries: Thirteenth, from Kincaid to University Street; University to County Road, now Franklin Boulevard; County Road to Eleventh, then Eleventh to Kincaid; Kincaid to Thirteenth.

27. The big promoter of Fairmount was George Melvin Miller, younger brother of Joaquin. Like Joaquin, George was a visionary with grandiose ideas —and a big *Guard* advertiser.

28. *Eugene City and Lane County Directory*. Portland, Eugene and Albany: compiled and published by W.G. Obenauer & Co., 1892, p. 15.

29. O.B. Tout, *The Eugene Directory*. Eugene, Oregon: Press of W.O. Yoran, 1902, p. 126. The Yoran Press was the printer of the Eugene *Register* from 1884 to 1899.

30. Henry Villard's benefactions were instrumental in making it possible for the University to get started. See Eugene *Morning Register*, "Lane County Edition, 1904," undated; and Eugene *Daily Guard*, "Special Edition," December 8, 1906.

31. Harrison R. Kincaid, *Sunshine and Shadow: The Autobiography of H.R. Kincaid*, Microfilm Oregon State Historical Society. Portland, Oregon: 1917.

32. *Register-Guard*, "75th Anniversary Edition," January 4, 1942.

33. Tout, *op. cit.*, pp. 86-110.

34. Henry D. Sheldon, *History of the University of Oregon*. Portland, Oregon: Binfords & Mort, 1940. All the other titles have been cited heretofore.

35. Albert G. Walling, *Illustrated History of Lane County, Oregon*. Portland, Oregon: Walling Printing and Lithographing House, 1884, p. 348.

CHAPTER 4

The Guard Is Founded, And Lapses—But 'Makes It'

The histories of newspapers have been told best in the biographies of and autobiographies by their editors and publishers. These narratives reveal more, or at least as much, as economic accounts and analyses of news events that the newspapers handled. Most of the major biographies have been those of metropolitan editors who founded major journals, exerted impact upon their cities, outshone their competitors, built empires large and small, and stayed around long enough to leave records and writings of their own that were easily retrievable.

In the history of the Eugene City *Guard* and Eugene City *Register* we have no such accessible material to help us gain information. Publishers and co-publishers came and went—at least 10 of them for the *Guard* from 1867 to 1906 and 13 for the *Register* from 1884 to 1907. The *Guard's* history in these years involved six different ownerships and the *Register's* involved five. So far as can be learned, the second *Guard* publisher was in charge only five weeks. Another appeared on the masthead with his senior partner for the full length of their ownership but was not once mentioned by that partner. A third co-partner was dropped after a few months without specific explanation.

For the *Register*, the co-founder later became a shoe merchant in Eugene, a fact that recalls an often-quoted derogatory quip that newspapers, to succeed, cannot be run like shoe stores. In the case of the *Register*, newspapering and shoe merchandising were profitable businesses for the paper's first commercially aggressive entrepreneur; and it is on record that he gave up the newspaper for the shoe business. Later, three other co-owners of the *Register*, who kept the paper only a short time, never put their names on the masthead.

THE GUARD.

VOL. 1. EUGENE CITY, OREGON, SATURDAY, JULY 13, 1867. NO. 7.

THE GUARD.

PUBLISHED EVERY SATURDAY, BY

J. B. ALEXANDER.

TERMS—Three dollars a year, invariably in advance.

Rates of Advertising.—Legal, and other transient advertisements, will be charged at the rate of $3 00 per square for the first insertion and, $1 00 for each subsequent insertion. Twelve lines or less of Minion type counted a square.

A liberal deduction from the above rates made to persons advertising by the year.

The number of insertions must be marked on all transient advertisements or they will be continued until ordered out, and charged for accordingly.

S. HEINSHWAY, M.D.,
PHYSICIAN & SURGEON
Office at Residence.
EUGENE CITY, - - OREGON.

DR. A. W. PATTERSON,
Office at Residence.
Eugene City, - - - - - - - - - Oregon.

MEDICAL NOTICE.
Dr. L. Danforth

HAS permantly located in Eugene City, and offers his professional services to the inhabitants of this place and vicinity.

Residence on Olive Street. Office on Willamette Street, one door north of A. A. Smith's store.

DR. A. N. FOLEY,
PHYSICIAN & SURGEON,
Office near M. E. Church,
EUGENE CITY, - - - OREGON.

UNDERWOOD & DORRIS,
ATTORNEYS AT LAW
Office on Willamette Street.
Eugene City, - - - - - - - Oregon.

Z. D. SERMAN,
ATTORNEY AT LAW,
Eugene City, - - - - - - Oregon
Office at the Court House.
Collections promptly attended to.

J. J. WALTON, Jr.,
Attorney & Counseller at Law.
Office at the Court House.
EUGENE CITY, ... Oregon.

NEW TANNERY,
J. T. WITTER,
Eighth St. (near the Bridge.)

LEATHER FOR SALE.
HIDES OF ALL KINDS TAKEN IN EXchange for Leather.
Eugene City June 1st, 1867. 1—tf

SHAVING & HAIR DRESSING.

THE UNDERSIGNED HAVING FITTED up his Shaving & Hair Dressing Saloon in a neat and comfortable manner begs leave to say to those who want a Good and Easy Shave or their hair cut in the latest and most approved style or an old-fashioned Shampoo, that he is just the man they want to see. Being an old hand at the Biz. he is enabled to work at reduced rates. Give me a call and if I don't suit you—I'm mistaken.

Remember the place—next door to the Telegraph Office.

W. J. MARCUS.
Eugene City, June 1st, 1867. 1—3m

H. M. RUSS,
CITY BOOT & SHOE
MANUFACTORY.

THE FINEST QUALITY OF FRENCH CALF BOOTS—pegged and sewed—made to order.

ALL of my work is
WARRANTED
To give satisfaction to my patrons.

SHOP on Wilamette Street, one door north of Wand & Co.'s Tin Shop,
Eugene City, June 1, 1867.—1tf.

Renfrew's
ST. CHARLES HOTEL.
Eugene City, Oregon.

THIS ESTABLISHED AND POPULAR Hotel is open for the accommodation of travelers and the public generally.

Commodious Rooms, Good Beds and a well Supplied Table,

Are among the inducements offered to guests at this Hotel.

The California and Oregon Stages

Have their Office at the St. Charles, and make it their point of starting and arrival.

Parties traveling in their own conveyances can have their Vehicles and Animals well cared for.

The Proprietor is thankful to the public generally for the patronage so liberally extended to him in the past and would respectfully solicit a continuance of the same.

This House is kept on the Restaurant principle—meals at all hours.

A. RENFREW, Proprietor.

W. J. J. SCOTT. - - - - F. B. DUNN

SCOTT & DUNN,
Wholesale and Retail
DEALERS IN
GENERAL MERCHANDISE.

WOULD RESPECTFULLY ANNOUNCE to the citizens of Lane and adjoining counties, that they have the most complete assortment and the greatest variety of Goods to be found in the upper valley. Our stock is large, well selected and bought cheap, and consists in part of

Hardware and Ladies' Dress Goods, Hoop Skirts and Hoop Iron, Skein Thread and Thimble Skeins, Needles, Pins and Carriage Bolts, Ladies' Shoes and Horse Shoes, and Infant's, Misses', Boys' & Mule Shoes, Hair Pins & Fine Tooth Combs. Ax Handles & Ladies' Hats, Sausage Stuffers & Swis Mull, Jaconette, Laces, Edgings, Fringes, Gloves, &c.,

A large stock of
Woolen Goods
Of every description.

BARN DOOR ROLLERS & HINGES, IRON, STEEL, GROCERIES, PAINTS, OILS, AXES, BRUSHES, &c. &c.

We are receiving new supplies by every boat, and intend to keep up with the demands of the country, and will not be undersold.

CASH PAID FOR
WOOL.
Call and try us.
SCOTT & DUNN.
Eugene City, June 1, 1867. 1-tf.

BUY AT
WALTON'S.

J. J. WALTON, ... C. W. WALTON.

WALTON & SON

WISH IT TO BE GENERALLY KNOWN that they have on hand a well selected stock of

General Merchandise,

which they are selling on terms and at prices to suit the times.

Their stock consists in part of

DRY GOODS,
GROCERIES,
HARDWARE,
QUEENSWARE,
STATIONERY,
CLOTHING,
HATS
CAPS, BOOTS, SHOES, FANCY GOODS, &c. &c.

Ladies and gentlemen desiring to purchase will do well to give us a call before making their purchases, and examine our goods and prices.
We are determined to sell goods
CHEAP AS THE CHEAPEST, for
CASH OR COUNTRY PRODUCE.

Come and see us at the old stand on Willamette street, next door to the Dennison House.

WALTON & SON.
Eugene City, June 1, 1867.—1tf.

MILLINERY!
(Sign of the Green Band-box, next door to Bristow & Co's Brick.)

MRS. U. C. MARCUS RESPECTFULly asks the ladies of Eugene City and vicinity to call and examine her stock of

Millinery Goods.

She will keep constantly on hand a supply of Bonnets of the latest and most fashionable styles. Also, a complete assortment of Dress, Cloak, Hat and Bonnet Trimmings, carefully selected in Portland by the most fashionable Milliner in the State. She is also prepared to render her services to the ladies in

Mantua making,

And promises satisfaction to all who patronize her.

Orders from the country attended to with dispatch.

Eugene City, June 1, 1867.—1m3.

A. W. PATTERSON. G. W. COOPER.

PATTERSON & COOPER,
DRUGGISTS,
(Successors to B. Jennings & Co.)

KEEP CONSTANTLY ON HAND A FULL and complete assortment of

Drugs,
Medicines,
Chemicals,
Paints,
Oils,
Dyes,
Liquors, etc., etc.

Of the Best and Purest Qualities.

Physicians Prescriptions and Orders ...

A Good Thing for Everybody Who who wish to Save Money!

Goods at Greatly Reduced Prices!

Cheap Cash Store!!

S. STEINHEISER

HAS just returned from San Francisco and opened, on Ninth Steet, in the building formerly occupied by Bristow & Co., next door to the Postoffice, his large and well selected stock of

General Merchandize:

Consisting of

Dry Goods,
Clothing,
Groceries,
Salem Cloth,
Domestic,
Prints,
Hats and Caps,
Trunks, Valices,
Glassware,
Crockery,
Hardware,
Cutlery,

Cigars, Tobacco, Hosiery, Canned Fruit, Fancy Goods, &c.

Ladies' & Gent's Furnishing Goods.

A large assortment of
Ladies' Cloak and Dress Bugle and Bead Trimming.

A great variety of
Ladies', Misses and Children's Gaiters and Balmoral Shoes,
Godo Borgia Chains and Ear Rings,

And a great many other articles too numerous to mention.

I most respectfully invite the citizens of Eugene City and the public generally to call and see before purchasing elsewhere. I intend to sell

Cheap for Cash.

My motto is, "Quick sales and small profits." Please call and convince yourselves; by doing so you will find it to your advantage and save forty per cent. in the worth of your money.

THE HIGHEST MARKET PRICE PAID FOR ALL KINDS OF
COUNTRY PRODUCE.
—ALSO—
FURS OF ALL KINDS WANTED.
The highest market price paid in
CASH for
WOOL.
S. STEINHEISER.
Eugene City, June 1, 1867.-1tf.

FURNITURE STORE,

At the old Stand of

J. F. Muntz, one door south of Osburn & Maxwell's Tin Shop.

On hand and to arrive,

Bedsteads,
Tables,
Chairs,
Stands,
Center Tables,
Lounges,
Sofas,
Bureaus, &c., &c.

From this date, we shall adopt the pre pay system, either for cash or produce at the market price. We have determined to sell CHEAPER than any other establishment this side of Salem; so bring along your ready pay, and you can get great bargains.

All kinds of
TURNING
done in good style and at the shortest notice.
CAMPBELL & GARDNER.
Eugene City, June 1, 1867. 1-tf

LAGER BEER SALOON.

THE PROPRIETORS BEG LEAVE TO REturn their thanks to their old customers for their former liberal patronage, and would say that they will still be found at

"THE LAGER"

ready to furnish them and the public generally with anything in their line.

Our Bar is always supplied with the best and finest LIQUORS in the country.

Whiskey,
Rum,
Gin,
Schnapps,
Hostetters,
Hoofland's,
Brandy,
Wine,
Lager,

and, in fact, any and everything that is "good to take."

We also have a large and full stock of
Oysters, Sardines, Nuts, Confectionaries, Cigars, Tobacco, Merschaum Pipes, Toys, Fancy Goods, etc.
Drop in and take a sip.
COLEMAN BROTHERS.

BELL & DEXTER,
BOOKSELLERS and STATIONERS
638 CLAY STREET,
SAN FRANCISCO, CALIFORNIA.

GENERAL AGENTS for American and Foreign Magazines, Newspapers and other Periodicals. Importers and Dealers in Books and Stationery of every description, Law books, Blank books, and School books.

Newspapers, Magazines, Reviews, Medical and Scintific Journals, or either Periodicals published in any part of the World, will be furnished to order. A circular will be sent on request, giving a more extended list of Magazines and Papers, with the price annexed. The following are some of the most popular:

	PER YEAR.
Harper's Monthly Magazine	$3 50
Godey's Lady's Book	2 50
Atlantic Monthly	3 00
Leslie's lady's Magazine	2 50
Ladies Depository	3 50
Hours at Home	3 00
Peterson's Ladies Magazine	2 50
Arthur's Home Magazine	2 50
Our Young Folks	2 00
Merry's Museum	1 50
The Playmate	1 50
Beadle's Monthly	3 00
Mad. Demorest's Magazine of Fashions	3 00
Eclectic Magazine	5 50
Ballou's Magazine	2 50
Every Saturday, monthly parts	4 50
All the Year Round, English edition	6
Once a Week, monthly p's	6
The Cornhill Magazine	6
Temple Bar, G. A. Sala's	6
London Society	6
Good Words	4
English Woman's domestic Magazine	7 50
Young English Woman	4 50
Intellectual Observer	7 50
Hall's Journal of Health	1 50
London Lancet	5 50
Braithwaite's Retrospect of Medicine	3
Am. Med. Jour Science & Medical News and Library	6
New York Medical Journal	5
N. A. Journal of Homeopathy	5
The Builder, monthly parts	11
Chambre's Journal	4 50
Blackwook's Edenburg Magazine	3 50
London Quarterly Review	3
Westminister Review	3
Edenburgh Review	3
North British Review	3
The four Foreign Reviews	10
Do and Blackwook's	12
North American Review	5 50
Catholic World	5 50
American Mining Gazette	5
United States Insurance Gazette	5
U. S. Service Magazine	8
Hunt's Merchant's Magazine	5 50
Banker's do	5 50
Guardian	12
Christian Remembrance	10
Churchman's Family Magazine	6
Church of England Magazine	4
Christian Examiner, Boston	5
American Agriculturalist	2
Working Farmer	150
American Farmer	1 50
Masonic Review	3
Phrenological Journal	2
Herald of Health	2
Yankee Notions, comic	2
Mr Merryman's Monthly	2
Nick Nax, monthly	2
Leslie's Budget of Fun	2
Illustrated London News	13
London Times, weekly	10
London Times, daily, last date	12
London Dispatch, weekly	13
Bell's Life in London	13
London Athenaeum	11
London Punch	7
Evening Mail, tri-weekly	25
London Mining Journal	13
Army and Navy Journal	6
Mining & Petroleum Standard & Gaslight Journal	3
Scottish American Journal	13 50
New England Farmer	2 50
Turf, Field and Farm	5
Wilkes' Spirit of the Times	4
New York Weekly Clipper	3 50
do do Gazette	2 50
do do Ledger	3 50
do do Mercury	3
do do Home Journal	3
do do Independent	3
do do Leader	3
dd do Staats Zietung	3
do do Weekly Tribune	3 50
do do do Times	2 50
do do do World	2 50
do do Herald for Cal's	3 50
Leslie's Illustrated Paper	3 50
do do German	3 50
Literary Companion	3 50
Flag of our Union	3 50
Waverley Magazine	4 50
National Republican	3 50
Portland Transcript	3
Boston Weekly Journal	3 50
California Police Gazette	6 00
California Golden Era	5 00
San Francisco Weekly Alta	5 00
dd do Bulletin	5 00
The Pacific Churchman	4 00
Sacramento Union, weekly	5 00

Saturday Review	$13	Church Journal	4
Public Opinion	11	Country Gentleman	2 50
The Engineer	13	Rural New Yorker	3 50
Every Saturday	4 50	Prairie Farmer	2 50
Round Table	5 50	Harper's Weekly	2 50
Littel's Living Age	7	Literary Album	3 50
Scientific American	3 50	Chimney Corner	3 50
American Artisan	3	Mo. Republican	3 50
Oil News	3 50	N. O. True Delta	5 50
The Nation	5 50	do Picayune	5 50
Banner of Light	3 50	Forney's Press	3 50
Irish American	3 50	Boston Pilot	3 50
Irish People, N. Y.	3	Cal. Mercury	4 00

Agency for the Art Union of London. Subscriptions received for the Annual Distribution of Paintings and other Works of Art.

Postmasters sending orders will be allowed a commission. Orders from the trade supplied on the best terms.

I SAY, STRANGER!

A. A. SMITH,
Dealer in
GENERAL MERCHANDISE,
EUGENE CITY, OREGON,

THANKFUL for the liberal patronage in the past, would call the attention of the public to his well selected assortment of

MERCHANDISE.

He will buy all kinds of

PRODUCE,

Will pay the highest market price, in CASH, for any quantity of

WOOL.

I will sell Goods CHEAPER than any merchant in Eugene City, for CASH.

A. A. SMITH.

TRAIN ON FINANCE.

The following is an extract from a speech delivered in the Gold Room of Geo. Fracis Train. Mr Train was called upon for a speech and he gave them his views without any reserve. The people will do well to hear what Wall street says and prepare for a near and terrible storm. After reviewing the financial condition of the country from 1861 to the present time and contrasting our situation then and now he supposes the crisis to have begun and says:

"Then comes the rush on National banks for greenbacks, and the greenbacks are not there. (Sensation.) What is the result? Does Congress help us? No—the lawyers are in power; what do they care? They add $400,000,000 bounty to the debt, and advance their own salaries to $5,000! Is the South to be admitted under the Military Bill? No; Stevens holds the reins. Where, then, are we floating? Congress sees McCulloch has made a mistake; and it is an administration blunder, the Jacobins intend to pass no bill of relief. They will pinch the country this year and bring on a financial crash in the fall—(remember this is the panic year of the never-failing sevens)—lay it on the Administration policy, and when every body is broken, Congress will meet in the winter and pass Randall's bill, putting greenbacks in the place of the $300,000,000 National bank bill. Pass another bill paying duties on imports in greenbacks, and then another bill paying interest on the $1,400,000,000 five-twenties in legal tenders. In other words, give the country one currency—that is, twenty-five hundred millions of legal tenders, instead of sixteen currencies as at present. (Applause.) This makes all happy for the Presidential elections of 1868. *Delirium tremens* requiers National whiskey to recuperate the system. The next war is to be financial. Land and labor against banks and bondholders—and the former own the notes The South had no debt. The West little. The greenback age wiped off their mortgages, and placed the load on the back of the bondholders. The debt, rests uneasily on the seashore and in Europe, and the shadow is on the wall.

Paying gold interest in greenbacks is repudiation you say. Why so? nearly all the States have done it, New York taking the lead. The finalty of all the recent Congressional legislation may be stated in two words. *Confiscation* and *Repudiation*. (Sensation.) The Chicago papers have already sounded the tocsin; we are growing poorer every day. The $2,500,000,000 debt only cost $1,250,000,000.—But bondholders ask specie payments.—The people who did the fighting hold no bonds, and ask for legal tenders. The rich arraged to have their bonds free from taxation. Hence the rich man with his millions of untaxed Governments, sends his children to the same school where the poor man, with no bonds, sends his.—Hence the poor man is obliged to pay for the education of the rich man's children as well as for his own. (Sensation.) But enough of this. You asked me for a speech, and you have got it. You have been dancing five years and the fiddler demands his pay. When the candle is lighted at both ends you had better sell it short.

DEMORALIZATION OF HAYTI.—The latest news from Hayti confirms the previously reported flight of Geffrard to Jamaica, after having sent in his resignation of the Presidency of that stormy republic. The election of another President was expected to take place immediately after the departure of Geffrard. The history of Hayti since the negro population obtained its freedom has been a series of sanguinary revolutions and civil wars, and the country is probably in a worse condition now than ever before. The negro leaders have never shown themselves capable of agreeing upon or establishing anything like a sound and substantial government. Life and property have always been exceedingly insecure and the constant danger of the new revolutions has tended to keep the country in deplorable condition. If the African race had any capacity for self-government they had the best possible opportunities of developing these talents in Hayti where they have had things their own way for more than twenty years past.

The trouble appears to be that their own way is a very disorderly and rebellious one. They have gone backwards in morals and education, and have attained proficiency in none of the arts of civilization except that of war and political intrigue. Under their own management their property and credit have alike deteriorated in value, and the nation has made itself an object of pity to those who expected better things of the race, and of ridicule to those who understood them better and foresaw the result of the wild experiment of negro self-government. The normal condition of the negro is such that it is only by constant association with superior races that anything like civilization can be imparted to the race. Even after such advantages there is an inevitable tendency to relapse into barbarity when the elevating influence is withdrawn.—N. Y. Sun.

THE REASON.—A Georgia nigger orator says down South they are going to mix the races like rum and molasses. That's what makes the Yankee ...

Page One, July 13, 1867
Earliest known edition of The Guard

City Edition

Eugene Register-Guard

LANE COUNTY'S HOME NEWSPAPER

Second Page One on Page 2A

97th Year, No. 30 | TWO SECTIONS—30 PAGES | Eugene, Oregon, Friday, November 22, 1963 | Price, 5 Cents

John F. Kennedy President 1961-63

Page One, November 22, 1963
An eloquent story told without words

Yet, to get a fair picture of Eugene's two newspapers in the years after 1867, we must as best we can tell what can be told about them. What can be found varies from much to almost nothing. The sum total, however, gives a representative picture of small-city journalism in the Oregon of the time.

Pioneer editors were careless about keeping files. Volume 1, Number 1 of the *Guard* has never been located, although the search for it has been going on for 30 years at least and although its June 1, 1867 date has now been verified. In the case of the short-lived Eugene City *Hawk-Eye* of 1873 and 1874 two single copies are known to be in Oregon libraries, one real copy and nine photocopies are in the Lane County Pioneer Museum and about a dozen issues are held by an 86-year-old niece of the *Hawk-Eye's* publisher.

George S. Turnbull, professor emeritus of journalism at the University of Oregon, considered March, 1867, as a possibility for John B. Alexander's starting the *Guard*, since one researcher in 1924 indicated that month.[1] Professor Turnbull later decided October, 1867 had a better claim.[2] And as long ago as August 27, 1887, Ira L. Campbell, ninth publisher or co-publisher, wrote,

> "The *Guard* with this issue enters upon its twenty-first year of existence. The past year has been the most successful in history."

Then Campbell forgot to change the volume entry and continued to issue "Volume 20."[3]

The oldest *Guard* file in Oregon, that held by the University, begins with Alexander's successor, a J.W. Skaggs, who was for years a Democratic politician in Lane County. That file opens with Saturday, November 21, 1868, as Volume 2, Number 5. By the next issue, November 28, Volume 2, Number 6, Skaggs was out and two new co-publishers, William Thompson and William Victor, were in.

Turnbull backtracked four issues of Volume 2 to October 24, 1868, and then deduced that the *Guard* could have been born October 24, 1867. This date appeared as good as any (and it is for Volume 2, Number 1). After the paper's 90th anniversary had passed, the *Register-Guard* accepted October 24, 1867, as its "birthday." This was all right, provided that Alexander in the first year had missed no issues. Turnbull's *History of Oregon Newspapers* was published in 1939, and from then until the winter of 1967 no hiatus was found. October 24 looked safe.

With the 100th birthday coming on fast, sure enough, the gap appeared. A sharp-eyed librarian at the University of Oregon, Mrs. Frances Schoen, who directs the newspaper collection, came upon an agate-line reference that perhaps the Bancroft Library of the University of California at Berkeley had Volume 1 of the Eugene *Guard*. It does—12 scattered copies—from Volume 1, Number 7 (July 13, 1867) to Volume 1, Number 48 (May 9, 1868). There were no others until the University of Oregon's copy of November 24, 1868. With only a few single-copy lapses after that date the *Guard* file thereafter is unbroken.[4] All the Volume 1 copies carry Alexander's name, with a few in 1868 bearing also the name of an unknown, William Beers.

The Bancroft Library file of the *Guard*—how the historian and publisher Hubert Howe Bancroft obtained it is not known—narrowed the *Guard's* first issue to June 1, 1867. A combing of the Portland *Oregonian* for the two weeks on either side of June 1 did the rest, for the half-dozen lines in the *Oregonian* of June 4 checked with the back-up from the seventh number of July 13. Advertising in Alexander's first volume gave further proof. The *Guard's* ads carry numerous printer's "keys," some of them reading "June 1, 1tf," others "June 8, 2tf," and "June 22, 4tf," and so on. These appear to have been Alexander's method of noting the start of an ad, the issue number, and intention to run "to further notice."[5]

In his issue of May 9, 1868 (Number 48, although the calendar indicated that it should have been Number 50), Alexander was recommending candidates for the 1868 Oregon primary. All we can do is surmise that he gave up the *Guard* then or after the primary, just as he had done two years earlier with his abortive Eugene City *News*.[6] The likelihood is that, after a summer's absence of the *Guard*, Skaggs tried again October 24, immediately before the November presidential election. The October 24 date, therefore, appears to be the "birthday of continuous publication." Unless more missing issues turn up for the summer of 1868, the *Register-Guard* is standing on October 24.[7]

John B. Alexander: Ill-Fated Publisher

Only from scattered secondary sources and the 12 Bancroft Library copies of the *Guard's* Volume 1, plus the lone issue of the Eugene City *News* of 1866, do we know anything about John Alexander. He had come to Oregon from Illinois in 1852, when he was already 32 years old, and later he learned the printer's trade on the rabid secessionist sheets of Eugene City. He appears also to have been a farmer, a surveyor, and a justice of the peace. Nothing is known of his financial situation. Although Walling mentioned the *Guard* in 1884 he included nothing about Alexander. Harrison Kincaid in his *Autobiography* wrote that Alexander founded the opposition paper as a Democratic organ; beyond that Kincaid didn't comment.

Two of Alexander's sons, William, 12, and Frank, 10, helped their father in putting out the first *Guards* and a decade later became publishers of the paper themselves in its fourth transfer. Still later a grandson, George L. Alexander, edited the Lebanon (Ore.) *Express*.[8]

Alexander's failure with the *News* and his dropping the *Guard* after a year lead to the inference that, while contemporaneous reports say he was a strong-willed Democrat, he was not competent enough to operate a newspaper. Skaggs had to revive the *Guard* late in 1868, but seems to have been less competent than Alexander.

Alexander's earliest *Guard* still extant carried four columns of ads in a five-column page one, one of ads and four of reading matter on page two, three of ads and two of reading matter on page three, and five columns of reading matter on page four. This made eight columns of advertising out of 20, hardly enough to appear lucrative. The open column on page one was given to a report by George Francis Train, a journalist, author, and lecturer of some national renown (or notoriety). Train's subject was post-Civil War finance. His piece was lifted by Alexander without credit to source; it attacked hard-money interests and called for Greenback expansion. The nub of it read:

> "Delirium tremens requires national whiskey to recuperate the system. The next war is to be financial. Land and labor against banks and bondholders. The people who did the fighting hold no bonds and ask legal tender." [9]

Page two carried two and a half columns of what appeared to be a letter to the editor (though unsigned and not clear as to whom the article was addressed). The writer drew on the Fourth of July observance of 1867 and, in extremist language, asked: "Have we any independence to celebrate" [sic, no question mark]. And, if there was an Independence Day, the writer said, it was actually the first Wednesday of March, 1789, and not July 4, 1776 [referring to the constitutional date of March 4 for inaugurating the President, although George Washington did not actually take office until April 30 1789]. Apparently meaning the recently seceded states, the writer found "Washington's Virginia disrobed of sovereignty and governed by a military tyrant [under Reconstruction]." He also found North Carolina, South Carolina, and Georgia among the 13 original states "dissolved of sovereignty." He concluded:

> "Can the citizens of the United States honestly rejoice whilst more than one-fourth of the states are taxed without representation, their state government destroyed, civil authority abolished, a military despotism placed over them, the oppression in comparison with which that of Great Britain to the colonies was a mere shadow." [Punctuation as in original.]

Alexander ran also on page two a lift from the Chicago *Herald* on Horace Greeley's testimony in favor of bail for Jefferson Davis (which Greeley supplied); and some shorts on frauds in New Orleans scrip and on the execution of the puppet Emperor Maximilian in Mexico.

Page three carried a half column of "Town and Country" briefs, three-fourths of a column of "State Items," three-fourths of a column of "Church Notices," and the ads. One ad, of a half column, boosted the Bohemia City mining region south of Eugene City with this come-on:

> "Quartz, Quartz, Quartz. JOHNSON AND STOWELL'S GENERAL MERCHANDISE. Take greenbacks or coin. Insurance. Agents for Oregon Stage. Money Orders."

Page four had no ads. Alexander filled it with a long article from the San Francisco *Examiner* under the headline, "The Mighty Men of Mass" (Massachusetts). The account was a vitriolic attack on "Banks, Boutwell, Butler, Sumner, Wilson," comparing these "ignoble" leaders of Reconstruction derogatorily with the Massachusetts Colonial patriots, John Adams, Samuel Adams, and James Otis.[10] Page four included in addition an attack on Horace Greeley taken from the Pittsburgh *Post*, and several poems.[11]

This was John B. Alexander's *Guard* of July 13, 1867. The paper's rabid anti-Reconstruction, pro-Southern views continued under seven of the founder's successors, until Ira L. Campbell bought the newspaper in 1878. In post-war Oregon, with the Republican Party steadily gaining strength, fulminations like these couldn't possibly insure success; in fact, all but one of Alexander's successors before Campbell had difficulties.

Perhaps as little is known of John B. Alexander as of any other newspaper founder in Oregon. The *Oregonian* gave his paper only its scant attention on June 4. And Harrison Kincaid apparently ignored his new competitor, unless we can infer that in an editorial June 8, 1867, Kincaid had Volume 1, Number 1 of the *Guard* in mind when he wrote a week later:

> "Some of our Democratic editors who pretend to be decent and reasonable men, whenever they undertake to say anything in regard to the action of Congress, it amounts to nothing more than 'rump! Rump! RUMP!' Is this a manly and respectable process of reasoning in their estimation, or are they simply afflicted with *rump* [italics in original] on the brain, for the word is neither euphonious nor elegant, and the use of it in the mouth of a rational man best indicates a very coarse taste."[12]

J.W. Skaggs: The Guard and Two Cords of Wood

J.W. Skaggs, he who resuscitated the moribund *Guard* a few weeks before Ulysses S. Grant was elected President, had been around Eugene City for some time. His name had appeared in campaign lists for various Lane County offices in the mid-1860s and continued to show up in the 1870s. One historian of Eugene says in an unattributed statement that Skaggs in his five weeks as publisher attacked high tariffs, the United States banking system, and federal "usurpation" of states' rights.[13]

Working for Skaggs as printers were William Thompson and William Victor. Many years later, when he was 83, Thompson said:

> "After I had worked there about two weeks the proprietor said to me, 'I can't make the paper go. It will give me a black eye if the paper suspends publication while I am the owner. If you will take it, I will give you not only the Washington hand-press and the type, but I will give you two bundles of paper and two cords of wood.' "[14]

Thompson did not say what, if anything, Skaggs offered the other printer, Victor, who was a half-breed Cherokee Indian. But on November 28, 1868, Thompson and Victor were joint

Four operators of The Eugene City Guard who kept the early Guard's tenuous lineage alive.

THE EUGENE CITY GUARD.

ESTABLISHED FOR THE DISSEMINATION OF DEMOCRATIC PRINCIPLES, AND TO EARN AN HONEST LIVING BY THE SWEAT OF OUR BROW

VOL. IX.—NO. 40 EUGENE CITY, OREGON, SATURDAY, JULY 22, 1876. $2.50 per year IN ADVANCE.

DETAILS OF CUSTER'S FIGHT

The Herald has the following additional details of Custer's fight: They took the flying savages in the flank, or doubling back on Reno. Reno crossed the Little Horn, and charged down the valley about a mile and a half, following what seemed to be the flying Indians. Certainly they were on a dead run, but all at once turned and charged the advancing soldiers. Reno halted his command and engaged the Indians. The fire was terrific and reminded those present of the engagement of the Wilderness. Reno says he never heard firing more terrible. In a moment his command was completely surrounded with howling devils on every side, firing at short range. Charley Reynolds a well known scout, afterwards killed, exclaimed: "We are gone up. There is no hope for us." Reno was evidently of the same opinion. He ordered his men to mount, and leading the way, they cut forward. Porter's atention was attracted by a dying man belonging to French's company, who was shot through the heart. The cavalry was flying, pursued on every hand by Indians. Porter sprang to his horse and throwing his arms around the horse's neck, he goaded the animal forward, passing and being passed by Indians in their chase for scalps. They reached the ford with little loss. McIntosh, mounted on a horse which had been wounded, was overtaken and pulled from his horse and plugged with pistol shots while lying at the feet of his murderers. In this state of confusion, three companies reached the ford, a narrow pass into which men and horses were crammed and jammed, with Indians firing into them at short range from the front, flank and rear.

While in the river, Lieut. Hodgson was wounded and his horse killed; he received another shot just as he reached the bank, and tumbled, back into the river, dead.

The ford being passed, a wild scramble commenced to reach the bluff beyond.

The side of the bluff was so steep that the men were compelled to cling to the necks of their animals to prevent sliding from their backs. Col. Smith declares the incline to be steepest he ever saw ascended by horses or mules. Though the Indians were yelling on every hand and firing into the retreating force at short range, they gained the summit and just as they reached it eight men shot on the way up fell from their horses. Lieut. Matthews at once set about building barracks for a hospital — dead animals and dead men were used for this purpose as well as stores from pack mules. Those who fell in the retreat were placed in Porter's charge and the number rapidly increased. DeWolf was killed just as he reached the summit, and Porter was left alone with no help, until Girard escaped from the thicket; when, with his assistance two amputations were performed.

The officers inform your correspondent that when Custer came in sight of the 1,800 lodge village of upwards 7,000 inhabitants, he swung his hat and said: "Hurrah! Custer's struck the biggest Indian village on the American continent." Halting here only for coffee, he pushed forward at a rapid gait. He took five companies for his peronal command, gave Renot three, and left four in reserve under Benton. Dr. Porter believes the result would have been the same had Custer charged with his whole regiment, only the massacre would have been more terrible. Reno instead of simply failing to accomplish any good result, so m sconducted his forces as to harrass, if not seriously and permanently mar all hopes of the future success of the expedition. He did not only deliberately, and without a shadow of excuse, fail to obey his written orders issued by Gederal Terry's personal directions, but he acted in positive disobedience of the strick injunctions of the department commander. Instead of conforming his line of march to the valley and water courses laid down in his written orders, he moved his command to the mouth of Little Powder river, then across to Tongue river and instead of following the latter stream down to its mouth there to unite with the main command, he, for some unacountable and unexplained reason, switched off from his prescribed course and marched across the country to Rosebud stream. He had been particularly cautioned not to approach as Custer had predicted Indians in the neighborhood. The effort to remedy Reno's blunder resulted in the terrible massacre already known. A court martial of Reno is hinted at.

"Details of Custer's Fight" from opposite page. Reprints such as this supplied the early Guard with its out-of-town news.

publishers. Thompson's brother, Walter Thompson, who was a judge in Oregon at the time, advised William not to take Skagg's offer. As William quoted him, Walter said:

> "'It's the height of presumption for you to take over that paper when it's foredoomed to failure.' "

William took the *Guard* anyhow, even, as he said, "if I had to cook my meals and live under a tree."[15]

Skaggs on November 21 seems to have given a hint about his intentions. He buried this "For Sale" ad deep in the "Town and County" section of the *Guard:*

> "Mr. J.W. Skaggs wishes to sell a good house north of Judge Risdons, and opposite Joseph Meador's, in Eugene City. Apply at this office."[16]

Thompson and Victor: Indian Fighter and Indian

With William Thompson's entry, the faltering *Guard* got a publisher who could have built up a newspaper had he not had a roving disposition and been less interested in newspapers than in climbing mountains, fighting Indians, and opening up the Pacific Northwest. He is still, today, the only owner of the *Guard* who ever published his memoirs. William Thompson became as much a part of Oregon as of the Eugene City *Guard.* He is indeed a character straight out of the history of the West.

Like many other pioneers Thompson had arrived in Oregon as a boy (he was born in Polk County, Missouri, November 2, 1846) during the migration of the 1850s. In an interview in Portland when he was 83 he told how his mother's brother, a General Henderson, had gone to Texas with Sam Houston and become prominent in Texas politics. Then, after his parents had reached Oregon they took up a land claim "about one and three-quarters miles from Hulings Miller's place" (near Coburg). Young Thompson, who was only 6, got to know Cincinnatus Miller, who was then only 13 himself. Thompson became the future Joaquin's great admirer. When Joaquin was running the *Democratic Register* and the *Review* Thompson, now 16, got a job as a printer's devil at $50 a year in wages the first year, $180 the second, and $360 the third. And before he became a printer, Thompson said, he and Miller had shared a 12x14-foot shack on the outskirts of Eugene and attended Columbia College together. Thompson also knew Harrison Kincaid and other leading Eugeneans. He was particularly impressed by Miller's sympathy for underdogs and Democrats.[17]

While Miller, before becoming an editor, was running a pony express from the Oro Fino mine country in Idaho to Walla Walla, Thompson was one of his agents, and when enemies later criticized Miller for his policies, Thompson defended him:

> "To the credit of Mr. Miller . . . thieves, robbers and murderers let him severely alone. . . . No one ever lost a dollar entrusted to Heine's care."[18]

This contrasts strongly with Unionist charges that Joaquin as an editor robbed his subscribers by pocketing subscription money.[19]

The shutdown of the *Democratic Register* and the uncertain future of the *Review* caused printing to "lose charms" for Thompson and, further, "my spirits bent to a 'Call of the Wild'." So he took off on treks into the Cascades and engaged in Indian skirmishes. On one occasion he climbed one of the Oregon mountain peaks and was so impressed that when he wrote his autobiography he said—almost as if he foresaw the logotype that the paper he owned in 1869 would be displaying a century later:

> ". . .We ascended one of the Three Sisters, snow mountains standing together and reaching to the realms of the clouds. Like mighty sentinels, white as the driven snow, they constitute one of the grandest sights to be seen on this or any continent."[20]

In 1868 Thompson was back in Eugene City as compositor and foreman in the plant of the shaky *Guard.* When Skaggs gave up, Thompson said, it was with an agreement that Thompson "promise to run the paper and keep it alive." This he did, made $1,200 in a year and sold to George J. Buys and an A. Eltzroth on December 24, 1869.[21]

When Thompson left Eugene City, he didn't even mention his half-breed partner, William Victor, unless his use of the plurals our and we in a parting editorial imply both Thompson and Victor. Thompson said:

> "TO THE PATRONS OF THE GUARD
>
> "With this issue our connection with the *Guard* ceases. No pecuniary stress has induced this step. We entered upon the publication of this paper without a dollar, amid the jeerings of enemies and the misgivings of friends. We have added several hundred dollars worth of material to the office, and leave it out of debt, with money ahead."[22]

In the same editorial Thompson promised that the new publishers would continue to put out a strong Democratic newspaper. Buys, he said, was an "experienced journalist and practical printer." Thompson was sure a party paper, "properly conducted [would be] a self-sustaining institution." It is a safe historical assumption to say that William Thompson kept the *Guard* from failure. Buys was able to keep the paper moving on the momentum Thompson had given it; Eltzroth did not remain Buy's partner long enough to be significant in the *Guard's* history.

With his $1,200 in *Guard* profits and with the support of General Joseph Lane, the secessionist nominee for vice president in 1860, Thompson went to Roseburg and started the Roseburg *Plaindealer.* Within two years he had a subscription list of 1,200.[23] He says the *Plaindealer* prospered, even though he made some enemies and was once shot in the left ear and shoulder and in the mouth. Then, in February, 1872,

Thompson was urged again, by both Lane and John Whiteaker (first statehood governor of Oregon) to take the Salem *Mercury* and make it "the leading Democratic Party organ in the state." He sold out in Roseburg for $4,000, went to Salem, built up a "large circulation," and started a daily.[24]

By January, 1873, the Modocs were getting out of hand, so Thompson once more took off to fight Indians. In his *Reminiscences* he dropped his newspaper story abruptly and spent pages recounting his struggles with the Modocs, troubles with the Bannocks and the Snakes, vigilante justice, and even his experiences as a farmer. At one time he was in the cattle business 95 miles south of The Dalles.[25]

At the time Thompson wrote his autobiography he was editor of the Alturas (Calif.) *Plaindealer*. The book rests today, seldom read, in the Oregon Collection of the University of Oregon Library. It is an unorganized memoir of a typical frontier newspaperman-soldier-farmer-wanderer of obvious talent who could not stay put. Thompson was overly sentimental, too, and there is poignancy in his summarizing of his part in Oregon's growth:

> "Reared in the wilderness and on the frontier of civilization, I was merely the product of environment, and lay claim to no particular distinction above those who were my companions. And yet, as I look over the past, I must be excused for a feeling of pride in having been a part, however insignificant, in the building here on the western rim of the continent, of the mighty Empire of the Pacific."[26]

George J. Buys: Strong-Minded Democrat

With Thompson's and Victor's departure the *Guard* passed to two co-publishers about whom almost no written records remain nearly a century later, even though the senior member of the new partnership kept the paper for nearly seven and a half years. George J. Buys and A. Eltzroth operated the *Guard* together only until July 9, 1870, when Eltzroth withdrew.

Everything about the relations of Buys and Eltzroth must be dug out of files and judged by inference. We do have a statement of Thompson and Victor that Buys and Eltzroth were experienced journalists, but "journalist" had a loose meaning in 1869. We know, too, from a prospectus of the *Guard* at the time Buys took over that he intended to extend its purview: "Divoted [sic] to Politics, Literature, Agriculture, Telegraphic and Local News, General Miscellany, Etc."[27] And as we shall see in the chapter on news coverage Buys gave the *Guard* its first test in covering a major national news story.[28]

Buys and Eltzroth announced their purchase in an editorial-page notice simply headed "Change":

> "Many changes have been made in the management of the *Guard* in the few years of its existence. It has met with many adverse winds which have threatened its destruction. But for the past eighteen months the business of the paper has been steadily carried on. In assuming control . . . we intend to make no promises that shall not be fulfilled. We shall do our utmost to furnish the people of Lane County with a good local paper; in politics, Democratic, first, last and always. . . . Able talent will be retained in the editorial chair, and the business will be managed in all instances to the best interests of the paper's friends."[29]

Buys had a knack for clear, positive statement. The trouble is that he never indicated anything about himself. Some six months later he and Eltzroth separated, but all he wrote on July 9, 1870, was that "the co-partnership . . . between George J. Buys and A. Eltzroth was, on the 4th of July, dissolved by mutual consent." Buys assumed all of Eltzroth's obligations.[30]

Later Buys inserted a long declaration of purpose under the nameplate, and this statement the paper carried throughout his years of ownership and for some time into the period of his successors. It read: "Established for the Dissemination of Democratic Principles and to Earn an Honest Living by the Sweat of Our Brow."[31]

The *Guard* and the *Oregon State Journal* faced some short-run competition from May 22, 1873, to June 13, 1874, this in the form of the Eugene City *Hawk-Eye.* Published by Thomas Gale and Henry H. Gale, brothers of the James Newton Gale of the *State Republican* in 1862, this was a four-column, four-page sheet running 12 inches in depth. It supported an Oregon Independent Party, which in 1874 ran a full slate of candidates from governor to congressman to county coroners; it was opposed to "corruption" in the Radical Republican Party of the Grant Administration and it picked up also an assortment of Democratic Party dissidents.

The *Hawk-Eye* gave indication of being a permanent newspaper, for its masthead indicated a $1-a-year subscription rate, special rates for long-time advertisers, and "job work a specialty." But the paper did not start soon enough to be listed in Rowell's *American Newspaper Directory* for 1873 nor last long enough to be among the 44 Oregon newspapers carried in Rowell's *Centennial Newspaper Exhibition* in 1876. Further, the *Hawk-Eye* did not even list its publishers by name.[32]

Buys in the *Guard* was scornful of the *Hawk-Eye.* One can believe in independence, Buys said, but not in "Independent" as the name for a party. He continued:

> "There can be no such thing as an independent party. Party signifies a number of persons united by some tie. It implies organization. There cannot be unity and organization when each individual acts independent of others."[33]

In another instance Buys criticized the "dishwatery" tone of the *Hawk-Eye.*[34]

From the *Hawk-Eye,* though, we do get helpful information not obtainable elsewhere about J.W. Skaggs, erstwhile publisher of the *Guard.* Skaggs in 1874 was a bookseller and stationer, was maintaining a stand in Ellsworth and Belshaw's Drug Store, and was running for Lane County treasurer with Independent support. Evidently Skaggs had broken with the Democrats, as had Joel Ware, years before an associate of B.J. Pengra and Harrison Kincaid, broken with the Republicans. The *Hawk-Eye* was supporting Ware for county clerk.[35]

After Oregon's spring primary, the Gale brothers, like so many of their predecessors in Eugene City journalism, suspended the *Hawk-Eye*. In their final issue they said:

> "The *Hawk-Eye* ran through the campaign at considerable extra expense, on the PROMISE of a number of 'leading men,' that we should not lose anything on extra printing. Some men forget promises remarkably soon? . . . With good will toward all and malice toward none, we lay down our quill."[36]

Eugene City's *Hawk-Eye* accomplished little, but however short a time it lasted it comes down as the city's twelfth newspaper.

While Buys was contesting with the *Hawk-Eye* he was also experimenting with a daily newspaper. Ira L. Campbell and his brother George have received credit for launching the permanent Eugene *Daily Guard* in 1891. Nevertheless, George Buys tried a *Daily Guard*, Volume 1, Number 1, apparently on Monday, May 11, 1874, during the same spring campaign in which the *Hawk-Eye* was operating. He delivered it by carrier, evenings, for 25 cents a week or for 50 cents "for the campaign." This note would imply only limited continuance of the daily, but we cannot be sure; there is no terminal date on record. The *Daily Guard* of 1874 was four columns, four pages, and of 15 inches depth. It called the *Hawk-Eye* "Nast's nastiest carricature [sic] in type."[37]

A check of Buys' files of the weekly for May 2, May 9, May 16 and for several weeks thereafter revealed no comment about a *Daily Guard*.[38]

Two More Alexanders: Downhill Once More

On May 12, 1877, Buys departed the *Guard* and the Alexander name returned to the masthead, this time in John B.

Alexander's sons, F.R. Alexander and W.R. Alexander. If the story about their helping their father start the paper in 1867 is accurate, at which time they were boys, the two were now in their twenties. And as the father had run the paper a year or less, so the sons were soon gone. On November 2, 1878, they sold to two other brothers, Ira L. and John R. Campbell. Eleven years old in 1878, the Eugene City *Guard* had gone through five managements, with eight publishers trying their luck with it. Among all of them, only William Thompson was able to make money.

All this reflects as much on political association of a newspaper as it reflects upon publishers' talent, although Thompson alone had any real newspaper gifts. While in frontier journalism sound business practice was rare, the fact remains that in the specific situation of the *Guard* the march of the publishers was a procession fighting the battles of the Democrats and then blaming the Democrats for not supporting the paper. Buys in leaving used much the same arguments that John Alexander had spouted in 1866 when his *News* folded. Buys' reasoning went:

> 1. For Democrats who want party success there is no surer path than to have a good newspaper.
> 2. Good newspapers need encouragement—"something that will rattle."
> 3. There are enough Democrats in Lane County to *sustain* [a popular word when it came to money; italics added] a good paper, but they don't contribute to it until they want jobs.
> 4. Every Democrat should take the paper and pay for it.[39]

So the young Alexanders were going to do what their father and Buys gave up trying to do. They promised to follow the policies of Thomas Jefferson, but they would be the mouthpiece of "no clique, faction or combination of aspirants to personal promotion." They would give the latest news and apply "industry, energy, and pluck."[40]

They had to give up, too. A year and a half after starting the Alexander brothers sold to the Campbell brothers, along with another valedictory tale of trouble:

> "We admonish those who have forgotten that it required cash to buy material and that printers, like other mortals, cannot live on air."[41]

The Alexanders had found newspaper work "more toilsome than the daily labor of the farmer, mechanic or the artisan, and . . . more meagerly rewarded. . . . The editor's work is never done."

Then they promised that the *Guard*, under the Campbells, would remain thoroughly Democratic. The Campbells were young men (actually about the same age as the Alexanders) of more than ordinary ability, they said, and "of undoubted integrity, inflexible Democrats and affable gentlemen."[42]

Ira and John Campbell: Competence and Dedication

Luckily, Ira and John Campbell were all the things the Alexander brothers said they were. So had William Thompson been. But the Campbells stayed with the paper, Ira for 26 years, until he died in 1904. John remained a little longer. He withdrew after 1906, when he first sold a part interest in the *Guard* and then helped to incorporate the Guard Printing Company. The Campbell brothers' ownership remained—until 1956—the longest single control of a newspaper in Eugene except for Harrison Kincaid's of the *Oregon State Journal.*

Purchase of the *Guard* by the Campbells proved to be another of those fortuitous changes that, in retrospect, rescued the paper. Skaggs had got it going again after the first Alexander faltered, and Thompson saved it from Skaggs. While 10 years later it would be inaccurate to say the Campbells saved the *Guard's* life, we can credit them with giving it direction. This took three forms: toning down the vituperative language so frequently used during Civil War and Reconstruction; expanding content and taking some notice of the local scene; and instituting sound management policies. It is often said that business management alone cannot build a newspaper. This is true, as we shall see in the first years of the Eugene City *Register*, which was well run for its first 11 years.[43] But poor management can ruin a newspaper or keep it from growing. Until Ira and John Campbell arrived, the *Guard* had had only Thompson's 13 months of profitable operation.

When the Campbells took over, the *Guard's* circulation (1879) was listed by Rowell as "KK", a code meaning 500—or perhaps more. Kincaid's *Oregon State Journal* had a lower circulation than the *Guard*, but Kincaid had been in Washington, D.C., through most of the 1870s. In 1883 the *Guard* was up to 900 circulation (claimed) as against the *State Journal's* 575. Two years later the *Guard* had 960 (claimed), with the *State Journal* reporting 800 and the new Eugene City *Register* (founded in 1884) 660. In 1887 the Campbells had pushed the *Guard* to 1,032; the *State Journal* was still at 800; and the *Register* had reached 720. In another ten years the *Weekly Guard* had reached 1,575; the *State Journal* and *Register* both were "JKL," Rowell's code for less than 1,000 each. Rowell's reasons for using letters to designate circulations were that small-city publishers submitted inaccurate or false reports, or no reports.

After Ira Campbell had died and John Campbell had sold the *Guard*, N.W. Ayer's certified circulation for the paper (1910) showed 2,425 for the daily and 1,725 for the weekly. For the *Register* the figures were 900 daily and 1,250 weekly. The *State Journal* in 1910 had ceased publication.[44]

The *Guard*, of course, had a circulation advantage in that it was one Democratic paper competing against two Republican papers through 20 years of the Campbell period. When it became a daily some years before the *Register* and because it was an evening newspaper, it gained an inside-the-city circulation advantage. The point is, it progressed—and in the face of competition in a town too small to support three newspapers. In news treatment the *Guard* was more lively than the other two;

and wisely, more toned down politically than it had been. It was the *Guard* that gave Eugene its best local coverage in the last 20 years of the century.

Ira L. Campbell *was* the *Guard* from 1878 to 1904, whatever the joint ownership with his brother implied. Oldtimers in Eugene today, and there are a few who can remember back to 1900 both as to the city and its journalism, mention only Ira. It was he who first gave the *Guard* character. Yet when he and John bought the paper Ira was only 22, simply a talented hometown youth who was to live all his life in Lane County and be more representative of small-city publishers than the Ed Howes or the Bill Whites. When he died of a stroke October 15, 1904, he was only 48.

Ira Campbell likely came by his Democratic party sympathies through his father, Andrew Jackson Campbell, about whom little is known. Campbell lived at Long Tom, Lane County, where Ira was born.[45] The father soon moved to Eugene City and operated a tool shed in an alley off the north side of East Ninth and opposite Kincaid's *State Journal* plant. Ira frequented Kincaid's shop, then went to Portland for a time to learn the printing trade, and returned to Eugene City. Kincaid called him, "the most practical, substantial, and reliable of men."[46]

Sentimentally (Kincaid was 68 when Ira died), the *State Journal* editor said he had known Ira "since he was a little boy." Kincaid stressed Campbell's kindness and honor and called him a "big brain—big intellectually as well as physically." Kincaid's memory was a bit shaky on *Guard* history, for he had Campbell in 1878 buying the "little weekly paper when it was 15 years old," which would have made the *Guard* a year older than the *State Journal;* and Kincaid said Ira ran the *Guard* 21 years, five years less than he actually did.

The young Ira Campbell in his "Salutatory" on taking over the *Guard* re-emphasized its Democratic party principles, but he added something new: "never to forget the courtesy due an opponent [and never to] sink our patriotic promptings in the dirty pool of partisanship."[47] These words were stronger than they sounded. Campbell meant them.

Another departure was the *Guard's* emphasis on local affairs:

> "Upon building up a live local paper, our best energies will be called forth. . . . We shall be found always advocating the interests of Lane County, and of Eugene City in particular."[48]

The first Campbell *Guard* carried about four columns of local news. Ira's intent was carried out, for it is easy to forget that reporting in 1878 was not a perfected technique in Oregon. Four columns of local news (even though "shorts" for the most part) must have taken some doing.

Ira Campbell did at least five things that raised the *Guard's* level of performance:

1. In 1887 he installed a power press run by a water motor, although he did not indicate how the device operated. (The *Guard's* location on Willamette Street was some distance from the Willamette River.)
2. On April 6, 1889, he increased the size of the *Guard* to seven 13-pica columns of 22-1/2-inch depth, the standard size for metropolitan newspapers. And as early as May 24, 1879, he had enlarged to eight pages of six columns. Much of the four pages in the middle, however, consisted of "patent insides" from syndicate services.[49]
3. Campbell gradually altered headline display and expanded news coverage; sports news and crime gained some prominence.[50]
4. On June 8, 1891, Campbell went daily, the *Guard* pacing the *Register* by three and a half years and in actuality by more than eight years, since the *Register's* first efforts at a daily faltered. For more than 20 years the *Guard* ran both a daily and a weekly, the *Weekly Guard*

continuing to September 29, 1910, and a *Twice-a-Week Guard* from October 3, 1910, to March, 1914.

5. Finally, Campbell was one of the prime movers in the organization of the Oregon Press Association, August 15, 1887.

Ira Campbell's work in at least two of these areas is best told as part of the chapter on specific news coverage, but his part in entering the daily field and in starting the Press Association fits in here to show him as a builder and promoter as much as newspaperman and political voice of Lane County Democrats.

Oregon already had 16 daily newspapers by the 1890s, within five of the number the state has in 1967. When Campbell expanded in 1891 Eugene was not big enough to support four newspapers comfortably, for at the time it was customary to count weeklies and dailies as two papers, even when under the same management. Then by 1895 the Eugene *Register* went daily too—to bring Eugene's claimed total to five. Campbell, however, was efficient, and his daily was a success. The *Register* had troubles, as we shall see; and the *State Journal* did not expand.

Campbell gave notice of his daily on Saturday, June 6, 1891, saying in the weekly that the expansion would come Monday afternoon. The message was directed TO ADVERTISERS, although he did give secondary mention to readers, who would gain additional news space. His main point was:

> "Advertisers who appreciate the benefits conferred by advertising will take advantage of the first issue of *The Daily Guard.*"

He promised to run off several thousand copies (weekly circulation was then a shade over 1,000) the first day and to keep the daily press-run large for a month. The expansion in news, he said, would be extensive: Circuit Court in session, University of Oregon commencement, a Civil War Veterans' encampment, and Fourth of July exercises. The daily would offer "great facilities for increased circulation."[51]

The *Daily Guard's* first subscription rates were 20 cents a week by carrier; 75 cents a month, by carrier or mail; and $7.50 a year, by mail. The *Register* was silent about Campbell's announcement.

As with the *Weekly Guard's* Volume 1, Number 1 in 1867, so the *Daily Guard's* Volume 1 disappeared. In 1963 only the University of Oregon among major Oregon libraries reported having the first six months of the daily, but in 1966 that file was gone. For what the *Daily Guard* ran in June, 1891, we must today rely on a feature story by Paul J. Deutschmann in the *Register-Guard's* New Year's edition of 1942. Deutschmann reported that the first *Daily Guard* carried sensational news of a flood in Texas and of crime in London; and stories on Eugene's rise to fourth place among Oregon cities, on the visit to Eugene of a pugilist named "Jack Dempsey," and—on business—about the booming Fairmount suburb east of the University of Oregon. Promoting Fairmount was George Melvin Miller, brother of Joaquin. George had become a Eugene real estate agent and, like Joaquin, exaggerated. He said that by 1895 Eugene, Fairmount, Glenwood, and Springfield were to be one. Only Fairmount ever was annexed, this being in 1905.[52]

Ira Campbell's work with the Press Association needs backgrounding.

One of the minor sidelights of the first Grover Cleveland administration (1885-1889) and the Democrats' return to power for the first time in 24 years was a stress on honesty in government; insofar as the West was concerned, frontier settlers would have to prove up their land claims. Many pioneers, Oregonians among them, had been squatting for years. This resulted eventually in government action for strict enforcement of laws governing publication of land notices. As a corollary, publication notices became a major source of revenue for small newspapers. Many of the new papers of Oregon relied almost wholly for support on their legal-ad revenues.

Allied with the land issue was the booming railroad development throughout Oregon. How better could newspaper gains be made solid than by tying economic opportunity to trade-association organization?

Ira and John Campbell and the Eugene City *Guard* were leaders in calling, for August 12, 1887, a meeting in the burgeoning settlement of Yaquina City to unite Oregon's newspapers for mutual business cooperation.[53] This session led to the incorporation of the Oregon Press Association, today the Oregon Newspaper Publishers Association. Interestingly, the Oregon Press Association was formed the same year as the American Newspaper Publishers Association.

Yaquina Bay in 1887 was the center of a railroad promotion for a line from the coast to Corvallis and then eastward to Idanha in the Central Oregon Cascades east of Salem. This line was to connect with the Union Pacific and Central Pacific (later Southern Pacific). It is said that the railroad sponsor, a Colonel J. Edgerton Hogg, was generous with passes for the press.[54] Editors in the 1880s were hardly scrupulous about "paid vacations."

Fourteen other Oregon publishers in addition to Campbell met in Yaquina. Fifteen more were granted charter membership in the association by mail. The Portland press, led by Harvey W. Scott of the *Oregonian*, shunned this upstart session of small-town publishers eager to help their own businesses by cooperating with each other and meeting in a boom resort along the underpopulated coast. What the event did was to illustrate Ira Campbell's faculty for cooperation.

Of the founding papers of the Press Association that had publishers in person in Yaquina, only six remained when the ONPA observed its fiftieth anniversary in La Grande in 1937. Besides the Campbells' *Guard* (*Register-Guard* in 1937), these were the Roseburg *News-Review*, Albany *Democrat-Herald*, Corvallis *Gazette-Times*, and Oregon City *Enterprise*. The Albany *Democrat* and Albany *Herald*, with two founding memberships, later were consolidated.[55]

Throughout August, 1887, the *Guard* ran extensive "Yaquina Correspondence"—the kind of puffery that today is paid advertising or free publicity to pad out real estate sections. For example:

> "YAQUINA CORRESPONDENCE
>
> "YAQUINA—The weather here is lovely, neither too hot or too cold. Improvements are constantly being made by the Oregon Development Company. . . . In the sweet bye and bye, which is to say a year or two at the most when the road is completed to its eastern terminus, then this place will boom, and don't you forget it. . . . The Oregon Development Company has built at their own expense a non-sectarian place of worship, a 32x64-foot building.
>
> "YAQUINA."[56]

No one can fault Ira Campbell for his business acumen. The above blurb was typical of its day, but in succeeding years Campbell's successors in the Oregon Newspaper Publishers Association were to do much to raise the business and news standards of the Oregon community press.

Campbell's enterprise was reflected in other ways. In Tout's Eugene City Directory of 1902 the *Guard* ran a major ad:

> "If you want to reach the people of Eugene and Lane County advertise in the *Guard.*"[57]

And the *Guard* cited *Printer's Ink* as crediting it with Lane County's largest circulation and with being a "recognized authority of newspaperdom."[58]

When Ira Campbell died in 1904, the *Register* put its Republicanism aside and paid the publisher this compliment:

> "Ira Campbell was one of the pioneer Oregon newspapermen who helped build up the state. He was generous and kind-hearted, and had friends all over the entire state who will miss him."[59]

When Campbell died the Oregon Press Association he had helped to found was meeting in Hood River. Campbell had hoped to attend, but illness prevented this. The association passed a testimonial honoring Campbell's service. It noted that he was the first charter member to die.[60]

Less than three years later the *Guard* again was sold. While it continued to progress as a newspaper it began once more to change hands frequently. The *Register* eventually passed it in circulation and kept its primacy until the 1920s.

Ira Campbell left an estate of less than $10,000. A reading of the probate record more than 60 years later reveals how modest the rewards of small-town newspapering were in the late Nineteenth Century, although, because the *Guard* was held in partnership when Campbell died, it is possible that the paper did not go through probate. Ira left personal property of less than $2,000 and six small parcels of Eugene real estate totaling $5,050, plus a $1,594 promissory note from Joaquin Miller's brother George, the real estate dealer and frequent advertiser. An inventory of the estate, filed March 23, 1906, showed no interest in the *Guard.* A month later, April 30, 1906, brothers John Campbell and Edward Campbell incorporated the paper with Charles H. Fisher.[61]

---

1. Flora Belle Ludington, *The Newspapers of Oregon, 1846-1870.* Eugene, Oregon: Koke-Tiffany Co., 1925, p. 9.
2. George S. Turnbull, *History of Oregon Newspapers.* Portland, Oregon: Binfords & Mort, 1939, pp. 279 ff.
3. *Guard*, August 27, 1887.
4. *Guard*, Volume 1, Numbers 7, 9, 10, 11, 13, 14, 15, 17, 33, 43, 45 and 48 (July 13, 1867, to May 9, 1868). Number 48 should have been Number 50, indicating two missed issues.
5. There is no consistency in these advertising "keys." As many lacked them as had them.
6. *Guard*, May 9, 1868, p. 45.
7. *Register-Guard*, "Volume 91, Number 67 is the *Register-Guard's* Right Number," December 29, 1957, p. 1. On this date the paper began numbering on the basis of October 24. Until 1957, its sequence was consistently inconsistent.
8. Turnbull, *op. cit.*, p. 274.

9. *Guard*, July 13, 1867.

Train, an extremist in almost all his activities, was ordered three years later to leave France for his part in the communistic policies of the commune.

Dictionary of American Biography, under the auspices of the American Council of Learned Societies. New York: Charles Scribner's Sons, 1936, Vol. 18, pp. 626-627.

10. *Guard*, July 13, 1867. Banks: Union general and governor of Massachusetts, member of Congress; Boutwell: Massachusetts congressman, leader in Andrew Johnson impeachment; Butler: Union general, Massachusetts governor, congressional head of impeachment forces; Sumner: Massachusetts senator, most ferocious of the impeachment group; Wilson: Massachusetts senator, personal foe of Andrew Johnson, vice president during Grant's first term.

11. *Ibid.*

12. *Oregon State Journal*, June 8, 1867, p. 2.

13. Lucia W. Moore, Nina W. McCornack, and Gladys W. McCready, *The Story of Eugene.* New York: Stratford House, 1949, p. 107. This source says that, simultaneously, 1868-1870, Skaggs was Lane County school superintendent.

14. Fred Lockley, "Impressions and Observations of *The Journal Man*," relating an interview with William Thompson in *Oregon Journal.* Portland, Oregon: August 14, 1929, p. 8.

15. *Ibid.*

16. *Guard*, November 21, 1868.

17. Lockley, *op. cit.*

18. William Thompson, *Reminiscences of a Pioneer.* San Francisco: 1912, p. 71.

19. See p. 23 *supra.*

20. Thompson, *op. cit.*, p. 70.

21. *Ibid.*

22. *Guard*, December 25, 1869.

23. Thompson, *op. cit.*, p. 71.

24. *Ibid.*, p. 73. The *Mercury* was one of five Oregon dailies in 1876.

25. *Ibid.*, p. 144.

26. *Ibid.*, p. 186.

27. *Guard*, December 25, 1869.

28. The disputed Presidential Election of 1876. See pp. *infra.*

29. *Guard*, December 25, 1869.

30. *Guard*, July 7, 1870.

31. *Guard*, May 5, 1877.

32. Eugene City *Hawk-Eye*, May 30, 1874. The source on ownership is Mrs. E.A. (Leonore) Barette, daughter of James Newton Gale. See Chapter Two, footnote 55.

33. *Guard*, May 2, 1874.

34. *Guard*, May 9, 1874.

35. *Hawk-Eye*, May 30, 1874. Ware at the turn of the century was United States commissioner in Eugene.

36. *Hawk-Eye*, June 13, 1874. This copy is owned by Mrs. Barette. See footnote 32, *supra.*

37. *Daily Guard*, May 16, 1874, Volume 1, Number 6.

38. Albert G. Walling, *Illustrated History of Lane County, Oregon.* Portland, Oregon: Walling Printing and Lithographing House, 1884, mentioned no *Hawk-Eye* nor *Daily Guard.* The *Hawk-Eye* is also unlisted by Turnbull, who gives the *Daily Guard* date as 1890.

39. *Guard*, May 12, 1877.

40. *Ibid.*

41. *Guard*, November 2, 1878.

42. *Ibid.*

43. See pp. 93-94 *infra.*

44. George P. Rowell & Son, *Rowell's American Newspaper Directory.* New York: 1879, 1883, 1885, 1887, 1897.

American Newspaper Annual and Directory. Philadelphia: N.W. Ayer & Son, 1910.

45. Long Tom is about 16 miles northwest of Eugene. The Long Tom River feeds into today's Fern Ridge Lake, a local recreation area; it is one of the smaller tributaries of the Willamette.

46. *Oregon State Journal*, October 22, 1904. Campbell obituary editorial.

47. *Guard*, November 9, 1878.

48. *Ibid.*

49. The seven-column paper was a change made simultaneously by the *Register.*

50. Here Campbell was recognizing developments in the national press. Even weeklies in as remote spots as Oregon could, if alert, avoid clipping entirely from other newspapers.

51. Eugene City *Guard*, June 6, 1891. After the circulation of the *Daily Guard* had had a chance to settle down, *Rowell's American Newspaper Directory.* New York: G.P. Rowell & Co., 1897, gave circulation as "less than 1,000"; Campbell claimed 1,575.

52. *Register-Guard*, January 4, 1942. Today a portion of Fairmount is part of a huge University of Oregon dormitory complex. The University of Oregon Library has no record of a reported loss of Volume 1 of the *Daily Guard.*

53. Yaquina City, at the mouth of Yaquina Bay, was adjacent to the present Newport, a key spot for tourists on the Oregon coast. It is about equidistant from Portland and Eugene.

54. Eric W. Allen, "Oregon Journalism in 1887." *Oregon Historical Quarterly*, Vol. 38 (September, 1937), p. 253.

55. *Ibid.*, p. 262.

56. *Daily Guard*, August 27, 1887.

57. O.B. Tout, *The Eugene Directory.* Eugene, Oregon: Press of W.O. Yoran, 1902, p. 1.

58. *Ibid.*

59. *Morning Register*, October 16, 1904.

60. *Ibid.*

61. Probate Record Number 1677, Lane County Oregon Archives, *In the Matter of the Estate of Ira L. Campbell, deceased*, October 15, 1904. John Campbell, who lived to November 23, 1913, left the *Guard* shortly after incorporation. The third brother, Edward L. Campbell, who died October 14, 1922, was Eugene's postmaster in World War I. Fisher was sole owner after 1907.

CHAPTER 5

The Eugene City Register—And Some Competitors

One may be amazed that the *Guard* survived its first 11 years. The careful reader of early files of the Eugene City *Register* will be amazed too—not that the *Register* succeeded financially at once but that so little ingenuity was needed to make a newspaper pay, even under the news standards of the time. It took until at least 1879 before anyone could be sure the *Guard* would live; the *Register* made money at once, but it took more than 15 years before it showed any editorial enterprise. The two papers were quite opposite; yet there were similarities.

Like the *Guard* before 1878, the *Register* changed hands often, although not right away. Like the *Guard* (and most community newspapers) the *Register* was a printing shop also—but more printing shop. Unlike the *Guard*, the *Register* had no trained editors to speak of until 1899, while the *Guard* had William Thompson and Ira Campbell, and perhaps George Buys. Unlike the *Guard*, the *Register* was almost always dull. Unlike the *Guard*, which faced no daily competition before it went daily itself, the *Register* was up against Campbell's daily paper before it was seven years old. Then, when the *Register* chose to go daily—in the midst of the Depression of 1893—it failed to succeed. Finally, with the daily on its hands, the *Register* ran into the same kind of ownership parade that had long frustrated the *Guard*.

Silas M. Yoran: Businessman

The *Register's* founder, on Wednesday, October 8, 1884, was Silas M. Yoran, who appears to have decided to start a newspaper because he felt a second Republican organ was needed in Eugene City. More likely, in the booming 1880s, he saw a newspaper and job printing establishment as a good business venture.[1] Yoran disregarded the fact that the *Oregon State Journal* was going strong and would continue to go strong for nearly a quarter century.

Yoran, a Eugenean who had come from Iowa only a year before, was 49 years old in 1884. He had opened a prosperous warehouse and, after 1893, ran a successful shoe business. For his printing firm he had a partner, John M. Hodson, who remained with Yoran only until 1888, after which Hodson became deputy collector of customs in Portland upon Benjamin Harrison's presidential victory.[2] Soon Yoran and one of his sons, William C., were listed as proprietors of the *Register* under the name of Yoran and Son.

The *Register* made a good profit, more because of its job work on the side than because of the advertising it carried. The inside of the paper included long pieces on Republican doctrine, heavy discussions of economic matters, and columns of canned fiction—the usual content of the "patent insides" of the period. The paper's beginning size was the standard format of the day, eight six-column pages 18 inches deep.

After his first year Yoran said he was satisfied. He hadn't expected a "great bonanza" and he was willing to earn his way to "the confidence and patronage of the people of Lane County."[3] In the year 1884-85, Yoran said, "half a million pages of printed matter [had come] from Yoran presses, . . . all the kinds known to a country publishing house."[4] The weekly newspaper made up about 40 per cent of these half-million pages, so Yoran and Hodson and then Yoran and Son had considerably more than an equal business in job printing. If not a bonanza, the *Register* must have been close to it.[5]

In 1885 Yoran and Hodson were planning another press within a few weeks and other equipment as needed. They were even continuing subscriptions without notice of intention to renew and were not cutting off unpaid subscriptions unless given notice.[6]

Silas Yoran and son William ran the *Register* together until March 25, 1891, when the father left in favor of his other business interests and turned the paper over to William and another son, George C. Yoran. The firm became Yoran Brothers. The biggest change from 1884 to 1891 was the *Register's* going to seven columns on April 3, 1889 (the same week that the *Guard* increased its size).[7] "Increasing patronage" was the reason. This was also the week the *Register* dropped "City" from its name to conform to Eugene's municipal change.

The senior Yoran continued to prosper. His shoe store was a big Eugene advertiser for years, and in 1892 Silas Yoran was a vice president of the Eugene National Bank.[8] He was also active in the Bank of Oregon and was vice president of the Eugene Loan & Savings Bank.[9] A few years later he became prominent in Republican Party politics, being named a presidential elector for Oregon in William McKinley's victorious campaign of 1896.[10] He was active in Eugene civic affairs and in 1903 became grand commander of the Oregon Grand Commandery of the Masonic Grand Lodge. Before coming to Oregon in 1883 Silas Yoran had lived in Iowa for 20 years. He had been a farmer and merchant there and had served for a time in the Iowa Legislature.[11]

Beginning in 1892 the *Register* began running into trouble and its course for the next seven years can be deduced only from inadequate information in the files. It quite evidently needed editorial competence to buck Ira L. Campbell and didn't have it. Since the *Guard* had gone daily and times were good—until 1893—the *Register* expanded to semi-weekly March 2, 1892, the Wednesday paper becoming Wednesday and Saturday. The Yorans cited a healthy growth in three years, kept the same subscription rate as the weekly ($2 a year), and promised to increase local news and "drop uninteresting story matter." The expansion to twice a week was more apparent than real, however; the eight-page weekly became a four-page semi-weekly, although the elimination of the patent insides was a help.[12] Later, when the 1893 business slump became serious the *Register* gave a "hard-times reduction" in subscription rates to $1.50 a year, and this could have caused distress for the paper.

The Yorans Sell: The Buyers Sell, Too

On January 1, 1895, the Yorans went daily and incorporated as the Register Publishing Company and then, without explanation, sold to C.J. Rowlands, L.S. Howard, and Howard Rowlands, youthful Eugeneans who were printers, knew nothing about the news side (and admitted it), and relied on their "practical knowledge" of the mechanical end and of business in general to run the paper. Messrs. Rowlands, Howard, and Rowlands didn't even put their names on the masthead.[13] In all previous accounts of Eugene newspaper history written heretofore, this particular transfer of *Register* ownership appears never to have been mentioned.

Suddenly, on April 26, 1895, the new owners (acting only as the Register Publishing Company) returned to weekly publication, dropping the semi-weekly but continuing the daily. Again promises were made to improve the paper, but for a second time there was little change. The four-page semi-weekly became an eight-page weekly.

On June 17, 1896, the names of Condon and Edwards appeared as owners of the *Register*—without announcement of sale by Rowlands, Howard, and Rowlands. These men were Chester D. Edwards and H.T. Condon. Turnbull in his *History of Oregon Newspapers* lists Seymour W. Condon as a partner of Edwards, but the *Register* ran only the name of H.T. Condon. In the first Eugene City Directory of 1892 H.T. Condon was listed as a clerk for John H. McClung, a Eugene merchant who was also mayor at one time; Seymour Condon had been district attorney in 1892. It is possible that Seymour Condon gave financial backing. Chester Edwards had at one time been an employe of Harrison Kincaid on the *Oregon State Journal.*[14]

Two years later Condon and Edwards broke up, with no other explanation than that Edwards would assume the *Register's* obligations.[15] But as early as July 7, 1896, less than a month after they had taken over the paper, Condon and Edwards had said they were giving up the *Daily Register.* Their tone, somewhat bitter, carried innuendoes reflecting back on the Yoran brothers for starting a daily. The *Register* said:

> "Every effort has been made to make it [the *Register*] a paying investment. . . . The daily has made its way, but it has been of little help to the proprietors. They have had labor for their pains. . . . Realizing that the field is too small for two daily papers such as the *Guard* and *Register*, and not caring to continue publication without receiving something over and above the actual running expenses, the management has decided to discontinue the publication of the same, with the view of turning its attention to the continued building up of the *Weekly Register*."[16]

Nevertheless, and again without notice, the *Daily Register* picked up once more in 1898 and was publishing on October 25. Then after a few weeks it stopped a second time, with a long hiatus continuing until December 1, 1899, when as the *Morning Register* it was renewed under new owners. This time the *Register* made a go of the daily.[17]

The Gilstraps: A Better Register

As the Campbell brothers had revived the *Guard* 21 years earlier, so a set of brothers were to restore the *Register*. There were four of them, Will G. Gilstrap, W. Frank Gilstrap, Otto Gilstrap, and Ernest Gilstrap, with at least two of the four—and sometimes three—being associated with the paper continuously until November 17, 1930. All were newspapermen and printers who had come to Oregon from Kansas in the late 1880s, with Will and Frank founding the Springfield *Messenger* in 1892. Otto at the time Will and Frank bought the *Register* was managing a hotel in Pendleton. His brothers called him to Eugene to be telegraph editor; this is the first indication in Eugene journalism that a copy editor of a national news wire was put on a desk.[18] For years thereafter it was a policy of the *Register* to devote page one to national and international news except in instances of gigantic local happenings.

The Gilstraps' first issue of the *Morning Register* came out December 1, 1899, as Volume 3, Number 90. This probably was accurate in view of the stops and starts of the *Daily Register* between its beginnings in 1895 and the Gilstraps' taking over. The brothers said in their first issue:

> "OUR BOW
>
> "With this issue we begin our morning daily. We have no lengthy speech to make. We consider the daily a plain business proposition. If you will look over our columns we believe you will agree with us that it looks like a business. . . .
>
> "We start with a big list of subscribers and expect to make a steady substantial growth.
>
> "We believe our telegraphic service will give you satisfaction and we expect to have the daily to all our patrons every morning before the breakfast hour. . . .
>
> "We launch our morning paper, trusting to the people of Eugene and Lane County to discover in its columns enough of merit to make it a permanent enterprise."[19]

The story of the Eugene *Morning Register* under the brothers Gilstrap bridges the period between the tiny Eugene and expanding Eugene. In less than five years Ira Campbell was gone and in less than ten years Harrison Kincaid gave up the *Oregon State Journal.* The *Register* after 1899 belonged to the new century and its significant competition with the *Guard* was post-Campbell competition. By World War I the *Morning Register* had become Eugene's leading paper in circulation; then, in the late 1920s, the *Guard* pushed past it once more.

The Eugene Broad Axe: Noisy Opponent

Oregon politics was a serious business in the 1890s and early 1900s, what with the People's Party, which outran the Democrats in 1892 by pollling more state votes than Grover Cleveland did. Later there arose the issues of direct primary, initiative, and referendum, as well as the federal income-tax amendment and municipal ownership. Journalistic repercussions over these conflicts resulted for 12 years from 1894 to 1906 in at least four newspapers entering the Eugene scene. These were the *Broad Axe* (*Broad Axe Tribune* at the start) and its successor, the *Weekly Citizen;* the *Weekly Record;* and the Eugene *Herald.* Only the *Broad Axe* and the *Citizen* published long enough to offer a sidelight to *Guard* and *Register* history.

The *Broad Axe*, started March 10, 1894, if its volume numbering is accurate, was a raucous Populist sheet that made a rather good effort to cover general news, although much of the content was "boilerplate." But it could get little advertising—barely 25 per cent. Considered along with its extremist political views in years when "Free Silver" was a frightening concept among businessmen, this fact gave the *Broad Axe* little chance. It obviously did not imperil the *Guard*, the *Register*, or the *State Journal*, and it was unlisted by both Rowell and Ayer.

Yet the paper survived for more than six years, under its founding name to February 28, 1900, and as a more moderate *Weekly Citizen* for seven months longer. The last known issue was October 31, 1900. In Oregon, only the University of Oregon has a scattered file, much of it worm-eaten.

Except for its publisher, James Franklin Amis—a name that rings with crusading spirit of a free press—the *Broad Axe* would merit no more than a footnote. James Franklin Amis, however, was a man of vitality. He had some of the marks of Joaquin Miller and Alexander Noltner and William Thompson of more than a generation earlier. In the 1890s, even with the Populist issue to help, he had no chance against the staid Ira Campbell (a solid Democrat) or against the Yorans or their successors. Besides, Amis was already 66 years old in 1894.[20]

Amis was a resident of Oregon for 60 years before his death in 1912. He was born in Clay County, Kentucky, and had fought in the Mexican War before coming to the Pacific Coast in the migration of 1852. Before his death he was one of the few surviving Mexican War veterans in Oregon. He "drew a government pension for years," the *Guard* pointed out somewhat unkindly in Amis' obituary.[21] The *Morning Register* ran only a classified notice of Amis' death, August 29, 1912.[22]

Amis talked about himself extensively in the *Broad Axe.* He had been a printer in early Eugene City and had been one of the underwriters for a press for the old *Democratic Herald* in 1859 and 1860, the *Democratic Register* in 1862, and the *Review* in 1862 and 1863. Amis wrote the articles of agreement whereby 20 incorporators put up $1,000 so that the *Democratic Herald* could get a hand-press. Amis had at least a $50 investment in this.

After the suppression of the first two papers and the *Review's* departure to Salem in 1865, the press remained unused for a time and then, in 1867, passed to John B. Alexander and the infant *Guard.* To Amis the *Guard* in 1894 was "simply a continuation of the original Democratic Herald instituted back of [sic] the '60's."[23] Amis of course was making the common error of tracing a newspaper's history with its equipment.

Amis did not say whether he ever worked for any of the *Guard's* first publishers, but he had been a Democrat and by 1894 was a noisy Populist. He might have had an open break with Ira Campbell. One difference arose over *Daily Guard* coverage of a Populist meeting November 17, 1894. The *Guard* had called it a "gloomy meeting," since "about the only business transacted was the subscribing of a subsidy fund of $25 a month for one year for the support of the *Broad Axe.*"[24]

Amis replied in high dudgeon. He accused Campbell of "viciousness" toward old political friends who had supported the *Guard* "through all its years of ups and downs for more than a quarter of a century." In season and out, Amis said, "the *Guard* tries to slur our people." As to Ira Campbell, he was a "barefoot boy at play, on the boom of saw logs in the mill race of Eugene" when Amis was fighting for the Democratic Party during the Civil War. And as to "subsidies," Amis had never been repaid for his investment in the first press that had come down from John Alexander. Perhaps, Amis added, the *Guard* was worried lest the *Broad Axe* become a serious future competitor.[25]

The *Broad Axe* didn't like the *Register* either. In connection with the same subsidy story, Amis said:

> "If the success of the *Register* depended upon 'merit,' the most charitable contributions it would receive would be to contribute to the charges incident to its funeral and burial."[26]

As a seven-column, four-page newspaper the *Broad Axe* carried plated material on activities of Congress, telegraphic notes about the Pacific Northwest, various features, and such local content as stories on McKenzie Highway needs and the University of Oregon. Its violent opinions aside, it was an adequate paper for its day. But the vitriolic style of the Civil War had no longer a place.

Beginning November 22, 1899, the *Broad Axe* was reduced to four pages of small format, four columns to a page. Amis put as good a face on the changes as he could: The "patent insides" had added nothing, many press association dispatches were old, and he was at all events carrying "the cream of all local happenings." Nevertheless, his advertising was still light—only seven of the 16 short-depth 16-inch columns. In addition, he was offering a joint subscription rate of $1.40 a year for the *Broad Axe* and either the "twice-a-week St. Louis *Republic* or the *National Watchman.*" For 65 cents more he would add the "thrice-a-week New York *World.*"[27]

Economic attrition was operating against the fighting Populist, now 71 years old.

A little more than three months later, in March, 1900, Amis changed the *Broad Axe* to the *Weekly Citizen*. He recalled how in 1894 "the *Guard*, the *State Journal*, and the *Register* heaped their columns of abuse upon the people's party organization . . . [how] it was an anarchist sheet and should not be sustained . . .

[how] all agreed that it must by common consent be fought to a finish."

"Yes," Amis said, "*Broad Axe* it was." But in 1900 he felt he no longer needed a broad axe to get along, since the "populist people are now treated with respect and their paper is allowed to go along like other papers. . . . Its editor, too, is less belligerently inclined."

Amis had thought, since he was reducing the *Broad Axe* in size, of changing the name to the *Hatchet.* He decided instead to "bury the hatchet" and to choose the name *Weekly Citizen.* He promised to be "a nice old man of peace and a good and quiet Citizen."

Yet even the "quiet Citizen" continued to have fire. The *Citizen* boldly proclaimed a policy of public ownership of utilities; destruction of criminal trusts; a graduated income tax; popular election of senators; national, state, and municipal ownership of public schools; currency reform; no tariff protection for trusts; and the initiative, referendum, and recall. Oregon within a few years became a leader among states in passing legislation of this type; and James Franklin Amis, the raucous opponent of the *Guard* and the *Register*, comes down as one more of those community editors who were some years ahead of their time.

Amis was no admirer of William G. Gilstrap, for only three months the new co-owner of the *Morning Register.* In an article gingerly skirting the edges of libel, the "quiet Citizen" recalled how he had once been looking for some newspaperman to run the business side of the *Broad Axe.* Gilstrap, Amis said, proposed that he would be willing to manage the Populist paper and print it on the press that in 1894 was putting out the just-established Springfield *Messenger.* But Amis felt that Gilstrap was "oily of tongue." He asked Gilstrap for recommendations, followed through on the names given him, and decided to "preclude him from any connection with the [*Broad Axe*]." [28]

Soon after the fall of 1900 the *Weekly Citizen* was no more. With it went the last remnants of frontier journalism in Eugene.

Other opponents of the *Guard* and *Register* have since tried to compete, some with apparent success for a time, but the days of objective coverage of news and increased expenses in newspaper operation were not far off. In the *Eugene City Directory* of 1902 James Franklin Amis was listed with his wife, B.F. Amis, both as printers; and with Eva Amis, a dressmaker—all of 396 West Seventh.[29] It was at that address 10 years later that one of the oldest in age of all pioneer Eugene journalists died. He had been born in 1828—eight years before Harrison Kincaid and at least 11 years before Joaquin Miller.

The Weekly Record and the Herald: Interludes

The Eugene *Weekly Record* was a third of the end-of-the-century sheets that lived only a short time, from November 17, 1897, to some date in 1899. Only one copy of Volume 1, Number 1 apparently is extant—in the Lane County Pioneer Museum in Eugene, this issue having been salvaged from the old Nineteenth Century Court House when its cornerstone was opened. The Oregon Historical Society has a running file from February 2, 1898, to January 18, 1899.

The *Weekly Record* was published by William W. Moore, who had been at one time a printer for the *Guard.*[30] The *Record* had offices in the McClung General Merchandise building at Willamette and Eighth Streets; it sold for 65 cents a year. Starting out as a four-column half-sheet, four pages, it expanded to seven columns standard size before its demise. The paper sought to be independent, and in a brief salutatory it said:

> "The *Record* . . . has no axe to grind. Its policy will be brevity. It will at all times furnish the latest news, county and state, besides a department page devoted to agriculture.
>
> "Nonpartisan in politics, its columns will be open to all at all times to the free discussion of timely topics."[31]

General news was extensive enough, although the content was devoted as much to telegraph copy as to agriculture. The

Record had only scanty advertising, one issue carrying only six columns of ads out of 28 columns total. The paper obviously could not compete with the major Eugene newspapers.[32]

The Eugene *Herald*, "Advocating Municipal Ownership of Public Utilities," had an even shorter life than the *Weekly Record.* Only four copies are readily available for three dates, March 19 and 26 and April 2, 1906 (issues 3, 4, and 5 of Volume 1). The *Herald* was hardly a newspaper, being only four pages of three columns and 10 inches in depth. Its publisher was listed as the "Special Committee of the Municipal League." We can infer only that the sheet was intended to be a specifically directed political broadside. It carried almost no advertising.[33]

The Emerald: Next to the Guard the Oldest

Despite these four more Eugene journalistic failures between 1894 and 1906, a fifth newspaper effort was made. It succeeded.

On February 12, 1900, a specialized newspaper called the *Oregon Weekly* appeared. It continued to June 14, 1909, and the following fall started up again as the *Oregon Emerald.* It continues to publish in 1967 in its sixty-eighth year as a flourishing *Oregon Daily Emerald.* In years in Eugene it has outlived every newspaper ever established in the city except the *Guard* and, if we count its merged-with-the-*Guard* years since 1930, the *Guard's* 83-year-old *Register* half.

This paper was the student journal of the University of Oregon. As early as 1902 the *Oregon Weekly* had gained a listing in Tout's *Directory* along with the *Guard, Register*, and *State Journal.* Soon thereafter it made Ayer's national *Directory.*

The *Emerald* never competed with the downtown newspapers. Its future lay in providing the city with the always fascinating news of campus developments, including University of Oregon squabbles big and little. On many occasions in the years ahead it found itself in the thick of fights over higher education. Its free use of the language off and on would bring it before the Legislature in investigations involving obscenity, and it would need the *Guard's* help in getting off those "hooks." But in 1966, even the powerful assistance of the then influential 99-year-old *Register-Guard* couldn't save the *Emerald's* 20-year-old managing editor, a woman, from being the first Oregon journalist ever to be found guilty of contempt of court for refusing to answer questions as to a source of news.[34]

More important to journalism than any of these things, however, the *Emerald* in the future was to provide a much improved *Guard*—and other Oregon newspapers, too—with a train of reporters and copy editors and business-side employes. One former *Emerald* worker became the *Register-Guard's* city editor and a distinguished specialist in communications research. Another *"Emeraldite"* editor in 1947, is today one of the *Register-Guard's* associate editors. A one-time *Emerald* columnist is today the *R-G's* managing editor.[35] In time the *Oregon Weekly* reached—as *Emerald*—a circulation greater than that of *Guard* and *Register* combined when the college paper joined the Eugene scene.

---

1. *Register-Guard*, "Register Began as Republic Paper in 1884." January 4, 1942.

2. *Portrait and Biographical Record of the Willamette Valley, Oregon*, illustrated. Chicago: Chapman Publishing Company, 1903. Hodson, born August 24, 1839, was a native of Ohio. Before coming to Oregon in 1883, he has been joint proprietor of the Winchester (Ind.) *Journal*. After Harrison's defeat in 1892, he went into the commercial printing business in Portland.

3. *Register*, October 7, 1885.

4. *Ibid.*

5. The *Register* had about 500 circulation its first year; at eight pages per issue this would make 208,000 pages of the 500,000 of printed matter Yoran mentioned. This is a mere deduction. The *Guard*, except in "house ads," did not mention its commercial-printing aspects.

6. *Register*, October 7, 1885.

7. The story of the increasing of sizes of small papers, with that of the ready-print insides, is one taken up frequently in general histories of journalism.

8. Joseph Gaston, *Centennial History of Oregon, 1811-1912*, illustrated. Chicago: S.J. Clarke Publishing Company, 1912, Vol. 2, pp. 597-598.

9. *Ibid.*

10. *Morning Register*, Silas M. Yoran obituary, June 24, 1922.

11. *Ibid.*

12. *Register*, March 2 and March 5, 1892.

13. *Register*, March 9, 1895.

14. George S. Turnbull, *History of Oregon Newspapers*. Portland, Oregon: Binfords & Mort, 1939, p. 279.

Eugene City and Lane County Directory. Portland, Eugene and Albany: compiled and published by W.G. Obenauer & Co., 1892, pp. 45 and 52.

15. *Daily Register*, July 7, 1896.

16. *Ibid.*

17. The University of Oregon Library does not have a full file of this second effort to issue the *Daily Register*. Issues are scattered and the starting date in 1898 is uncertain. One cannot be sure the last issue of October 25, 1898, was the last until December 1, 1899.

18. *Register-Guard*, "Frank Gilstrap of the *Register*," obituary editorial, November 15, 1948.

19. *Morning Register*, December 1, 1899.

20. This account of the *Guard's* Populist competitor was followed through as a result of a conversation with Martin Schmitt, curator of special collections for the University of Oregon Library. Professor Schmitt had mentioned, "There was a Populist paper in Eugene run by a man named Amis, but we haven't much on him. Have you run into him?" At the time the answer was "No."

21. *Daily Guard*, August 29, 1912.

22. *Morning Register*, August 30, 1912.

23. *Broad Axe*, November 24, 1894.

24. *Ibid. Daily Guard*, November 18, 1894.

25. *Broad Axe*, November 24, 1894.

26. *Ibid.*

27. *Broad Axe*, November 22, 1899.

28. *Broad Axe*, March 7, 1900.

29. O.B. Tout, *The Eugene Directory*. Eugene, Oregon: Press of W.O. Yoran, 1902, p. 10.

30. *Eugene City and Lane County Directory*, *op. cit.*, p. 86.

31. *Weekly Record*, November 17, 1897.

32. *Weekly Record*, January 26, 1898, and January 4, 1899.

33. *Herald*, March 26, 1906.

34. Annette Buchanan.

35. The late Paul J. Deutschmann, *Register-Guard* city editor, 1942 and 1946, later assistant professor of journalism, University of Oregon, and professor of journalism, Michigan State University; Robert B. Frazier, *Register-Guard* associate editor; William L. Wasmann, managing editor.

CHAPTER 6

News Of The Early Years—1867-1907

The oldest existing issue of the Eugene City *Guard* that is still available in a bound file in Oregon—the whole of it—would have fit into slightly more than 20 columns of the 192-column *Register-Guard* of October 24, 1966, Volume 100, Number 1. This old copy, Volume 2, Number 5, of November 21, 1868, is the one that we know starts the *Guard* in unbroken sequence, no more breakdowns such as John Alexander suffered, despite close shaves. J.W. Skaggs, whatever his deficiencies were, was wise enough to turn the *Guard* over to William Thompson for the "two cords of wood" and insure the publication of Volume 2, Number 6, on November 28.

This comparison of Skaggs' last issue with the *Register-Guard* of today is quite unfair, of course. It is noted only to stress the mighty change from struggling frontier newspaper to affluent sub-metropolitan daily. Important, too, is the need to tell how the paper grew physically, how its coverage and its policies changed, how its circulation expanded, how its advertising developed, and how its staff increased. By "staff" we mean here the employes, not the owners.

Thirty-one years after 1867, only six years before Ira L. Campbell's death, the Eugene *Guard*, daily or weekly, was not greatly different from the *Guard* of the beginning. It was still four pages, seven columns instead of six, 21 inches deep instead of 18. Space had increased from 24 columns to 28, from 432 column inches to 589. Advertising was up from 45.5 per cent to a healthy 62.5 per cent, although the nature of the ads hadn't changed much; they were still heavy in the profit-making "legals" and in questionable patent-medicine palliatives. The *Guard* and *Register* did not differ much in their handling of advertising; but, older by 17 years, the *Guard* carried a higher percentage of advertising, chiefly as a result of the legals. The *Register*, as noted, was the more extensive printing business.

News and editorial presentation changed somewhat more in the *Guard's* first third of a century. Under Campbell the vitriol of the beginning days had disappeared, while the *Register* was never editorially frenetic. Campbell for years ran scores of local "shorts"—most of them unheadlined—on the courts, on personalities, on Eugene and Lane County events, and about the University of Oregon. Much earlier than the *Register* he cut out the fiction and "lift" from Eastern newspapers. Only occasionally, at least until the Spanish-American War, would a headline "break a column-rule." Even in mid-1898 the American engagement with Spain failed to get many heads of more than two columns. Eugene's newspapers were unprepared for sensational display or for news pictures, although a few halftones and line-drawings were appearing.

Over-all, Eugene's newspapers were sadly inadequate by today's standards. They were in 1900 still awaiting municipal growth, the coming of press association service, the gradual increasing of staff, the formulating of advertising standards, and the meshing of all these factors. The changes could not really be noticed until Campbell's successors [1] took over the *Guard* and the Gilstraps bought the *Register*.

The *Guard's* contents in the early years are nevertheless revealing. Overriding all else for more than a dozen years was the paper's extreme hatred of the Radical Republicans; its continual castigation of corruption in Washington; its total disregard (if not hatred) of the Negro; later, in the 1880s, its affection for Grover Cleveland; and, in local matters, an occasional burst of enterprise. Its devotion to the University of Oregon after the school got off to its hesitant start in 1876 was unbounded.

Harvey W. Scott of the Portland *Oregonian* described well in his *History of the Oregon Country* the nature of the Democratic press during Reconstruction.[2] The *Guard* fitted the pattern. It opposed civil and political rights for the Negro and advocated repudiation of the Civil War debt.[3] When it appeared certain

DAILY EUGENE GUARD.

50 Cents..... A Month.

VOL. 14. EUGENE, OREGON, SATURDAY EVENING, APRIL 30, 1898. NO 24

AT HARRISBURG.—Hon E M Veatch Union nominee of this district for Congressman, will speak at Harrisburg Monday afternoon, May 1st.

STOCK TAKEN TO PASTURE—Apply to A M Hendricks, Oak street, between 14th and 15th, Eugene.

WOOD FOR SALE.—Inquire of M S Hubble, drayman.

OUR BOYS IN BLUE.

The Godspeed With Which Our Soldiers Go to the Front

THE PRIDE OF EUGENE.

Commencing about 7 o'clock last evening anvils were fired in various portions of the business part of the city, and about the same time the streets began to fill not only with residents of the city, but from the country adjacent, until a solid sea of faces was visible. It is said by many that the largest night crowd that ever assembled in Eugene was seen last night.

About 7:30 the band led the way to the school grounds and was followed by the large crowd, who listened attentively and appreciated every portion of the happily arranged impromptu program. Company C and the resident staff officers of the Second regiment were given a position directly in front of the platform, from which point of vantage they were able to enjoy to its fullest their public leave taking. The introductory remarks by Mayor Kuykendall, and short talks by J M Shelly, S H Friendly, S M Yoran and C J Dodd were so blended as to inspire a patriotic feeling in the breasts of all. N R Gaylord made a very fitting presentation of a drum to this company and a feeling response made by Captain Moon. The music of the occasion was furnished by the band, and a quartet which led the audience in patriotic songs.

THE BANQUET.

Marching to the banquet rooms in the Hendricks block the boys were greeted by their hostess most charmingly, and the event was one of peculiar pleasure and interest. The ladies of the W R C and Patriotic League deserve every praise for their noble work.

THE DANCE.

To Misses Maud Shelly, Edith Hofman, Ina Craig, Reta Applegate, Pearl Park, Blanch Straight and Jessie Gilstrap is due the honor of successfully carrying out a most elaborate surprise farewell dancing party for the boys after the banquet. A program of 12 numbers was carried out, and the boys enjoyed to its fullest what will probably be their last home dance for some time.

Having some money left over after paying expenses the young ladies have ordered a tree which will be planted in the city park in honor of Company C. The G A R and W R C will be invited to attend and speeches and music by the band will add to the occasion.

The following program will be rendered.

Music by Band.

Introductory remarks by Hon S H Friendly.

Prayer.

Music, choir.

Address, L T Harris.

Music, male quartet.

Dedicatory address, Hon S M Yoran.

Music, choir.

Music by Band.

J W Geary post and corps and others will meet at 7:30 at the corner of Oak and Ninth streets, and march from there to the park.

THE LEAVE-TAKING.

Early this morning the entire city again turned out and accompanied "our boys" to the 10:30 train, on which they left for Portland. Their special car was literally covered with bunting, flags and banners. No demonstration was held at the depot, other than music by the band, and the good byes said. Tears glistened in the eyes of the soldiers as well as those left behind, but the brave are ever tender, and the Godspeed wished the boys carried much more effectiveness by their manly bearing. Never before in the history of Eugene has such a popular demonstration been given. Every business house closed from 10 to 11, and it was well, for no one was left in the city, a popular human chord carrying all to the S P depot. The actions of our boys will be watched with interest and no one fears the result. They are the right sort of men to represent any community.

The Blue and Gray.

For the first time, so far as we know, since 1865 in this state, we had a solid union of the old Union and Confederate veterans in line marching through the streets of Eugene this morning. It was a grand scene to see old soldiers who had been pitted against each other in the bloody strife at Gettysburg, Cold Harbor, Atlanta, Vicksburg, The Wilderness and other bloody fields, marching shoulder to shoulder in honor of the boys of Co C, who have enlisted for the Spanish war. The old veterans gave three solid cheers for McKinley and then three just as solid for Fitzhugh Lee.

ENTHUSIASM EN ROUTE.—Today's north bound local, carrying Company A of Roseburg and Company C of Eugene, to Portland, was received by a large crowd at every station along the line, and anvils were fired and bunting and flags displayed galore.

S of V's and G A R, Attention!

The members of Geo A Custer Camp, Sons of Veterans, and J W Geary Post, No 7 G A R, will meet at G A R Hall Monday evening, May 2d at 7 o'clock p m, sharp, to attend the tree planting exercises in honor of Co C, O N G.

All sons of veterans are invited to meet at the same time and place and accompany the camp.

By order of E F CHAPMAN, Com'd.
R H MILLER, Capt.

APPOINTMENTS RECEIVED.—Notice was received today that Rev W S Gilbert of this city had been appointed Chaplain of the First Regiment, Oregon Volunteers, and that Lieutenant R S Huston would report to Captain Moon as his First Lieutenant. Each of their salaries will be $125.00 per month. Both gentlemen wired their acceptance at once, and will leave for Portland on tomorrow's 4:15 overland. Their appointment will be received with pleasure by all.

HEAVY FIRING.

Key West Reports Heavy Firing to Southeast.

PORTUGUESE ENLISTING.

Nothing Has Been Heard From Dewey.

Chasing Merchantman.

WASHINGTON, D C, April 30; 5:40 p m—Key West, Florida, reports heavy firing to the Southeast, and sees an American torpedo boat chasing a Spanish merchantman.

FIRED AT HAVANA.

A torpedo boat fired five shots at Havana today.

NOTHING HEARD.

The Spanish government forbids the transmission of news regarding naval movements, therefore nothing has been heard from Admiral Dewey.

ENLISTING.

Portuguese are rapidly enlisting in the Spanish army.

FRESH EVERY DAY—Cream puffs, lady fingers and doughnuts, at Chicago Bakery.

WILL FIGHT.

The Flying Squadron After the Spanish Fleet.

MARIEL, CUBA, BOMBARDED.

American Colony Driven From Madrid.

SPAIN'S DISABLED VESSELS.

Special to the Guard

KEY WEST, Fla, April 30, 4:20 p m.—Commander Schley's flying squadron has put to sea to intercept the Spanish fleet. This probably means a naval battle.

BOMBARDED.

The town of Mariel, Cuba, has been bombarded by the American fleet.

Fortress Cabanas is a scene of desolation.

DRIVEN FROM MADRID.

The American colony has been driven from Madrid, Spain, by a mob.

VESSELS DISABLED.

Three Spanish vessels were disabled in yesterday's Cape Verde island collision and are being towed to the Canary Islands.

HONORS EVEN.

The Spanish gunboat Ligar today engaged and defeated an American torpedo boat near Cardenas, Cuba.

The American gunboat Dolphin captured the Spanish gunboat Galle today.

OFFICERS APPOINTED.

George Yoran Gets the Lieutenant-Coloneship.

SUMMERS COLONEL.

Special to the Guard.

PORTLAND, April 30.—Governor Lord has made the following appointments.

Colonel—O Summers, of Portland, salary $3,500.

Lieutenant Colonel—Geo O Yoran, of Eugene, salary $3,000.

Majors—P G Eastwick and C U Gantenbein, of Portland and Percy Willis of Salem, salary $2,500 each.

DEVLISH WORK.

Special to the Guard.

PORTLAND, Or, April 30.—An attempt was made last night to blow up Wolff & Zwicker's torpedo boats here. Believed to be the work of a Spanish sympathizer.

DRIED FRUIT WANTED.—Commissioners Wilkins and Kuykendall are very desirous of securing fine specimens of Lane county dried fruit to exhibit at the Omaha exposition. If either commissioner is notified the fruit will be sent for.

LADIES' RIDING SCHOOL.—We are informed that a ladies' equestrian riding school will be organized in Eugene in the near future. Thirty pupils are wanted.

POSTPONED.—The Ladies Musical Club has postponed their next meeting to Monday, May 9. The club expects to have a concert May 19, in which they will be assisted by Miss Nealey Stevens, a celebrated pianist of San Francisco.

RESIDENCE BURNED.—An unoccupied house on the Summers' place, about two miles north of this city was burned this morning between 1 and 2 o'clock. The fire was probably of incendiary origin. Mr Summers is in California. Loss $125.

The Mexican Medicine Co this morning had among other banners on the street, "Say au revoir and not good bye," and "Company C, Eugene hearts are with you." They hit a popular chord.

Al Kuykendall returned to Salem this morning.

"ON TO HAVANA."

Pacific Coast States Ask President for Cruisers.

SPAIN'S THREAT ALARMING.

Special to the GUARD.

WASHINGTON, D. C., April 30; 4:10 p. m.—Senators Perkins and White, of California, Senators Wilson and Turner of Washington, and Senator McBride, of Oregon, called upon President McKinley and Navy Department, urging that auxilliary cruisers be placed on the Pacific Coast.

Spain's threat to bombard coast cities is giving considerable alarm.

ON TO HAVANA.

"On to Havana" is the war cry everywhere now.

A San Francisco Examiner's special of today says Havana has been fired upon but no response was given.

General Sahfler will invade Havana next Wednesday.

WILL BOMBARD

Pacific Coast Cities Threatened by Spaniards.

TROOPS CONCENTRATING.

Madrid Government Claims Germany Will Help Her.

Insurgents Enlisting in Spanish Army.

Special to the Guard

WASHINGTON, D C, April 30; 12:15 p m—A New York World special says that prominent Spaniards favor the immediate bombardment of Pacific Coast cities, thus crippling the American forces now advancing on Cuba.

INSURGENTS ENLISTING.

A special from Havana says hundreds of insurgents are enlisting in the Spanish army. Starvation is said to be the cause.

EXPECTS GERMANY'S AID.

A special to the New York Journal from Madrid, Spain, says that prominent Spanish officials say that Germany will aid Spain when the crisis comes.

TROOPS CONCENTRATING.

More troops left Mobile, Alabama, this morning for Tampa, Florida.

Two companies of infantry and one of cavalry broke camp at Chicamauga Park this forenoon.

INDIAN OUTBREAK.

An Indian outbreak is threatened in South Dakota since the withdrawal of troops.

TORPEDO BOATS

Government Orders 100 of These Destroyers.

MANZANILLO CAPTURED

38,000 Spanish Soldiers Sick in Cuba.

HEAVY RAINS IN CUBA

Special to the Guard.

WASHINGTON, April 30; 5 p m.—The government has ordered one hundred new torpedo boats, to be finished as fast as possible.

CAPTURED.

NEW YORK, April 30; 5 p m.—A Journal special says the Insurgents have captured Manzanillo, Cuba.

SPANISH SOLDIERS SICK.

There are thirty-eight thousand Spanish soldiers sick in Cuba.

WANTS PROTECTION.

The British consul at Santiago, Cuba, has asked his government for a war ship.

HEAVY RAINS.

Heavy rains are reported in the interior of Cuba.

CAPE FOUND.—A ladies cape was found at the depot this forenoon. The owner can have the same by calling at this office.

that the Fifteenth Amendment (1870) eliminating race as a consideration for suffrage would pass the *Guard* charged:

> "The purpose of Radicalism [is] to down utterly the constitutional safeguards of state power. . . . We shall have to gulp down the Fifteenth Amendment."[4]

Scott said that Oregon's Democratic press during Reconstruction advocated that government "be put into the hands of those who had sought to overthrow it," and urged that "Jefferson Davis be put on the payroll of the Army in [his] retirement."[5] The *Guard*, however, did not appear to go to that extreme.

The single issue during Reconstruction that showed the young Eugene City newspaper at its best arose over the Election of 1876 and the disputed electoral votes involving Rutherford B. Hayes and Samuel J. Tilden. Historically the Hayes-Tilden fight involved challenged returns from Louisiana, Florida, and South Carolina, and a lone vote in Oregon. Hayes needed every one from the four states to carry the Electoral College by 185 to 184. To George J. Buys, then publishing the *Guard*, it was the Oregon vote that elected Hayes. From an Oregon Democrat's point of view this might well have been the case, since the Oregon vote was the only one not involving the Carpetbaggers.

The *Guard* outdid itself in covering this election, its issues from November 11, 1876, until after March 4, 1877, being filled with news of the struggle; most of the content was extremely biased, of course. We cannot tell whether any of the *Guard's* reports were received by telegraph, were clipped from other papers (credit was seldom given), or were written by Buys and his staff. It is enough to say that the spate of information was there, week after week. Even in frontier days, when news was emotionally surcharged, a newspaper with scant facilities could show itself to advantage. In sum, the *Guard's* Hayes-Tilden stories stand up as to accuracy in accounts of the election in histories of Oregon prepared nearly a half-century later.[6]

The *Guard* had come out for Tilden immediately upon the New York governor's nomination for the Presidency in June. It said:

> "The whole country has associated its mind with Tilden and reform. Coast and South will give Tilden full strength. It will be the Republicans who will be lost in the Hayes of November."[7]

On November 11, 1876, in its first post-election issue, the *Guard* reported, "Tilden Probably Elected." By November 18, Buys was certain, "Tilden Elected." On November 25 he was less sure, a one-word heading reading, "Uncertain."[8] In its coverage the paper ran full county-by-county tabulations of Oregon's presidential vote and precinct-by-precinct totals in Lane County, a distinctive bit of enterprise for a weekly in 1876.[9] Lane County went to Hayes by three votes, 949-946.

Two weeks later the *Guard's* news was related to Louisiana: "A Dark Page from History—Fraud in Louisiana Vote."[10] There *was* fraud, in Louisiana and in Florida and in South Carolina; but the Southern angle was pushed aside out West when the dispute involving Oregon broke wide open.

The Oregon conflict concerned one John H. Watts, United States postmaster at Lafayette, Yamhill County, who had been one of the three victorious Hayes electors; however, he had been ineligible to enter the Oregon electoral contest, since Article II, Section 2 of the United States Constitution provides that "no person holding an office or trust or profit under the United States shall be appointed an elector." Watts conveniently had resigned his postmastership a week after the election—and before the canvass of the Oregon vote to certify the three electors. The state issue, then, was, Would the resignation after the fact legalize Watts' ineligibility to run in the first place? The Democrats, and obviously the *Guard*, held, "No." The Republicans held that the people's will had spoken in Oregon for Hayes and, at worst, Watts' spot should be declared vacant and the two legitimately chosen electors should have authority to fill the vacancy. This is what the other two did; they reappointed Watts.

The governor, Lafayette F. Grover (a Democrat) then set Watts' election aside and the *Guard* cheered. Grover certified the highest running Tilden elector in Watts' place, he being E.A. Cronin of Portland. Grover granted certificates of election to the two undisputed Hayes electors, J.C. Cartwright of Wasco County and W.H. Odell of Marion County, and to Cronin. The row arose when Cartwright and Odell wouldn't accept Cronin and a two-to-one division for Hayes. Cronin, meanwhile, refused to give up his certification.

The ruckus reached Washington and was thrown into the total conflict including the Southern states. Governor Grover testified before the United States Senate Committee on Privilege to defend his appointment of Cronin. Of Grover's stand the *Guard* said:

> "His action in the Watts-Cronin case [has] made him and Oregon both famous and henceforth people at a distance will turn with inquisitive interest to a place that furnishes such men as our governor and minds capable of scotching the most unscrupulous combination of fraud and corruption that have ever disgraced our country. The 'half-civilized Westerner' will hereafter be counted a factor in politics."[11]

Grover and the *Guard* and all the Democrats nationally availed nothing. The Electoral Commission resolved the Oregon fight, set Cronin aside, and accepted Watts' vote for Hayes. From the Oregon Democrats' point of view this is the vote that put Hayes into the Presidency.

Buys foresaw the result and on February 24, 1877, he called the Electoral Commission a "nondescript commission," and he added that "human depravity and national degradation have touched bottom." He went on:

> "Watts will be recognized as a legal elector, our State laws will be spurned, and the Constitution of the United States will be disregarded and everything tending to perpetuate Radicalism, usurpation and fraud will be decided legal and what favors the success of honest government will be as dust in the balance. . . . We cannot see that our country can outlive the shame, the folly, the degradation of being subjected to the whims—worse, the loathsome rascality of a few unscrupulous traitors."[12]

Whatever the merits of the Watts case or the Cronin case, George Buys' *Guard* handled the news event excellently. We can discount the political bias and judge the coverage as technique. But it took a Hayes-Tilden crisis to bring out the *Guard's* reserve potential. Run-of-the-mill news of Eugene City and Oregon was treated indifferently.

After Buys sold out to the Alexander brothers in the spring of 1877 the *Guard's* coverage declined noticeably. When President Hayes called a special session of Congress in the fall to consider a military deficiency appropriation the *Guard* ran the speech in full, but with no comment. In the same issue it reported that 179 students had enrolled in the one-year-old University of Oregon, which it said was "flourishing," was "under the best discipline," and was being served by "a corps of teachers [who] cannot be excelled in the state." When a fire occurred up the Willamette River a scant four miles from Eugene all that was published was, "The smoke house of Mrs. Laird on the Middle Fork of the Willamette burned."[13] This was the kind of reporting that was most frequent throughout the *Guard's* first 30 years.

Yet any Eugenean who is devoted to the lore of the little city 70 to 100 years ago can, by browsing through *Guard* files, find occasional news or feature pieces that do show reporting depth. Every once in a while the *Guard* could write up the news interestingly—if it had a mind to and took the time.

President Benjamin Harrison Comes: He Slights Eugene

One delightful story was an account, on May 9, 1891, of an abortive reception for Benjamin Harrison, twenty-third President, who passed through Eugene at 6:10 a.m. May 5. (This was only a month before Ira Campbell founded the *Daily Guard.*) The President was en route from San Francisco to Portland on a Western tour, and Eugene had prepared a grand reception. Presumably arrangements for Harrison's stop had been made in advance and the President's entourage notified. A firebell was set to ring at 5 a.m., and within an hour a throng had congregated at the foot of Willamette Street. "At least 2,000 persons were present," the *Guard* reported.

All through the presidential way-stop it was raining, not an uncommon circumstance in early May. The greeters didn't mind that. What they did mind was that Benjamin Harrison did not appear on the platform.

"Flags and evergreens were everywhere," the *Guard* said. "The band played. . . . Bombs were fired. . . . The reception committee included Mayor [John H.] McClung, S.M. Yoran, and S.H. Friendly.[14] No one appeared. They waited and waited, with the same barren result."

The *Guard's* headline read:

"AN INSULT TO EUGENE

"The President's Train Stops 20 Minutes—
Benjamin Does Not Appear—The Citizens
Indignant at the Affront

The news story was highly colored:

> "Someone saw Wannamaker through a window complacently reading a paper. . . . Harrison was presumably enjoying his bed. . . . [It was] a contemptible manner to be treated."[15]

The Eugene civic committee boarded the train to see what could be done. It reported back that the presidential party had sent a telegram from California saying that Mr. Harrison could not appear. Mayor McClung and other Eugeneans denied having received such a dispatch.

During the 20-minute stop a McKenzie River fishing party also boarded the train and delivered "a basket of as fine trout as ever was lifted from the water." Later in the day an irate greeter sent a telegram to Harrison in Portland.

> "EUGENE, May 5—Send back the basket of trout and we will send suckers instead.
>
> "INDIGNANT EUGENE."[16]

A year and a half later the new Eugene *Daily Guard* reported the results of the Benjamin Harrison-Grover Cleveland-James Weaver (Populist) presidential election of 1892. In Eugene the results were: Harrison 591, Weaver 392, Cleveland 134; in Lane County they were: Harrison 1,902, Weaver 1,324, Cleveland 828. The county at large was not irritated by Harrison's slight. The Populist strength of 1892 reflected the extent of debtor-class sentiment in Oregon.[17]

The Spanish-American War: News Display Broadens

Imperceptible as news coverage changes are from day to day, we begin to observe in the *Guard* and the *Register* from this time on a more open approach—particularly in the *Guard.* The Mergenthaler Linotype machine had been perfected in the 1880s, and although it did not reach Eugene until after 1900, the city's newspapers were being affected by typographical changes elsewhere. The influence of the sensationalism of the 1890s could be noticed in Eugene by frequent use of double-column display on page one, in headlines up to 48-point, and in bulletin treatment of important news.

The Spanish-American War was a major factor toward speeding changes, just as it was on a larger scale in the circulation struggle between Joseph Pulitzer and William Randolph Hearst in New York.

The *Guard* reflected both the war and the expanding news front the most, for it was by 1898 a going daily, whereas the *Register* was in the throes of its interim difficulties between the Yorans and the Gilstraps. But even the *Weekly Register* was moving ahead. The *Oregon State Journal* showed little forward momentum in news coverage, since Harrison R. Kincaid was busy from 1895 to 1899 as secretary of state in Salem and after 1900 as a county judge in Eugene. The *Journal* remained to its end the typographically unimaginative paper it had always been.

The *Daily Guard* and the *Weekly Register* had no copy desks in 1898.[18] When the Spanish-American War broke out in April, headline treatment on occasion went to four-column spreads in the *Guard*, but the news was published in short dispatches, many repetitive and none integrated into what in newsroom idiom we today call "roundup." The *Guard* in April showed some enterprise in setting off some of the news from Cuba in two-column bold-faced boxes, indented, under the heading, LATEST WAR NEWS.[19] But for the most part the reader had to shift for himself. Any person today who feels frustrated in trying to tie events together in daily press reports—especially in community newspapers—need only to peruse files of 70 years ago to learn how much press association "general leads" and copy-desk editing advances have improved readability.[20]

Upon the declaration of war the *Daily Guard* used three single-column heads for closely related items, the essence of which was told in one of the headline decks: "President McKinley Signs War Resolution." Separate stories carried the House vote (310-6) and the Senate vote (42-35) and other aspects of the war. No mention was made of the newsworthy factor of the narrow seven-vote Senate margin. Only one of the three stories carried a credit, "Special to the Guard."[21]

Oregon had an important local angle in the Spanish-American War in the race of the battleship *Oregon* from the North Pacific around Cape Horn to assist American naval forces in the Caribbean. The *Oregon's* voyage had all the human-interest trappings that would today make columns of feature news. Even in 1898 some American newspapers made much of the voyage: Would the *Oregon* reach Cuba in time? The event carries its share of footnotes in American histories, and the *Oregon* itself became a showpiece in Portland harbor until it was used for scrap in World War II.

The *Oregon* news received only cursory treatment in the Eugene newspapers, usually in buried brevities, and one can make out the battleship's progress only with difficulty. On April 28 the *Register* ran a one-sentence "special dispatch" from Buenos Aires:

> "A Spanish torpedo boat left here April 22 going to meet the *Oregon*, now on way around Cape Horn to join the American fleet at Havana."[22]

Later the *Guard* carried an item that the *Oregon* was being recalled to the Pacific. This proved inaccurate, for the battleship reached the war zone in time to take part in the victories of Admiral William T. Sampson and Commodore W.S. Schley's fleet at Santiago de Cuba in July.[23]

On May 31, under a Key West (Fla.) dateline, the *Guard* ran a story that "the battleship *Oregon* and cruiser (*sic*, singular) *New York* and *New Orleans* have just left here at full speed supposedly to join Captain Schley's fleet at Santiago de Cuba."[24] This was followed six days later with a bit more color—at least in the headline—in news from Kingston, Jamaica:

> "OUR OWN OREGON
> "She Destroys the Spanish Torpedo Boat Terror"[25]

However, the *Register* three days after this reported that "advices say" the *Oregon* encountered and sank the *Terror;* yet, under a Cape Haytien dateline there was a denial of the sinking, with no source of the denial given.[26] In none of these items were there subsequent follow-ups.

Thus the *Oregon* stories continued. It is easy nearly 70 years later to attribute these omissins to lack of news sense among Eugene editors. Why didn't they extract this colorful sidelight of the war and play it apart from the run of the news? This could be answered with other questions: Did they have time? Did they know how? Or, did they have adequate staff? If we answer "No" to all three of these—a reasonable judgment—we put a better light on what on the surface seems weak handling of significant news.

The *Oregon* story wasn't entirely missed, however. On July 9, 1898, the *Oregon State Journal* ran a 36-line poem lifted from *Frank Leslie's Weekly:* "The Race of the *Oregon.*" It closed on this stirring note:

> "When your boys shall ask what the guns are for,
> Then tell them the tale of the Spanish War
> And the breathless millions that looked upon
> The matchless race of the *Oregon.*"[27]

A few weeks later the Northern Pacific Railway put an ad in the *Register:* THE BATTLESHIP OREGON. The *Oregon* in its 18,000-mile trip had made many records, said the ad. So was the N.P.'s "80-page vest-pocket-size *Army and Navy Book* [telling the *Oregon* story]. This is a tribute to the enterprise of the Company and the value of the book."[28]

The *Daily Guard* and the *Register* did a better job in covering other phases of the war, particularly in reports of activities of Oregon's troops. News appeared on the state's quota of volunteers—730; on troops who wrote home to friends; about departures for the Philippines; and about Eugene's celebrations of the Manila and Cuba victories in July 4 rallies. Buried among these items was one in the *Register* reading:

> "Robert Eastland of Eugene received a letter from Horace Burnett in which he [Burnett] says he was sick all through the voyage, and that Honolulu is a hot town."[29]

Horace Burnett was a 23-year-old Eugenean who had served an apprenticeship as a typesetter on the *Oregon State Journal,* held his first paying job as a typesetter on the *Guard* in 1897, returned to the *State Journal* after a few months to become city editor, and then in 1898 enlisted in Company C, Second Oregon Volunteers. He served in the Philippines during the war and in 1899 returned to Oregon journalism. With the *Guard*, the *Register*, and the *Register-Guard*, he was to remain in Eugene until after World War II. At one time Burnett was a stockholder in the *Morning Register.*[30]

Assassination: William McKinley's Death

The assassination of William McKinley in 1901 while the President was attending the Pan-American Exposition in Buffalo, N.Y., provides an example of how limited the coverage of such a tragic event was then as compared with the story of John F. Kennedy's death in Dallas 62 years later. Both the *Guard* and the *Register* handled the McKinley murder in as great depth as their facilities permitted; yet more might have been done with it had the papers been resilient in their makeup. Continuity was given in coverage, for McKinley was the lead for nearly two weeks, and editorial expression of grief was profound. But years of custom in running news secondary to advertising on page one were not to be overcome in the Eugene of 1901. Even the shooting of a President could not break the display straitjacket this early, and an ad-less news page was not to appear in Eugene for nearly another decade.

McKinley was shot in the Buffalo Temple of Music on Friday, September 6, 1901. The *Guard* as an afternoon paper with a three-hour time-zone advantage, broke the story in Eugene. Its two-column head read into the middle of page one, columns 3 and 4:

"PRESIDENT McKINLEY SHOT
"Well-Dressed Stranger Shook Hands,
Then Fired Two Shots Into the
President's Body
"WOUNDS THOUGHT FATAL"

The account ran double-column measure all the way down the page. The source was given only as "Special to the Guard." The only picture was a half-tone two-column portrait that appears similar to the "front-porch-campaign" portrait used in 1896. News content included three separate Buffalo leads of maximum length of three paragraphs each, plus one item out of New York. One bulletin reported the shooting; the second said that McKinley was "resting easier" but that either of the two bullets which entered his body could be fatal; the third reported that the assassin was a Polish anarchist (unnamed). The third item also included a brief biography of McKinley (in brackets). The New York story mentioned flurries in the Stock Exchange.

That was all.[31]

The *Morning Register* report of September 7 differed only slightly from the *Guard's*. The *Register* carried also a two-column headline, "Assassinated the President," with four decks, but the news ran in single-column measure down columns 3 and 4 and carrying into 5. A two-column half-tone profile of McKinley had better reproduction than the *Guard's* photograph. Inside, the *Register* carried two editorials. The first, "Shot the President," was emotional: "The nation rises up as one man and cries for the blood of the foul-handed assassin."

The second editorial, "President's Day at the Pan-American Exposition," was commentary prepared before the shooting and not revised in spite of news developments, even though the *Register* had had more than 12 hours to handle the news for its morning edition.

This detail is useful in revealing advances made in newspaper mechanics and editing since 1901, the speed-up of emotional tempo as shown in treatment of John Kennedy's death in 1963, photographic changes, and newspaper tendencies today toward "blanket coverage." The Eugene newspapers throughout the week before McKinley died on September 14 offered no local coverage other than editorial comment.

The *Guard* did not vary its McKinley display, the same two-column position holding daily until September 21—through the long waiting period in which the President gained and lapsed, the notifying of Theodore Roosevelt of McKinley's death and Roosevelt's becoming President, the funeral, the arrest of Leon Czolgosz, and the national hunt to run down anarchists, among them Emma Goldman. Finally, on September 21, the Boer War took over lead position. [32]

The *Register* dropped back to single-column headlines on September 8 and continued this moderate display thereafter. Both newspapers used "turned rules" when McKinley died, a typographical practice to show bereavement that is now seldom used. [33]

Locally, the McKinley death did lead to one editorial exchange between the newspapers to show that occasional intemperate attacks by editors upon each other had not yet ceased. The *Guard* on September 11 commented upon a "partial confession" that assassin Leon Czolgosz had made in which he said there did exist an "anarchist plot" in America. This in turn had led to news stories that the government would ruthlessly hunt down all would-be murderers. To be opposed to anarchism was all right, said the *Guard*. But the paper then offered reasons why the United States faced such perils: "There are too many millionaires taking wealth from the people." Further, too strong government intervention would be a danger to free speech. [34]

This brought an angry response from the *Register*. To it the *Guard's* utterances were "startling." The *Register* implied:

> "[The *Guard* believes] we cannot suppress anarchy because this is a country of free speech. . . . Will the people of Lane County, irrespective of party, endorse such an incendiary statement? We think not!" [35]

The *Guard* in turn charged misinterpretation, that the *Register* was trying to create prejudice against the *Guard*. And to this the *Register* replied, "The *Guard* is worried." [36]

Slowly, as with the Kennedy assassination, the shock of McKinley's death wore away and other news superseded it. To believe, however, that an assassination in 1963 caused a greater national trauma than in 1901 could be inaccurate. The files show otherwise, and we can ask some rhetorical questions: What if Ira L. Campbell and the Gilstraps in September 1901 had had the *Register-Guard's* news and desk staff and physical plant of November 22, 1963? How would they then have handled the murder of William McKinley? Perhaps the *Register*, when it attacked the *Guard* for its effort to analyze anarchism, had missed an earlier *Guard* editorial:

> "The shooting of three presidents in 36 years is a horrible record for this, the most enlightened country of the earth."[37]

Technology: The Associated Press Comes to Eugene

Meanwhile, the years immediately after 1900 were years in Eugene in which both newspapers proudly displayed national and international news, this practice being influenced by the papers' acquiring leased wire service for the first time. Although the Associated Press had been serving member newspapers (mostly metropolitan) for a long time before 1900, it was not until that year that the present-day corporate AP was formed under the laws of New York State and was stabilized under Melville E. Stone. The Associated Press in 1900 served about 700 daily newspapers in the United States out of nearly 2,200 then publishing, and its membership increased to 1,250 by 1920.[38] The Eugene dailies were among the first to get AP service during this expansion, the *Morning Register* leading, on Friday, November 7, 1902. The first story to carry a "By the Associated Press" credit-line in boldface agate type was one on an election fraud in the New York mayoral race.[39] The *Register* carried no news promotion about its service, so it is possible that AP had been received but not credited before November 7. Such promotional restraint is noteworthy, for the *Register* was not reluctant in boosting its own merits. Two years later the paper was less bashful:

> "No other city on this coast the size of Eugene can boast of a morning paper . . . expending as much money annually for telegraphic service as is paid annually by the *Register* for its Associated Press, and which service gives our patrons such general satisfaction."[40]

The *Guard* did not get the Associated Press until 1906, when on October 30 it added "Member of the Associated Press" to its editorial-page masthead but, like the *Register* earlier, made no comment about the addition. Unlike the *Register*, however, the *Guard* did not regularly use a credit line on its telegraphic news.[41] The *Guard* by late 1906 had passed from the hands of the Campbell brothers, and the Associated Press membership can be clarified by an editorial note run nearly six months later:

> "No matter how fast Eugene and Lane County grow, the *Daily* and *Weekly Guard* will keep fully abreast of the procession."[42]

A press association franchise clearly would be part of this procession.

How impressive the Associated Press memberships were to Eugene's editors can be seen in a local story relating to the *Register's* coverage of the Russo-Japanese War in 1904. Paul Cowles, Western Division manager for the AP, who had been in the Far East, had come to Oregon to report on the increase in the association's foreign service. The *Register* might have had its own reporter in Portland to hear Cowles, for its news from there was undatelined under the head:

"IT COSTS MONEY FOR WAR NEWS"

The report, a promotional one, carried no specific figures as to costs, but it was worth a great deal as a "status item." Cowles criticized the Japanese censorship and lauded his general manager (Melville Stone) for the AP's achievement in gaining access to news from Russia through intercession with the czar. Then, forecasting brashly, Cowles was reported as saying:

> "The time of the special correspondent as a big factor in a modern war is past, and the work of the news association is far superior, more accurate, and more satisfactory." [43]

Cowles was wrong. The individual newspaper correspondent was not superseded in future wars, but little newspapers like the *Guard* and the *Register* could not afford them anyhow. Associated Press news such as Cowles was promoting was heady wine to these booming newspapers from 1900 to 1910. When the *Register's* first 20 years ended in 1904 the Gilstraps could run a four-column spread, "Roosevelt Elected," and use all of page one to cover a national election except for what the paper gave over to advertising. And the *Guard*, age 37, was using seven-column maps of the Far Eastern War Zone. [44]

---

1. Charles H. Fisher, E.J. Finneran, then a receivership, then Fisher a second time, with Joseph E. Shelton. See pp. 149-157 *infra*.
2. Harvey W. Scott, *History of the Oregon Country*. Cambridge, Massachusetts: Riverside Press 1924, Vol. 5, p. 34.
3. *Ibid.*
Guard, March 6 and March 13, 1869, October 30, 1869.
4. *Guard*, March 27, 1869.
5. Scott, *op. cit.*
6. Charles Henry Carey, *History of Oregon*. Chicago, Portland, Oregon: Pioneer Historical Publishing Company, 1922, pp. 817, ff.
7. *Guard*, July 1, 1876.
8. *Guard*, November 11, 18, and 25, 1876.
9. *Ibid.* The tabulation of November 11, only four days after the election, showed a 62 per cent return covering 17 of Oregon's then 23 counties. In 16 of these the early result held up in official returns; only in Lane, where Tilden held a six-vote margin, was there a reversal to give Hayes the county by three votes. Hayes carried Oregon on full returns, 15,214 to 14,156. The *Guard* carried county-by-county returns for congressman-at-large Richard Williams (Republican, Portland) winning over Lafayette Lane (Democrat, Lane), son of secessionist Joseph Lane.
10. *Guard*, December 2, 1876.
11. *Guard*, January 20, 1877. Grover resigned the governorship within a few days and was elected by the Oregon Legislature to serve in the United States Senate, term 1877-1883.
12. *Guard*, February 24, 1877.

13. *Guard*, October 27, 1877.

14. The 2,000-attendance estimate must have been exaggerated, unless two of every three persons in Eugene were out at this hour, or unless a great crowd came from county points. McClung and Friendly of the committee were prominent merchants and Yoran, as noted, owned the *Register*. The full committee contained 20 names.

15. John Wanamaker (the *Guard* misspelled his name) was the Philadelphia department store owner who was Harrison's postmaster general. The story also carried oblique references to "Uncle Jerry Rusk" not showing himself. Rusk, of Wisconsin, was secretary of agriculture.

16. *Guard*, May 9, 1891.

17. *Daily Guard*, November 10, 1892.

18. See reference to Otto Gilstrap, p. 95 *supra*.

19. *Daily Guard*, April 19, 1898.

20. Readability and ease in helping readers follow news is one of the continuing technical studies conducted by newspaper and press association executives today.

21. *Daily Guard*, April 19, 1898.

22. *Register*, April 28, 1898.

23. *Daily Guard*, May 31, 1898.

24. *Ibid.*

25. *Daily Guard*, June 6, 1898. The *Terror* was a steel torpedo boat of 380 tons, carrying six guns.

26. *Register*, June 9, 1898, under June 6 dateline.

27. *Oregon State Journal*, July 9, 1898.

28. *Register*, August 18, 1898. The book sold for 10 cents through R. McMurphy, general agent, Northern Pacific Passenger Department, St. Paul, Minn.

29. *Register*, June 30, 1898, p. 5.

30. *Register-Guard*, January 4, 1942. Burnett was one of the few of the *Register* staff to remain with the *Register-Guard* after the consolidation. It was said of him at one time that he "knows everybody in Lane County."

George S. Turnbull, *History of Oregon Newspapers*. Portland, Oregon: Binfords & Mort, 1939, p. 278.

31. *Daily Guard*, September 6, 1901.

32. *Daily Guard*, September 6 to 21, 1901, inclusive.

33. *Morning Register*, September 7 to 21, 1901, inclusive.

34. *Daily Guard*, September 11, 1901.

35. *Morning Register*, September 12, 1901.

36. *Daily Guard*, September 12, 1901; *Morning Register*, September 13, 1901.

37. *Daily Guard*, September 7, 1901.

38. Alfred McClung Lee, *The Daily Newspaper in America*. New York: The Macmillan Company, 1937, p. 526.

39. Seth Low was mayor of New York City in 1902-03.

40. *Morning Register*, "An Improved Register," in *Anniversary Edition, 1846-1904*, p. 22; no date of month given.

41. *Daily Guard*, October 30, 1906.

42. *Daily Guard*, March 2, 1907.

43. *Morning Register*, September 9, 1904.

44. *Morning Register*, November 9, 1904; Semi-Weekly *Guard*, April 16, 1904.

CHAPTER 7

Eugene—Boom Town, 1900-1920

Eugene's most optimistic years were those from 1900 to 1920, chiefly the first decade. In the 1890s the city had grown only 4.9 per cent, from 3,086 to 3,236, while Oregon from 1890 to 1900 showed a 31.8 per cent gain, from 313,767 to 413,536. Lane County was up 29 per cent, 15,198 to 19,604, and was fourth in population after Multnomah (Portland), Marion (Salem), and Clackamas (Oregon City).

In the next 10 years the population picture changed abruptly. Eugene soared to 9,009, up 178.4 per cent; Oregon rose to 672,765, or 62.7 per cent; Lane County jumped to 33,783, for 72.3 per cent. For the first time Eugene and the head of the Willamette Valley were outpacing the rest of Oregon. More than 2,000 behind Astoria in the race for city position at one time, Eugene almost caught the coast city in 1910 (9,009 to 9,599), only to fall behind in the next decade and not pass Astoria until 1930.

The Lane County and Eugene growth in the 1900-10 decade was reflected in an expansive boastfulness quite different from the relative moderation mid-Twentieth Century residents became accustomed to use in describing their region. The "Emerald Empire" of later years was restrained metaphor compared with the descriptions at the turn of the century. The R.L. Polk Company, American city directory publishers, issued an advertising-packed *Eugene City and Lane County Directory* of 471 pages in 1910, nearly 100 pages fatter than a later directory in 1918, after the bloom of the expansion had faded. The Polk descriptions were effusive:

1. "The City has always been prosperous." (This wasn't quite true.)

2. "The City now has a population of 12,000." (This was a 33 per cent over-estimate on the 1910 census and a figure not to be reached until 1930.)

3. "Construction of the 200-mile Natron-Klamath cutoff, to become the main line of the Southern Pacific [is] among the chief factors which bring Eugene pre-eminently to the fore as one of the important inland cities of the state." (The cutoff did not open until the 1920s.)

4. "The University of Oregon is one of the most completely equipped educational institutions in the United States." (This statement simply exaggerated.)

The directory emphasized construction in 1909: that a $75,000 federal building was being erected; that postal receipts were up 19.6 per cent; that there "are no saloons"; that 60 blocks of "bitylithic" pavement had been laid; that the Booth-Kelly Company was the "largest lumber-making concern on the Coast"; that a railroad was being projected to Florence to open the Siuslaw basin; and that "the water courses and mountain fastnesses of Lane County, reached from Eugene, afford an exceptionally attractive rendezvous for anglers and sportsmen." [1]

None of this commentary was actually inaccurate. Taken in context the descriptions showed the great hopes that lay ahead. All these developments—and more—were to come for Eugene and Lane County, although more slowly than the optimists of 1910 foresaw. World War I, of course, was a delaying factor.

Changes in the city proper included the annexation of the Fairmount area east of the University of Oregon in 1905.[2] The city limits reached south in numbered streets to Twenty-third, from which point there was little extension until after World War II. Eastward, with Fairmount added, the city reached to Fairmount Boulevard and a promontory called Judkins Point abutting the river; the limits have moved beyond this point only slightly in the half-century since, Glenwood never having come in.[3] Westward, Eugene had reached to Polk Street but not yet

Chambers. Northward, it stopped at the river, which Eugene would not vault until the 1960s.

On April 8, 1908, voters approved a $300,000 bond issue to pay for a municipal water system, the forerunner of today's Eugene Water and Electric Board. The decision to have a publicly owned utility came as a political aftermath of a typhoid epidemic in 1906. The *Guard* supported municipal ownership, while the *Register* opposed it. Both newspapers were filled throughout the period from 1905 to 1908 with arguments about municipal supplying of water. Today, however, Eugeneans regard the Water and Electric Board as one of the city's proudest achievements in city administration. [4]

Eugene remained a decidedly optimistic city in 1918, although the directory exaggerations were down from five pages to less than one. As for population, it had gone up only slightly to a shade more than 10,000. [5]

The *Guard* and the *Register* both reflected this early-century zeal. The years from 1904 to 1907 brought the first special promotional editions of each paper, two by the *Register* and one by the *Guard.* Newspaper special editions to advance the home community, frequently little more than a means of getting advertising, have always been journalistic perennials. However, Eugene's boom after 1900 was substantive enough to warrant these special sections abounding in community pride. Their size, editorial content, and pictorialization give them historical value far exceeding their worth in news content.

The *Register* was first, with a 64-page, tabloid-size LANE COUNTY EDITION issued in 1904 without specific date and for the purpose of covering *Fifty-eight Years of Growth and Progress for Eugene, the City of Destiny and Future Metropolis of the Willamette Valley.* [6] Although the *Register* reported for 1905 only 1,000 circulation daily and 1,600 for its semi-weekly edition, it ran off 10,000 copies of the special edition and said, "Fully half the number will be sent East as an advertising medium." The edition was printed on coated paper, mostly in black and white but with a blue-and-white cover and with a number of full-page rotogravure ads in brown. There was a superfluity of formal pictures of pioneers and business men and of city and county landscapes and building scenes. Writing was pedestrian and overdrawn. Still, the issue was crammed full of facts and, on a smaller scale, did a better job for Lane County than Walling's history had done 20 years earlier. [7]

The *Register* had intended to commemorate 20 years of its own and 40 years of Eugene's history as an incorporated city, but the Gilstraps became enthusiastic about their endeavor and extended the purview all the way back to 1846 and the arrival of Eugene Skinner. The paper was quite carried away:

> "With everything pointing to a destiny as here marked out, we confidently believe that twenty years from now another anniversary edition of the *Morning Register* will show a still greater contrast between Eugene and Lane County of 1904 and 1924 than is shown between the periods of 1846 and 1904. . . . The Eugene of 1924 should have a population of 50,000 and the Willamette Valley over a million population." [8]

The *Daily Guard* followed two years later with a 24-page standard-size SPECIAL ILLUSTRATED EDITION of three sections. In news space this carried approximately the same total content as the *Register's* issue of 1904, the *Guard* having more editorial matter and less advertising. Its issue was also on coated paper and was a supplement to the regular newspaper of December 8, 1906. Though covering the same promotional ground as the *Register*, the *Guard* did a more competent editorial job. Old Harrison R. Kincaid came over from the *State Journal* and wrote seven solid columns on Oregon, Lane County, and Eugene; Professor F.G. Young wrote a comprehensive piece on 30 years of the University of Oregon.

The particular occasion for the *Guard* edition was less apparent than that for the *Register's*. Possibly the paper engaged in its promotion because 1906 had been a banner year worthy of attention: bank deposits from December 1, 1905, to December 1,1906, jumping from $1,406,243.43 to $2,128,658.72, post office business soaring 12 per cent, and retail trade going up 10 per cent. It is possible, too, that the *Guard* was exhibiting some of the new owner's enterprise, Charles H. Fisher having taken control eight months earlier. No mention was made of this.[9]

Three months later the *Morning Register* issued another tabloid special edition, this one a 60-page INDUSTRIAL EDITION. Somewhat different from that of 1904, it stressed news more than it promoted settlement, but as in 1904 its advertising was heavy and its chauvinism evident:

> "Lane has an area seven times larger than the state of Rhode Island, yet it has only 30,000 population as compared with 400,000 in the Island state. If Rhode Island can support 400,000 Lane county should accomodate [sic] 2,800,000 people."[10]

Whatever their extremes of exaggeration, the three special editions reflect their day: city, county, and newspaper hopes for the future. Their compendiums of facts, even when discounted, tell what the Willamette Valley economy was like. The issues are fruitful sources of biographical material. And they reveal their publishers' public service sense more than 20 years before the *Guard* adopted "Citizen of Its Community" as a standard.[11]

---

1. *Eugene City and Lane County Directory*. Portland, Oregon: R.L. Polk and Company, 1910. Includes Cottage Grove, Junction City and Springfield.
2. City of Eugene, *Annexation Records*, 1905.
3. Glenwood in 1967, faced with numerous urban-fringe problems, was the subject of a series of *Register-Guard* articles. The community's difficulty lies in elimination of pollution. It is an area of light industry, which historically has been slow in development because of its being subject to flood. Population is about 1,500. Residents have several times voted against annexation to Eugene.
4. W.A. Moore, *Thirty-six Years of Progress: A History of Eugene's Water and Electric Utilities Development*, promotion brochure. Eugene, Oregon: Eugene Water and Electric Board, 1947. See also *Guard* and *Register* files, 1904-1908.

5. U.S. Bureau of the Census, *Fourteenth Census, 1920*. Washington: G.P.O., 1921-1923. The exact figure was 10,593. Astoria had pulled ahead in the teens, to 14,027; Salem, only 5,000 ahead of Eugene in 1910, was at 17,679 in 1920.

6. *Morning Register*, Lane County Edition, 1904. No date given.

7. Albert G. Walling, *Illustrated History of Lane County, Oregon*. Portland, Oregon: Walling Printing and Lithography House, 1884.

8. *Morning Register, op. cit.*, p. 22. The United States Census showed 18,901 for Eugene in 1930 and for Oregon that year 953,786. Eugene did not reach 50,000 until 1960 (50,977). The *Register* promotion was also tied to the Lewis and Clark Exposition in Oregon in 1905.

9. *Daily Guard*, December 8, 1906.

10. *Morning Register*, "Industrial Edition," March 15, 1907, p. 26. Lane County is only 4.3 times larger than Rhode Island; and the *Register* understated Rhode Island's population, 542,610 in 1910. As to Lane County, it passed 200,000 population in 1966. See *Register-Guard*, December 16, 1966.

11. Subjects covered in the various editions: forest wealth and lumbering in Lane County; agriculture (horticulture, gardening, dairying, the stock industry—even goats); mining; Eugene business and commerce; public schools and the University of Oregon; "booster" organizations (the Commercial Club, founded in 1902 as a predecessor of the Chamber of Commerce); the Oregon National Guard and military affairs; the Siuslaw region on the coast; medicine and hospitals; Eugene's municipal structure; major cities of Lane County; Oregon laws; public power sites; fraternal organizations; and libraries. (The University of Oregon had 537 students and 91 faculty members in 1907.)

CHAPTER 8

Charles H. Fisher—Man Of Talent

After Ira L. Campbell's death the *Guard* within a year and a half went through another ownership change, the first of six more switches in the next 21 years. Again the shuffling was to handicap the paper immeasurably, but in a growing Eugene the *Guard* inched forward despite handicaps. In one instance early in 1916 it narrowly missed bankruptcy.

Piecing this record together leads to philosophical observations: Talent alone is not enough to build a successful newspaper, for in Charles H. Fisher the *Guard* had true editorial competence over 15 years split between Fisher's two separated ownerships; Fisher bought the paper in 1906, sold it in 1913, and then bailed it out of receivership by repurchasing it in 1916. Optimism in the future of a city is not enough, especially when optimism reaches beyond good business sense and the community's immediate potential, as it did when E.J. Finneran owned the *Guard* from 1913 to 1916. Bad luck can be fatal—at best, perilous—as it was for the *Guard* when World War I struck and upset Lane County's economy just as the owner of the paper had overextended his resources. Then the death of a publisher at an unfortunate moment can force changes; as Ira Campbell died in the paper's service in 1904, so Fisher died in 1924.

The events of the years 1904-1924, therefore, followed an up-and-down-and-up pattern. Everything seems in retrospect to have been right for the *Guard*, then wrong, then right again, and then, because Fisher died, uncertain once more. Yet one thread carried through: Whoever controlled the Eugene *Daily Guard* at any given moment acted for it in the best way he knew how at the time he owned it—even though, as in Finneran's case, what he did turned out to be financially disastrous.

THE EUGENE DAILY GUARD

VOL. 52. EUGENE, OREGON, FRIDAY EVENING, APRIL 6, 1917. NO. 92.

President Proclaims State Of War

Cuba and Brazil Will Probably Enter World Conflict

CALL TO ARMS IS ADDRESSED TO MEN OF NATION

Chief Executive Issues Sweeping Orders for Defense of United States and Aggressive Warfare Against Germany.

LIBERAL TREATMENT OF ALIEN ENEMIES URGED

So Long as Unnaturalized German Citizens Show Respect for America and Preserve Peace Internment Improbable

(By The Associated Press)

Washington, April 6.—President Wilson today signed the resolution of congress declaring a state of war between the United States and Germany.

The resolution was signed by the president at 1:11 o'clock.

All the naval militia and naval reserves were called to the colors with the president's signing of the war resolution.

The president also signed a proclamation formally declaring a state of war between the United States and Germany. In the proclamation he called upon American citizens to give support to all measures of the government.

War Officially Recognized.

...

Text of Proclamation.

...

Vigilance Is Urged.

...

(Continued on page six)

WOODROW WILSON,
President of United States, Who Today Proclaimed His Country in State of War With Germany.

SUBMARINES IN GULF OF MEXICO PLAN TO STRIKE

Washington Government Informed That Kaiser's Craft Await Declaration of War to Launch Blow at America.

Brownsville, Texas, April 6.—Pro-American sentiment is spreading rapidly in Mexico and General Carranza is reported to be considering routing Germans out of the Mexican army, according to information sent to Washington today by United States Consul Jensen in Matamoros, just across the river.

Washington, April 6.—Persistent but hitherto unconfirmed reports of German submarines waiting in the Gulf of Mexico for the opening of hostilities with the United States were further supported today by advices to the government from Europe.

...

LASSEN IN ERUPTION

Redding, Cal., April 6.—Lassen Peak shot a giant column of inky smoke skyward today. ...

65 ARRESTS ORDERED.

Washington, April 6.—Orders for the arrest of about 65 Germans in this country have been sent out by the department of justice. ...

WAR BRIDE TAKEN BY COLONEL HAMMOND

Ceremonies Are Completed in 15 Minutes at Bogart Residence; Mrs. Titus Is Bride.

Surrounded by immediate relatives and simple decorations, and with the expectation of a call to arms at any moment, Colonel Creed C. Hammond, commander of the Coast Artillery corps of the Oregon national guard, and past exalted ruler of the Eugene Elks, married Mrs. Bertha Titus, at the B. L. Bogart residence, 862 Pearl street, at 1:30 o'clock this afternoon. The ceremonies were completed within 15 minutes. Rev. A. M. Spangler, pastor of the Congregational church, officiated.

...

NEGRO ARRESTED ON CHARGE OF TREASON

Federal Agents on Trail of Germans Masquerading in South as Bible Agents.

(By The Associated Press)

Nashville, Tenn., April 6.—A Columbia, Tenn., special despatch says Andrew J. Armstrong, a negro, is in custody upon the charge of rebellion and treason in default of $20,000 bond.

TWO SUSPECTS HELD.

(By The Associated Press)

Birmingham, Ala., April 6.—With the arrest of a white man and a negro here late yesterday, federal agents who have the two men in custody have announced they have evidence of a movement by German agents to incite negroes in the south.

...

UNITED STATES OFFICERS SEIZE GERMAN SHIPS

All Vessels Interned in American Ports at Beginning of War Are Taken on Orders From Washington.

VESSELS TO BE HELD AS MATTER OF SAFETY

So Far There Has Been No Decision Whether Government Shall Take Them Over for Merchant Marine.

(By The Associated Press)

New York, April 6.—The seizure of German merchant vessels that took refuge in Atlantic ports at the beginning of the war began this morning almost immediately after congress passed the resolution declaring a state of war between the United States and Germany.

...

(Continued on page three)

9000 RUSSIANS ARE CAPTURED BY ENEMY

Berlin War Office Announces Success of Forces in Attack on Stokhod Bridgehead.

(By The Associated Press)

Berlin, April 6. Via London.—More than 9000 Russians, 15 guns and 150 machine guns and mine throwers were captured by the Germans in their attack on the Russian bridgehead on the Stokhod, the war office announces.

GERMANS ON OFFENSIVE.

...

TURKS IN RETREAT.

...

Local Doctors Now Enrolled in Federal Reserve Corps

...

CUBA TO BE NEXT TO TAKE UP ARMS AGAINST TEUTON

President Menocal Sends Special Message to Congress Asking That Body to Declare State of War Exists.

LOYALTY TO AMERICA IS BASIS FOR ACTION

Friendship for United States Will Not Permit Country to Remain Neutral in War Against Germany, He Says.

New York, April 6.—With the formal declaration by Cuba of a state of war with Germany, the Cuban government, following the course of the United States, intends to seize three German ships now in Havana harbor. This was announced today by the republic of Cuba news bureau here, a Cuban government agency.

(By The Associated Press)

Havana, April 6.—President Menocal this afternoon sent a message to congress asking that body to declare that a state of war exists between Cuba and Germany.

...

Cuba Not Indifferent.

...

(Continued on page six)

DECLARATION OF STATE OF WAR IS LIKELY IN BRAZIL

Anti-German Excitement in Rio Janeiro Is Intense as Result of Sinking of Parana by Submarine.

ATTACK UPON NEUTRAL CRAFT IS MADE AT NIGHT

Three Members of Crew From Vessel Destroyed When Flying Flag of Southern Republic Are Reported Missing.

(By The Associated Press)

Cherbourg, April 5, 12 midnight.—The Brazilian steamer Parana was sunk during the night. Three members of her crew are missing.

The Parana was a vessel of 4461 tons. She was built in 1893 and was owned in Rio Janeiro.

RIO JANEIRO EXCITED

...

LOYALTY TO NATION IS SHOWN IN GREAT PATRIOTIC PAGEANT

Eugene Citizens Turn Out en Masse in Enthusiastic Demonstration on Eve of Declaration of War by Congress

Men, women and children yesterday afternoon paraded the streets of Eugene in a great patriotic demonstration planned to give expression of the spirit of loyalty to the nation on the eve of a declaration of war by congress. ...

(Continued on page three)

Mexican Spits on American Flag; to Serve Six Months

Trenton, N. J., April 6.—Philip Madino, a Mexican, was to day sentenced to six months in the work-house by a police justice for spitting on the American flag.

RAILROAD STRIKE THREATENED.

...

FRITZEN SENTENCED.

...

STATE OF WAR IS VOTED BY HOUSE AT 3 A.M. TODAY

Members After Long Debate Cast Ballot for Clash With Germany; 375 For and 50 Against Resolution.

ONLY WOMAN MEMBER SIDES WITH PACIFISTS

Miss Rankin Unable to Answer When Roll Is Called Because of Emotion; Clerk Goes to Her Seat.

(By The Associated Press)

Washington, April 6.—War between the United States and Germany became an actuality today when President Wilson approved the war resolution adopted by a vote of 373 to 50 by the house a few minutes after 3 o'clock this morning.

...

(Continued on page three)

34 MEN ARE KILLED IN MINE EXPLOSION

Toll of Disaster at Coal Creek, Near Fernie, British Columbia, Is Heavy.

(By The Associated Press)

Fernie, B. C., April 6.—An explosion in No. 3 mine at Coal Creek last night killed 34 men. ...

BASEBALL TODAY

AT LOS ANGELES.

Los Angeles, April 6.—The score:

Los Angeles . .

Oakland . . . .

R. H. E.

Batteries—Oakland, Burns and Murray; Los Angeles, Brown and Boles.

AT SALT LAKE.

Salt Lake, April 6.—The score:

Portland . . . .

Salt Lake . . .

Batteries—Portland, Houck and O'Brien. Salt Lake, Evans and Hannah.

AT SAN FRANCISCO.

San Francisco, April 6.—The score:

San Francisco

Vernon . . . . .

Batteries—Vernon, Johnson and Simon; San Francisco, Steen and Baker.

Page One, April 6, 1917

Finally, in 1927, after another interim ownership of Paul and Eugene Kelty, the *Guard* was sold to a complete outsider. A young man of ideals, ability, and courage from Cleveland, Ohio, bought it. Within a few months he called to Eugene another young man to handle the news-editorial side—a reporter with an excess of energy, ability, and zeal. Sixty years of changes came to a halt, the owner from the big city put the *Guard* permanently on its feet and went on to buy the *Register*. Within a few more years the Eugene *Register-Guard* had become a journalistic power in Oregon.

Fisher: College Editor to Publisher

The Fisher story comes first. For in Charles Fisher's two periods in Eugene he laid the groundwork to make the *Guard* "the best newspaper property in the state," including possibly Portland.

Ira Campbell's brother John did not keep the *Guard* long after Ira's death. For a time John brought in another brother, Edward L. Campbell, to help carry the load until the Campbell family could sell the paper. Edward Campbell during World War I became postmaster of Eugene.[1] The Campbell brothers' names remained on the masthead as publishers from October 15, 1904, to May 5, 1906, and the only noticeable change was the appearance of the words, "An Independent Newspaper." [2] Through the first third of the paper's 100 years it had always been outspokenly Democratic, and Ira Campbell's party membership had been mentioned in his obituary.[3] On May 7, 1906, the words Guard Printing Company appeared, with no news story or comment on the incorporation.[4]

The articles of incorporation had been filed April 30, 1906, with John R. Campbell, Edward L. Campbell, and Charles H. Fisher as officers. Fisher held the controlling interest in the $20,000 capital stock, 200 shares of $100 each. The Guard Printing Company was to remain the corporate name until 1927 when it became the Guard Publishing Company. The stock has always been privately held.[5]

By June 9, 1906, the plain Roman logotype of many years gave way to a designed nameplate showing an eagle above one of the Oregon state mottoes, "She Flies with Her Own Wings."[6] On June 12, the daily, which had been six columns, joined the weekly in becoming a standard seven-column newspaper.[7] Headlines started to become expansive spreads.

The purchaser, Charles H. Fisher, was aggressive and incisive, an editor who during his ownerships was to be a force in Eugene until he died. Fisher did not add his name below Guard Printing Company until March 2, 1907, but in the 10-month interval he made many changes. As early as June 26, 1906, in announcing the installation of new machinery (a better press), he referred to Eugene's boom and journalism's part in it:

> "Good papers help in the van of the procession, the herald of the good times coming. Eugene will have to hustle, grant electric railway franchises and do many other things that will shock the moss-backs into nervous prostration to keep up with the newspapers."[8]

By fall the *Guard* was promising to install still more equipment—the "latest Linotype machine on the market within the next two weeks." Its business was "over 50 per cent greater in every department than it was six months ago." Fisher kept his promise, for within the two weeks a headline read, "New Linotype at Work in Guard office."[9] In December came the big special edition we have noted. The following March "Member of the Associated Press" appeared for the first time.

Charles H. Fisher was one of that rare brand of small-city editors and publishers who, decades later, stir the imagination and admiration of even the hardest-headed realist. With a greater desire for the state or national spotlight he might have had the competence to become a William Allen White. He quite clearly had abilities far beyond those of most newspapermen in cities of Eugene's size. He was the best-educated man to run the *Guard* in the 60 years before 1927. He had editorial sense and business sense both, and he made the *Guard* distinguished one way and profitable the other. He was the first *Guard* editor to give strong support to higher education. His vision went beyond one city and, looking toward a broader life for himself, he bought and sold several newspapers. When, three years after he had sold the *Guard* in 1913, the paper lapsed under successor Finneran's management, he took it back and rebuilt it. He gained appointment to the University of Oregon Board of Regents. He fought the Ku Klux Klan in the 1920s even though as a Democrat he found his own party's candidate for the governorship (Walter Pierce) playing for Klan votes.

Few newspapermen in the Eugene of 1967 remember Charles Fisher. One is George Turnbull, who as a young professor of journalism at the University of Oregon during Fisher's second ownership of the *Guard* regarded him as a "good, hard-boiled, conscientious editor, with a sound news sense."[10] Another whose memories go back to the early 1920s is strong-minded E.G. Boehnke, for many years a commercial printer in Eugene, who in 1922 worked in the ad alley of the *Guard*. "Fisher weighed values and acted on his own views," Boehnke recalls. "He was well-educated and had a sharp pen. He was a good force in Eugene."[11] Boehnke, then only 29 years old, remembers particularly Fisher's opposition to the Klan.

Like William Thompson a half-century earlier, Charles Fisher belonged to Pacific Northwest journalism as much as to Eugene's. He was born in the Missouri River county of Clay in agricultural South Dakota, August 18, 1865, and came to Oregon with his parents, Jesse L. and Mary Fisher, when he was 12. They settled in Roseburg, where Charles went to rural schools and then, in 1885, enrolled in the "prep course" of the nine-year-old University of Oregon.[12] At the University he was elected editor of the Laurean Literary Society, his assignment being to send accounts of the society's meetings to Harrison Kincaid's *Oregon State Journal*. He did not get a degree, but his university experience stirred Fisher's interest in journalism.[13]

In 1886 Fisher returned to Roseburg, taught school for a time, and then bought a run-down newspaper in Oakland, Ore., a few miles north in Douglas County. He called it the *Umpqua Courier* and ran it with a Washington hand-press. In 1887 he returned to Roseburg, went into partnership with a Floyd Flood and started Oregon's first semi-weekly newspaper, the Roseburg *Herald*. He later consolidated the *Herald* with the Roseburg *Review* and in 1896 made the *Review* a daily. The paper continues today as the Roseburg *News-Review*, one of the Scripps League Newspapers.[14]

Fisher's activities in Roseburg, he said more than 20 years later, gave him confidence in his own "ability to go into any town and publish a paper that the people would have to read." To prove his point, perhaps, but giving in 1901 the reason that he had to move for reasons of health, Fisher went to Boise, Idaho, where he formed a stock company to expand the weekly *Idaho Capital News* (founded in 1888) into a daily afternoon paper with Democratic leanings. His partner in this enterprise was R.S. Sheridan of Roseburg. Fisher kept an interest in the Roseburg *Review* when he went to Idaho. The *Idaho Capital News*, now no longer published, was once the state's leading newspaper in circulation.[15]

Possibly it was the Eugene *Daily Guard's* need for a new publisher after Ira Campbell's death; or, possibly it was that after he had proved to himself that he could publish a newspaper anywhere that Fisher decided to return to Oregon. To purchase the *Guard* he sold his Boise paper and his remaining interest in Roseburg and entered the Eugene field.[16] This time he stayed in one place for seven years.

Metropolitan: No Ads on Page One

We have already noted some of the quick changes Fisher made in the *Guard*. Another was his "going metropolitan" in 1910 and taking all advertising off page one. On May 30 that year he ran a curiosity-whetting editorial:

> "Tomorrow there will be some radical improvements in the makeup of the *Daily Guard.* We won't tell our readers in advance, only promising that the paper tomorrow will have a more metropolitan appearance than ever before. The *Guard* is keeping pace with the queen city of Western Oregon."

The next day, there was the brand new page one! As Fisher said, "For the first time since its establishment the *Guard* is carrying no ads on page one. There will be none hereafter." [17] In both instances of adless news pages in Eugene, *Guard* and *Register*, the last advertiser to depart from the page was Alton Hampton, operator of a major clothing store in Eugene, Springfield, and Cottage Grove. Hampton's last *Register* ad on the page had been a four-column by ten-inch "Saturday Special—Big Clothing Sale."[18] In the *Guard* the last Hampton ad on the page, also four-by-ten, was couched in status terms and not on price: "To the Young Men Who Are About to Graduate from the University of Oregon and Eugene High School—We'd Like to Have a Hand in Getting You Ready to Graduate."[19]

On May 31 Alton Hampton's clothing ad was inside that day's *Guard*—a full seven-column by ten-inch display atop the editorial page, with an editorial boost to help: "Mr. Alton Hampton has taken another position . . . because his growing business demands more space than could be given him on the front page."[20] By this time full-page ads inside were becoming commonplace in both Eugene newspapers. Typographical facility, business enterprise, and editorial needs had united.

How did these changes affect the news? The *Guard's* lead story of May 30, impacted by the advertising, carried a modest display headline on a record airplane flight of the aviation pioneer Glenn H. Curtiss in taking off from Albany, N.Y., and landing in New York City 152 minutes and 137 miles later. The lead story of May 31, uninhibited by an ad, was a prominent one, even with the same modest two-column headline as that

Willamette Street near Seventh Avenue about 1900

given Curtiss. Theodore Roosevelt, on world tour, was in London giving advice to Great Britain on how to run the world: "Stay in Egypt and keep order." Britain, said T.R., had given Egypt "its best government in 2,000 years." The former President also eulogized Britain for its administration of backward Uganda and the Sudan. Self-determination of peoples had not yet become conflict news in 1910.

The University: Guard and Register Fight for It

Fisher's interest in education and his incisiveness in writing appear frequently in the *Daily Guard* in these years. Oregon by 1910 had instituted its progressive legislative reforms of initiative and referendum, and a news development with regard to the referendum arose in 1911 over the University of Oregon. The State Legislature that year passed a $328,259.92 appropriation to extend facilities and activities of the University and to increase faculty salaries. However, anti-public education people who had opposed the appropriation sought to block its implementation by circulating petitions calling for a referendum to stay action. In June a story appeared stating that Burns Detective Agency investigators had uncovered "4,000 forged petitions and 8,000 tainted ones." Fraud appeared patent.[21]

The *Guard* struck out editorially in what was an early example of many defenses of higher education it would make in the next half-century. In its history, the support of education—especially of the University of Oregon—has been one of the newspaper's tenets. Who happened to be editor at any moment has not altered policy.[22] Fisher attacked the scandal of the bogus petitions on two fronts.

> "1. No practice can bring into disrepute Oregon's advanced legislation so fast as fraud in initiative or referendum petitions.
>
> "2. The guilt of the perpetrators of this outrage is only the more reprehensible because it was calculated to deprive one of the worthiest institutions in the state of needed

financial aid. . . . The men who stooped to practice fraud in their efforts to hamper an institution of higher learning brand themselves not only as habitual crooks and insidious foes of popular government but as dastardly enemies of education as well."[23]

Fisher gave credit to honest signers who, though misguided, thought a referendum to block the expenditure for the University was a way to save money. They had acted in good faith, he said, but he was against skullduggery.

The case went to court, with S.W. Friendly, a leading Eugene merchant and regent of the University of Oregon, suing as a citizen. He asked for an injunction against Ben W. Olcott, secretary of state, to forbid him from putting the petition referendum on the ballot in the 1912 general election. In December, 1911, a permanent injunction was granted by Circuit Judge William Galloway of Marion County (Salem). In his decision, Galloway rebuked Olcott for considering forged petitions at all and thereby throwing the burden of proof back on Friendly to prove that the petitioners themselves had agreed that some of the signatures were "confessedly fraudulent." Of 13,615 names, 3,098 were shown to be outright forgeries or duplications, while 5,105 were names on sheets of paper that did not indicate exactly what kind of relief was being sought. The court held:

"The court is of the opinion that he who knowingly files a fraudulent petition is no less morally culpable than he who traffics in counterfeit money." [24]

The case then was carried to the Oregon Supreme Court, with amazing repercussions. On April 23, 1912, the high court reversed Judge Galloway, vacated the injunction, and ordered the petitions reinstated. The court reasoned on purely technical grounds, that S.H. Friendly had no personal right to seek a remedy against a public official, the secretary of state, since he had been unable to show any personal property or other loss. It added, "The drastic remedy of injunction can only be invoked by the state acting through a public officer."[25]

The Supreme Court did not consider the substance of the fraud charges at any point.

Both the *Guard* and the *Register* were furious, the *Guard's* headline on the decision reading, "Fraud and Forgery Triumph in Supreme Court of State of Oregon."[26] The *Register* was more moderate, at least in the headline, "Court's Ruling Grieves Eugene; Suprise Over Ignoring Fraud."[27] Fisher showed in his editorial response the bluntness and clarity with which he could strike:

> "The supreme court of the state of Oregon has placed the seal of its approval upon forgery and fraud, bare-faced and inexcusable. . . . It has invoked a technical point of law. . . . [There was] no reason to render such a decision except to legalize the fraud and hamper the growth of the university. The decision was purely political, to invoke the commendation of that element of the state's citizenship which contends that anything labeled as a referendum or initiative petition should be sacred. . . .
>
> "There is no comfort for any citizen except the law-breaker, the forger, and the grafter. . . .
>
> "As far as the university is concerned, it is going to live and prosper, because it is doing a great and good work. Its friends are legion, and they will be drawn closer to it by the onslaught of its foes. . . . The people of the whole state have its destinies in their hands. . . . The burden of fighting [the university's] battles should not fall on the [people of Eugene]."[28]

Fisher then named names: those in Cottage Grove who had acted in spite because they had failed to get a new county; allies at Oregon Agricultural College in Corvallis who abetted enemies of the University in Lane County; and an H.J. Parkinson, "a discredited labor leader and tool of those carrying out a program of spite" against higher education.[29]

> The *Register*—always milder than the *Guard*—reported: "Sensations of shock gave way to dum [sic] amazement over the audacity of so flimsy a ruling emanating as it did from the councils of supposedly austere and erudite nestors of legal lore."[30]

The *Register* raised a point not mentioned by the *Guard.* The Supreme Court's decision had come out four days after the Oregon general primary election of April 19, in which Secretary of State Olcott had won renomination on the Republican ticket by defeating Frank S. Fields. The *Register* continued:

> "Why was this decision postponed until after the primary? Did the court wait until the people [Republican voters] had clarified its insight? . . . No one will believe that politics was not played to secure the delay of the decision. . . . The whole opposition to the University's case has so smelled to heaven that such a finale is eminently fitting."[31]

The case then was taken up by Governor Oswald West, who urged that a second appeal be taken to the Supreme Court. So the University of Oregon started over, but on July 24, 1912, the court ruled that the referendum should go on the ballot, since there were, by careful check, 7,615 good names on the petitions; the law called for only 6,135.[32]

The University of Oregon lost this fight, *Guard* and *Register* support availing nothing. An effort was made to have an initiative petition passed in November calling for a general state levy to provide funds to be apportioned evenly between the University and the Agricultural College and thereby to take higher education out of politics. That measure—entitled a "millage levy"—failed by 2,000 votes. S.H. Friendly was quoted in November:

> "A state is judged by its higher educational system. Oregon's university does not compare favorably with that of

California or that of Washington, both of which are sustained by a millage tax."[33]

And Fisher "put it on the line" for the 1913 Legislature: "It is up to the Legislature to pass needed appropriations at once with the emergency clause. Either that or slaughter the University."[34]

Henry D. Sheldon in his *History of the University of Oregon* written in 1940 makes no mention of the *Guard's* and the *Register's* great support in the 1911 and 1912 fraudulent-petition fight. But he does say that "the resulting publicity . . . aroused a strong interest in the consolidation of the two institutions of higher education." The concept of "extreme economy" in all state affairs had many supporters, among them W.S. U'Ren, the father of Oregon's direct legislation.[35]

This struggle, with the resulting consolidation concept growing out of it, was only a precursor of the most serious conflict that the University of Oregon was to go through in its own now 91-year history. Twenty-one years after the petition fight the University of Oregon was to need every bit of *Register-Guard* support in a battle that threatened its very existence. And it is not too rhetorical a question to ask, Where would higher education in Oregon stand in 1967 vis-a-vis comparable state universities without the years of help given it by Eugene's newspapers and men like Charles H. Fisher and the editors of the *Morning Register* and their successors? In 1932 and 1933 the consolidated newspaper, stronger than Fisher's and the Gilstraps', would win in its defense of the University.

Journalism Education: "To Instill Proper Ethics"

When the University of Oregon in 1912 became one of the country's first state universities to establish an independent School of Journalism, Fisher and the *Daily Guard* were quick to support education for journalism. The early journalism schools were not always accepted with favor by the "old hands" among newspapermen (many still are not today), but Oregon publishers for the most part welcomed journalism instruction. Perhaps Fisher's support of the "J-School" could be attributed to his own education and his literary-society editorship in Eugene a quarter of a century earlier. In any event, he called the new school "a step in the right direction." As Fisher viewed the need for training of young journalists, the American press was no longer a "flotsam and jetsam of professional life for failures, broken-down politicians, and preachers." He added:

> "Anything that is done to raise the standard of journalism will be of public benefit. Trained and educated workers will bear fruit in better newspapers, and if the proper ethics of the profession are instilled into the students the tendency will be toward more independent honest journalism."[36]

Fisher foresaw journalism education as opening entirely new careers to students, careers beyond the newspaper. He tied in the need for journalism schools with an earlier-evidenced need for schools of law, medicine and theology, three areas that he regarded as no more equal in importance than journalism. As a result, he said, Oregon in the future would have better newspapers. He did not mention that the *Guard* would be one of the beneficiaries of journalism education, as time would show it to be. And, as is recognized today, national expansion of journalism schools beyond the newspaper into public relations, television and radio, publication management, and "communications" in general has shown Charles Fisher to have guessed correctly.

The first head of the Oregon School of Journalism was a Wisconsin newspaperman, Eric W. Allen, who came to Oregon in 1912, was promoted to dean of the school in 1916, and served until his death in 1944. Allen and the *Guard* and *Register* always maintained close relations, which in turn have continued in the 23 years since the dean's death.[37] In the early days of the school students occasionally put out both Eugene newspapers.

In more recent years *Register-Guard* staff members have served at intervals on the University's journalism faculty.[38]

---

1. *Eugene City and Lane County Directory.* Portland, Oregon: R.L. Polk and Company, 1918.

2. *Daily Guard,* May 5, 1906.

3. *Morning Register,* October 15, 1904.

4. *Daily Guard,* May 7, 1906.

5. *Corporate Records,* Lane County Court House, Eugene; and *Minute Books,* Guard Printing Company, 1906.

6. *Daily Guard,* June 9, 1906.

7. *Daily Guard,* June 12, 1906.

8. *Daily Guard,* June 26, 1906. The "good times coming" quotation recalls an editorial by Edwin L. Godkin in *The Nation* in 1869 upon the death of Henry J. Raymond of the New York *Times,* in which Godkin likened Raymond as a symbol of a new journalistic day.

9. *Daily Guard,* November 12, 1906.

10. Interview with George Turnbull, November 10, 1966. Turnbull served on the University of Oregon journalism faculty from 1917 to his retirement in 1948 and was dean from 1944 to 1948.

11. Interview with E.G. Boehnke, November 1, 1966. Boehnke was for a long time chairman of the Lane County Republican Committee and was once Oregon State Republican chairman.

12. University of Oregon Registrar and Alumni Office records. There were no high schools in Oregon in 1885; the University operated a preparatory course for students seeking degrees.

13. "Opportunities Everywhere," *Oregon Exchanges,* Volume 3, (November, 1919), pp. 3-6.

14. *Ibid.* Between 1887 and 1896 Fisher was on one occasion sold out to Flood, who continued with a new partner, J.R.N. Bell; but Fisher later returned and bought out both partners. When he left Roseburg he sold an operating interest to an L. Wimberly. He appears to have enjoyed buying in and out of newspapers, a practice possible in his day for a publisher who liked changes of scenery.

15. *Ibid.*

George S. Turnbull, *History of Oregon Newspapers.* Portland, Oregon: Binfords & Mort, 1939, pp. 238-239. In 1905 the *Idaho Capital News* had 2,788 sworn circulation daily and 3,834 weekly, total 6,622; the morning *Idaho Statesman,* a pioneer paper in the state and today's leading daily, then had 3,401 daily and 1,399 weekly, total, 4,800, publisher's estimate.

16. "Opportunities Everywhere," *op. cit.*, p. 4.

17. *Daily Guard,* May 30 and 31. Actually the Gilstraps of the *Register* beat the *Guard* to a no-advertising news-page by a full month, but the *Guard* made news out of the change while the *Register* merely changed. *Morning Register,* April 30 and May 1, 1910.

18. *Morning Register,* April 30, 1910. "Hart-Schaffner & Marx suits, $25 to $12.50; shirts, $1 to 75c; socks down to 12-1/2c; Stetson hats, $4 to $8."

19. *Daily Guard*, May 30, 1910. Historically, the tradition of giving page one to advertising has had a strong pulling force in journalism. Not until the mid-1960s did the prestigious London *Times* change to a full news-page.

20. *Daily Guard*, May 31, 1910.

21. *Daily Guard*, June 11, 1911.

22. See pp. 237-252 *infra* for detailed analysis of the Zorn-MacPherson battle involving the State System of Higher Education in 1932, with the *Register-Guard* taking a leading part.

23. *Daily Guard*, June 14, 1911.

24. The *Morning Register* joined the *Guard* in the case. On December 22, 1911, it ran in full the decision of *Friendly v. Olcott*, seven columns. It also ran an editorial from the Medford *Tribune* backing the University and blaming the fraud on persons in Cottage Grove who were angry because Eugene had successfully opposed separation of Cottage Grove from Lane County so that it might be the county seat of a proposed Nesmith County. The petitions had been circulated for spite, the *Tribune* said. (One of the three remaining buildings on the "Old Campus" of the University of Oregon today bears the name of S.H. Friendly Hall.)

25. *Friendly v. Olcott* (1912), (61 Oregon Reports 580).

26. *Daily Guard*, April 23, 1912.

27. *Morning Register*, April 24, 1912.

28. *Daily Guard*, April 24, 1912.

29. *Ibid.* See also footnote 22.

30. *Morning Register*, April 24, 1912.

31. *Ibid.*

32. Henry D. Sheldon, *History of the University of Oregon*. Portland, Oregon: Binfords & Mort, 1940, 156 ff. Sheldon discusses the petition fight in his treatment of the University years 1902-1917.

33. *Daily Guard*, November 11, 1912.

34. *Daily Guard*, November 14, 1912.

35. Sheldon, *op. cit.*, p. 156.

36. *Daily Guard*, "Oregon's School of Journalism," August 29, 1912.

37. George S. Turnbull, *Journalists in the Making: A History of the School of Journalism at the University of Oregon*. Eugene, Oregon: School of Journalism, University of Oregon, 1965.

38. William M. Tugman, managing editor and editor of the *Register-Guard*, 1927-1954, was at various times a lecturer on the School of Journalism faculty. William L. Wasmann, present managing editor, and Robert B. Frazier, present associate editor, have taught courses in reporting and editing. The author of this book was for 15 years, 1945-1960, Sunday news editor of the *Register-Guard*.

CHAPTER 9

E.J. Finneran—Too Far Too Fast

Charles H. Fisher did make mistakes, however, in his management of the *Guard*, and one was to cause the paper a severe setback. In 1911 he had join him a young metropolitan newspaperman with big ideas, with sound enough editorial judgments but with business visions that quickly outran the *Guard's* and Eugene's immediate potential. This was E.J. Finneran, of Boston and Kansas City, to whom Fisher offered a one-half interest in the paper. Finneran was to handle the business side. The announcement of appointment was carried only on the editorial page, with no accompanying news story:

> "He [Mr. Finneran] will devote his attention mainly to the advertising and business departments, having had many years of experience in that particular line of work. We are sure that his association with Mr. Fisher in the publication of the *Guard* will be to the material benefit of the paper in all respects."[1]

It is not clear whether a subsequent conflict developed between the co-publishers, for the minutes of the Guard Printing Company for this period show only changes in stock ownership when Fisher later withdrew. Two interpretations of events are possible:

> 1. When Finneran came to Eugene he might have had an understanding that "if the field looked good he would take over," that is, buy Fisher's remaining half-interest.[2] The *Guard's* rise did exceed Finneran's expectations and this is what happened; Fisher left the paper March 1, 1913.

2. After arriving Finneran might have begun pressing for a rapid expansion of facilities, and this could have led to a "buy-or-sell" argument—Fisher from Finneran or the other way around. Fisher finally sold.[3] The *Guard's* report of this sale said Fisher was "retiring" (although he was still less than 50 years old). The account added: "Mr. Finneran's ambition is to make the *Guard* the best paper published in a city the size of Eugene in the United States. [He is] looking to material improvements and will soon begin to put his ideas into material form."[4]

Fisher's stated reason for leaving was that he wanted a "real vacation." He planned to go to Cuba and the Canal Zone and to the East. He said also he "might build a business building on Willamette Street." He certainly was going to remain a resident of Eugene. But in an editorial he wrote words that, with our benefit of hindsight, have *double entendre:*

> "The *Guard* has become a permanent institution greater than any one man who labors to produce it, and it will not suffer by the change in editorial management. . . . Mr. Finneran is a young man of ability and a newspaper worker of experience."[5]

Another point is that Fisher wasn't really retiring at all but was merely eager to change scenes again, "looking for a paper at the right price which he could take hold of, put on its feet and turn into a valuable property. . . ."[6] This is a plausible explanation. How long his vacation trip was we do not know, but he did not return to Eugene. Within a short time Fisher had bought an ailing *Capital-Journal* in Salem for $36,000, paying one-third down, later paying off the difference, and by 1918 getting its circulation up from 1,700 to 5,350.[7] He obtained the *Capital-Journal* from Andy Hofer and Colonel Ernst Hofer, operators of ready-print for small newspapers who had a nation-wide business.

No question remains about what happened to the *Guard* under Finneran. His expansive ideas resulted in the paper's purchasing a Duplex tubular perfecting press that used extensive stereotyping equipment and was capable of turning out 30,000 sixteen-page papers an hour. At this time the *Guard's* circulation was still only about 2,500 to 3,000. Observers said that a pressman, "once he had started the machine, had to keep an extra sharp eye on it or he'd find himself with an extra thousand papers on his hands."[8] Thinking that the boom of the previous decade would continue, Finneran also expanded the *Guard's* floor space in the Eugene Theatre Block at 478 Willamette Street, which it was renting. There does not appear to be any evidence that Finneran altered Fisher's editorial policies. The *Guard* appears to have remained "an honest vehicle of the news, an organ of the plain people."[9]

Unhappily, the European War broke out in 1914, business became uneasy—especially as a result of the German blockade—and Finneran found himself hopelessly extended. The fact that economic fears were unfounded in the long run and that the war created a boom in America did not help the *Guard* in time. By 1916 Finneran was more than $20,000 in debt to an unknown number of creditors who, fearing the paper might not be able to meet obligations, were threatening legal action.[10]

A suit was brought in Lane County Circuit Court, January 3, 1916, by George Midgley and Henry Hollenbeck, representing the building the *Guard* occupied. They asked $916.99. Finneran acknowledged the obligation, which represented unpaid rent at $160 a month, but on which only $290 had been paid on account. When the creditors asked for a receivership "to manage and control the future business of the *Guard*," Finneran's lawyers agreed. A default judgment of $626.99 was granted in the Circuit Court January 27, 1916, and the receivership was set up the next day.[11] Finneran gave this explanation:

> "I thought it was the best thing to do under the circumstances that surrounded my personal condition. . . . I

wanted it in order that the *Guard* might be conserved in the interest of the people of Eugene and Lane County. . . .

"There is not one thing in the history of this paper at which any person can point with suspicion. . . .

"The good that I have in a measure been responsible for, I simply ask that you do not forget; for the mistakes I have made I ask your forbearance and charity. . . . I trust that the depression which we have all felt will pass like the morning mists."[12]

The court (Judge F.M. Calkins of Medford sitting for Judge George F. Skipworth of Eugene) appointed E.J. Adams, an investment man, to operate the *Guard* and to take control January 29, 1916. Finneran left Eugene for Seattle. He did not thereafter appear in the *Guard's* history. The company's *Minute Books* are blank on any monetary disposition of his obligations.

The *Guard* was circumspect in reporting details of its troubles, but the *Register* carried a complete story, namely that the *Guard* creditors were the ones who did not want to force a shutdown of the paper. The creditors cited such good but intangible assets as advertising contracts and readership, a going job-printing business, and an Associated Press franchise. They feared that Finneran might not be able to continue meeting his payroll or to obtain further supplies on credit. If a large number of creditors should sue, they might be able to close the *Guard* down. The *Register* ran this story on page eight.[13]

The receivership lasted only a little more than two months. On April 11, 1916, Charles Fisher repurchased the newspaper in association with Joseph E. Shelton, who resigned from the *Register*, where for two years he had been news editor, to take over direct operations of the *Guard*. Shelton had been in Eugene for four years and had been with the *Guard* as advertising manager under Finneran in 1912 and 1913.[14] Fisher, however, did not return to Eugene immediately but remained in Salem for three more years and continued to publish the *Capital-Journal*. The arrangement to repurchase the *Guard* resulted in Fisher's taking the title of president; Shelton's in becoming secretary and manager; and Fisher's wife, Effie, becoming vice-president. Fisher took 159 shares in the Guard Printing Company, Shelton 40 shares, and Mrs. Fisher one share. Fisher and Shelton were authorized to borrow enough money to pay off the company's indebtedness. Thereupon Judge Skipworth discharged Adams as receiver and turned the newspaper over to its new owners.[15]

This quick adjustment of the receivership difficulty leads to the inference that Fisher was personally motivated to save the Eugene *Daily Guard.*

Journalism: Not So Cold-Blooded

Adams in his short service as a newspaperman apparently liked journalism. He wrote a cordial "good-bye" editorial saying that he felt gratified and that he had been able to push circulation up a bit. He found it "really unnecessary to introduce the new owners, both of whom know and are known in this community, and whose very names insure the future of the *Guard* as a live, patent force for all that's good in our community life."[16]

Fisher and Shelton stressed, too, that they were not "strangers," and they added, somewhat flatteringly:

> "The *Guard* will be mindful of the duty it owes to the people . . . and at no time will it lose sight of the interests of . . . the great, common masses of whom God made so many."

They talked of serving no special interest, of bringing about harmony and advocating high moral standards, of not overlooking religious elements, and of being politically democratic "but not a Democratic organ."[17] For a paper that had narrowly escaped bankruptcy the soft approach was masterful.

The news story of the sale to Fisher and Shelton indicated that the mechanical equipment, "which comprises one of the best plants in the state of Oregon, will be retained." However, the 30,000-paper press was larger than the *Guard* could possibly use; in 1918 Fisher and Shelton traded Finneran's press to the Aberdeen (Wash.) *World* for a Cox Duplex that printed directly from type.[18]

Fisher's return to newspaper ownership in Eugene is another of those events in press history that may show journalism to be more than cold-blooded business. The *Guard* was worth saving and two men who worked for it, one as former proprietor, thought enough of it to rescue it. The *Morning Register*, however, was somewhat unkind. Although technically objective, its four-paragraph story on an inside page read:

"EVENING PAPER PASSES
"OUT OF RECEIVERSHIP

"The *Daily Guard* has changed hands again. J.E. Shelton, of this city, and Charles H. Fisher, of Salem, purchased the stock."

The remainder was bare fact. There was no editorial.[19]

Journalism Students Take Over: "The Dean for Governor"

The most interesting episode of Adams' brief receivership was that in its last week the students of the University of Oregon School of Journalism put out the *Guard* for five days. This operation was under the direction of Dean Eric W. Allen and Professor Colin V. Dyment, the *Guard* news and editorial staff withdrawing completely, although the business and mechanics staff remained on duty. It is possible that Adams permitted this student-editorship engagement because he knew that on April 11 Fisher was returning. The students therefore took over some of the load and themselves gained valuable experience. There was nothing, however, in the paper's announcement of April 3 of the student operation to indicate the corporate change that followed.[20]

This exercise appears to have been the first of a number of on-the-job-experience activities carried on between the journalism school and the Eugene newspapers for years to come. The

Register took part in these, too, but its policy was not to tell when University students were putting out the paper; for all *Register* readers could tell, no changes were ever evident. Undergraduates, given the relatively small size of the *Guard* or *Register* a half-century ago and the stimulus of a professional challenge showed they could edit a daily newspaper.

All the students said in April, 1916, was "We Are in Charge." They promised in editorials that they "would not run opinions counter to the policy of the *Guard*," a fair enough concession. But when they did take a stand, they said, "our opinions are our own."[21]

The students "opinionated," among other things, on the Oregon loganberry crop, namely, that the problem of selling Oregon loganberries was not in getting them to market but in getting people in the East to eat them. This view was based upon press reports out of New York and Chicago that there "was absolutely no demand" for 175,000 pounds of evaporated Oregon loganberries.[22] Also, a year before the United States entry into World War I the students were urging preparedness: "It is good to observe that the nation is becoming interested in military preparedness."[23] Then, in editorializing on educational matters, they came out against a move to have the dean of the University of Oregon faculty, John Straub, run for governor of Oregon, as a number of political leaders were urging. To the students, Dean Straub was "too good a man and too kind a man for the job." While he would make an excellent governor and bring to the office an "unblemished record," his friends "should not let him throw away his position of high honor and permanent dignity to chase after the will-o'-the-wisp of political preferment."[24]

When the week had ended, receiver Adams expressed satisfaction with his experiment. The students had "peppered the page with thought; . . . all they had to say we cannot endorse, but in the main their ideas were good, their reasoning logical, and their conclusions sound." If Adams had any criticism, it was that students don't read newspapers carefully. Several stale news accounts, published before the students took charge, had been run a second time. But then, Adams agreed, the general public probably didn't notice the duplication any more than the students.[25]

The *Register-Guard* is too big mechanically for this sort of undergraduate enterprise 50 years later. Limiting the question to news and editorial operations and setting aside necessity for speed, accuracy, and technical precision, we can ask, Could University of Oregon journalism students put out the *Guard* today? They probably could. Young men without college educations were editors of the *Guard* many times while they were still in their early twenties. William Thompson was 23 when he rescued the paper from J.W. Skaggs in 1868; Ira Campbell was 22 when he took over from George Buys in 1878; Charles Fisher was buying newspapers in Roseburg at 21. Frank Jenkins,[26] was 22 when he became editor of the *Register* in 1912. It could be that this backward-look at the student-produced *Guard* of 1916 gives some insights into youth and journalism in the 1960s. Responsibility in journalism when held back too long can lead to irresponsibility.

---

1. *Daily Guard*, "Business Notice," June 12, 1911, p. 4.
2. *Daily Guard*, "Fisher Retires from *Daily Guard*," March 1, 1913.
3. "Opportunities Everywhere," *Oregon Exchanges*, Vol. 3, (November, 1919), p. 4.
4. *Daily Guard*, March 1, 1913.
5. *Daily Guard*, "A Word of Parting," March 1, 1913, p. 4.
6. "Opportunities Everywhere," *op. cit.*

George S. Turnbull, *History of Oregon Newspapers*. Portland, Oregon: Binfords & Mort, 1939, p. 139.

Capital-Journal, founded in 1888 by Will H. Parry, a native Oregonian who went into real estate and years later became a member of the Federal Trade Commission, is another newspaper of many ownerships that survived and is a highly regarded Oregon daily of today.

7. Turnbull, *op. cit.*, p. 277.
8. *Ibid.*
9. As expressed by Fisher in his departure; *Daily Guard*, "A Word of Parting," March 1, 1913, p. 4.
10. *Morning Register*, January 29, 1916; not reported in *Daily Guard*.

11. *George Midgley and Henry Hollenbeck d/b/a Eugene Theatre Company v. Guard Printing Company.* Circuit Court of Lane County, Oregon, Case No. 10010 (to collect money) and Case No. 10071 (receivership) January 27 and 28, 1916.

12. *Daily Guard*, "A Word of Explanation," signed "E.J. Finneran," January 28, 1916, p. 4. Midgley Millwork and Glass firm still operates in Eugene.

13. *Morning Register*, January 29, 1916. The *Register* also ran a history of the *Daily Guard* since Ira Campbell started it in 1891.

14. *Who's Who in Oregon*, 1929-1930. Oregon City: Oregon City Enterprises, Volume 1.

15. In an inventory filed by the Guard Printing Company in the receivership petition, Finneran listed *Guard* assets at $49,325, of which $35,291 was in machinery. Midgley and Hollenbeck v. *Guard* Printing Company, *op. cit.*

16. *Daily Guard*, "Good Bye," April 11, 1916.

17. *Daily Guard*, Fisher's unsigned editorial, April 11, 1916.

18. *Daily Guard*, April 11, 1916, p. 1.

"Opportunities Everywhere," *op. cit.*

19. *Morning Register*, April 12, 1916, p. 8.

20. *Daily Guard*, April 3, 1916, p. 4.

The students must have missed classes for a full week, the spring vacation in 1916 running from April 7 through April 15. University of Oregon, *Catalogue, 1915-1916; Announcements, 1916-1917.* Salem, Oregon: State Printing Department, 1916, p. 6.

21. *Daily Guard*, April 3, 1916, p. 4.

22. *Daily Guard*, "Loganberries to the Front," April 3, 1916, p. 4.

23. *Daily Guard*, "A Factor in Preparedness," April 8, 1916.

24. *Daily Guard*, "Straub for Governor?" April 8, 1916.

25. *Daily Guard*, "The All-Student Staff," April 8, 1916.

26. See pp. 173-174 *infra.*

CHAPTER 10

Fisher, Shelton, And The Keltys— The Guard Rebuilds

The Fisher-Shelton control of the *Guard* continued for eight years, until July 3, 1924, when the Fisher estate and Shelton sold the paper to Paul R. and Eugene S. Kelty of Portland, father and son. The Kelty ownership, which lasted less than three years, was to be the final one before continuity came under the Baker family. In the 11 years from 1916 to 1927 Fisher and Shelton brought the *Guard* back to financial stability, while the Keltys held its position. By 1927 the Eugene *Guard* had become an excellent long-term investment.

Fisher remained in Salem with the *Capital-Journal* until April 1, 1919. He sold the Salem paper to George Putnam of Medford and returned to Eugene to join Shelton, who had been running both news and business staffs since the end of the receivership. The only public indication of Fisher's taking up the *Guard* again in person came on September 19, 1919, when the masthead dropped "president" from Fisher's name and "manager" from Shelton's and became "Charles H. Fisher—Joseph E. Shelton," without rank designation.[1]

Two possible reasons can be given for Fisher's selling the *Capital-Journal.* The more plausible is that operating two newspapers was too heavy a load, particularly since Fisher in 1919 had become a member of the University of Oregon Board of Regents and had numerous duties calling him to Eugene other than the *Guard.* Another reason, offered in the anonymously written sketch of Fisher in *Oregon Exchanges* in 1919, after his return, is that he felt Salem to be growing too rapidly toward metropolitan size and that he preferred the smaller field of Eugene.[2] If this was so, Fisher was overestimating Salem, for its population margin over Eugene was hardly enough to call it "metropolitan" without saying the same for Eugene.[3] In either case, Fisher was back at his *Guard* desk. Although gushy and trite about it, the writer who welcomed him home put the greeting in warm words:

> "He is back behind a flat-top desk in his Eugene office, with a partner to worry over most of the details of the business, with a paper that is big enough to make him all the money he needs, and which will print the pungent little editorials he loves to write, with a comfortable home a little way down the street, and with a neat little touring car at the curb outside the office door to carry him off to the never-never land any time he gets tired of being an editor."[4]

Fisher's partner complimented him. Although by 1916 Joseph Shelton had more than a quarter of a century of newspaper experience, both news- and business-side, he was more a management-type man, less intellectual and volatile, and more one who would serve the *Guard's* public relations needs. But, like Fisher, he understood small newspapers.

A native of Indian Mound, Tenn., Shelton was nearly eight years younger than Fisher. In years when his future partner had been operating newspapers in Oregon and Idaho, Shelton had wandered through Missouri, Kentucky, and Arizona: *Daily Era* in Cape Girardeau, Mo.; *Leader* in Springfield, Mo.; *Daily Commercial* in Louisville; *Daily Democrat* in Paducah, Ky.; *Gazette* in Phoenix, Ariz.; and an unnamed newspaper in Union, Mo. From 1891 to 1911, when he came to Oregon as advertising manager of the *Guard*, Shelton had been a newspaper part-owner, secretary-treasurer, telegraph editor, managing editor, and an editor.[5]

Together Fisher and Shelton took the *Guard* through World War I and post-war crises. Had not Fisher died in 1924 they might have enjoyed many more years with the paper.

Shelton after leaving the *Guard* entered the commercial printing business in Eugene as the senior member of the firm of Shelton, Turnbull, and Fuller, which was founded in 1924. At this time the *Guard* gave up its commercial-printing facilities and printed the newspaper only. The Shelton printing firm under the name of Shelton-Turnbull continues today as one of Eugene's major printing establishments, although there is no longer any connection with the three founders or their heirs. Shelton also became an advocate of automobile travel and was manager of the Oregon State Motor Association from 1929 to 1933. For a time he edited a story magazine called *Tumbleweed.* He moved to Portland in the 1930s and then retired to Arizona, living in Phoenix until he was past 80.

Charles Fisher's death as a result of complications arising from an appendectomy was the first passing of any Eugene *Daily Guard* publisher to bring statewide testimonials from public officials, educators, and newpapermen. Under instructions he had previously given, the *Guard* did not suspend an issue but closed only for the funeral. The paper quoted Fisher:

> "A newspaper [is] of far more importance in the world than the man or men who own it. [He] desired always that its functions be not interfered with."[6]

The *Guard* published, although on Monday, April 7, 1924, the University of Oregon canceled all morning classes. President Prince L. Campbell of the University called Fisher "an editorial writer of unusual force and ability, a man of strong opinions. . . absolutely fearless in expressing those opinions."[7]

The *Morning Register*, against whose Republican policies Fisher had often used sharp words, lauded him for his often-expressed view that "criticism hurts no one and helps most people and most institutions."[8]

Another, one whom Fisher had not hesitated to criticize in 1922 (for yielding to the Ku Klux Klan), was Governor Walter

M. Pierce. Pierce's testimonial, although somewhat wooden, might have been dodged had not the Governor been sincere:

> "In the passing of Charles H. Fisher, citizen of Oregon and Regent of the State University, I feel a sense of loss. . . ."[9]

Others who praised Fisher's service to city and state were Circuit Judge George F. Skipworth and executives of the Associated Press, United Press Associations, and International News Service. Even the Portland *Oregonian*, also the recipient earlier of *Guard* attack for the *Oregonian's* softness on the Klan, said:

> "In the death of Charles H. Fisher, editor of the Eugene *Guard*, a capable western journalist passed from the controversies and discussions of life. Under his direction the *Guard* was widely read and possessed the attributes of a real newspaper. It reflected the energetic personality of one who understood his profession. . . .
>
> "The talents of Mr. Fisher were distinctive and eluded the common mold. His editorial views were independently individual, and even those who could not agree with his conclusions found interest and vigor in his writing. . . ."[10]

Eleven years before his death, however, Charles Fisher had expressed his views better than any who lauded him in death. In quoting an unidentified editor he had written:

> "A great newspaperman once said that nothing could induce him to write what shallow-minded persons wished him to say; rather, he persisted in writing that which they needed to be told. In my humble way I have tried to follow this rule."[11]

The Ku Klux Klan in Oregon: Faces Unmasked

Charles Fisher's greatest achievement was his editorial battle against the Ku Klux Klan in Oregon. In his dealing with news of national interest as well as state interest, the Klan issue is the one most to be remembered for all the 15 years he owned the *Guard.*

To Fisher and George Putnam, to whom he sold the *Capital-Journal*, Oregon remains historically in debt. The Putnam battle against the Klan has been told in book form.[12] Fisher's has not. His fight was not so drum-beating as Putnam's, but in 1922 he joined his Salem colleague and a scattered few other small-city editors in Oregon in a crusade perilous in implications. Fisher proved that he could tell readers what they had to be told.

The spread of the post-World War I Ku Klux Klan was one of those waves of the hysteria of "pure Americanism" that made sensational news in the early 1920s. That the Klan could make inroads into the Deep South and parts of the Middle West was not surprising, but that it could be transplanted into Oregon was somewhat of a phenomenon. In any case, reports of its doings and fears that its reactionary forces could destroy civil liberties filled newspapers across the nation at the time. On a national journalistic level the New York *World* in 1922 received a Pulitzer Award for Meritorious Public Service for its exposés of the Klan.[13]

Oregon in 1921 and 1922 would appear on the surface to offer little of promise for an organization feeding on race prejudice, religious bigotry, and ignorance and reaction in general. The state had few Catholics and almost no Negroes; its literacy rate was 98 per cent or more; its educational system was sound, although regionally narrow and unsparked by challenging ideas. Nevertheless, Oregon was still far removed from heavily traveled routes of communication. As one historian of the Ku Klux Klan wrote in 1924 about Oregonians:

> "Their mental attitudes, in spite of their freer Western life, are not essentially different from those of the people of Texas, Missouri, Kansas, and Indiana. The anti-Catholic tradition has been generally familiar to them from childhood. . . . There are few great trunk lines and it is easy to

> imagine that social traditions would remain largely unchallenged, in spite of an admirable educational system, in these narrow and shut-in valleys."[14]

The Klan importation into Oregon was planted in Medford, Jackson County, in January, 1921, ostensibly to help public officials enforce the prohibition laws. Within a year the organization had spread throughout the state and, as "The Federation of Patriotic Societies," was becoming a strong political force. Night-riding outrages became common, particularly in Jackson County and elsewhere in southern Oregon. For the most part the Oregon press did little to warn the citizenry about what was taking place. The Klan story was brought into the open, however, when on February 16, 1922, George Putnam in Salem attacked the Portland press for failure to get into the fight against the Federation of Patriotic Societies.[15]

Fisher in the *Daily Guard* was somewhat slower in joining the battle, perhaps because he was more an intellectual than Putnam and less quick on the trigger. When he did lend his strength to fight the Klan he was just as forthright.

The news break Fisher acted on came May 13, 1922, when Governor Ben W. Olcott (the secretary of state whom Fisher had opposed in the University of Oregon petition fight in 1911 and 1912) publicly attacked the Klan. The Governor, a Republican and a Protestant, issued a proclamation calling on all police officers, sheriffs, and judges to see that "all unlawfully disguised men be kept from the streets."[16] Olcott made direct reference to the Klan:

> "Dangerous forces are insidiously gaining a foothold in Oregon and these forces, . . . parading under the name of the Ku Klux Klan are endeavoring to usurp the reins of government and are stirring up fanaticism, race hatred, religious prejudice, and all the evil influences which tend toward factional strife and civil terror."[17]

Charles Fisher
His greatest battle was against the Ku Klux Klan

The *Guard* gave banner headlines to the story; the *Register* carried one-column headlines. Then followed Klan denials: F.L. Gifford of Portland, exalted cyclops of Ku Klux Klan No. 1 in Oregon, saying it was "law-abiding" and directed only toward "maintaining white supremacy and the Christian Religion."[18]

Closely related to the governor's statement was the forthcoming 1922 Oregon spring primary on May 19, in which Olcott was opposed by Charles Hall of Marshfield, Ore.,[19] a state senator, for the Republican gubernatorial nomination. Hall carried overt Klan support. The election turned out to be a seesaw affair, with Hall leading in first returns. Hall did carry Lane County by 200 votes, an indication of Klan strength locally that an editor more timid than Fisher might have bowed to. Eventually it was Eastern Oregon that tilted the results in favor of Olcott; by May 23 the governor was enough ahead (42,728 to 42,481), with so few precincts still to report, that renomination was assured.

The *Register*, however, had failed to wait to see if Hall would hold his early lead. Two days before Olcott's renomination was certain, the paper explained "how it happened" that the governor had "lost":

> "Just a week before the votes were counted Governor Olcott took a spade, went out in the yard and dug a hole and buried himself in it—for that was substantially the result of his anti-Klan proclamation. . . . Before the proclamation he was a 'copper-riveted' cinch."[20]

The *Register* in effect justified the Klan. Its only menace, the paper said, lay "in its face-covering regalia, which tempts outsiders to use the Klan disguise for their own purposes."[21]

The *Guard*, being Democratic and not directly concerned with results of the Republican primary, had, first, waited to comment until Olcott had won. And, second, it took the *Register* editorial as a cue to move in on the Klan itself. Fisher wrote his own version of "how it happened":

> "Every hide-bound partisan paper puts its foot in it occasionally by giving expression to its real convictions at the wrong time. It looked Sunday morning as if Governor Olcott was a dead one and Hall, Ku Klux chieftan, with the aid of the self-styled patriotic societies, . . . had won the election. That was naturally the proper time for our esteemed conter[illegible]ary to break the silence it had maintained during the primary campaign in the fear it might guess wrong.
>
> "Consequently it proceeded to eulogize the klan and its allies, and to berate Governor Olcott for bringing about his own defeat in attacking those brave and true men who are so diffident about the good deeds they are performing that they are simply overwhelmed with embarrassment when their faces are unmasked, and who love all humanity —except the people whose opinions differ from their own, and therefore should be mobbed."[22]

Then the *Guard* re-ran the *Register* editorial in full and closed ironically:

> "[This is] a splendid example of fearless journalism. An editorial on how it happened the [Register] editor spoke up too soon would be more edifying."[23]

In the meantime, while the Olcott-Hall decision was still in doubt, the Portland *Oregonian* announced editorially that it would support the Republican nominee for the governorship whoever won. To Fisher this was as much as to say that party success was more important than principle, "even [though] that party, with Klan leaders at its head, would be only republican in name." He continued:

> "The *Oregonian* has never been able to reject anything handed out to it with th[illegible]l republicanism, whether the label was true or fa[illegible]his explains why papers of

> statewide circulation have so little influence in elections. . . .
>
> "It is always the case that newspapers which rise above party considerations when principles are involved exercise great influence over their readers, and that the other type, represented by the *Oregonian*, in time come to be read solely for their news, and little or no attention is paid to their editorial pages."[24]

This criticism of editorial partisanship, while specifically directed after a heated campaign, was actually a general one that was hardly new, even as long ago as 1922. The rise in importance of the news pages and the consequent decline of the editorial pages had been noted back as far as the turn of the century. Fisher and Putnam and other opponents of the Klan[25] were striving for an editorial ideal that has always been rare in its expression.

Hall made an effort to have a recount of the primary vote, but this fizzled, and the campaign settled down to Governor Olcott versus Democrat Walter M. Pierce, an Eastern Oregon state senator from La Grande. In January, 1923, after Pierce, with the help of Klan votes, had defeated Olcott and become governor, Fisher described him as a "typical eastern Oregon hustler—rancher, school superintendent, and lawyer." The *Guard's* editorial greeting the new governor was almost wholly biographical; it mentioned almost nothing about Pierce's talent, and it concluded on a mildly hopeful note: "Maybe he'll be all right."[26]

The Compulsory School Bill: Fisher Bores In

Pierce's success and Olcott's defeat did not come until after one of the most heated campaigns in Oregon's history, with religion and the Klan displacing fundamental issues in state government, taxes, of course, being one. The key conflict of the campaign was to center upon an initiative measure known as the Compulsory Education Bill, a proposition that provided for compulsory attendance of all Oregon primary-school children in publicly supported schools. The bill, to all intents and purposes, would have killed all parochial and other private schools. Supported by the Klan, the proposal was obviously aimed at the Catholics, although it struck at all denominations; military academies were also imperiled, as were private secular schools. The strength of the Klan can be seen in the fact that candidate Pierce during the campaign decided to come out for the bill, that it carried in November, 115,506 to 103,685, and that Pierce won the governorship by 20,000 votes.[27] The effective date of the Compulsory Education Act was to be 1926, but litigation on constitutionality followed and the Oregon law was overturned by the Supreme Court of the United States in 1925.

The confusion of the campaign frustrated and angered Fisher, who threw all his editorial force into the *Guard's* efforts to have it defeated.

For 15 days in late summer (September 9 to 23) Hall was in the spotlight again, this time as the Compulsory Education Bill candidate for governor on an Independent ticket. He had been put forth September 9 in a maneuver to draw votes from Olcott, even though there was doubt whether under Oregon law a defeated candidate in a primary could run independently.[28] However, Hall accepted this nomination September 12, the last day for filing as an Independent. The *Guard* ran the story of September 9 on page eight and the one of September 12 on page two, an apparent policy control of unwelcome but significant news that would be frowned upon under objective interpretations of 1967.[29] A few days later the Eugene Compulsory Education League ran a two-column full-measure ad to get its message across.[30] And a day before the ad was run Fisher editorialized that the campaign had become hopelessly ensnagged:

> "It is impossible even to have an honest and open discussion of those matters which should most vitally concern the welfare of the general public, while elections are decided on issues raised by busy and mischievous agitators."[31]

Within a week Hall withdrew his Independent candidacy—and this the *Guard* bannered: SEN. HALL QUITS CONTEST. The main deck read: "Withdraws in Support of Pierce."[32] This action brought from the *Guard* an editorial calling for modification of the direct primary law to protect the integrity of parties and to draw up principles on which candidates must campaign in order to avoid the "travesty" Hall had made of the election.[33]

Toward election day Fisher let wishful thinking mislead him, for he forecast defeat of the school bill: "The people are generally awakening to the menace of the proposal if [it is] enacted into law." He was wrong in his expectation, but the *Guard's* editorial was another of those blunt expressions that so marked Fisher's editorship. The editorial was two columns long. Here, paraphrased were its principal points.

1. Proponents of the school bill were frankly declaring it to be a first step in the elimination of Reed College [Portland] and Willamette University [Salem], and colleges at Forest Grove [Pacific University], Newberg [Pacific College, now George Fox College], McMinnville [Linfield College], Albany [Albany College], and Eugene Bible College.

2. The law would bring about a demoralization of the public schools—with secret bosses controlling puppets.

3. The proposal was substantively wrong, since there was a school law on the books, with private schools supervised. Every resident of Oregon had to support public schools through taxes; if he desired a private school the fees came out of his own pocket.

4. Every citizen should have the right to direct the education of his own children, "in accordance with his best judgment and the dictates of his conscience."

5. The school bill was being promoted by false and misleading advertising.

6. If the bill passed, taxes would go up as a result of increased public school attendance.

7. The bill possibly would carry Lane County, in which case "we will send to the outside world a message of hate as well as selfishness, in attempting to crush all private schools and colleges in the interest of tax-supported state schools. That will be the interpretation."[34]

The school bill was passed and the case went to court. Today the record of this case that a few small-city newspaper editors of Oregon fought against is carried in due-process sections of books on constitutional law. The first victory for the private schools came March 31, 1924, when a three-judge United States District Court in Portland held the Oregon school law to be a violation of the due-process clause of the Fourteenth Amendment.[35] In 1925 the Supreme Court of the United States affirmed the Oregon Federal District Court decision.[36]

Charles H. Fisher of the Eugene *Daily Guard* was in a hospital in Eugene Monday, March 31, 1924, the day the District Court issued an injunction against Governor Pierce and the Oregon attorney general. And the newspaper that weekend had moved into a new building at 1037-41 Willamette Street. The news story of the decision in Portland (an eight-column banner) was the lead on page one of the first *Daily Guard* to be published from the first non-rented plant the paper had ever had. Fisher missed the vindication of his stand in the school battle of 1922, and of course there could be no editorial. He never edited the *Guard* from its new location, for he died April 5.[37]

Another Sale: The Guard Passes to Eugene and Paul Kelty

Joseph E. Shelton, the Charles H. Fisher estate, and Mrs. Effie Fisher, the widow, sold the *Daily Guard* July 3, 1924, to Paul R. Kelty and Eugene S. Kelty, Paul's son. The senior Kelty had long been news editor of the Portland *Oregonian*, while the son had in 1922 been graduated from the University of Oregon School of Journalism. In the intervening two years Eugene Kelty had been a bond broker. Paul Kelty became editor of the *Guard* and Eugene business manager. Mrs. Fisher, however, did not sell the new *Guard* building.[38]

Shelton gave health as a principal reason for his selling, a condition caused by the strain of running the paper alone after Fisher's death but influenced also by exertions related to moving into the new building. These might not have been the full answers, for it is quite as likely that Shelton's loss of Fisher as a partner was an unexpected shock. The two had made the best team the *Guard* had had up to that time, and the Fisher-Shelton combination for eight years had been successful in competition with the *Register*, quite apart from superior news and editorial policy.

As late as 1918 the *Register* had led the *Guard* in audited circulation, 3,433 to 3,124.[39] When Fisher died the balance favored the *Guard*, 5,065 to 4,944. Under the Kelty regime the *Guard* once more fell behind, with 5,917 in 1927 to the *Register's* 6,667.[40] The intense competitive situation in the boom period of the 1920s was a difficult one. In a two-newspaper city, with rural motor-route delivery to subscribers coming in as highway development proceeded, a morning newspaper had a circulation advantage. This could account for some of the *Register's* gains. Eugene and Lane County were continuing to grow, too, but not sharply enough at this time to account for the big circulation jumps of both papers. What it shook down to was that the economics of publishing competitive newspapers in small cities was becoming an expensive proposition. In a general way we see here the trend toward the consolidation to come six years later in Eugene.

The Keltys' declaration of purpose for the *Guard* was similar to many such statements. It stressed independence, virility, positive outlook, non-partisanship in politics, and the promising future of Eugene as a city. The most perceptive point was that the "Eugene *Daily Guard* is one of the most valuable present and potential newspaper properties in the Pacific Northwest."[41] Paul and Eugene Kelty were right about this, but they did not remain long enough to realize the *Guard's* potential. One observer years later said that Paul Kelty was really too much a Portlander and metropolitan newspaperman editorially oriented to enjoy the small city.

The senior Kelty's newspaper background, when compared with that of previous editors in Eugene, was prodigious. He was a nephew of Harvey W. Scott of the *Oregonian* and in 1896, at age 24, had been given the job of telegraph editor of the Portland *Telegram*, an afternoon paper owned by the *Oregonian*. The story told is that Scott gave Kelty the job simply because the nephew told Scott he wanted to become a newspaperman. Kelty had never had a day of experience, but he made good.

By 1898 Kelty was city editor of the *Telegram* and by 1904 managing editor. Then, to gain experience outside Oregon, he went to Los Angeles in 1905 to work for Hearst's Los Angeles *Examiner*. He covered the San Francisco earthquake for the *Examiner* in 1906 and in the next two years became news editor, city editor, and managing editor. But in 1908 Kelty was back in Portland as news editor of the *Oregonian*. This was two years before Harvey Scott's death. In the succeeding 16 years Paul Kelty was responsible for much of the news success of the *Oregonian*. His biggest achievement came in foreseeing the United States break in relations with Germany in 1917. Kelty prepared a news page on the forthcoming story and had it made up in advance; when the break came he "beat all the Pacific Coast papers."[42]

But the Eugene *Guard* wasn't Paul Kelty's spot. The paper remained sound enough, however, and when Alton Baker arrived it could be that Kelty was satisfied to make a profitable sale and get out of ownership. He spent some time from late 1928 to the spring of 1930 as managing editor of the *Register*, but then he returned to Portland as the *Oregonian's* executive news editor. In 1931 Kelty became editor of the *Oregonian* and remained in that position until he retired in 1939.[43]

Kelty's name was to appear once more on the Eugene scene after 1930. In 1932 he was one of the leaders among Oregon journalists to serve nobly in convincing the State Board of

Higher Education to restore the University of Oregon School of Journalism to degree-granting status after it had been cut off in a money-saving move during the Depression.[44] Kelty died in McMinnville, Ore., March 11, 1944.

Two major changes in the nameplate came within a few weeks of the Keltys' purchase of the *Guard.* On July 16 the *Daily Guard* dropped "Daily" from the name and became the Eugene *Guard.* The word "Daily" had been carried ever since June 8, 1891, when Ira L. Campbell expanded his horizons. Then on September 22, 1924, the all-capitals Roman logotype gave way to another version of Old English, this time with the Oregon seal, *The Union, 1859,* spliced between Eugene and *Guard.* The seal in 1928 yielded to the Three Sisters, but a Roman-face nameplate has not been used in the past 43 years.[45]

---

1. *Daily Guard,* September 19, 1919.
2. "Opportunities Everywhere," *Oregon Exchanges,* Vol. 3, (November, 1919), p. 6.
3. Salem's population exceeded Eugene's in 1920 by 17,679 to 10,593 and in 1930 by 26,266 to 18,901.
4. "Opportunities Everywhere," *op. cit.*
5. *Who's Who in Oregon, 1929-1930.* Oregon City: Oregon City Enterprises, Vol. 1.
6. *Daily Guard,* April 5, 1924.
7. *Daily Guard,* April 7, 1924.
8. *Morning Register,* April 7, 1924.
9. *Daily Guard,* April 7, 1924.
10. Portland *Oregonian,* "An Editorial Thirty," April 7, 1924, p. 8.
11. *Daily Guard,* March 1, 1913.
12. George S. Turnbull, *An Oregon Crusader.* Portland, Oregon: Binfords & Mort, 1955, pp. 63-172.
13. John Hohenberg, ed. *The Pulitzer Prize Story.* New York: Columbia University Press, 1959, pp. 70 ff.
14. John Moffatt Mecklin, *The Ku Klux Klan: A Study of the American Mind.* New York: Harcourt, Brace, and Company, 1924, p. 45. Mecklin was a professor of sociology at Dartmouth; his criticism of Oregon at the time was severe.
15. Turnbull, *op. cit.,* p. 66, quoting the Salem *Capital-Journal* of February 16, 1922.
16. Old residents of Eugene recall with interest the Klan parades, in full regalia, down Willamette Streets in the 1920s.
17. *Daily Guard,* May 13, 1922, and thereafter; *Morning Register* May 14, 1922, and thereafter.

18. *Morning Register*, May 16, 1922.
19. Marshfield, on the Oregon coast 120 miles southwest of Eugene, is today named Coos Bay, Ore.
20. *Morning Register*, "How It Happened," May 21, 1922.
21. *Ibid.*
22. *Daily Guard*, "How It Happened," May 25, 1922.
23. *Ibid.*
24. *Daily Guard*, "*Oregonian* and Its Partisanship," May 23, 1922.
25. Other small-city editors who fought the Klan included Robert W. Sawyer of the Bend *Bulletin* and Robert W. Ruhl of the Medford *Mail-Tribune*.
26. *Daily Guard*, "The New Governor of Oregon," January 10, 1923.
27. *Daily Guard*, November 7, 1922. The official vote on the Education Bill is taken from the *Oregon Blue Book*, 1955, p. 282.
28. This issue has never been tested in Oregon courts.
29. *Daily Guard*, September 11 and 12, 1922.
30. *Daily Guard*, September 15, 1922.
31. *Daily Guard*, September 14, 1922.
32. *Daily Guard*, September 22, 1922.
33. *Daily Guard*, "Senator Hall Withdraws in Support of Pierce," September 22, 1927.
34. *Daily Guard*, "School Bill and Lane County," November 4, 1922.
35. *Society of Sisters of the Holy Names of Jesus and Mary v. Pierce, Governor; Hill Military Academy v. Pierce.* 296 Federal Reporter 928 (1924).
36. *Pierce v. Society of Sisters of the Holy Names of Jesus and Mary.* 268 U.S. Reports 510; 45 S. Ct., 571; 39 A.L.R. 468; carried also in Walter F. Dodd, Cases and Materials on Constitutional Law, 4th Ed. St. Paul, Minn., 1949, p. 1047.
37. *Daily Guard*, March 31, 1924.
38. Paul Kelty, his wife Mary E., and Eugene Kelty each took one share of *Guard* stock, while 197 shares were held in pledge for completion of the sale. Paul later assumed 148 of these and Eugene 49. The transaction also included a note of $30,000 to Mrs. Fisher on the building. The *Guard* newspaper bought $41,307 to Mrs. Fisher on her half-share; this, with Shelton's half, put the value of the paper at more than $80,000. The job-printing part of the Guard Printing Company was Shelton's. Its value is not known, but would have to be subtracted from the $80,000. *Minutes of the Guard Printing Company*, July 3, 1924. Also, *In Re Estate of Charles H. Fisher*, deceased April 5, 1924, Probate Court of the State of Oregon, Lane County, Document No. 4,120, January 8, 1925.
39. *American Newspaper Annual and Directory.* Philadelphia: N.W. Ayer & Son, 1918.
40. *Ibid.*, 1927.
41. *Daily Guard*, "The Guard and Its New Owners," July 7, 1924.
42. F.W. McKechnie, "Leaders of the Oregon Press: Paul R. Kelty," *Oregon Exchanges*, Volume 2, (December, 1918), p. 16.
43. "Paul R. Kelty Dies at McMinnville," *Oregon Publisher*, Volume 12 (March, 1944), p. 2.
44. See pp. 241-243 *infra*.
45. *Guard*, July 16, 1924.

CHAPTER 11

The Morning Register: 1899 To 1930

From the day the Gilstrap brothers[1] started the *Morning Register* December 1, 1899, through the first quarter of the Twentieth Century the *Guard's* competitor exemplified undisturbed steadiness. No changes in control upset its course, for although two of the brothers withdrew in 1911 and 1918, respectively, there were four of them, and the remaining two continued in service. One competent and modest outsider, Frank Jenkins, joined the staff in 1910, became editor in January 1912 and president in 1918, and remained until the *Register* was sold in 1930.

Always soundly Republican, the *Register* was uninclined to upset conservative apple carts. Its news policy and its makeup were ever the same, until in 1930 the *Guard's* competition forced it out of its single-top-head practice into experimentation with spread heads. Its reports were long and solid, well packed with details that the *Guard* frequently lacked, and it had also the time advantage of the morning field and space advantage of a Sunday edition.

But like all "solid" newspapers the *Register* from 1900 to 1930 wasn't the kind of paper to produce readable history. Conservative Eugeneans might have regarded it as a "better paper," but that was opinion. Where the *Guard* showed zip the *Register* evidenced calm; and there seemed to be room for both.

Sometimes the difference could be incomprehensible. On December 8, 1922, when fire destroyed 40 square blocks of Astoria, with a loss of $15,000,000, the *Register* the next morning gave the story its standard single-column headline in column one of page one and equated it with three other news stories on the page.[2] The *Guard* had used an 8-column, 120-point banner. Old-time journalists in Eugene have explained that, according to *Register* policy, the fact that the Astoria fire was on page one at all was proof enough of the magnitude of the news. The *Register* under ordinary circumstances reserved the front page for national and foreign news.

George Turnbull, historian of Oregon journalism, described the *Morning Register:*

> "It was never necessary for the news editor to 'dummy' the front page, for the makeup scheme was always the same. . . . *Register* readers had been brought up on that sort of thing, and apparently they liked it." [3]

The readers apparently did like it. This type of news handling in any event made it possible for the *Register* to use its Associated Press service to the full by stressing foreign news and thereby avoiding nasty squabbles like the Klan issue.

The fact remains, however, that what must have helped the *Register* more than its news decorum were the *Guard's* troubles caused by the deaths of two publishers, with the subsequent sales and purchases of the paper and with the threatened financial failure. Although the circulation differences between the papers were usually slight, the *Register* actually held a lead only when the *Guard* was changing hands.

Solid the *Register* was. For a small-city daily in its day it was well-edited, too. But sparkle it never had. One could not foresee at the time what would happen; but, looking back, we can understand why it was that when the right moment for consolidation came it would be the *Guard* that would become the dominant Eugene newspaper.

The senior Gilstrap brothers were Will G. and W. Frank, with Will retiring December 31, 1911, and Frank selling his interest in the paper in 1918. Otto Gilstrap and Ernest Gilstrap remained until the *Guard* bought the paper. The change in 1911 was the more important, for it was then that Will G. Gilstrap sold his majority stock to Frank Jenkins and to Otto and Ernest. Jenkins became editor. [4]

A young man of 22, Frank Jenkins subsequently became one of the most successful, active, and widely known editors in Oregon journalism, with more noteworthy phases of his career coming after he had left Eugene in 1930 to become publisher and president of Southern Oregon Newspapers. This corporation published the Klamath Falls *Herald* and *News* and Roseburg *News-Review* and held a stock interest in the Medford *Mail-Tribune.* Jenkins still lives in Klamath Falls and is the only surviving former editor of all who ever served the Eugene *Guard* or the *Register.* [5]

Frank Jenkins was a native of Knoxville, Iowa. He was born September 26, 1890. He attended Simpson College, Indianola, Iowa, before coming to Eugene in 1910 to join the *Register.* A man who made friends easily, Jenkins soon became recognized as an editor of talent. It was with his father, B.K. Jenkins, that he invested in the *Register* when Will Gilstrap left.

Will Gilstrap gave no specific reasons for his departure. In a long, sentimental editorial he said he was not sure what field he would go into, but he emphasized that he had spent 20 years in Oregon journalism and he closed with a 16-line poem, the last four of which read:

> "We'll go our way, each to his coming task,
> Content to know that, whatsoever betide,
> Each did his best, that's all the world could ask
> Of those who have true motives as their guide." [6]

The senior Gilstrap brother had done much for the *Register.* He had made the daily pay; he had brought the first Associated Press membership to Eugene; he had installed new press equipment, which he said was 10 years in advance of circulation needs; he had added departmental pages, one of which (agriculture) was aimed at building up county circulation; and he had enlarged to seven standard columns. On the occasion of the press installation he wrote:

> "Great oaks from little acorns grow. Eleven years ago, when the present owners of the *Register* bought the plant it was chiefly a pile of old, wornout material, the paper was a weekly, and a weakly one at that, with very little circulation and less of advertising patronage." [7]

After W. Frank Gilstrap sold his stock in 1918 and Jenkins became president, the *Register*, though remaining exceptionally conservative, became more effective. Jenkins, like others, saw Eugene as "the best newspaper field in Oregon, excepting Portland." With the advantage of a morning paper, he saw the possibility of extending the *Register's* delivery area from the Cascades to the coast, north toward Albany, and south toward Roseburg. He carried a page of Lane County news daily, believed in "circulation on merit and without 'clubbing arrangements,' " and stressed "uplift." The *Register* had "no desire to be a propagandist," he said. [8]

One of the *Register's* features was an editorial column, "About Ourselves," in which Jenkins talked in simple language about ideals and aims. He liked "chatting informally with readers." [9] This was a type of journalism that, while "uplift" and pleasing, was hardly able to meet strong competition.

During the 1920s the *Register*, like the *Guard*, needed additional space to handle its expanding circulation. Since 1899 it had occupied part of the Brown Block, a wooden structure at East Ninth Avenue (now Broadway) and Oak Street. In February, 1923, it purchased this building, with plans to enlarge it, but in April three years later it decided to build an entirely new building on the east side of Oak between Ninth and Tenth. It moved into this in July, 1926, at which time the *Register* installed a 30,000-paper-an-hour four-deck tubular press capable of printing 16-page sections.[10] It is possible that building expansion for both papers about the same time, along with the other competitive factors, made it more difficult for both papers economically.

Circulation figures for the decade are intensely revealing. Between 1921 and 1925 the *Register* gained from 4,511 in circulation to 5,469; the *Guard*, revived by Charles Fisher, gained from 3,293 to 5,116. From a lead of more than 1,200 the *Register* faded to a lead of only 353; and, as noted earlier, the *Guard* before Fisher's death had taken a momentary edge. In 1922 alone, during the Klan fight, which the *Register* played softly, the aggressive *Guard* jumped its circulation 1,200, while the *Register* gained less than 100. During the Kelty ownership of the *Guard* the *Register* managed to move ahead a bit faster, going to 6,667 while the *Guard* reached only 5,917; the *Register* then led by 750. But within three years after the Alton Baker purchase of the *Guard*, 1927 to 1930, the *Guard* surged to 7,777, while the *Register* went only to 7,694.[11]

Six months before the *Register* sold out to the *Guard* it ran a house ad showing a circulation gain of 88.3 per cent in the prosperous 1920s, from 4,348 in 1920 to 8,190 in 1930 (the second figure being 496 higher than Ayer reported). The *Guard's* gain for the same 10 years (Ayer figures) showed 136.1 per cent. The *Guard* at the time carried no promotional advertising on circulation.[12]

In the final year before the consolidation the *Register* made two major efforts to meet *Guard* competition. Beginning September 16, 1929, it went on an all-day basis by adding an afternoon edition and keeping the morning edition. Since the *Guard* had the afternoon Associated Press service, the *Register* had to add United Press for its afternoon paper. It ran its editorials, editorial features, and other non-news matter through all editions and gave readers the choice of six papers a week: Sunday and mornings, except Monday; or Sunday and afternoons, except Saturday. The operation, with the financial crisis that set off the Depression coming within a few weeks, proved to be unworkable.[13]

Within seven months the *Register* gave up its morning edition and from April to November, 1930, fought it out with the

Guard as an afternoon paper only. In dropping out of the morning field the *Register* said:

> "Believing that the evening field is the only field with a future for daily newspapers in towns of the class of Eugene, the *Register* is discontinuing its morning edition. The afternoon edition proved so lusty a youngster that the publishers lost interest in the older sister." [14]

This account gives some indication of the pressures operating in Eugene during the late 1920s. But before the general economic forces leading toward consolidation of the Eugene rivals reached a peak, the historical interpretation must be that the purchasing newspaper up to the last few months before November 17, 1930, might have been either the *Guard* or the *Register*. The differences between the two, in days when competition was easier, would not seem to have been material factors in the *Guard's* eventually becoming the paper to buy out the opposition. Rather, as we shall see, it was a matter of newspaper know-how on the business side and news and editorial purpose on the information side—and the fact that it was the *Guard* that in 1927 was sold to the community-minded newcomer.

Until 1927 every proprietor but one of the many who had owned the *Guard* since 1867 had been small-city oriented—printer, political advocate, small-business man, or community journalist of variable talent. The same was true of all the owners of the *Register* from 1884 to 1930. Only E.J. Finneran in 1911 had come out of the big city, and he was too expansionist, visionary, and financially unwise.

When Alton Baker came from Cleveland he brought a metropolitan knowledge of the newspaper business that, intelligently applied in the small city at the right time, made it difficult if not impossible for the earlier generations to compete. The story of the Eugene *Register-Guard*, then, becomes the story of the second part of this history—the Alton Baker story.

Part One In Retrospect

The First 60 Years—the Assessment

Such a sharp break in direction took place in 1927 when the *Guard* changed hands for the tenth time that the tendency in Eugene today, even among those having knowledge of the city's journalism, is to think historically only of the past 40 years. Except for the members of the Lane County Pioneer Historical Society—and many of these are in their seventies and eighties—Eugene's daily newspaper means *Register-Guard* alone. These first chapters, therefore, redress a historical balance. They also raise a summary question: How did the many owners and co-owners of the *Guard* and *Register* measure up against each other during the first 60 years?

Of all who operated either newspaper Charles H. Fisher alone brought to Eugene journalism the combination of business ability, understanding of the purposes of a newspaper, and forthright courage to have been potentially a successful publisher in the period from the 1930s to the 1960s. Fisher was born 25 years too soon. By all measurements he ranks first among *Guard* or *Register* owners in the formative years.

Second would come solid Ira L. Campbell, and then the Indian fighter William Thompson, despite Thompson's brief tenure. Fourth would be the *Register* group of the four Gilstrap brothers and Frank Jenkins. Their limitations lay principally in lack of venturesomeness and crusading zeal when such was called for. After we have named these men we drop off sharply to others who, for a few weeks or a few years, did little more than publish a community newspaper.

George Buys put up one grand battle in the Hayes-Tilden controversy of 1876, but he withdrew the next spring and left nothing tangible. The Yorans of the *Register* were business men only, whose real contributions to Eugene lay in merchandising, banking, and commercial printing. John M. Hodson, Silas M. Yoran's founding partner, had journalistic ability, but he left early to join the customs service and then became a printer in

Portland. The Condons and Chester Edwards of the *Register,* as well as the Messrs. Rowlands, Howard, and Rowlands did little more than hold the fort in the years between the Yorans and the Gilstraps. Neither ownership in these two cases was willing to fight to keep the *Register* alive as a going daily after the Yorans had initiated it.

E.J. Finneran almost caused the *Guard* to go into bankruptcy, as had J.W. Skaggs so many years before. John B. Alexander has a part in this history only because he founded the *Guard.* The general history of journalism is replete with names of publishers whose only achievement is that they put out the first issue but couldn't *sustain* the paper—to use again the word the Alexander family was fond of. Alexander himself was quite likely the least qualified of all the *Guard's* publishers. He simply dropped a newspaper twice—the Eugene City *News* first. As for Alexander's sons, they, too, could not measure up to the *Guard's* needs, even in 1877.

Joseph E. Shelton in the modern day was a competent newspaperman, but as Charles Fisher's partner he was outshone. There is no way of telling what Shelton might have achieved as sole owner after Fisher's death had he decided to keep the *Guard* instead of selling to the Keltys and founding the highly successful Shelton-Turnbull printing establishment.

Paul R. Kelty and Eugene S. Kelty were sound newspapermen; but, again, their tenure with the *Guard* was not long enough to indicate how the paper would have fared had they not sold in 1927. We must measure Paul Kelty's accomplishments as an employed executive on the news side in Portland, Los Angeles, and back in Portland, and they were outstanding.

That the Eugene *Register,* despite its lack of aggressive journalism, continued for 46 years as the *Guard's* chief competitor, is not surprising. After all, it was a conservatively run business (Will Gilstrap said as much in taking over in 1899). Most of the time in the first quarter of the century it was better managed than the *Guard;* and it had the advantage of being on the Republican side of stable Oregon thought. It disturbed no one, which is what numerous "successful" newspapers do in any case.

That the *Guard* got through the more acute crises of its threescore years to 1927 is something of a newspaper phenomenon. Four times it could have gone under, twice within its first 17 months under Alexander and Skaggs, with the young Alexanders in 1878, and with Finneran in 1916.

It is as much because William Thompson, Ira Campbell, and Charles Fisher each in his turn saved the *Guard* as for all else they accomplished that Fisher must get first place, Campbell second, and Thompson third in the paper's first 60 years.

There is a saying in journalism that newspapers, like people, have lives of their own and should grow to full stature. It is always painful to see any newspaper die, for, profit-making business that it must strive to be and frequently is not, it is by nature more than a business institution dealing in wares. The Eugene *Guard* was always fortunate. It was always saved. It took it a long, long time "to get there." But "get there" it did—and always as a private, individually controlled enterprise. No newspaper chain ever entered the picture.

The 40 years after 1927 were to give the newspaper power and honor and stature.

---

1. See pp. 95-96 *supra*.

2. *Morning Register*, December 9, 1922; *Daily Guard*, December 8, 1922. The Astoria fire set back the Columbia River city so that it never fully recovered. Astoria dropped in population from 14,027 in 1920 to 10,349 in 1930 and today still has less population than it had nearly 50 years ago.

3. Turnbull, *History of Oregon Newspapers*, *op. cit.*, p. 280.

4. *Morning Register*, "Editor Gilstrap Retires," December 24, 1911.

5. The Scripps League Newspapers today publish the Klamath Falls *Herald and News* and the Roseburg *News-Review*.

6. *Morning Register*, December 31, 1911.

7. *Ibid.*, "Greater Morning Register," June 25, 1910.

8. Frank Jenkins, "Covering the Morning Field," *Oregon Exchanges*, Volume 1, Number 1, p. 3 (June 1917).

9. Miriam Page, "Letting in the Laity," interview with Frank Jenkins, *Oregon Exchanges*, Volume 1, Number 5, p. 1 (March 1918). For W. Frank Gilstrap's retirement, see *Oregon Exchanges*, Volume 1, Number 8, p. 8 (June 1918).

10. *Oregon Exchanges*, "Building Bought," February 1923, p. 14; "Eugene Register Building New Home," April 1926, p. 10, and July 1926, p. 28.
11. Ayer, *Directory, op. cit.*, years 1921 through 1930.
12. *Register*, May 25, 1930.
13. *Ibid.*, September 16, 1929. Also, *Oregon Exchanges*, "Register Enters Evening Field," October 1929, p. 16.
14. *Oregon Exchanges*, "Register Gives up A.M. Field," April 1930, p. 38.

Part Two

CHAPTER 12

The Alton F. Baker Purchase: Last Sale Of The Guard

Alton F. Baker, son of the general manager of the Cleveland *Plain Dealer*, was in 1926 a young man of 32 eager for an opportunity to operate a newspaper of his own. Coming from a closely-knit family of extensive journalistic background and having had himself six years of experience on the *Plain Dealer* after World War I, Baker was well prepared to do an exceptional job with whatever newspaper he purchased. The city he chose to come to could conceivably have been one of many. It turned out to be Eugene, Oregon. For the Eugene *Guard*, Baker's decision to buy it was one more of those fortiutous circumstances in the newspaper's history as we have seen: 1868, 1878, 1906, and 1916. Yet it was not chance in 1927 that brought Alton Baker to Eugene. The young publisher knew what kind of city he wanted, and Eugene at the right time offered the right opportunity.

For Baker the city he went to had to be small enough to make it possible for him to buy a paper with limited family resources. Newspaper properties in the 1920s were no longer coming cheap; and Baker, while he was from a well-to-do family, was not the son of a metropolitan press-tycoon. His father, Elbert H. Baker, was a highly talented executive who had made a paying property out of the *Plain Dealer*, but he was not an owner. So Alton Baker's future, if he wanted to be a publisher, could hardly rest in Cleveland.

The city to be chosen would have to be one in which a newspaper property was for sale. There usually are enough of these around the country to provide a choice, but not if choice is limited to promising small cities that also offer promising newspaper investments. Paul Kelty had written in 1924 upon buying the *Guard* that it was one of the most valuable present and potential newspaper properties in the Pacific Northwest. Kelty was correct, as the *Guard's* increase in business under his control showed. His willingness to sell in 1927, then, was Alton Baker's opportunity.

The city chosen would have to be one on main lines of communication, as Eugene was, being on the principal north-south route of the Pacific Coast. The city would have to be far enough from a dominating metropolitan center so as not to be swallowed up by the larger community, as Eugene again was, being 120 miles from Portland. Eugene offered a trade hinterland of its own of more than 4,000 square miles. Finally, the city would, ideally, be in a progressive, developing state with economic potential as yet untapped, as Oregon was; and, again ideally, in a center of culture, which the University of Oregon offered.

All these points are supported in retrospect by Charles A. Sprague, publisher of the *Oregon Statesman* in Salem since 1929 and governor of Oregon from 1939 to 1943. Charles Sprague had come to Oregon from Eastern Washington State, where he owned a weekly at Ritzville; he also was interested in the 1920s in entering the daily field. Sprague at the time was associated with the Corvallis *Gazette-Times*, and he too might have been interesting in buying into Eugene had he known about the *Guard* possibilities at the time. As it happened, Sprague bought the Salem newspaper, and the *Guard* and *Oregon Statesman* have grown in parallel 70 miles distant from each other. Along with the Salem *Capital-Journal* the two have given Oregon journalism a regional standard in small-city journalism matched by few newspapers of their size in any state.

Developments shortly after Baker bought the *Guard* made Eugene a one-newspaper city,[1] whereas Salem remains today one of the few competitive newspaper cities of its size in the country. As a result, the *Register-Guard* became much bigger than either of the Salem newspapers, although slightly smaller than *Statesman* and *Capital-Journal* combined. The *Guard* and *Statesman*—centenarians both—would offer a fascinating joint study, with each in a different field recognizing the opportunities and obligations of regional newspapers.[2]

To get back again to the Eugene of 1927: The city provided everything that an enterprising young publisher could ask. All these potentialities young Baker was able to determine in advance, for an older brother, Frank Baker, had come West 15 years before Alton to purchase the *Tacoma* (Wash.) *Tribune* and later to buy the Tacoma *Ledger* and Tacoma *Evening News.* Frank Baker understood Pacific Northwest journalism's possibilities and he, Elbert Baker of the *Plain Dealer*, and Alton scouted Eugene in 1926 and decided the *Guard* was the paper to buy.[3]

On March 1, 1927, the Eugene *Guard* changed hands again, for the last time in its 60 years—and no more in the coming 40. The price paid for it was a shade less than $100,000, less than $20,000 more than it had brought when the Fisher Estate and Joseph Shelton sold to the Keltys in 1924. The paper in 1924, however, had included a job plant, which was part of its value under Fisher and Shelton, so the increment in the *Guard* proper was actually more than $20,000.[4] Alton Baker was to remain permanently in the city, and he brought to the *Guard* the combination of talent and purpose we have mentioned earlier—enough of both to conquer even the Depression, which ensued before Baker really had had a chance to get himself adjusted. Further, the depth of depression was not reached until two to three years after the new publisher had obligated himself to buy the *Register.*

Alton F. Baker, Sr.
Longest tenure as publisher—1927 to 1961

This is the news story that accompanied the Baker purchase, the account being covered by a modest one-column top headline on page one, column five, without pictures:

EUGENE GUARD
PURCHASED BY
ALTON BAKER
New Owner Member of
Noted Family of
Newspaper People
Paul R. Kelty and Eugene
S. Kelty Dispose of
Their interests

"Alton F. Baker, of Cleveland O., today purchased The Eugene *Guard* from Paul R. Kelty and Eugene S. Kelty, its owners since July, 1924. In assuming ownership, Mr. Baker announced that the newspaper will continue to be conducted in accordance with its present editorial and news policies, and that Paul R. Kelty has been invited to remain permanently as editor if he so desires. Both Paul R. and Eugene S. Kelty will remain temporarily.

"Mr. Baker has been actively connected with the Cleveland *Plain Dealer*, whose publisher is his father, Elbert H. Baker. Frank S. Baker, publisher of the Tacoma *News-Tribune* and the Tacoma *Ledger*, is a brother of *The Guard's* new owner. Mr. Baker's wife and four children will join him here in the near future.

" 'I have come to Eugene because I believe it to be one of the coming important cities of the Pacific Northwest,' said Mr. Baker, 'and I have bought *The Guard* because I believe it to be a first-class newspaper property, with a great future. It is my intention to conduct the newspaper in accordance with its present high standard and to improve it as the field grows. Both my father and my brother, who like myself are familiar with newspapers and newspaper fields, have investigated Eugene and *The*

Guard, and they believe, as I do, that there is a real opportunity here.'

"Paul R. Kelty said: 'We bought *The Guard* when its circulation was 2800. It is now 7000. The volume of business has doubled since we have had it. We have published every day the best paper we could, and the public has responded. We are grateful. Mr. Baker is a splendid young man. He comes of a noted newspaper family and by inheritance as well as by training is a thorough newspaper man. We know that Eugene and this newspaper field will be as good to him as they have been to us, and that is saying much.' "[5]

To understand the *Guard* that Alton Baker had in mind in 1927 we must first tell the story of his father, Elbert Baker of Cleveland. For Alton gained his concepts of the purpose of a newspaper in his formative days in Ohio. What he did in Eugene was principally to apply these concepts in a newspaper of his own. The principles have been carried on through the grandsons of Elbert Baker, and we have in today's Eugene *Register-Guard* the third generation of the Baker family.

Elbert H. Baker, a native of Norwalk, Ohio, was born July 25, 1854, and he began his newspaper career in 1877 as a bookkeeper for the Cleveland *Herald.* He later switched to the advertising department and in 1882 left the *Herald* to become advertising manager of the Cleveland *Leader.* This was the nature of his experience for the 21 years to 1898. By then, at age 44, he had proved himself a competent newspaper executive, but there was nothing in his career that could single Baker out as outstanding.

However, in 1898 the Cleveland *Plain Dealer*, the distinguished paper that had given the humorist Artemus Ward (Charles Farrar Browne) to American journalism during the Civil War, was in financial difficulties. The *Plain Dealer's* owner was Liberty E. Holden, a civic-minded capitalist and former college teacher of English who had bought the paper in

1884 to gain a medium to expound his views on how to improve the City of Cleveland. Holden was in effect a preacher of civic righteousness.[6] The paper, however, wasn't making money, and the Holden family finally decided, after 11 years, that it needed business and editorial management that Liberty E. Holden himself was not trained for.

It was at this point that the owner made one of the most interesting arrangements to be recorded in newspaper administration. Holden brought Elbert Baker to the *Plain Dealer* and put him in charge of the business side, at the same time transferring one Charles E. Kennedy to the editorial side. Kennedy had been in the *Plain Dealer* advertising department, but previously he had had experience as a managing editor of the St. Louis *Post-Dispatch.* Holden drew up a contract with Baker and Kennedy making them co-lessees of the *Plain Dealer*, they gaining the right to run the paper as they saw fit, without owner interference. This kind of operation—in effect complete delegation of authority to a management team—was something new in turn-of-the-century concepts of ownership. It proved to be the making of the *Plain Dealer.*

Kennedy remained for eight years, leaving the paper in 1906 after a break with Albert F. Holden, Liberty's son, over a matter of "meddling" with the lease. Baker remained with the *Plain Dealer* until his death, September 27, 1933.[7] After Kennedy's departure Baker became both editor and publisher, although he took the title of general manager. Actually, he set both news and editorial policy as well as business policy. In 1920 Elbert Baker became president of the *Plain Dealer* corporation, the Forest City Publishing Company. By 1930, upon retirement from active duty, he became chairman of the board.[8]

In the 32 years that Elbert Baker managed the *Plain Dealer* his son Alton was growing from boyhood to manhood and observing the direction his father was giving to journalism in Cleveland. The *Plain Dealer* achieved "a new sense of harmony with its times and its community . . . and by the force of his own [Baker's] character and ability [he made] a new and better

Plain Dealer out of the old."[9] The *Register-Guard's* ideal of "citizen of its community," then, seems to date to Elbert Baker's indoctrination of Alton. Many years later, when Alton Baker, Jr., in 1966 accepted for the *Register-Guard* the University of Missouri's award for distinguished service in journalism, he said he believed the motto to be that of the late William M. Tugman, for 27 years managing editor and editor of the *Guard* and *Register-Guard.*[10] It is possible that Tugman first put "Citizen of Its Community" on the *Guard's* editorial page. But Tugman appears only to have been enunciating the principles of Cleveland's Elbert Baker as carried out by Alton in Eugene.

Elbert's concepts of journalism were evidenced almost at once. In 1899, only a year after he had signed his lease, Holden became discouraged and thought it might be better to sell out entirely, for the *Plain Dealer* under the arrangement with Baker and Kennedy had not yet begun to make money. Baker, however, argued the matter. "No," he said, "it is wiser to hang on, to plow back all income gains into the newspaper." He urged that policy even if it meant a loss to the lessees and a smaller return to the lessor for an indefinite time. Interestingly, Kennedy, the editorial lessee, was inclined to support Holden; but Baker was the more persuasive. Holden agreed to keep the paper. After all, Baker had shown an increase in *Plain Dealer* revenue of $62,000.[11]

Baker squeezed water out of circulation and reported exact figures to advertisers, an unusual tactic in days before the Audit Bureau of Circulations but one that did much to raise confidence in the *Plain Dealer's* integrity. He also gave figures on volume of business. Receipts increased by $87,000 in Baker's second year and $120,000 the third. As to circulation, the true daily figures at the time were 18,000, with the Sunday edition not over 32,000. Both were below totals previously quoted to advertisers.[12] These revelations cost the *Plain Dealer* only two advertisers, and one of these returned within a year.

Baker also set up an advertising rate card, another new device at the time. Rates would apply equally to all advertisers, with preferences to none. In future years Baker said proudly, "There never has been one broken rate, not even one slightly cracked."[13] The *Plain Dealer's* rate-card principle nearly 30 years later enabled Alton Baker to prove to suspicious Eugene businessmen that the *Guard* in 1927 would treat all advertisers alike. This practice as much as any changes in the news-editorial department—and they were many—helped Alton to outstrip the *Register* so rapidly when he came to Eugene.

Elbert Baker and Kennedy took over in Cleveland only two years after Adolph S. Ochs had purchased the New York *Times*, and, as admirers of Ochs, the lessees applied in Ohio many of the ideas Ochs had put to use in New York. News became an important element in the *Plain Dealer*—"news unbiased, untrammeled, and down to the minute." The *Plain Dealer* before 1898 had not reached for news beyond Ohio, but Baker and Kennedy contracted for the New York *World's* telegraph service,[14] as well as for a leased wire from the Chicago *Daily News*.[15] For the first time Cleveland got a diet of national and world news more extensive than that provided by the press associations.

The *Plain Dealer* also separated news from opinion, with Baker insisting that the paper's opponents gain "equal representation with friends" rather than mere "lip service to their activities."[16] In fact, the *Plain Dealer's* historian, Arthur Shaw, wrote:

> "In Baker's early days with the *Plain Dealer* the only other outstanding newspaper publisher insisting on his standard in this respect was Adolph Ochs of the New York *Times*." [17]

For reporters, the Baker-Kennedy instructions were to have "neither friends to serve nor enemies to punish. . . . Their business was to write the news." So, noting again: Few Eugeneans of a future generation who saw this news policy applied in their city realized where the *Register-Guard's* frequently blunt reporting methods had first been fashioned. Charles H. Fisher had given hints of such practice, but not with Alton Baker's metropolitan touch.

Apart from his newspaper, Elbert Baker was intensely active in outside affairs, all except partisan elective politics, and these activities, too, were carried on in Oregon by Alton. Elbert did not believe that a newspaperman in public office could render suitable service to the office and to the newspaper at the same time.[18] Rather, he operated the *Plain Dealer* with an eye toward broad improvements in Cleveland and Ohio. He supported the initiative and referendum and the recall of judges; the proposals that brought to Cleveland the headquarters of a Federal Reserve District; a modernized street-numbering system; workmen's compensation; an end to the practice of prison contract-labor; and annexation of suburban communities to the central city.

Baker also played a material part in settling a nasty franchise conflict between the City of Cleveland and the East Ohio Gas Company in 1913. And he helped to bring about municipal home rule, Cleveland in 1913 becoming the first Ohio city to gain a home rule provision in its charter.[19]

Baker likewise inaugurated a practice of recommending the *Plain Dealer's* choices of candidates in elections. At the beginning the recommendations were limited to the general elections and did not include the primaries. The *Plain Dealer* in starting this policy in 1908 is said to have been the first Ohio newspaper to do so. The publisher's reasons were that a newspaper "can't evade decisions," even though to recommend one local candidate over another could be perilous when the paper was dealing with readers who were emotionally involved in the outcome of an election.[20]

This election-recommendation practice was one of the first aggressive actions the Alton Baker regime took in Eugene in 1927 within three months after Alton had bought the *Guard.* As we shall see, some of the *Guard's* and *Register-Guard's* greatest conflicts with readers and with the Eugene and Lane County political "establishments" resulted from the consistent policy of measuring candidates—from county assessor to President of the United States—not in isolated campaigns but in election after election, general or special.

All these *Plain Dealer* activities made Elbert Baker's paper a staunch supporter of the liberal reform movements early in the century. His name was linked frequently in Ohio with men widely known historically: Tom L. Johnson, the "reform mayor" of Cleveland; Brand Whitlock, mayor of Toledo and World War I ambassador to Belgium; and Newton D. Baker (no relation to Elbert), secretary of war under Woodrow Wilson.[21]

In private community affairs Elbert Baker was likewise active. He was a solicitor for the Cleveland Community Fund, treasurer of the YMCA, a director of the Cleveland Life Insurance Company, member of the Cleveland Chamber of Commerce, and a trustee of the Euclid Avenue Congregational Church. He sponsored a civic program to bring about the straightening of the Cuyahoga River. In national newspaper circles he was a director of the American Newspaper Publishers Association from 1904 to 1924 and president of the ANPA from 1912 to 1914. He was a director of the Associated Press for 17 years, from 1916 until his death in 1933.

After Liberty Holden's death in 1913, Baker, though a nonowner, was in effect *The Plain Dealer.* Shaw says in the centennial history of the paper, published in 1942, that Baker was the "fourth builder of the Plain Dealer"—more responsible for its growth than any predecessors, J.W. Gray, William Wirt Armstrong, and Holden himself.[22] Late in life Baker was nominated for the Ohio State University School of Journalism Hall of Fame.

> Shortly before his death Elbert was quoted:
>
> "I may be a bit old-fashioned, but I like to see a paper striving to improve the community in which it is located. This is sound principle."[23]

This was the background that Alton Baker brought to Eugene. What was said of the father in *Editor & Publisher's* obituary in 1933 could be said of the son, that what Elbert did for Cleveland Alton did for Eugene: give the city "fresh inspiration, modernize its point of view, and establish the claim of [providing] in fact a metropolitan newspaper."[24] We may even conjecture that, as the *Plain Dealer's* owners were willing to delegate much of management to Elbert Baker, so, when Alton became an owner he did not hesitate to give free rein to his managing editor and editor. As a result, many Eugeneans gave considerable credit to William M. Tugman for building the modern *Register-Guard.* This was a fact, and Alton Baker did not mind that, for delegation was to him a professional responsibility. Liberty Holden had delegated to Elbert Baker; likewise, Alton turned over news and editorial management to his executive. In each case the newspaper gained.

Alton F. Baker: The Early Days

Alton Baker was the youngest of four children of Elbert. The eldest son, Frank, had come to Tacoma and had scouted the coast journalistic scene for Alton in 1926. Another brother was Elbert Baker, Jr., of Cleveland; and a sister was Louise Baker Hastings, of Shaker Heights, Ohio. With Elbert, Sr., all were deeply interested in helping the young man to succeed in his Oregon venture.

Alton was born in Willoughby, Ohio, February 14, 1894, attended Ohio schools, and went to Cornell University, from which he was graduated. During World War I, despite a leg injury that left him with a permanent limp, Alton volunteered in the American Field Service and was attached to the French Army. Later he became a first lieutenant with the United States Army Air Corps in France. After the war he returned to Ohio and in 1919 married Mildred Moody, of Binghampton, N.Y., whom he had met on a visit there.

The Bakers had five children, four sons and a daughter. Years later, the eldest son, Alton, Jr., and his brother, Edwin M.

(Ted) Baker, succeeded their father as publisher and general manager, respectively, of the *Register-Guard.* The youngest son, Richard M. Baker, after a short term as managing editor of the *Guard,* took over his own paper in 1963 in California, the El Cajon *Californian,* outside San Diego. The second son, Herbert Baker, started in newspaper work with the *Register-Guard* but switched to medicine and is now a practicing physician in Eugene. The daughter, Louise Baker Little, lives in Eugene.

Alton's purchase of the Eugene *Guard* came from his share of family funds which, in 1927, made it possible for him to buy from the Keltys for something less than $100,000.[25] Guard Printing Company records show only the stock transfer to Alton, Elbert H. Baker, and Mildred Baker, so the exact amount paid is not recorded. The $100,000 was only slightly more than the estimated $82,000 that the Keltys had paid in 1924.

Shortly after Baker's purchase the corporation became the Guard Publishing Company, a procedural move that broadened the corporation's direction and eliminated the small-city tie to the job-printing business that had gone with Shelton in 1924. With these changes accomplished and with his start as a small-city publisher taken, the 33-year-old Alton was on his own.[26] When on November 17, 1930, Baker also purchased the *Register* for $244,000—in retrospect, a high price in a declining economy—that decision for consolidation was his, singly. The fact that Baker carried this load of the combined *Register-Guard,* with its heavy debt, through the Depression—is sufficient evidence that he had talents equal to this father's.

Enemies of the *Register-Guard* in Eugene have intimated on occasion that the *Register-Guard* made its way only because of Elbert Baker and the Cleveland *Plain Dealer.* This is disproved, however, by records showing how, year by year, Alton Baker whittled down his loan. The loan was held by the Southern Oregon Newspapers, the Roseburg and Klamath Falls company that the Eugene *Register* publishers took over after 1930 following their selling out in Eugene. As late as 1941, the *Register-*

Guard still owed $105,000; and it was not until 1945 that the newspaper was clear of the *Register* obligation.[27]

In addition, Mrs. Effie Fisher, widow of Charles Fisher, held a $30,000 mortgage on the *Guard* building on Willamette Street. This, too, Alton had to pay out of earnings of the newspaper. A sidelight here shows Baker's concern for people. Interest on the newspaper building was good income for Mrs. Fisher, so Baker kept the smaller loan alive while he cleared the larger one on the *Register* purchase first.

Either way, Baker's first 15 to 20 years in Eugene were hard ones: publishing a strong-minded newspaper forever trying to push a city faster than many conservative residents wanted to be pushed; meeting heavy obligations during depression; and rearing a large family. But Baker turned back almost all his income margin into the newspaper and kept his own salary down; he gave his small staff its head, particularly in news and editorial matters; and he turned out a product that Eugene and Lane County had to read. From 1931 to 1942 the *Register-Guard* had short term competition from the Eugene *Daily News*, but the *News* never had the quality of staff of the *Register-Guard*, and its financial base was always tenuous.

Minutes of the Guard Publishing Company are revealing in the cold figures of salary that Alton Baker allowed himself in these first years in Eugene. A salary of $150 a week in 1931 was a healthy one, but not necessarily for the owner of a newspaper that could readily have yielded its owner more had he been less concerned with debt liquidation and freedom from all obligation to creditors.

Well-to-do background or not, Baker knew what it was to live on little, a little that from 1931 on was to become less. From January 1, 1931, to November 22, 1933, Baker kept reducing his own income from the paper, to $135 a week, to $110, to $100, to $95, and finally to $85.50 a week.[28] Finally the turn in the Depression came, Baker began raising his own salary, and the company was able to declare a dividend of $1,121.85 for 1934. Later, in 1935, Baker himself passed $10,000 in salaried income for the first time. He had weathered the early troubles. While obligations were still difficult to meet, the financial future of the *Register-Guard* was assured and it became the business success Alton had hoped for in 1927. And in the face of its difficulties the *Register-Guard* threw all its news and editorial energies into the crisis that imperiled the future of the University of Oregon. A newspaper concerned only with economic survival would hardly have dared to take on the vested educational establishment of the State of Oregon in order to rescue a foundering university before the paper's own future was secured. This is what the *Register-Guard* had courage to do. The paper made some educational history in its own right.[29]

Policies Toward Employes

Baker could not operate through these years by assuming responsibility for both the business and news-editorial functions of his newspaper. When he bought the *Guard*, he kept on as many of the old employes as wanted to remain, and he gave assurance later that if they would bear with him the hardships of the depression period he would grant, in effect, tenure of employment. This was something decidedly distinctive among newspapers of the day—large or small. One employe, for example, was helped through the University of Oregon in the 1920s and remains with the paper today. The *Register-Guard* sports editor for nearly 30 years, Dick Strite, came over from the faltering Eugene *Daily News* in 1937 and remained until his death in 1965. One of the stockholders of the *Register*, Horace Burnett, did not go to Roseburg or Klamath Falls with Ernest and Otto Gilstrap and Frank Jenkins but remained with the *Register-Guard* until his own career ended in the 1940s. As we have noted, Burnett's journalistic career in Eugene antedated the Spanish-American War. At one time or another he covered probably all the news sources spanning 50 years. Another longtime employe who joined the paper before Baker's purchase is Robert Bertsch, now promotion manager.

Paul and Eugene Kelty were invited to stay on after March 1, 1927, but the former owners left of their own volition within a few weeks.

Many employes in the various departments stay with the paper throughout their entire working careers. This gives the *Guard* a deep reservoir of highly competent, broadly experienced staff members to complement the flow of new people needed to keep the complex mechanism of the medium-sized metropolitan daily working smoothly. Alton Baker was noted for his esteem of employes with long service records.

In 1946 he formed the *Register-Guard* 20-year-Club.[30] Its members meet annually for dinner, initiation of new members and the opportunity for all present to advise members of the Baker family on the finer points of operating their newspaper!

As the years passed the *Register-Guard* became a "feeder lot" for able newspapermen ambitious to rise beyond the small-city daily and to enter metropolitan journalism, related journalistic fields, or other fields. The talent flow to the *Register-Guard*, helped by graduates of the University of Oregon, was under Baker's ownership always greater than the paper's limited needs could absorb, so many employes, of course, had to move on. This the management always recognized, and its managing editor 20 years later said the paper had no intention of "holding the younger men on the *Register-Guard* for more than a few years." The paper wanted reporters and desk men "who aspire to the New York *Times* staff some day or who dream of serving in Washington or in some foreign capital."[31]

As a result, the *Register-Guard* in the years since 1927—and particularly after World War II—gave starts to newspapermen who eventually became justices of the Oregon Supreme Court, professors of law in state universities, directors of communication research and professors of journalism, staff members of *Time*, managing editors of other Oregon newspapers, executives of major trade journals, and staff members of quality newspapers of the level of the Milwaukee *Journal*, Washington *Post*, and (as the paper hoped) the New York *Times*. This course of career development is not necessarily exceptional among American newspapers, except that the *Register-Guard* was to provide an inordinate amount of such advancement in consideration of its size.

---

1. A morning newspaper, the Eugene *Daily News*, competed with the *Register-Guard* after the *Guard* had bought the *Register*. The *News* published from 1931 to 1942. See p. 220 *infra*.
2. Interview with Charles A. Sprague, Salem, December 8, 1966.
3. Frank Baker had worked for the *Plain Dealer*, 1904-1906, and was publisher of the Boston *Traveler*, 1906-1912, before going to Tacoma. The Tacoma papers became the present Tacoma *News-Tribune* in 1937. The *Register-Guard* and the Tacoma papers have always been corporately separate, although each corporation has held minority stock interest in the other. A brief history of Tacoma journalism has been written: Paul W. Harvey, *Tacoma Headlines: An Account of Tacoma News and Newspapers from 1873 to 1962*, illustrated. Tacoma, Washington: The Tacoma *News-Tribune*, 1962.
4. Corporate minutes of the Guard Publishing Company do not show specific amounts of purchases but only stock transfers. Much of this information comes from interviews with Alton Baker, Jr., and Mrs. Alton Baker, Sr.
5. *Guard*, March 1, 1972.
6. Archer H. Shaw, *The Plain Dealer: One Hundred Years in Cleveland*. New York: A.A. Knopf, 1942, p. 263.
7. Shaw, *op. cit.*, pp. 272 ff.
8. "Elbert H. Baker Dies in Cleveland," *Editor & Publisher*, Volume 66 (September 30, 1933), p. 7. The Forest City Publishing Company continues to be the name of the *Plain Dealer* corporation. Although the contemporary story of the *Plain Dealer* does not bear on the Eugene *Register-Guard*, it is of interest to note that early in 1967 Samuel I. Newhouse, the chain publisher who also owns the Portland *Oregonian* and the *Oregon Journal*, bought the *Plain Dealer* for a reported $50,000,000, the highest price ever paid for an American metropoitan newspaper. "Newhouse Pays $50 Million for Cleveland Plain Dealer," *Editor & Publisher*, Vol. 100, (March 4, 1967), p. 11.
9. Shaw, *op. cit.*, p. 279.
10. Alton Baker, Jr., *The Newspaper as a Citizen*, address at University of Missouri School of Journalism, Columbia, May 5, 1966.
11. Shaw, *op. cit.*, pp. 274-275.
12. *Editor & Publisher*, Vol. 66 (September 30, 1933), *op. cit.*
13. *Ibid.*
14. *Ibid.*
15. Shaw, *op. cit.*, p. 275.
16. *Ibid.*, p. 277.
17. *Ibid.*
18. *Ibid.*, p. 278.
19. *Ibid.*, pp. 314 ff.
20. *Ibid.*, p. 318.
21. *Ibid.*, p. 313.

22. *Ibid.*, p. 270.
23. *Editor & Publisher*, Vol. 66, (September 30, 1933), *op. cit.*
24. *Ibid.*
25. Interview with Mrs. Alton F. Baker, Sr., November 29, 1966.
26. *Minutes*, Guard Printing Company, March 1, 1927, and Guard Publishing Company, October 27, 1927.
27. *Minutes*, Guard Publishing Company, 1927-1952, inclusive.
28. *Minutes*, Guard Publishing Company, January 1, 1931, to November 22, 1933.
29. See "Zorn-MacPherson: Crisis in 1932," Chapter 16 *infra.*
30. See "*Register-Guard 20-Year Club,*" Appendix.
31. Quoted material is from Ralph D. Casey, "Interview with William M. Tugman, managing editor, *Register-Guard,*" prepared for the Commission on the Freedom of the Press, Summer 1946.

CHAPTER 13

The Coming Of William M. Tugman

Alton Baker's major problem in 1927 was to find an editor. Paul Kelty left the *Guard* within three weeks of his sale to Baker, and for two months thereafter the new publisher ran the paper alone.

In the six years in which Baker had worked on the *Plain Dealer* both as a reporter and solicitor of advertising, he found that his interests lay in business management. He needed in Eugene a managing editor, and to the employe whom he brought to this spot he gave a *carte blanche* to edit the *Guard.*

This policy, considering conditions under which many newspapers have operated—then or now—was professional in the extreme. Cynics in Eugene have often asked, "Didn't Alton Baker interfere in editorial policy?" The answer is "No." As Elbert Baker managed the *Plain Dealer*, so Alton was to manage the *Guard:* to give to his managing editor a free hand within broad outlines of sound newspaper practice. Therein lies the secret of *Register-Guard* news and editorial growth and respect in the years after 1927. *Guard* circulation has risen sevenfold; advertising has soared; the Baker sons have assumed control; and two associate editors now complement the managing editor in handling news-editorial operations. The *Register-Guard* is today a semi-metropolitan newspaper and, like many newspapers in a single-ownership city, is quite institutionalized. But in the generation after Alton Baker's arrival the paper was principally a two-executive operation, the young publisher with grave financial problems and the equally young managing editor with news and opinion as his domain.

It is true that Baker's news executives often pursued a policy that was frequently aggressive in the extreme and that upset local die-hards, with consequent difficulties for the owner. The

The University Rule Prohibiting Students who Cannot Swim From Canoeing is Sound and Should be Enforced

THE WEATHER

The Eugene Guard

OUR SERVICE

6:30 P. M.—If your copy of The Guard does not arrive by 6:30 p. m., phone 1200 and a copy of the paper will be sent. We have special messengers to insure delivery in every part of the city of Eugene.

VOL. 73 — TODAY'S NEWS TODAY — EUGENE, OREGON, FRIDAY, MAY 20, 1927. — PRICE: ON STREETS 3c; ON TRAINS AND NEWS STANDS, 5c. — NO. 111

LINDBERGH OFF FOR PARIS

Andrews Quits Post as Chief of Prohibition

CITY NEWS

Final Exams Near—

COMMENCEMENT dates for the two junior high schools and the Eugene high school will be as follows: Roosevelt, Wednesday, June 1; Eugene high, June 2; Woodrow Wilson, June 3, according to the announcement today from the office of David John Jones, city superintendent of schools. Examination questions for the "finals" at the two junior high schools are now being prepared by the city superintendent. The final examination schedule for the lower grades will begin on Tuesday, May 31, with spelling and arithmetic in the morning and geography in the afternoon; Wednesday, June 1, history in the morning and grammar in the afternoon; while the examination on hygiene will be given Thursday morning, June 2. Report cards will be distributed at two o'clock Friday.

RESIGNATION IS EFFECTIVE ON AUGUST 1

Former Lieutenant Governor Of New York Will Succeed Him

WASHINGTON, May 20.—(AP)—Lincoln C. Andrews, assistant secretary of the treasury in charge of prohibition enforcement has resigned, effective August 1, and Seymour Lowman, former lieutenant governor of New York, will succeed him.

This shift was announced late today at the treasury, together with announcement that James M. Doran, prohibition bureau chemist, had been designated prohibition commissioner. He succeeds Roy A. Haynes, who has been acting commissioner for several months.

Secretary Mellon expects Mr. Haynes to resign, although the resignation has not yet been formally presented.

Mr. Lowman's appointment must yet be officially made by the president although the treasury said the office had been offered to him and that he had accepted.

Graduation Plans Made

McAdoo and Hughes not Candidates

NEW YORK, May 20.—(AP)—The New York Times says Tammany Hall has been informed that William G. McAdoo will not seek the democratic nomination for president next year. The Times quotes George W. Olvany, Tammany leader, as saying:

"A close friend of McAdoo was in here today. He told me that McAdoo was not in the race for the nomination."

NEW YORK, May 20.—(By The Associated Press) — Charles E. Hughes, republican nominee for president of the United States in 1916 in a formal statement today referring to published reports of his possible candidacy for the presidency next year said "I am too old to run for president and I would neither seek nor accept the nomination."

"I am for President Coolidge first, last and all the time," he added, "and I believe that he will be renominated and re-elected."

JUNIOR WEEK-END FESTIVITIES ARE ON AT UNIVERSITY

PRICES SPEED UP RECEIVING STATION PLAN

General Satisfaction With Proposal is Felt in This District

HE'S ON HIS WAY IN PARIS TRIP

Youthful, open-faced, pink-cheeked, is Captain Charles A. Lindbergh. He's but 25 years of age.

Youthful Aviator Has Close Calls As he Hops Off

Plane Barely Misses Road Scraper, Then Skims Telegraph Wires; No Radio Equipment is Taken Along

HALIFAX, N. S., May 20.—(A.P.)—Captain Lindbergh left Nova Scotia on his non-stop flight to Paris at Mainadieu at the easternmost tip of Nova Scotia, at 5 o'clock Atlantic daylight time (4 o'clock Eastern daylight time). The "flying fool" headed away for Cape Race, Newfoundland, across 200 miles of sea. The weather had cleared slightly as the American flyer left the coast, and watchers said he was flying very high.

The flying log of Lindbergh's plane follows:

7:52 a. m.—Left New York for Paris.
9:05 a. m.—Sighted over East Greenwich, R. I.
9:40 a. m.—Sighted over Halifax, Mass.
12:25 p. m.—Reported over Meteghan, N. S.
1:05 p. m.—Reported over Springfield, N. S.
1:50 p. m.—Over Milford, N. S.
3:05 p. m.—Passing over Mulgrave, N. S. and Straits of Canso for Cape Breton.

Start is Dramatic

ROOSEVELT FIELD, N. Y., May 20.—(AP)—Charles A. Lindbergh, captain in the Missouri national guard, but "Slim" to his buddies, set out today on an unmarked air trail for Paris. The Missourian, who plays a lone hand, had no one to show him the way as he hurled his Ryan monoplane, the "Spirit of St. Louis" into the muggy air ...

... hoped for several weeks to get off on a hop to Paris wished Lindbergh good luck, as did Commander Richard E. Byrd, who will follow the trail blazed by the youth in a few days. Commander Byrd's careful preparations to have the America act as escort for the Spirit of St. Louis finally ...

Plane Clears Wires

Plenty of Gasoline

Weather is Better

Has no Radio

France Lights Way to Paris

Chances Held Slight

Flight to India Starts

MOOSE GROUPS TO MEET HERE SUNDAY

Story Hero Is Eugenean

Comfort of Jail Extended to Vet

Park Watering Topic

(TURN TO PAGE 5)

BASEBALL RESULTS

COAST TENNIS MEN PLAY HERE TODAY

Local Girl Honored

Liquor Sentence Hard

Records to be Filed

Oakridge Asks Road

Pioneer of Lane Dies at Hospital

Liquor Fine is Paid

Sinclair to Serve Term

(TURN TO PAGE 3)

Abe Martin

NEWBERG STUDENTS ON STRIKE OTHER OREGON COUNTRY NEWS

Rail Decision Awaited

(TURN TO PAGE 7)

Page One, May 20, 1927

fact is that Alton Baker backed his editor, though he must have disagreed with the editor's judgments on occasion. Fundamentally the two agreed on the basic principles of what a newspaper is and should do.

The man whom Baker brought in, on May 13, 1927, was William Masten Tugman, also an Ohioan, who was six months older than Alton. As individuals the publisher and his managing editor were in many ways almost antithetical: Baker, quiet and shy, never himself voluntarily in the foregound, always courteous, yet firm and determined in his goals; Tugman, forward, frequently belligerent, considerably a showman, literarily sensitive and articulate, and sharp and satirical of editorial pen.

Baker set guidelines and worked as an individual apart from the public eye. He sought a firm groundwork for the paper and moved to advance the City of Eugene through unpublicized services. Tugman was forever telling Eugene, Lane County, the University of Oregon, and assorted state and national leaders how things ought to be. He never shunned the limelight—as editor, reporter, outdoors man, or amateur actor. He would cover major news himself and attach his own by-line. Editorially, Tugman knew Baker would support him in actions the *Guard* and *Register-Guard* took; he never hesitated to run the news with force and take on the editorial page the liberties he felt a newspaper should take. Until after World War II, if the *Register-Guard* had major news faults, they lay in Tugman's relative inattention to the mundane subjects of society and sports.

Since Baker's business policies, however sound, seldom gained much publicity, it was Tugman who in many Eugene circles became the better known. This was particularly true among the political leaders of the community, those most affected by *Register-Guard* publicity. Many readers, not knowing the relations between the two men, tended to think of the managing editor as THE *Guard*. This was not so, for the paper's standards were Baker's. Tugman implemented policy, and the two made an excellent combination. We shall take up later the ways in which

Baker made his influence felt in his more quiet way. But first let us consider the managing editor who, by Baker's choice, became the first person other than an owner or co-owner ever to have his name below the publisher's on the masthead.

Tugman: His Early Career

William M. Tugman (in his years in Eugene he was almost always called "Bill," even by those who did not know him well), was born in Cincinnati, August 22, 1893. He was graduated from Harvard College in 1914, where he had been an avid student of municipal government. So thorough was his understanding of city affairs that as a newspaperman he often knew more about how cities should be run—and could be run—than the politicians themselves. When toward mid-century he edited the *Register-Guard* in the burgeoning Lane County he couldn't refrain from putting forth improvement programs or from trying to stop actions that might be detrimental to the area.

From 1914 to World War I Tugman worked for the Springfield (Mass.) *Republican*, then a still-distinguished New England paper not too many years removed from earlier greatness. Tugman also worked for the Providence (R.I.) *Journal*, another of New England's famous papers. Just before the war he was a correspondent with General John J. Pershing's forces on the Mexican border; later, in Europe, he became a captain of field artillery.

After the war Tugman returned to Ohio and became a police reporter for the *Plain Dealer*. It was then that he met Alton Baker, and the two, so temperamentally different, became close friends and associates. Both served the *Plain Dealer* the same number of years; and both were actively together on the *Register-Guard* about the same length of time. Shortly after Tugman left the paper in 1954 Baker turned over active management to his sons and became chairman of the board. And both died in the same year, Tugman on May 9, 1961, and Baker October 27, 1961.

Baker knew exactly what his friend could do for the *Guard* when he asked him to give up the *Plain Dealer* job and join the newspaper in Oregon.[1]

Few Eugeneans outside newspaper circles knew how capable an editor Baker was enticing west. Tugman's energy and Baker's purpose soon faced the rather narrow-gauged *Register* management with the knowledge that the *Guard* was putting out a far more provocative paper than the Keltys had.

In fact, a little more than a year after Baker had arrived, the *Register*, itself needing a managing editor, brought Paul Kelty to that paper. This put the former *Guard* owner in service of the Gilstraps and Frank Jenkins against the much younger Tugman. Tugman as a new Oregon arrival didn't have the state background of Kelty nor Kelty's years of associations. Kelty's move to the opposition so soon after his sale of the *Guard* worried Alton Baker. Details are lacking about this upsetting problem, but Alton took it up with his father.[2] Elbert Baker replied with strong support of Tugman and Alton's choice of him as managing editor. Much of Elbert's letter must be left to inference, but he said:

> "My dear son,
>
> "You are absolutely right in your conclusions all the way. Kelty will be unable materially to help them [the *Register* owners] and I will pit Bill against Kelty any day. . . . Of course, it goes without saying that while we did not ask Kelty to agree not to go into the business again in Eugene, by the mere fact of selling everything . . . to us for a price that was more really than it was worth, he put himself under a moral obligation."[3]

The Mellett Case: Tugman Investigates a Murder

The exchange between Elbert and Alton relates directly to the capabilities of the new managing editor under difficult conditions, so a detailed account of one of Bill Tugman's pre-*Guard* experiences will show why there was no question at all *vis-a-vis* Kelty. Let us go back two years:

On July 16, 1926, in Canton, Ohio, Don Mellett, publisher of the Canton *Daily News*, was shot and killed by an employed thug hired by an underworld mob. Corruption in Canton was closely tied in with liquor running, vice, gambling, narcotics, and other forms of racketeering. High local political officials were involved, and the crusading Don Mellett was getting too close to crime syndicate sources for the comfort of gang leaders. The Canton police department, among other groups, was deeply involved.

Newspapers in their general frailties long have accepted the fact of rampant crime and have done little to correct it except through sporadic crusades, but when one of their own is injured or killed editors rise as a body of avengers. So it was in Ohio with Mellett's death. Mellett's successor in Canton was Charles E. Morris, who took it upon himself to run down the killer and the accomplices. Morris before coming to Canton had been associated with the Ohio News League, which in Washington served four Ohio newspapers owned by James M. Cox. He had been Cox's secretary for four years when Cox was governor of Ohio. Cox had been the Democratic nominee for the presidency in 1920.

Canton was depressed over Mellett's murder, and since no action against the gangsters could be obtained from public officials, Morris brought in a Chicago investigator, Joseph Roach, who had broken vice rings in Terre Haute, Ind. Roach in turn supplied leads to district attorneys, including the prosecutor in Cuyahoga County (Cleveland), who brought in federal officers.

The Stark County (Canton) grand jury failed to indict. Roach then went to court in a civil action in behalf of Mellett's widow and named names: Ben Rudner, a liquor runner and conspirator in Mellett's death; Louis Mazer, a go-between for Rudner and the hired murderer; Pat McDermott, the murderer (who didn't even know Mellett); Carl Studer, another vice leader;

and C.B. McClintock, the Stark County prosecutor who had not taken action.

Into this vicious situation Cleveland and other Ohio newspapers sent their own reportorial sleuths. The issue to them was the peril to liberty of the press under threat of gangland control. The two most courageous reporter-investigators were William M. Tugman of the *Plain Dealer* and Ned Doyle of the Cleveland *Press* (Scripps-Howard). In the process the premature release of McDermott's name enabled him to go into hiding. Tugman and Doyle, operating on their own, worked through the McDermott relatives. They spent weeks digging into all angles of the Canton mess, yet never writing a line of copy but turning over irrefutable evidence to Stark County officials. Tugman and Doyle prevailed upon McDermott's brothers to reveal his whereabouts and turn him over to the district attorney. The reporters pledged that they would do all they could to get McDermott "a square deal" if he had anything to tell about Ohio crime and if he would tell it.

On December 24, 1926, a jury in Stark County Common Pleas Court found McDermott guilty of first degree murder. Because of the help he gave in getting at the syndicate, the jury recommended mercy. McDermott received a life sentence in the Ohio penitentiary.

Tugman's work helped further to bring about a cleanup in the Canton police department, the removal of the chief, and the ousting of the civil service commission.[4] For his part in the Mellett investigation the future managing editor of the Eugene *Guard* helped to bring to the attention of the American press "the fact that Canton [was] but a typical American city, one spot in the country that organized crime seeks to dominate," and he helped to direct the press "to the effort to break up organized crime wherever found."[5]

Editor & Publisher ran Tugman's picture in a depth account of the Mellett case and said:

"The murder of Don R. Mellett was intended to serve notice on newspaper editors to keep silent against obvious misconduct. Instead, the murder . . . aroused newspapers to further vigilance. . . . Don Mellett was a true martyr and his name should not vanish but live to inspire youth in journalism."[6]

Bill Tugman possibly was inspired by the Mellett case to keep a watchful eye on things local when he moved to Oregon less than six months later. He never again had an assassination to deal with, but he had learned how to probe and he had learned it was not necessary to yield supinely to power. Except among newspaper friends in Eugene Tugman said little about the Canton affair. When he did he always gave less importance to his share in the detective work than was really the case. Today, more than 40 years later, the murder of Don Mellett is merely a footnote to regional journalism in Ohio, although a Don Mellett memorial lecture was set up at New York University in tribute to the Canton editor.[7]

Tugman on the Scene: Who Runs This Town?

So in May of 1927 Tugman arrived in Eugene. This is what he was: courageous, dedicated to the rights of the individual; well educated, editorially articulate, interested in almost all subject matter, sensitive to the finer points of civic beauty and public virtue; positive, often tactless, and undeferential. In today's idiom he would be called an *activist.*

Two stories, both probably apocryphal, illustrate Tugman's impact.

When within three months of Baker's arrival and a few weeks of Tugman's, the *Guard* emulated the *Plain Dealer* in making recommendations in a minor special election, a group of Eugene officials are said to have "summoned" the managing editor. The conversation—one-way advice from the Establishment to the young Tugman—is reported to have gone something like this:

> "Mr. Tugman, the *Guard* is showing a lot of new life and spirit. We like your editorials. They have lots of punch. You run plenty of good news, too, and you sure write better than anyone on a newspaper here for a long time. But some of the boys got to talking things over the other night. We are wondering just how long to wait before taking things up with you, how long before we should let you young whippersnapper know who runs this town."

In the next 27 years there were many in Eugene who would swear that Bill Tugman ran the town—or thought he did, or wanted to. He did none of the three. He did drive (propel might be a better word) to make Eugene better. He had many successes and enough failures to have discouraged lesser men.

The second story, apart from independence, had some shades of arrogance.

Tugman was reportedly visited early by membership representatives of the three major service clubs, Rotary, Kiwanis, and Lions. Each in turn pressed the merits of the respective group and stressed the young editor's qualifications for service. Tugman, affable, asked, "How much?" He signed a personal check for all three.

> In due course the three were back, this time in a body.
>
> "There must be some misunderstanding," so the story goes. "Each of our clubs would welcome you, Mr. Tugman, but we are obliged to tell you you must choose. We shall abide by your selection, but each hopes you will join his club."
>
> "Have you cleared the checks?" Bill is said to have asked.
>
> "No, we didn't know what to do."
>
> "Do you have them with you?"
>
> "No, but we can get them."
>
> "Will you, please?"

William M. Tugman
His policies frequently upset local die-hards

The three soon returned with the checks. Whereupon Tugman tore up all three and continued:

"I appreciate your interest, gentlemen, but if I cannot join all service clubs, as an editor I cannot favor one. You are very courteous, and I thank you." [8]

Tugman never did join any business group, though he addressed them all, regaled them and needled them, summarized news events of the year for them as a special New Year's speaker, and gave generously of news space to service-club coverage. Apparently a residue of Tugman's attitude toward business clubs remains today, for in the news and editorial departments the newspaper is not represented in any. All Tugman ever belonged to were "non-directional" social dinner and "heavy-thought" groups like the Knights of the Round Table, or outdoor groups like the Order of the Antelope, or dramatic groups like the Very Little Theatre. He also had his own pet organization for deflating those who "needed to be taken down a few pegs," the Order of the Buggy Ride. Organizations like these fitted his personality better.

The *Guard*, however, did much for the business community through Alton Baker's membership in Rotary and the Eugene Chamber of Commerce. But that is a later story, as is Baker's work in the Boy Scouts of America. Tugman's ironic scorn toward service organizations was part of his individualism.

Yet, Tugman was inconsistent, for years later, when he had an opportunity to join the status-minded American Society of Newspaper Editors he did apply for membership among "those stuffed shirts" (as he wrote to a close friend).[9] In the ASNE he showed rare courage during the American press' struggle against McCarthyism.

The truth is, Alton Baker and Bill Tugman couldn't possibly have "run Eugene." No two newspapermen could do that in a city of 18,000 that was growing rapidly to 50,000. What happened between 1927 and 1961 for Baker and 1927 and 1954 for Tugman was that they moved down complementary avenues. One was quiet and effective, the other belligerent and effective.

The two worked down many fronts, all of which helped toward Eugene's material growth and toward a broadening of its municipal conscience.

Baker had behind him moral purpose and the confidence gained through his family's being part of the building of a larger American newspaper. Tugman had behind him rigid academic training and the rough-and-tumble experience of on-the-line reporting. Even the eventual outspoken opposition and scorn of leading politicians, including Senator Wayne Morse, could not deflect Tugman—whether he was right or wrong.

---

1. *Register-Guard*, "Bill Tugman Dies; Age 67," May 10, 1961, p. 1.
Who's Who in Oregon, 1929-30. Oregon City: Oregon City Enterprises, Vol. 1, p. 221.

2. There were many other worries relating to competition with the *Register*, among them advertising rates and, on another occasion, the *Register's* offering to buy the *Guard*. Alton Baker, Jr., recalls that Alton, Sr., said he had come to Eugene to stay, not to sell out. In 1930, the situation had reversed itself. These matters, however, did not concern personnel.

3. Letter, Elbert Baker to Alton Baker, from Cleveland *Plain Dealer*, September 11, 1928. The father-to-son and son-to-father correspondence was always quite formal and the son's replies were genuinely deferential, facts that indicate the respect in which members of the family held each other.

4. Herve W. Miner, "Mellett's Successor Avenged Slain Editor," *Editor & Publisher*, Volume 59, (January 1, 1927), p. 5.

5. *Ibid.*

6. "Don Mellett's Victory," *Editor & Publisher*, Vol. 59, (January 1, 1927), p. 30.

7. Actually, few newspaper editors have ever been openly murdered in American journalistic history. The most famous assassination was that of the Rev. Elijah P. Lovejoy, editor of the Alton (Ill.) *Observer*, who was hanged by a pro-slavery mob from Missouri, November 7, 1837, and whose name remains a heroic one in the story of the Abolitionist movement.

8. The author cannot trace the source of these anecdotes. Possibly they came from Tugman himself many years ago, or from someone else at a Tugman soiree. There likely is a grain of truth in them—as in many others—but Bill could stretch the truth in relating stories like these.

9. Tugman correspondence, University of Oregon Library, Special Collections; name of addressee withheld.

CHAPTER 14

Guard And Register-Guard—Getting Established

Many Eugeneans who regard themselves as "old-timers"—and this group might include all who have lived in the city at least 25 years—like to think they can recall events of 35 to 40 years ago. Memories, however, are short, and inaccurate. As concerns the Eugene *Guard*, these memories seldom ante-date 1932, the year the newly combined *Register-Guard* rose to the defense of the University of Oregon over an abortive political effort to move the University to Corvallis and consolidate it with Oregon State College. As far as the Baker-owned newspaper is concerned, even vivid memories of townspeople and staff date their recollections only to 1932. "Now, during the Depression," people will say, or "during the Kerr affair [referring to the "enemy" president of Oregon State College] the *Guard* was a pillar of strength."[1]

Yet, there were five years before the *Register-Guard's* first great crusade, and in these five years the paper was facing problems far more fundamental to it as a business than as an aggressive news organization. Baker had first to get his newspaper financially buttressed. Not that news coverage was disregarded or that editorial opinion was not forceful; but the *Register's* competition had to be met and new business practices had to be instituted. The Baker regime started then with the publisher's influence uppermost. It was only later that Tugman's news-editorial force became obvious.

The First Problem: Circulation

What records remain for this period rest almost wholly in letters between Alton and Elbert Baker, neither of whom was a prolific correspondent. Tugman's correspondence, while extensive (Bill was a "packrat" who apparently never threw anything away), is almost barren of anything as "unimportant" as a cost crisis. Tugman operated at a "higher level of thought"—the resources of Eugene, the need for an auditorium, the sad condition of Willamette Street paving, and even the blooming of rhododendrons in November.

While Baker was striving to lay his base, Tugman was covering news as if he were still in Cleveland; yet Baker never restricted Tugman's news coverage. Editorial expense was necessary. One story, recalled by Baker's sons and subject to lapses of accuracy in the retelling, has Alton Baker disturbed because of an excessive long-distance telephone bill run up by Tugman in his zeal to get more background on some national story that the Associated Press had not covered in depth. The story might or might not have been important, for Tugman was subject to whims. Baker is said to have shown Tugman the bill, mentioned that "we're only a small paper now," and asked, "Bill, couldn't we use the United States mails once in a while?"[2] That wasn't Tugman's style, at least on news that agitated him, and for the most part Baker let editorial expense set its own limits. This practice—one that assumes that good business methods provide for meeting editorial expense—still prevails.

Meanwhile, Baker's business difficulties from 1927 on were many. *Guard* circulation, joyously proclaimed before Alton bought the paper as more than 7,000, was short of that. Official N.W. Ayer figures showed only 5,917 for 1926 and 6,887 for 1927, while the *Register* for the two years had 6,687 and 7,010, plus 6,850 and 7,176 for 1926 and 1927 for its Sunday edition.[3] Baker overcame the lead by 1929, a factor important in the consolidation.

There arose also the question of Eugene's population, which the boosters in 1926 had somewhat oversold and which in 1927 wasn't up to what the *Guard* had hoped for to sustain advertising and circulation. Elbert Baker in an undated, handwritten letter to Alton in the spring of 1927 asked in a disturbed vein:

"I have just been going over the new Rand-McNally 1927 Atlas and they give the population of Eugene as 11,000. Is that census 1920? What is the real honest-to-goodness population now? When we talked with [the] bank and others last September they talked 20,000 strong and said the new shops [Southern Pacific] would bring 4,000 more. It is quite worth while to guess as near as possible.

"I have been trying to estimate what we might hope to reach in circulation without foolish cost, and the actual population has much to do with it. Do you have a pre-date for circulation in towns of the county that you could reach with the evening [paper] or beyond the county line where you can arrive several hours earlier than the *Register?*" [4]

Alton replied to his father June 15:

"As to the honest-to-goodness population of Eugene, apparently no one knows."[5]

The 20,000-plus figure was that of the Pacific Northwest Bell Telephone Company. At the same time the Eugene Water Board was estimating 22,000 (based on 4,500 meters). It all added up to a question of how much circulation the *Guard* could reasonably expect. Alton was less disturbed than his father. He thought the *Guard* could get 400 more than the 3,600 it had in Eugene proper. It led the *Register*, 3,600 to 2,800 in Eugene, but the morning paper had a big out-county margin.[6]

The circulation problem, further, was more involved than the mere matter of population potential. Baker was this early putting city carriers on the "little merchant" system. The boys needed training, and part of their responsibility was to obtain regular payment from subscribers and to discontinue credit. This caused, as Alton said, "some stops." The *Guard* also took out "about 300 dead timber" [padded circulation] in the city and outlying territory. Alton was hoping to make that up within three or four months.[7]

The young publisher had still other circulation problems. Three years earlier the *Guard* had picked up some 400 subscribers in an automobile contest, subscriptions to run for five years. These Baker had to honor, though the money for the subscriptions had long since been absorbed. The Audit Bureau of Circulations was, after the change in *Guard* ownership, questioning the validity of this contest circulation. Alton Baker was sure his figures would be honored by the ABC; but he received a quick lesson in the inadvisability of contest circulation.[8]

In 1927 Baker had the paper on a strict "paid circulation" policy, well within the standards of the Audit Bureau of Circulations, which permitted brief arrearages.[9]

While the policy may have cost the paper a subscriber from time to time, it also worked to the paper's advantage. Advertisers came to recognize the accuracy of *Guard* figures so that merchants buying space on *Guard* pages knew exactly what they were getting for their money.

Advertising: The Rate Card

Guard records are skimpy in the matter of Alton's parallel tightening up of the paper's advertising structure. The big issue was the paper's institution of a rate card, which we have mentioned in the discussion of the Cleveland *Plain Dealer.* A fixed standard rate for all advertisers was a new experience for Eugene merchants, and some objected strenuously. The chief of these was the McMoran and Washburne department store, then Eugene's leading retail advertiser.[10] Carl Washburne, a power in Eugene, had to all accounts been a beneficiary of preferred rates and was not inclined to take kindly to any loss in his store's position. Washburne, further, was reported to have had at one time an investment interest in the *Guard,* but the corporation records do not show this, either before or after the Baker purchase.

Alton Baker stood firm, despite Washburne's threat to withdraw advertising, and the rate card became an established fact. The result was a surge of confidence in the new management among Eugene stores. Alton Baker, Jr., recalls today that one of the *Register-Guard's* biggest advertisers has had confidence in the paper for 40 years because of Baker's standing up to Washburne.

Another factor here lay in Washburne's preference for the morning field against the evening, and this might have been a greater problem for Baker than the rate question. Elbert Baker's correspondence is filled with emphasis on the superiority, in small cities, of the evening newspaper over the morning as an advertising medium, and that for a city like Eugene Sunday is poorer than morning. The second point could have been a rationalization because of the *Guard's* lack of a Sunday edition. Elbert Baker wrote:

> "I have such absolute confidence in the outcome of the evening paper vs. the morning that I know there can in the long run be but one answer [*Guard* surpassing the *Register*]. I do not think it will take you more than two years. . . . The big thing with Washburne or anyone else is to sell them out and out evening against morning and to prove to them that there is where the real results lie."[11]

Simultaneously in 1928 there was rumor in Eugene that McMoran and Washburne was interested in the *Register*, and Elbert Baker said:

> "It is a very bad thing, both for the big store and for the newspaper, to have the big store an interest in the publication, at least so far as common stock is concerned. . . . The town is much better off, you are much better off, McMoran and Washburne are both better off, each to attend to his own business."[12]

The father advised Alton to keep close watch so that the store did not get an advantage through the *Register*.

Alton was also facing a crisis in actual rates to be charged. Here, however, he delayed for a time in raising rates and worked instead toward a 16-page paper on Fridays, along with more 12-page papers during the week—sizes that seem absurdly small 40 years later. He sought at least a 60 per cent ratio of advertising to news and feature content. Today this ratio has not changed materially, although frequently fat issues of the *Register-Guard* pass 70 per cent in advertising.[13]

With a firm rate structure established, the *Guard* then adopted a Cleveland *Plain Dealer* practice of a cash discount to advertisers who paid by the tenth of each month. This appeared to be the easiest and fairest way to make concessions to all advertisers, and the *Register-Guard* continues to do this, even though many American businesses no longer give cash discounts.[14]

Mechanical Needs: No New Press Yet

Another immediate problem concerned the *Guard's* need for a new press. Within six months after his arrival Alton could see that the equipment the *Guard* then had would not meet future needs, and in October he was considering the purchase of a rebuilt Hoe or Goss press capable of printing 24 pages. Elbert Baker in this instance urged his son to go ahead, one reason being preparation for future growth,[15] and another—status. "It would . . . make a real impression on your community when you got it installed and in operation," the father said.[16] But in this case the son was conservative, for he replied:

> "We are not in too much of a hurry about this press, . . . but it is a problem that we will have to face sooner or later, and all I am trying to do now . . . is to decide when the time is ready for a new press [and] which is the best one to install."[17]

As things developed, with the Depression following, it was many years before the *Guard* had mechanical equipment adequate for its needs. The Willamette Street building that Charles Fisher had bought in 1924 was not big enough for a huge press and the paper had to get along with the rebuilt Duplex tubular one which Alton Baker bought, at the urging of his father, in 1928. The old tubular press was used until 1952, when the *Guard* moved to its present location at Tenth and High. As late as the mid-1940s the *Guard* was getting along with five Linotype machines. Nor was it able to have its own engraving plant for many years. Baker contracted with a Eugene engraver, Herbert Wiltshire, for all cuts carried in the *Guard.* The Wiltshire firm was taken over by the *Register-Guard* in 1961.

"The Other Fellow Is Worried": The Register's Reaction

Then there was the matter of the *Register's* reaction to all these *Guard* maneuvers. It is possible that Baker's sounder business practices worried the *Register* more than anything the *Guard* was doing editorially. Tugman covered the news more aggressively, but the *Guard's* news strength was not immediately apparent; besides, Eugene conservatives were quite satisfied with the *Register's* moderation. Baker probably would have preferred a more typographically conservative *Guard* than Charles Fisher had edited in the early Twenties, but Tugman favored more display and Elbert Baker, too, was urging his son to put out a lively paper. The father liked The Three Sisters logotype when it appeared in 1928 and, as to typography, said:

> "Don't worry too much about being sensational. I don't mean . . . to go to extremes or to do anything that would shock your town, but try at all times to look like an evening paper and look alive."[18]

The father put his son's position in Eugene in metaphor. The *Guard* was in the position of Ulysses S. Grant before Fort Donelson in 1862. Alton, like Grant, was "new to a large command" and was "probably scared stiff." But suddenly it dawned: "This other fellow was as badly scared as he was."[19]

The "other fellow" apparently was scared, for by late 1929 the *Register* moved to meet the *Guard's* pressure by entering the evening field.[20] Despite the *Register's* boastfulness, "offering for the first time in small-city newspaper history on the Pacific Coast an all-day publication service,"[21] it was losing ground to Baker. Its timing for both morning and afternoon editions was inopportune, the economic crash of 1929 coming within a few weeks, while the necessity of carrying United Press service for the afternoon *Register* (the *Guard* held the afternoon Associated Press franchise) further strained the *Register's* resources. In a little more than six months the *Register* dropped its 31-year-old morning edition and tried to compete with the *Guard* back-to-back on the *Guard's* established afternoon ground.

The changeover came April 30 and May 1, 1930. The last *Morning Register*, of April 30, carried the standard single-column headlines that for so many years had been the paper's makeup trademark. There was no announcement that this was the end of the morning paper.[22] On May 1 the *Register* came out with "4 P.M. City Edition" in its page one "ear," along with a banner headline on a wholly un-*Register* kind of story: "Farmer and Wife Die as Blast Demolishes Home," datelined out of Vancouver, Wash., and credited to United Press. A four-column secondary banner was more in *Register* style: "Air Line May Come Here" (today's United Airlines).[23]

It is easy in retrospect to note the trend in Eugene. These *Register* gyrations were merely a prelude to ultimate consolidation. At the time, however, the purchase of one of the papers by the other might have gone either way.

Alton Baker, Jr., today's publisher, was a boy of 11 when the consolidation came, but the problems his father faced had a great impact upon him. Nearly 36 years later Alton, Jr., said in an address in Missouri:

> "In 1930, my father, then 35, and perhaps with more spunk than good sense, purchased the *Morning Register.* [24] How that purchase came about is an interesting story in itself.
>
> "An emissary from the *Register* called on my father one day and asked if he would like to sell the *Guard.* My father, in his blunt way, told the emissary he hadn't come all the way from Cleveland to sell a newspaper. He was here to stay. The next day the emissary was back again and quietly asked my father if he would like to buy the *Register.* He said yes and the transaction was made.
>
> ". . .One of my clearest recollections as a young chap was seeing my father pace the floor at home night after night wondering where the next dollar would come from, not only to pay on the mortgage, but for payroll purposes as well." [25]

In buying the *Register* the *Guard* picked up the opposition's Sunday edition, which it continued. The *Sunday Register* had had a circulation of 7,744. By the time of consolidation the *Guard* had outrun the *Register* in circulation by nearly 500 copies, 8,107 to 7,617.[26] Of the combined circulations (15,724) some 3,000 was immediately lost because of overlapping or for other reasons and in 1931 the *Register-Guard* had 12,741. Sunday circulation, however, jumped nearly 5,000—to 12,668.[27]

Most of the *Register's* value to the *Guard* lay in its good will and in the *Guard's* gaining the Eugene field to itself. (The subsequent competition of the Eugene *Daily News* through most of the 1930s was never a threat to the *Register-Guard's* dominance.) It is probably true that the $244,000 paid for the *Register* was more than the paper was worth, as Elbert Baker had said, but once Alton Baker had ridden out the Depression the ultimate value of the *Register* was clear. Guard Publishing Company records show the specific physical assets acquired, but these were not measurable in great amounts, although the clearing of Associated Press membership in the *Guard's* favor was a distinct gain.[28]

News stories announcing the consolidation in the last issues of the *Guard* and the *Register* of November 17, 1930, were coldly factual and word for word the same. The *Guard's* Tugman continued as managing editor, while Frank Jenkins and Ernest Gilstrap of the *Register* said they planned to remain in Eugene. They moved soon to Klamath Falls and Medford, however. The purchasers promised to "follow scrupuously the ideal of a newspaper as a citizen of its community," and in this Baker never wavered. The "best features" of each paper were to be continued. Then followed a truncated history of the papers, with the *Guard* being erroneously traced back to Alexander Blakely and the *Democratic Herald* of 1859.

One could not tell from this low-key twin announcement what a journalistic power in Oregon was being fashioned.[29]

Tugman set forth the purposes of the combined newspaper on November 23, 1930, in the first of hundreds of editorials in the coming generation to bear his imprint and his influence. Summarized, the goals were:

1. To emphasize news of the Eugene home community and then the world at large, "intelligently, adequately, and impartially." Instructions to reporters would be "to get all the news and to give every person concerned in the news the chance to give his side of the story."

2. To limit to the editorial page and to the editorial columns only the views of the editors. The *Register-Guard* said: "We look upon the custom of editorial comment not merely as a privilege but as a duty. It is our habit to discuss important public matters not dogmatically, insisting that ours is the only possible view, but with the utmost candor, asking nobody to agree with us but only to credit us with sincerity."

Many critics in future years were to dispute this issue of dogmatism, and some few would attribute motive and doubt the *Register-Guard's* candor; but, to note again, the *Register-Guard* always has given its opponents the right to be heard in their disputes with it.

Then Tugman discussed consolidation—in 1967 the still unended trend toward single-newspaper cities. It was in line with efficient operation the country over, he said, a matter hardly to be disputed unless the dispute were over the word *efficient*. Consolidation for the *Register-Guard* carried "increased responsibilities and increased opportunities." The paper would seek to achieve the "ideal which we have set on the masthead—a newspaper which is thoroughly reliable and effective in its news services, which is fearless but not unreasonable in its editorial expression, which is in fact not merely an institution but a friendly trustworthy personality in your home and in your community."[30]

---

1. See Chapter Sixteen.
2. Conversation with Alton Baker, Jr., and Edwin M. Baker, date unknown.
3. *Directory of Newspapers and Periodicals*, Philadelphia: N.W. Ayer & Sons, 1927 and 1928.
4. Undated letter, Elbert to Alton Baker, 1927, urging also that the son go to 6-point type instead of 6-1/2-point to save space on classified advertising. As to population, the exact census figure for Eugene in 1930 was 18,901.
5. Letter, Alton to Elbert Baker, June 15, 1927.
6. *Ibid.*, paraphrase of further details in letter.
7. *Ibid.*
8. *Ibid.*, dated July 15, 1927.
9. *Ibid.*, October 24, 1927.
10. During the 1930s, McMoran and Washburne sold out to the J.C. Penney Company.
11. Letter, Elbert to Alton Baker, March 19, 1928.
12. *Ibid.*
13. Letters, undated, Alton to Elbert and Elbert to Alton Baker, 1928.
14. Elbert and Alton Baker correspondence, including copies of letters to Frank S. Baker of Tacoma, November 11, 1932; on current practice, interview with Edwin M. Baker, 1966.
15. Letter, Elbert to Alton Baker, October 18, 1927.
16. *Ibid.*
17. Letter, Alton to Elbert Baker, October 24, 1927.

18. Letter, Elbert to Alton Baker, March 19, 1928.

19. *Ibid.*

20. Eugene *Register*, "Register Will Inaugurate Afternoon Edition Monday," September 15, 1929. See also pp. 172-177 *supra*.

21. *Ibid.*

22. *Morning Register*, April 30, 1930.

23. *Morning Register*, May 1, 1930.

24. Alton Baker, Jr., *The Newspaper as a Citizen*, address at University of Missouri School of Journalism, Columbia, Mo., May 5, 1966.

25. *Ibid.*

26. *Directory of Newspapers and Periodicals*, Philadelphia: N.W. Ayer & Sons, 1931.

27. *Ibid.*

28. Records of the Guard Publishing Company, November 17, 1930. The *Guard* obtained all *Register* trade names, subscription lists, accounts payable and receivable, all correspondence, newsprint on hand, and paper and ink. All *Register* files and its library, title to advertising and paper contracts, and title to news and syndicate contracts were also included.

29. *Guard* and *Register*, both November 17, 1930.

30. *Register-Guard*, "The *Register-Guard*," November 23, 1930.

CHAPTER 15

The Guard Goes Into Action

The Eugene *Register-Guard* that November day in 1930 had started its 37-year course. The outlines of the course were evident, though, in the nearly four years before consolidation. Even as Baker was struggling with his management problems Tugman was giving editorial impetus. No one should have been surprised at what happened after 1930.

"You Will Like Eugene"

Long before Baker and Tugman were able to make their influence felt through the *Register-Guard*, they had set a tone that expressed strong feelings for the city. It is easy to observe on the surface the paper's continuous editorial effort for municipal betterment, with many of its suggestions resisted by entrenched interests. But there was also an acceptance of Eugene as the *Guard* found it, a recognition that the city was a good place to live in. Tugman put this feeling into words within ten days of his arrival. Rambunctious he would become; yet he had great sensitivity and a capacity to express this sensitivity in words. He liked what he saw. Those whom he met in his first days in Oregon told him, not in a chamber-of-commerce spirit but in a way that he found characteristic of the people, "You will like Eugene."

The comment came from strangers whom the managing editor later would know well, from passengers he met on the train west, and from passers-by on Eugene's streets. So it turned out that one of the strong-willed editor's first editorials was a gentle, literary piece. Tugman wrote:

> "This is a piece by a newcomer for newcomers, primarily, because there are many of them in Eugene, but the

older residents may listen in also, if they have a mind to, because often through the eyes of a newcomer there is a new view of things which have become old. . . . Nothing is left undone to make the newcomer feel he is welcome in the community. There is one expression which epitomizes the friendly spirit of the city.

" 'You will like Eugene.'

"There is a wish and not a boast in this expression as the stranger hears it first. . . . It is said so quietly and followed up with such practical helpfulness in every way that it is absolutely convincing.

"It may have its origin in Eugene's experience as a university town, or it may go back much farther to the pioneers who conceived the city. The fact is, it is there. As Eugene grows, this spirit will be one of its greatest assets. Much can be said of natural advantages and resources. No man can predict how populous or how rich it may become, but greatness is not measured only in census returns and industrial figures. These things are to be desired and they probably will come. And if in the process of physical growth Eugene retains this quality which makes it so desirable as a home city it will indeed have achieved greatness among great cities. . . . We are proud to pass the word on to the new newcomers." [1]

This was from the typewriter of the editor who would in the next 27 years wheedle the town, and bludgeon it, laud it and castigate it, satirize it gently and attack it with cruel irony, win admirers and arouse deep personal enmities. But this early—after ten days—he liked it. He grew to love it. Later, for self-protection perhaps, Tugman's gentleness had to be kept under wraps. But on May 23, 1927, these were the words of the tough Cleveland police reporter who less than a year before had uncovered the corruption of Canton, Ohio, and had helped to solve the murder of a newspaper editor. Tugman worked with Alton Baker and for the newspaper to make the Eugene of the late century finer than even they had found it. Few in Eugene ever knew this part of William M. Tugman.

Tugman had the same feeling for the region. One of the *Register-Guard's* first "major mistakes," on November 25, 1930, a week after consolidation, came in a "typo," a report that "25 inches of snow had fallen" at McCredie Springs, 50 miles up the Willamette River beyond Oakridge. The story should have said five inches, which was not enough to destroy the November-blooming rhododendrons.

A protest came, of course, from resort-minded McCredie, with an accompanying box of rhododendrons to prove the point. The *Register-Guard* was always ready to acknowledge overt errors, and this was its first. With the admission went these words:

> "What a country! . . . We cannot say that we have no winter in this part of Oregon; neither can we say that winter really comes to this part of Oregon. We see it passing by. . . .
>
> "Even in the valleys far back in the mountains rhododendrons are blooming. . . . It grows harder to remember winter as the devastating enemy which sweeps down from Medicine Hat across the Dakotas and over Lake Superior and down through the Soo and on across the St. Lawrence Valley and across the Alleghenies, an enemy that blasts and blackens the countryside. . . .
>
> "We cannot be sorry for the typographical error that brought us the box of winter rhododendrons. . . . It's news in Oregon whenever it gets down to freezing." [2]

These were the light touches. They continued for years to brighten *Register-Guard* pages, for Tugman conceived of *alter-egos* in the form of Ajax McGurk, the philosopher; Adrian and Chrystal Fuddle and their son, Herbert Hoover Fuddle, the beset family of "Mortgage Ridge" (which was perilously close to Tugman's neighborhood); and the Order of the Buggy-Ride, for those who needed to be taken down a bit. The *Register-Guard* and Eugene eventually became too big for these approaches, and at no time could the humorless in town appreciate them.

At the same time, however, a firmer note was evident in the newspaper's columns, long before the *Guard* became the *Register-Guard.*

Politics: Within Six Weeks

If any one factor in *Guard* policy may be said to have caused the greatest reaction to the paper through the years it has been its willingness to voice views on public issues. Call it "politics," if we wish.

From 1927 to 1967 the paper has come forth with a stand upon the occasion of nearly every election: presidential or off-year congressional; the spring primaries that—every fourth year—always make national headlines with New Hampshire's in March, Wisconsin's in April, Oregon's in May, and California's in June; or local special elections on anything from a school budget to an annexation. The candidates and issues discussed and analyzed have run into the hundreds. The letters-to-the editor columns, which the *Register-Guard* calls "The Mail Bag," have run on for pages, and only in the past few years have the editors seriously considered cutting down on contributors in number of letters accepted or in space used. The *Register-Guard* as a result has been a fruitful subject for graduate theses in journalism, some of them provocative, on such subjects as the editorial influence of William M. Tugman, the change in the paper's attitude toward Senator Wayne Morse, and the general influence of the editorial page.

Feelings, of course, often run high. The *Register-Guard* nevertheless has persisted in expressing an independent opinion, for the editors consider this an obligation, part of the "newspaper-as-a-citizen" goal. When on occasion the *Register-Guard* has not offered an opinion it has said that, too; then some readers, perhaps unable to make up their own minds, have charged the *R-G* with being wishy-washy.

One study of the Baker ownership put the start of this election comment as the presidential-year primary of May 18, 1928, the first general primary after Tugman took over as managing editor. Beginning May 14, 1928, the paper carried a series of editorials dealing with the candidates and making recommendations.[3] Actually, the *Guard's* new managing editor was too impatient a man to wait a full year before expressing views on what was good for Eugene, Lane County, and Oregon. The first significant editorial analyzing the election scene came June 18, 1927, five weeks after Tugman's arrival and three and a half months after Baker's. One could hardly blame the City Establishment for resenting the *Guard's* effrontery and considering Tugman a whippersnapper.

At issue that June day in a school election were two positions on the Eugene School Board, with two members seeking re-election against two opponents who charged the sitting members with interfering in the employment and discipline of teachers. Tugman could hardly have made a run-down on school politics in his short time in Eugene, and in fact the editorial was objective and made no outright recommendations.

What was pertinent was the paper's reportorial dissection of the four candidates: the sitting board members being 1) "C.W. Mullen, a middle-aged retired contractor and director of the Bank of Commerce," and 2) "W.F. Reed, a 55-year-old fruit grower and dairyman, father of six children, two of whom were school teachers but for which 'nepotism' he has no apologies"; and the opponents being 1) "Dr. Harry W. Titus, a 33-year-old dentist from an old Eugene family, graduate of the University of Oregon and the Northern Pacific Dental College, a war veteran and father of two," and 2) "Newton Anderson, a newcomer to Eugene, in town two years, the head of a Eugene laundry, with three sons, one a graduate of Eugene high school."

This was a tight, truncated run-down and the *Guard* said, in effect, "Take your pick." It could see only a "rumbling, mumbling undercurrent of criticism rather than a specific campaign of opposition against the incumbents. . . . We have tried merely to outline a reasonable process by which each individual [voter] can reach his own conclusion. . . . There is no community interest more important than the schools. There is no public office where it is so important to have the highest standards of ability and performance." [4]

The dentist, Titus, won over the incumbent contractor and the fruit grower and father of two teachers, Reed, won reelection over the newly arrived laundry operator. Whether the *Guard's* biographical details of dentist versus contractor and father of teachers versus laundryman—there is a status difference—had an influence on the outcome cannot be determined two score years later. Outright endorsements frequently are not necessary. Nevertheless, the approach was new, dynamic, and interesting. People read this kind of election presentation. They would approve of it or disapprove, often depending on what the voting results were, whether those whom readers wanted to win won or lost. In hotly contested elections reader reaction could become intense.

The *Guard*, however, never wavered in telling "who is running and who he is," and "what the issue is." Even critics of the *Guard* have agreed that the voter has been helped. Albert H. Currey, associate editor of the *Register-Guard*, believes that the newspaper today runs more material on candidates and on their views than any newspaper of like size in the country. For a period of days before every election it uses full section-pages to carry biographies, photographs, analyses of issues, and candidates' statements.

The Eugene Auditorium: And Other Matters

On June 28, 1927, within nine days of the school election, Oregon voted in a general referendum involving a state income tax, among a wide set of other issues; and tied in with these were a number of local questions. The most important proposition before Eugene residents was a vote to provide funds for a municipal auditorium.

Here the *Guard* began another new method—joining editorial support or opposition to page one news coverage before the vote. Use of space did not concern the paper, even in the 12-page issues of 1927. So extensive was the state and local referendum coverage from June 21 through June 29 (with analyses of results of the voting on the 28th) that general news had a hard time getting in. For example, on June 22 the *Guard* bannered on page one opposing views on the need for an income tax as expressed by Governor I.L. Patterson, in favor of the state entering this field, and C.C. Chapman, conservative editor of the *Oregon Voter*, in opposition to the tax.[5] Chapman regarded the income tax as a "slap in the face of industry." The Patterson-Chapman income tax series ran at length for three issues. The news display followed acceptance by the governor and the editor of the *Oregon Voter* of the *Guard's* offer to provide space for a three-day discussion of vital Oregon financial problems.

Editorially the *Guard* supported Patterson and the income tax. The tax carried in Lane County, 3,596 to 2,593, but lost statewide 67,039 to 48,745.[6] The income tax issue was referred again in a general election of 1928 and lost a second time, 132,961 to 118,696.[7] Eventually, of course, Oregon joined the income tax states, but not without a struggle; the *Guard* consistently led the pro-tax forces.

Amid all this, on June 27, 1927, one Hugh D'Autremont, a 23-year-old Southern Pacific mail-train robber in Southern Oregon, was found guilty of murder for a crime committed October 11, 1923. A jury recommended life imprisonment. So concerned, however, was the *Guard* with the income tax referendum that the D'Autremont news received only a single-column headline on page one, column two, despite the fact that, historically, the D'Autremont crime remains one of the most notorious in Oregon history. Twin brothers of Hugh, Ray and Roy, also were involved in the killing, in which mail-car workers had been slain.

The income tax story was not the only one played. On June 24 the Eugene auditorium story carried a banner headline when the Oregon Supreme Court held it to be legal to put on the ballot in a special election an initiative to authorize $500,000 in bonds to construct and maintain a public municipal auditorium on or near the University of Oregon campus. Previously a lower court had held that such a bond issue could be voted on only in a general election, not "in the next special election," as the June initiative provided. The *Guard* was overjoyed that the vote would be held June 28. It followed the Supreme Court story on June 27 with a 36-inch editorial on page one, two-column measure across a six-column display: "Build Public Hall for Eugene!" The essence of the paper's argument was that "having such a hall means that Eugene can become known as one of the great meeting places of the world." The $500,000 involved appeared inconsequential.

The auditorium bonds were defeated, 1,735 to 1,540, and the *Guard* lost this first effort to unloose the town's pocketbook. Forty years later, for all its progress otherwise, Eugene still has no municipal auditorium. The best it can do is to schedule concerts in the University's McArthur Court, a basketball pavilion; in the limited South Eugene High School auditorium; or, if a major speaker only is involved (as, for instance, Hubert H. Humphrey on the Vietnam crisis in 1966), to set up a platform outdoors on the football field and hope it doesn't rain. Today a Lane County Auditorium Committee, directed by Jarrold A. Kieffer, assistant to the President of the University of Oregon, is working to raise auditorium funds. The amount now needed is estimated at $3,500,000.

The *Guard* was ahead of its time in 1927. It would be ahead on many issues in the years thereafter.

State income tax and auditorium were only part of the *Guard's* big news and editorial drive during the new management's first few months. These issues were also at stake:

1. The need for $1,250,000 to expand the Eugene Water Board's municipal power plant on the McKenzie River. The paper said: "The problems of cities are not unlike

those of individuals. There come times when cities must look ahead and spend more money under the heading of investment. . . . We believe the return from the power plant expansion will be ample and swift."[8] Power was a more concrete issue with the voters and sale of power was a revenue producer. This issue the people supported, 1,856 to 447.

2. The recall of Lane County Sheriff Frank E. Taylor, submitted when 3,000 names were attached to a recall petition. This was a political vendetta that the *Guard* avoided getting into. The sheriff was saved, 3,749 to 3,575.

3. A general levy of one mill to improve Eugene's street lighting system. The *Guard* was for this, since "1,000-candle-power globes instead of 250s will provide more attractive and safer streets outside the downtown." This passed 1,474 to 1,299.

4. Thirty-year term bonds to build four new wooden bridges across Eugene's Amazon Creek—a winding slough that for years had had bad habits of flooding the city's south and west sides. The *Guard* said "No." It held that wooden bridges would be out of existence within 30 years, while on term bonds interest charges would pile up. Eugene voters agreed with the paper, 1,858 to 955.

5. A proposition to authorize the City Council to sell the City Hall at Eleventh and Willamette Streets preparatory to moving to the city park in a new city-county building. The *Guard* again said, "No." This was not because Eugene didn't need a new city hall but because Eugene Civic Center plans were "too hazy to warrant sale [of the City Hall] now. The plan may have merit some day." Once more the voters agreed and the City Hall sale went down, 1,679 to 859. Eventually the need for a new building was met. Eugene in the 1960s has one of Oregon's most attractive municipal buildings, directly across the street from

a Lane County Court House that has won architectural recognition.

6. A state referendum to repeal Oregon's then constitutional limitation of Negro suffrage. This the *Guard* favored, as did the voters, 69,373 to 41,887, many years before civil rights issues became national matters. Nevertheless, the strong negative vote on a Negro question as recently as 1927 reflected the still strong Southern biases that prevailed in Oregon for many years.

7. A state referendum to close Nestucca Bay (at the Southern boundary of Tillamook County along the North Oregon Coast) to net fishing by professionals. Sportsmen were leading a fight to close this region. The *Guard* advised another negative vote. The State Fish Commission held the closure to be unnecessary, while it would wipe out a 600,000-pound-a-year salmon catch. The *Guard's* argument was that conservationists should work on a statewide basis for controls of commercial fishing and not single out one coastal point. The Nestucca closing carried the state, 53,684 to 47,552; the *Guard's* point of view prevailed in Lane County, 2,492 to 2,341.[9]

The Eugene *Guard's* first venture into election recommendations won surprising support. Its view carried in four of the local issues and failed only in the auditorium referendum. On the income tax and on the fishing issue its stand won in Lane County even though losing in Oregon. On the seventh, the recall, it had no opinion. On Negro suffrage its view carried.

This percentage was better than the *Guard* was frequently to show on measure recommendations in later years. Whatever the results—in 1927 when the paper started its analyses, in 1954 when Bill Tugman left, or in 1967 when the present editors continue this "depth" policy of news and editorial consideration of major measures—the *Register-Guard* has consistently put forth its arguments. It maintains strongly that it tries "not to pontificate . . . but to give the paper's editorial columns the character of a respected citizen in whose opinions others are interested."

Twenty-five years after 1927 Tugman was asked to interpret the influence the newspaper had had in the hundreds of elections in which it had made recommendations. He replied:

> "Our recommendations are never offered as anything more than our own opinions and conclusions and solely for the benefit of those who may consider them helpful. Voting records over many years show that the public very definitely has a mind of its own; there may be cases where the newspaper recommendation 'tips the scales,' but we make no such claims.
>
> "In our opinion the most important thing we do in advance of every election is the FRONT PAGE EXPLANATION OF COMPLEX MEASURES, and the NEWS PAGE ROUNDUP of all candidates with their pictures and statements of their policy or program. The editorial page findings and the final front page summary of these findings are offered mainly as a service to those who may have some confidence in our opinions.
>
> "Never have we tried to pick winners, either as to men or measures. The record is dotted with lost candidates and lost causes. And even in those cases where the voters seem to have followed *Register-Guard* recommendations, we would have to confess that sometimes they haven't turned out too good." [10]

The practice has continued now on the occasion of every election—for 40 years. No contest for office, far or near; no program put to the voters, major or minor, is without *Register-Guard* attention, extensive or limited, whether the paper makes a recommendation or not. Up through 1952, the *Guard* and *Register-Guard* had made 562 recommendations in 699 election contests in the 25 years. It was on the winning side in 199 out of 240 local elections (82.92 per cent) and in 254 out of 322 state and national elections (78.88 per cent). These covered contests for individual public offices and votes for measures. No study of this nature has been made of *Register-Guard* election influence in the past 15 years, 13 of the years being under the editorship of Alton Baker, Jr., and associate editorships of Robert B. Frazier and Albert H. Currey.[11]

In its election coverage the paper eats up columns of space. Currey is probably right in his belief that the *Register-Guard* does a more extensive job along these avenues than any paper of its size.[12]

The results can be noted in the City of Eugene in 1967, even without the auditorium—and that will come, too. The loss of an issue here and an issue there—or of a contest for office—hasn't made too much difference. We shall take up in detail later one of the major civic victories (a zoning fight) and one of the major defeats (proposal for a county manager).

In the general election of 1928 the *Guard* under Baker and Tugman made its first presidential election recommendation. It was for Herbert Hoover over Alfred E. Smith. Through the years it would call itself an "Independent newspaper," but it did lean Republican. Its critics have said that its Republicanism was predetermined. Yet the *Register-Guard* has supported Democrats, and Tugman was on record as saying he later was sorry the paper backed Alfred M. Landon in 1936. The 1928 support of Hoover did, however, mean the end of the *Guard* as a Democratic newspaper, which it still was in 1924 under Paul Kelty. Kelty supported John W. Davis over Calvin Coolidge and the senior Robert M. La Follette.[13]

---

1. The *Guard*, "You Will Like Eugene," May 23, 1927.
2. *Register-Guard*, "Rhododendrons at McCredie," November 23, 1930.
3. Paul Edward Bluemle, *The Effect of the Editorial Recommendations of William M. Tugman in the Eugene Guard and Register-Guard on Voting Results in Lane County, Oregon, in Primary and General Elections During the Years 1928-1952*. Eugene: School of Journalism, University of Oregon unpublished master of arts thesis, June, 1953.
4. The *Guard*, "The School Election," June 18, 1927.

5. *The Oregon Voter,* published in Portland, was a widely organized periodical devoted to analyzing political and economic issues.

6. *Guard,* June 29, 1927, p. 1.

Oregon Blue Book, 1955, p. 282.

7. *Ibid.*

8. *Guard,* "Vote Up the Power Bonds," June 24, 1927, p. 4.

9. *Guard,* June 29, 1927.

Oregon Blue Book, op. cit.

10. Bluemle, *op. cit.*, interview in 1952 with William M. Tugman in which the thesis author quotes the editor, p. 189.

Register-Guard, "Question on Timing of Recommendations," November 5, 1952, p. 14A.

11. Interview with Albert H. Currey, January 13, 1967.

12. *Ibid.*

13. *Register-Guard.*

CHAPTER 16

Zorn-MacPherson: Crisis In 1932

Under a modest headline on page one in a United Press story no longer than five inches the *Register-Guard* reported on May 6, 1932:

MOVING OF U. O. TO
CORVALLIS PROPOSED

The news was out of Salem. It concerned the circulating of 600 initiative petitions calling for 18,000 signatures that proposed to merge the University of Oregon with Oregon State College and to centralize all administration in Corvallis. The initiative would go on the general election ballot in November. University operations in Eugene would be converted into an all-state normal school. Oregon's normal schools in Ashland and La Grande would become junior colleges, while the normal school in Monmouth (20 miles north of Corvallis) would be discontinued and its buildings disposed of.

The University of Oregon Law School, of which Wayne L. Morse was then dean, was to be merged with the Willamette University Law School in Salem. The new Oregon State Board of Higher Education (established in 1929 to unify all college educational administration in place of separate boards of regents) was to continue operating the reorganized institutions. All activities of the Board were to be conducted in a chancellor's office in Corvallis, the chancellor still to be appointed.

Sponsors of the initiative were the Marion County Tax Equalization League, whose president was a Henry Zorn of Aurora. Zorn was supported by Hector MacPherson, member of the Oregon House of Representatives from Linn County. MacPherson had once been a professor of economics at Oregon State College.

These were the simple facts.

That brief item, however, generated a wind that tore Oregon higher education apart. The ensuing quarrel engendered hard feelings that remained open wounds for at least 15 to 20 years. Though the initiative failed at the polls, Eugene and Corvallis took years before they could again have a way of educational life together. A year and a half after that May news story and a year after the defeat of the Zorn-MacPherson initiative a courageously challenging speech by Wayne Morse at a University of Oregon Homecoming brought about the resignation of the president of the Board of Higher Education and public humiliation of the State System's first chancellor, William Jasper Kerr.

Wayne Morse in turn became a mighty campus hero who was to go on to more than 30 years of state and national prominence. The University of Oregon faculty, long whipped and cowed, found heroes in James H. Gilbert, dean of the College of Liberal Arts, and in a host of professors who, despite depression, had the courage to defy political pressure.

The Eugene *Register-Guard* joined the battle. Throwing its full news and editorial strength behind the faculty and alumni and tub-thumping without cessation for months, the newspaper helped to save the University of Oregon for Eugene and eventually to "urge" William Jasper Kerr out of the chancellorship. Thirty-five years later, Wayne Morse, who in 1952 broke violently with the *Register-Guard* over national issues—including his departure from the Republican Party—readily conceded the *Guard's* service in 1932 and 1933. "Tugman [the *Register-Guard*] was a great strength in the University crisis," Morse said. "We couldn't have done what we did without the paper. The support for the University was terrific. We [the faculty] met day after day with Tugman to keep the paper informed on the battle." [1]

The Zorn-MacPherson crisis and the subsequent inter-institutional warfare in Oregon higher education developed, in its nonpolitical phases, out of events leading directly from changes in the education structure in 1929 and from the economic crisis of the Depression. Over-simplified, the issues were "administrative efficiency" and the need to cut educational expenses. Conflict arose out of differing views as to methods, and the issues got all tangled up with entrenched interests and personal motivations.

From the University of Oregon and *Register-Guard* points of view the "arch villain" in the affair Zorn-MacPherson was William Jasper Kerr, for 25 years president of Oregon State College before he became the first chancellor September 7, 1932, by a bare majority of the State Board (4 to 3, with one abstention).[2] In three years of operation before 1932 the Board had run its own executive office in addition to setting educational policy.

The appointment of Kerr as chancellor, within a week after the resignation of Arnold Bennett Hall as president of the University of Oregon, September 1, 1932, was part of the cause of the commotion. While the Zorn-MacPherson initiative was pending and the chancellorship decision still unsettled, it had been understood—with a sort of "gentleman's agreement"—that neither Kerr nor Hall was a candidate for chancellor. Hall, worn by the educational conflicts and personal pressures, had resigned to become director of governmental research for the Brookings Institution in Washington.

If by any chance the Zorn-MacPherson consolidation vote might have passed, Kerr as chancellor of the combined College and University would have carried with him obvious implications that the University of Oregon, transferred from Eugene, would not share equally. If the initiative failed, as it did by a 6 to 1 margin, the University would be dominated by an "enemy" chancellor favoring his own Oregon State. Either way, Kerr as chancellor set up an impossible situation. Not once did the *Register-Guard* hesitate to point this out.[3] Even upon Kerr's appointment the newspaper was unyielding, although under normal circumstances a new appointee enjoys a sort of "honeymoon," however brief. On September 7, the *Register-Guard* wrote:

> "President Hall resigned. The state board, after a few hours of deliberation, announced the appointment of Dr. Kerr as chancellor. The resistance which was roused a month ago, the bitter denunciation of the Kerr campaign vanishes before systematic pressures. Success rewards one of the most adroit sieges ever seen." [The *Register-Guard* believed firmly that Kerr, on the surface neutral as to Zorn-MacPherson, trafficked with the consolidation supporters in order to win the chancellorship.] [4]

These are the outlines of the Zorn-MacPherson struggle, some knowledge of which is necessary in order to understand the depth of feeling in Oregon in 1932 and the *Register-Guard's* involvement. From May until November, day after day, Zorn-MacPherson and the Kerr chancellorship appointment dominated the paper. Franklin D. Roosevelt was nominated for the Presidency and campaigned for his first term in these months. The notorious Thalia Massie rape and murder case (years later the subject of a full-length book), with Clarence Darrow on the scene, was getting headlines out of Honolulu. Clarence W. Spears, the belligerent football coach, was throwing the University of Oregon overboard to coach at the University of Wisconsin. Willis C. Hawley, Eugene's congressman for 20 years, who was co-author of the Smoot-Hawley tariff of 1930, lost his seat in Congress as a depression casualty. Adolf Hitler was agitating his way toward power in Germany.

These events and more were crowding for news space in the summer and fall of 1932. The *Register-Guard* reported them, but not vigorously. It was Zorn-MacPherson and the peril of this initiative to the University of Oregon that ruled the *Register-Guard's* news pages and its editorial columns. What was involved was "the integrity of higher education in the state."

As to the other news of 1932, after all, it was a depression year, pages were few, and something had to give. Bill Tugman, above all others in Oregon journalism, had a crusade, and he never let go. The press as a whole in Oregon opposed the initiative, with a few exceptions, but to Tugman and the *Guard* this was life and death.

The managing editor became so immersed in Zorn-MacPherson that years later he could recite its chronology, chapter and verse, step by step. The University of Oregon won and retained its identity, and for this it owed much to the *Register-Guard.* Such a judgment does not detract at all from the other Oregon newspapers and the help they gave. For only the Corvallis *Gazette-Times* strongly favored the initiative; it must be admitted that in each case, Corvallis and Eugene, local emotional bias was involved.

To the point, therefore, is an account of the major events of the battle.

"Allocation": Looking for Efficiency

Dean James H. Gilbert of Oregon's College of Liberal Arts attributed some of the consolidation agitation to a sharper depression decline in enrollment at Oregon State than at the University of Oregon, in part because of losses among students enrolled in agriculture and in part because of the transfer of business administration instruction to Eugene in a money-saving school-allocation adjustment. Oregon State in 1931-32 lost 29 per cent in enrollment as against the University's loss of 18 per cent, Gilbert recalled.[5]

Along with the State Board's transfer of business administration to Eugene, however, had gone a closing down of major instruction in science at the University and the abolition of the 20-year-old School of Journalism, in addition to the initiative proposal to discontinue the Law School by yielding it to Willamette. The committee on curricula for the State Board of Higher Education had recommended early in 1932 that Oregon journalism students transfer to the University of Washington. In fairness to Oregon State, it should be noted that simultaneously the State Board called also for elimination of lower-division journalism instruction at Corvallis.[6]

This action, even before Zorn-MacPherson, caused the Oregon press to mount a concerted drive to have journalism instruction restored. The *Register-Guard* lent its support, although in this instance the bulk of the campaign was in the hands of the Oregon State Editorial Association. One of the leaders on the association's School of Journalism Committee was Paul R. Kelty, the former *Guard* publisher who in 1932 was editor of the *Oregonian.*[7] The State Board of Higher Education reconsidered its journalism decision and on April 30, 1932, restored the school in Eugene. This news the *Register-Guard* bannered: "School of Journalism Restored." Tugman's account, over his own by-line, quoted C.C. Colt, chairman of the curricula committee:

> " 'Abolition of the journalism school was a serious mistake. The school is an outstanding one of its kind, and it would be a shame to permit the original order [for discontinuance] to stand.' "[8]

The restoration and the use of the word *outstanding* might have had reference to an editorial in the *Register-Guard* almost a month earlier in which the paper had paid tribute to Dean Eric W. Allen upon his completion of 20 years of service to journalism education in Oregon. This editorial said, in part:

> "It [tribute to Dean Allen] was in striking contrast to the decision of the state board that professional training [in journalism] should be curtailed as a 'luxury service.' The newspaper people do NOT regard the University's school as a 'luxury service,' and their tribute to Dean Allen illustrated their viewpoint."[9]

This newspaper pressure in behalf of the journalism school rankled in the minds of some educational administrators for some time. While journalism was restored to Eugene at once, pressure to put science back did not come for some years, nor did Oregon State College get business administration back until much later. It is difficult here to assess the self-interest issues involved in the 1932 conflict, for the state press was a direct party to almost all of it.

The subsequent introduction of the Zorn-MacPherson initiative within a week after the journalism school's victory was likely only a coincidence, but one cannot tell. After all, feelings were beginning to run high on many fronts over the State College versus University curriculum allocations and financial issues. And the policies of the Oregon press at large were being widely attacked by Zorn-MacPherson supporters. Dean Gilbert recalled that the consolidation forces were certain "that the organs of opinion were dominated by 'higher education interests.' "[10] MacPherson was quoted as saying that the Oregon newspapers were dominated by the "higher educational machine" as thoroughly as were the "leading Russian journals by the Soviet government." MacPherson charged that ever since the University School of Journalism was established in 1912 "its services have always been available to newspapers of the state, both large and small." He resented the fact that the school's graduates manned the editorial staffs of the papers (there certainly was considerable truth in this as to the *Register-Guard*) and "these loyal alumni could scarcely be expected to view with complacency a measure which threatened the extinction of the institution where they had received a broad general education combined with superior professional training."

There was no specific reference in the *Register-Guard* to this specific charge by MacPherson as Dean Gilbert recalled it. But the newspaper throughout the summer and fall was completely undeferential to the co-sponsor of the initiative. At times its attitude was scornful of MacPherson and even belittling. Tugman was a master of innuendo, a literary technique he exercised frequently through the years. MacPherson's first name didn't help him, and from time to time the *Register-Guard's* editorials addressed him as "Hector," the "eminent Hector," the "zealous Hector," the "versatile Hector," and the "voluble Hector." One of the first comments, two days after the initiative was proposed, read:

> "The eminent Hector MacPherson seems to think there is something undemocratic in [two great schools]. Every state needs, especially in these trying times of social and industrial change, the two types of thought and leadership [arts and letters at Eugene and technical training at Corvallis], and neither one could be merged with the other without distinct loss to the state."[11]

News stories and editorials in the *Register-Guard* in the following six months make fascinating reading a third of a century later. The *R-G* aimed its most telling attacks against Oregon State's William Jasper Kerr. As early as May 1, five days before the Zorn-MacPherson initiative was announced, the paper had called for appointment of a State System chancellor—"one free of antagonisms and bitterness, one free of bias and prejudice."[12]

The pitch of the editorial was that neither Kerr nor the University's Arnold Bennett Hall could be considered to manage the new State System of Higher Education. The *Register-Guard* called for an informal agreement that the two men voluntarily withdraw themselves from consideration. When four months later Kerr was appointed chancellor after Hall's resignation, all that the *Register-Guard* would say in his favor was that "much will depend on deeds." The paper continued:

> "There is . . . one important point on which definite assurance is needed even from the beginning. That has to do with Dr. Kerr's attitude toward the Zorn bill, which threatens the virtual destruction of the University of Oregon and three fine normal schools. . . . If the Kerr chancellorship is to start with the general confidence it deserves, a frank and positive statement must be forthcoming now. Sixty years of sacrifice have gone into the institution."[13]

The deeds were not forthcoming, at least to the *Guard*, University of Oregon faculty, and Eugene townspeople. Kerr, ostensibly neutral toward the bill, could not be budged into making an outright statement opposing it.

Within two days of Kerr's appointment two members of the State Board who had opposed the chancellor's appointment resigned in protest. One was Albert Burch of Medford, a member since the Board was established in 1929; the other was E.C. Sammons of Portland, a banker, who said flatly he was leaving in protest over the politics involved in the choice of Kerr and in Hall's departure from Eugene. Burch was more oblique: he would "be out of the state in the next few months." There were rumors that others might quit the Board, too, including Mrs. Walter Pierce of La Grande, wife of the former Oregon governor.[14]

The possible crippling of the Board because of the minority's reaction disturbed the *Guard*, which had hoped the other members would stay, since replacements under the existing conditions would be difficult. "No public service is more difficult or thankless," the *Guard* said.[15]

Meanwhile, the newspaper praised the resigned Arnold Bennett Hall highly. Among other accomplishments Hall had: helped to bring the Murray Warner Museum of Oriental Art to Eugene; gained for the University during his presidency $1,500,000 from national foundations; provided for dormitory expansion; buried "any yearnings he had to become chancellor"; and refused to take the Brookings Foundation job until the chancellor issue had been decided.[16]

The Financial Loss of Zorn-MacPherson

Coverage of the Zorn-MacPherson crisis included *Register-Guard* depth analysis of the total political, economic, and social meaning of transferring the University to Corvallis:

1. How a $3,500,000 investment in buildings in Eugene, plus $2,000,000 in general housing and fraternities would

be lost, while Corvallis would have to expand by $6,000,000 to handle a nearly doubled enrollment, while a normal school in Eugene would "rattle around in a University-size plant."

2. How losses to the three normal schools would exceed $1,000,000.

3. How losses among professors, Eugene business establishments, and residents dependent upon the University would reach $10,000,000.

4. How a subscription of $250,000 for a building for the Murray Warner collection ($1,000,000 of it from Eugeneans) would have to be sacrificed.

5. How impossible it would be to shift enrollments of large blocks of students from one section of Oregon to another.

6. How Eugene, Ashland, La Grande, and Monmouth were uniting forces to oppose the merger.

7. How 5,000 Lane County citizens rallied in the Eugene Armory to organize to save the University.

8. How the curricula of the two schools could not be adjusted without disturbing the overall structure of higher education in the state.

And so on—even to the distress of University of Oregon Mothers over the fact that the University might be lost.[17]

The *Register-Guard* made much of Governor Julius Meier's personal opposition to Zorn-MacPherson. (Meier, of the famous Oregon family that had formed Portland's distinguished Meier & Frank Department Store in 1857, had been elected governor in 1930 as an Independent candidate.) The governor called upon history to support the keeping of the University in Eugene. He noted that when the Legislature in the early 1870s located the University in the city it was to remain there "permanently," in return for which "Eugene residents have constructed [buildings] and have contributed to the development of the school.

. . . In my opinion it is incumbent upon the State of Oregon and its people to observe and keep inviolate their agreement."[18]

Statements about the initiative from individuals, apart from the major sponsors in the Marion County Tax Equalization and Reduction League, were negative or noncommittal. From Kerr the only comment the *Register-Guard* could get was that, so far as he knew, the Oregon State College staff had nothing to do with the movement. Kerr insisted that he himself was neutral, but this the *Guard* never did believe.[19] The Oregon State Board of Higher Education said it was opposed to the initiative.[20] Alumni of Oregon State College declined to take an official stand; the Corvallis Chamber of Commerce said it was not supporting the merger.

The *Register-Guard* put pressure on Henry Zorn to disclose who were the proposal's financial supporters (apparently Corvallis business men), but Zorn replied that "he did not care to tell." He said: "The Marion County League is a branch of the State Tax Reduction League." But when the State League was approached its official reply was that it was "too busy with other matters."[21]

The *Guard*, therefore, was never able to reveal specifically who the "moneyed interests" behind the measure were, although its inference was that, besides the Corvallis business men, Portland financial backers were in the picture, as well as "tax-poor people" who saw Zorn-MacPherson as a means of gaining relief, plus others with self-interest motives.[22]

Tugman and MacPherson Meet

In mid-June came a confrontation in Salem between Hector MacPherson and William M. Tugman of the *Guard*. They appeared for their respective sides before a meeting of the Oregon State Grange. Actually this session was loaded against the initiative, for Tugman was joined by State Senator H.C. Wheeler of Pleasant Hill (Lane County) and W.A. Ayres, market master of the Eugene Producers Public Market.

MacPherson, taking an idealist stand, said consolidation would raise Oregon's standards of higher education. He declared:

> "We have neither a university nor a college worthy of the name now. I doubt whether there is one man on either faculty who will come up to the first rate educators."

Then MacPherson attacked higher education public relations, particularly rivalry in journalism. To him the "corralled Oregon State Editorial Association was used to disseminate propaganda for one school or another. . . . Consolidation would eliminate this bad political influence and fight[ing] for control of the press."

Tugman ignored MacPherson's arguments and went affirmatively on the offensive. He repeated economic arguments against merger as previously outlined in the *Register-Guard* and said the State Board of Higher Education needed a trial of more than three years to adjust the state's educational needs within the existing university-college structure.[23]

On June 14 Tugman turned reporter again and covered an appeal to the Oregon Supreme Court on the wording of the ballot measure. One Curtis Ross, a lawyer representing a Clarence W. Keene of Silverton, a taxpayer, said the word *consolidate* in the initiative was mere "bait" to cover up the actual displacing of the University, and that the Zorn bill actually "*creates* new schools [junior colleges, italics added] not now existing," that it put the State Board in Corvallis in a mere geographical transfer from Salem, and that it left the state still with as many campuses as it already had."[24]

Within two days the Supreme Court ruled: the ballot title was "misleading and deceptive." The Court itself rewrote the title and made it read, "Bill *moving* the University of Oregon, normal and law schools, and *establishing* junior colleges" [italics added].[25]

Cloak and Dagger: The Petition 'Theft'

The Supreme Court's action made it necessary for backers of the initiative to start anew on petitions, with 17,888 needed as a minimum to be sure that the measure got on the November ballot. With only three weeks to go—July 7 being the deadline—this was a major matter. But the sponsors rounded up petition circulators, each to be paid 10 cents per name obtained; they succeeded in making the deadline.

This last-minute rallying was not without its comic overtones. Over the July 4 holiday huge boxes of petitions mysteriously disappeared from a Portland office in which they were stored. Initiative supporters accused Eugene opponents of the measure of stealing the petitions, but an investigation revealed the whole operation to be a hoax perpetrated by a watchman (Robert Tallman) who had been hired to guard the signatures and who had reported the "theft" to Portland police.[26] Opponents of Zorn-MacPherson accused petition circulators of deliberately arranging the "theft" because of their inability to secure enough signatures. An effort was made to charge larceny of the petitions by a Cyril Brownell, a perpetrator in collusion with the watchman, but a Portland judge ruled in August that since the whole affair was a fake no crime had been committed.[27]

So the news continued throughout the summer, with repetition of argument following repetition of argument. The *Register-Guard* would not be satisfied, it said, for Zorn-MacPherson to be defeated, which by fall appeared certain. Tugman, using the strongest arguments he could, wanted the initiative to be "snowed," so that an effort like this could "never be made again."[28]

The bill did fail, by a negative majority of 292,486 to 47,275, slightly more than 6 to 1.[29] In Lane and Benton Counties, the two most deeply involved, the vote on the merger of the schools was clearly an indicator of self-interest. Lane opposed Zorn-MacPherson by 23,653 to 638, or 37 to 1; Benton favored it by 5,629 to 1,576, or 3.6 to 1. Benton, however, was the only county among Oregon's 36 to support the bill. Portland's Multnomah voted no, 105,344 to 17,595; Salem's Marion voted no, 16,883 to 3,646; even Albany's Linn, Hector MacPherson's home base, voted no, 7,947 to 1,640. The one county, that although it was negative, to show a strong minority vote for the transfer was Polk, just north of Benton. There the initiative lost by a relatively small margin of 3,210 to 2,653.

The *Register-Guard* has never been a newspaper to crow over a victory, and after the election the subject of Zorn-MacPherson dropped sharply from the news and editorial columns. For that matter, the initiative was voted upon along with the Roosevelt-Hoover presidential contest, and the *Guard* turned its attention finally to other pressing matters. William M. Tugman, however, had amassed an enormous personal file on all phases of the initiative. These papers—letters, documents, and memoranda—he saved through the years and Tugman's files eventually were turned over to the Special Collections Division of the University of Oregon Library. They have not yet been indexed. Tugman before his death in 1961 made a tape-recording of his recollections of the struggle and this material, heavily colored with the editor's own views, is still held in a closed file.

The Initiative Record: Still Undocumented

In 1940, Henry D. Sheldon, former dean of the University of Oregon School of Education, wrote a factual history of the University, but he limited the Zorn-MacPherson episode and its sequels to a few pages.[30] Eight years afterward the issue was still a sensitive one in Eugene and Corvallis. Dean James H. Gilbert reviewed the struggle before the Eugene Knights of the Round Table in 1962 and his address is catalogued in the Oregon Library. It is interesting to observe that, as one closer to the battle on the University's side than was Tugman, Dean Gilbert possibly showed more objectivity in his analysis than did the *Register-Guard's* managing editor.

The affair today has passed pretty much into memory. Most of the leading participants are deceased, although a few, including Dean Gilbert and Wayne Morse, remember the conflict clearly. Until a documented study is made, the *Register-Guard* files and those of other Oregon newspapers will continue to provide the most useful information. The formal documents of the State Board of Higher Education are so stripped of color that, though accurate, they do not reveal the intensity of feeling at the time. Yet the *Register-Guard* was so deeply drawn into the fight that its coverage must be considered with its bias in mind; the same care would have to be shown if the files of the Corvallis *Gazette-Times* were consulted. It is possible also that a present-day history of the University of Oregon would show leanings toward the Eugene side—or even diluted. A history of higher education in Oregon by some neutral scholar might be the one way to get this immense story told, with all its nuances. For example, the question still remains, Who did put up all the money for the initiative?

As an account in newspaper history, the Zorn-MacPherson story's big point is that it gave the *Register-Guard* its first great crusade under Alton Baker's still new ownership and Bill Tugman's editorial direction. Zorn-MacPherson brings to present *Guard* staff members a feeling of pride. This was the way the newspaper fought "when the chips were down." It makes little difference that in 1932 the senior staff members of 1967 were boys or, at best, in their twenties. The case was one of "no holds barred," to save a university for its city and to hold the state to a moral obligation assumed from 1872 to 1876 when the University of Oregon had trouble raising $50,000 to open its doors. True, the people by initiative or the Legislature by statute, as MacPherson said, could put the state university wherever they wanted. Oregon in 1932 wouldn't buy the idea of saving money or of efficiency despite depression.

If Zorn-MacPherson had passed Oregon would have had an entirely different development in higher education. One can even toy with the idea that it would today have a "multiversity" in Corvallis, and it is possible that the junior college idea would have had a testing period many years in advance of its actual start in Oregon in the 1960s. One can even conjecture that, had the initiative won, the single campus in Corvallis by now would have had to be split up into regional campuses anyway, with the state restoring, perhaps, something in Eugene like Oregon State University—Eugene. But all such thoughts are historically hypothetical.

---

1. Interview with U.S. Senator Wayne Morse, Washington, D.C., February 23, 1967.

2. *Register-Guard*, September 7, 1932.

Minutes, Oregon State Board of Higher Education, September, 1932.

3. *Register-Guard*, "Out in the Open, Now! U.O. Can't Accept Kerr as Chancellor," May 11, 1932.

4. *Register-Guard*, "Hall Out; Kerr Goes In," September 7, 1932.

5. James H. Gilbert, *The Crisis of 1932: The Zorn MacPherson Bill.* Unpublished, undated address to Eugene Knights of the Round Table, in University of Oregon Special Collections, p. 3.

6. Turnbull, George S., *Journalists in the Making: A History of the School of Journalism at the University of Oregon.* Eugene, Oregon: University of Oregon School of Journalism, 1965, pp. 44-45.

7. *Ibid.*, p. 45.

8. *Register-Guard*, April 30, 1932, p. 1.

9. *Register-Guard*, "20 Years of Public Service," April 3, 1932.

10. Gilbert, *op. cit.*, p. 22.

MacPherson, Hector, *Oregon Taxpayer; a Monthly Review of Oregon Problems*, Vol. 1-3, No. 6; August, 1932 - June 1934. Albany, Oregon.

11. *Register-Guard*, "Folly Dressed as Reform," May 8, 1932, the paper's first anti-consolidation editorial.

12. *Register-Guard*, "Chancellor Imperative Now," May 1, 1932.

13. *Register-Guard*, "Hall Out, Kerr In," September 7, 1932.

14. *Register-Guard*, "Burch Resigns as Member of Board," September 9, 1932, p. 1; "Sammons Says He Will Quit Board," September 10, 1932, p. 1.

15. *Register-Guard*, "Burch and Sammons Quit," September 11, 1932.

16. *Register-Guard*, "Dr. Hall's Great Service," September 18, 1932.

17. *Register-Guard*, May 8 - June 15, 1932.

18. Letter from Governor Julius Meier to Henry Zorn, June 23, 1932.

19. *Register-Guard*, "Kerr Issues Statement on Merger Plan," June 7, 1932.

20. *Register-Guard*, June 5, 1932.

21. *Register-Guard*, "What's Behind the Initiative?"

22. *Ibid.*

23. *Register-Guard*, "Faculties Are Held Inferior by MacPherson," June 13, 1932.

24. *Register-Guard*, "Attack on Merger Ballot Title Made at Salem," June 14, 1932.

25. *Register-Guard*, "Court Knocks Out Ballot Titles," "Deception is Rebuked," June 15, 1932.

26. Gilbert, *op. cit.*, p. 9. *Register-Guard*, July 4-7, 1932.

27. Gilbert, *op. cit.*, p. 10. *Register-Guard*, August 3 and 6, 1932.

28. *Register-Guard*, "The Zorn Bill Will Fail," September 23, 1932.

29. *Oregon Blue Book*, 1933-34, p. 132.

30. Henry D. Sheldon, *History of the University of Oregon*. Portland, Oregon: Binfords & Mort, 1940.

CHAPTER 17

Crusade Against Kerr—The Initiative's Sequel

For a while after the defeat of the initiative events in Oregon higher education moved along more quietly, but discontent continued to simmer under the surface, particularly on the part of the University of Oregon faculty against Chancellor William Jasper Kerr. Before the election in November, 1932, Kerr had moved from Corvallis to Eugene (as a peace gesture), and early in 1933 the State Board had transferred the chancellor's office there from Salem. On the surface this appeared to be a good way to soothe feelings and to provide Kerr with a better insight into University problems. Kerr requested at the time "that no new presidents be contracted for by the State Board at the college and university [to fill his vacant position caused by his becoming chancellor and the Eugene vacancy caused by Arnold Bennett Hall's resignation] . . . in the interest of economy and because of other conditions." He asked for support of the people of Oregon, of the Board, and of the five Oregon colleges. And he had "no delusions about the task."[1] Much of this the *Register-Guard* reported as far back as September, 1932. And although much of its comment was negative, the paper hoped that his having a home in Eugene "will do much to allay distrust."[2]

Depression problems, however, were not easily alleviated. Sheldon noted how budgetary conditions became worse in 1933, how losses from tax revenues for education dropped nearly $500,000, how enrollment declines cost a $285,148 loss from fees, and how the Oregon Legislature in 1933 diverted more than $50,000 more from educational millage funds to the state general fund. Meanwhile, University of Oregon faculty salaries had been cut from 5 to 30 per cent, vacancies gone unfilled, teaching assistants dropped, and physical repairs neglected. The faculty regarded the chancellor's attitude in handling these problems as authoritarian and imperious. Kerr definitely irritated a faculty that had for years been accustomed to operate under a weak executive rein.

When the faculty feared that Kerr's budget in 1933 would sacrifice teaching quality to administrative efficiency its Advisory Council proposed an alternate budget.[3] The professors felt, further, that Kerr was favoring Oregon State College over the University. In addition, smouldering resentment between staff and chancellor made communications almost impossible.[4]

The situation occasionally drew news coverage, but for the most part remained under the surface until the fall of 1933. Also, in the course of the year, Governor Julius Meier appointed a new president of the State Board of Higher Education, Roscoe Nelson, an idealistic Portland lawyer of high integrity but subject to influence by those in the power circles of higher education. Wayne Morse recalled many years later that one of the first things Kerr did was "to do a job on Nelson" and to win the Board president to his side in the chancellor-faculty row in Eugene. And after the subsequent blowup, Morse said, Nelson admitted that Kerr had succeeded in misleading him.[5]

The Homecoming Speech: Morse's Philippic

The situation exploded at Homecoming, 1933, in an episode that threw Eugene and the University into turmoil, made Morse the faculty's champion—the voice of courage it had been waiting for—and brought the *Register-Guard* once more into the battle on the University's side.

Roscoe Nelson had appeared before University students and faculty in a pre-Homecoming assembly Novemer 2, ostensibly to plead for harmony, but, as Morse says, the Board president had been "primed" by Kerr to make an antagonistic speech.[6] Nelson warned against what he called University "carping and censoriousness," and he attacked "self-anointed Jeremiahs" who were opposing the chancellor. He added:

> "While Xanthippe was doubtless a virtuous housewife, I prefer Mae West. . . . Men of boundless egotism and minds tainted with unsated ambition [are] determined that the unified system adopted by the people [for an administrative chancellorship over all schools] shall not succeed. [They are] sabotaging the efforts of W.J. Kerr, chancellor of higher education."[7]

Nelson said he was in favor of academic freedom, but he declared the taxpayers had a right to place limits on this autonomy. He deplored faculty feuds and a revival of "prejudices" (apparently a reference back to Zorn-MacPherson), and he called *Catalines* "the little coterie which he said was seeking to frustrate these [Kerr's] aims." Then he told the University:

> "Cease to fill the role of a giant Achilles, sulking in his tent above which flies a flag on which are emblazoned 'negation' and 'defeatism.' Peevishness and churlishness are not consonant with sportsmanship and magnanimity."[8]

That afternoon Nelson went to Oregon State College, where in the friendly environment of Corvallis he regaled college students and faculty with a report on the University's transgressions. Nelson said the faculty in Eugene was "being misled by two or three men with inordinate influence who, like the drum in a band, make an immense noise while being empty." He referred to jealousy in Eugene over who should become president of the University of Oregon and he said that, under Kerr, no president of the University or the College should be named. He urged that each have a "representative chairman" to report to the chancellor.

Nelson even went so far as to praise the *Oregon State Barometer*, the College newspaper, for its sense of responsibility and to call the *Oregon Daily Emerald*, the University newspaper, "carping, critical and censorious." The chancellor was "leaning over backward to be fair," was "sincere and honest," and "had left his friends and home of 25 years to give his service to the state at Eugene."[9]

The *Register-Guard* ran these speech reports in full, and while its news objectivity could not be criticized, the contents were themselves inflammatory in Eugene. Wayne Morse, who heard both speeches, is said to have told Professor Orlando John Hollis, later Morse's successor as dean of the Law School, while they were returning from Corvallis: "Orlando, I won't take that."[10] Interviewed in 1967, Morse did not recall the exact words he used, but in substance they represented his reaction to Nelson's speeches.

At the Homecoming alumni luncheon November 4, 1933, with Kerr in attendance, Dean Morse lashed out at Nelson. He was advised by the University of Oregon faculty Advisory Council not to make a dangerous and cutting speech in retaliation (Morse was then only 33 and his academic future at this point in his career was not securely based), and it was not known exactly what the dean would say. Not knowing what the penalty for his response might be, Morse went ahead anyway.

The *Register-Guard* that same afternoon ran the text of Dean Morse's speech in full—29 column inches of it—not a minor feat for a small newspaper to get that much into type on a Saturday football afternoon. Morse, in language that as he showed later in the United States Senate would mark him as a master of invective, castigated Nelson for making "insulting, insinuating, and unfair" attacks upon the faculty of the University of Oregon. He called Nelson "a man who has been duped [by William Jasper Kerr]." He threw back at the State Board president the metaphor *Cataline* and challenged Nelson to name the "faculty *Catalines* and prove a case against them. . . . If he [Nelson] cannot do so, then let him, like the gentleman I know him to be at heart, apologize to the faculty of the University of Oregon and resign from the board."

Morse charged that Nelson, by speaking as he did in Corvallis, had destroyed any effectiveness he might have had as a harmonizer; he asked whether Nelson knew that not once had Kerr cooperated with the faculty or asked it for recommendations on academic problems or policies; he asked whether Nelson knew that the budgets [of Oregon State College and the University] "reeked with partiality for the College"; and he asked whether, if Kerr wanted presidents at Eugene or Corvallis, Nelson would recognize that then the University should have a voice in dealing with the chancellor. Going further, Morse named five downtown business men in Eugene who, he said, "were unjustifiably purporting to speak for this faculty" in peace approaches. He concluded:

> "For too long a time this faculty . . . has suffered encroachments upon its rights. But now Mr. Nelson has declared war on this faculty and the faculty will respond fearlessly. We have stood by and witnessed the selection of a chancellor in a plot so rotten that it stinks to high heaven; . . . politics with all its nefarious practices must be kicked out of higher education." [11]

As an aside in the speech Morse praised the *Oregon Daily Emerald* and the Eugene *Register-Guard* for their support. His words here are of importance, for they represent a peak of cordial relations between William M. Tugman and Wayne Morse. The future Senator's split with Tugman would not come for another 19 years, but one can understand the break better when it is known how close the young Bill Tugman and the young Dean Morse were in 1933. Morse said:

> "I shall not dwell upon his [Nelson's] smarting attack on a downtown editor, supposedly Mr. Tugman, because Bill Tugman needs no defense. During the turmoil in higher education, Tugman has sometimes stood almost alone like a beacon light sending its searching and penetrating rays over the fields of corruption in Oregon's system of higher education." [12]

Nelson Resigns and Morse Is Vindicated

The faculty gave Morse a standing ovation and the dean's speech became a legend in Eugene. Among other things, the faculty opened its meeting to the press, a special consideration that it was not to renew for 34 years. When, after more than a year of badgering by activist students during 1966 and 1967, the University faculty chose to open its doors to newspapers, the occasion was a general meeting on May 3, 1967.[13]

On Monday, November 6, 1933, the faculty unanimously (146 attending) passed a resolution giving full support to Dean Morse and demanding Roscoe Nelson's resignation as chairman of the State Board of Higher Education. The resolution was prepared by C. Valentine Boyer, professor of English, and was joined in by James H. Gilbert, Harvey G. Townsend (philosophy), Henry D. Sheldon, and Morse himself. Dean Gilbert said, "Never in many years has the University faculty exhibited more solidarity of interest and *esprit de corps* than during the past few trying days."[14]

Even before the faculty voted, the *Register-Guard* had come out behind Morse. On the Sunday after the dean's speech it ran an editorial under the heading, "A Challenge Is Accepted," and said:

> "When Roscoe Nelson went out of his way to attack members of the University of Oregon faculty and student body for failure . . . to submit to the stultifying influence of a hostile administration, he challenged the university and its friends to put up or shut up.
>
> "Through Dean Wayne Morse, the university—faculty, students, and friends—has answered that challenge with a ringing cry of battle. The reception given Dean Morse's speech indicated that now there can be no question but that opposition to Dr. Kerr as chancellor . . . is shared by a united faculty and not the grumbling of a carping few, as charged by Mr. Nelson."[15]

Throughout the following week the *Register-Guard* ran news stories and editorials on the aftermath of the Morse speech. On November 8 came a two and one-half column editorial starting double measure on page one and continuing inside, summarizing the whole inter-institutional conflict to days long before Zorn-MacPherson and stressing how, when the University was founded in 1876 "the people of Eugene and Lane County gave what they had to give in cash or farm produce or labor . . . to complete the first building"; how they fought for it through the decades; and how, after the "mistake in the selection of Dr. Kerr was made . . . every effort was made by both townspeople and faculty to achieve harmony." The *Register-Guard* called for any leadership at all that would bring peace.[16]

The same day, November 8, Roscoe Nelson resigned as president of the State Board of Higher Education.[17] And on November 9 came more editorials and a news story, these attacking William Jasper Kerr and calling for his departure as chancellor:

> "There can be NO COMPROMISE with facts as we in the state have learned them by bitter experience. The break with the old regime must be complete. Retirement must meet complete retirement [referring to suggestions that Kerr's face be saved by having him return to the presidency of Oregon State College]. The New Man and the New Deal must not be hampered."[18]

One of the editorials went into the fine points of academic freedom. The point of argument, of course, was related to the Kerr imbroglio, but the particular message was one to be repeated by the *Guard* often through the years. Few newspaper editors were as continually outspoken as William M. Tugman when it came to defending the college professor in his right to liberty of thought and the expression of it. The nub of this editorial was:

> "A university or a college is not like any other business—at least on the teaching side. A great school is an associa-

tion of scholars, men and women of equal intellectual ability and achievement. . . . The president or chancellor should be himself a scholar of sound merit with a grasp of scholarship in all the parallel lines of education. . . . [But] the president or chancellor is NOT the 'Boss' as is the head of a factory. . . . He is an executive surrounded by a staff of experts. . . . He is dealing with people who have the highest sense of professional duty and responsibility. . . .

"That is the principle for which the faculty of the University have risked their bread and butter. It is not trivial. It is valid to vital education. The state is not hiring these highly trained people to be 'yes men.' . . . We pay these faculties to get the benefit of what they know and can do. Politics and expedience cannot be allowed to interfere with getting the best out of them."[19]

We shall see this *Register-Guard* defense of free thought arise again in the Joseph R. McCarthy crisis nearly 20 years later, but it is impossible to catalog all the newspaper's views on the principle. Let there appear any demagogue or petty authoritarian (the second of which the *Register-Guard* was convinced Kerr was) and the newspaper was always ready to declare war. How much the open society of the University of Oregon owed to William M. Tugman and Alton Baker's support can, of course, never be measured. It was enormous. What is also unmeasured is the question of how much the University of Oregon community in future years realized the extent to which journalism helped to make its free atmosphere possible.

Oregon's Press Joins In: Kerr Should Resign

Meanwhile, the Oregon press had cast its collective decision in the Nelson-Kerr conflict. By November 8 at least 11 of the state's dailies, in addition to the *Register-Guard*, had come out for Kerr's departure as well as Nelson's. They included the Bend *Bulletin*, Albany *Democrat-Herald*, Coos Bay *Times*, The Dalles *Chronicle*, *Astorian-Budget* (Astoria), Eugene *Morning News* (the *R-G* competitor started in 1931), Oregon City *Enterprise*, Klamath Falls *Herald*, Pendleton *East Oregonian* and the more prestigious Portland *Oregonian* and Salem *Capital-Journal.* Only the Corvallis *Gazette-Times* stood staunchly by Kerr to attack Wayne Morse. The *Register-Guard* ran the *Gazette-Times* editorial in full.[20]

Sequels to the big Homecoming fight and Wayne Morse's philippic were anti-climactic. Kerr, who had a hard shell and, whatever his faults were, was a man of stiff-necked pride, refused to resign under pressure. Nor was the State Board about to yield to an angry faculty and the crusading *Register-Guard.* Not until after another year and a half did Kerr, then approaching 70, step down from the chancellorship.

In the interval an abortive effort was made to discipline Wayne Morse for insubordination. In December, 1933, a committee of the State Board was named to look into charges against Morse, and the Board's official minutes carry this report. Thereafter, however, the record is blank, for nothing happened. Morse was called to appear at a closed hearing, but he insisted on a public airing of his case, which the Board would not give. Morse flatly refused to come to a closed hearing. The dean recalls that he had a dinner with Willard Marks, Governor Meier's new appointment as president of the Board to succeed Roscoe Nelson, and told Marks about the facts of Kerr's chancellorship and the rights of the faculty in academic affairs.

> "There was no investigation," Morse said. "Any complaint against me had to go from the Board to the public in the first instance."[21]

Further, Morse recalls, he threatened if discharged as dean to open a law office in downtown Eugene and carry on his fight.[22] This proved unnecessary. The dean had won his perilous gamble. There is no way to judge a generation later whether Morse realized he had the strength he did or that he knew both faculty and *Register-Guard* would rally behind him sufficiently to win over Kerr and the power structure. Dean Orlando John Hollis, Morse's successor in the Law School after Morse was elected to the United States Senate in 1944, said he believed the faculty supported his colleague out of sheer conviction.[23] Morse said in 1967 that he had no prior commitments of support, and we have noted above that the Advisory Council had warned him of the danger of making his speech. The *Register-Guard's* handling of the news indicates that developments on November 4 were spontaneous—and for the University and Morse fortuitous.

Kerr, while he held on as chancellor, could not prevent after November, 1933, the appointment of a University of Oregon or an Oregon State College president. This Board decision came about in part because the Eugene chapter of the American Association of University Professors asked for an inquiry into the Oregon situation and the AAUP worked for a "satisfactory settlement." The AAUP criticized the State Board for making the Kerr appointment in the first place.

On January 16, 1934, Professor C. Valentine Boyer became acting president of the University, and in April that year Boyer's position was made permanent. Kerr than agreed to retire as chancellor as soon as a suitable replacement could be found for him.[24]

The *Register-Guard* agreed with the selection of Boyer. Although he had been strongly on the faculty side in the Kerr episode, Boyer had not been as aggressive as Dean James H. Gilbert or Morse. Morse supported Gilbert for the presidency, and there have remained through the years unverified stories that Morse himself wanted the presidency, in 1934 or later. Morse believes that "the downtown group," men whom he had named as "soft" toward Kerr for business reasons, wanted a more moderate president. (Boyer had served in an inter-institutional capacity with the State College in matters of arts and letters in 1932 before the educational conflict broke.) Morse's view is that the "downtown group" argued that Gilbert and he had lost future influence by being too much in the heat of the Kerr battle and that the businessmen "won Tugman and the *Register-Guard* over to support of Boyer." Tugman, Morse said, then took "the downtown line." [25]

Both William M. Tugman and Alton Baker, Sr., are now deceased, so this difference today must remain moot. It is possible, however, that Boyer was picked over Gilbert only after the latter had refused to be considered for the presidency. Any University president would have to serve for a time under Kerr, and Gilbert would not under any conditions "take the presidency if William Jasper Kerr remained as chancellor." [26]

The *Register-Guard's* coverage of the higher education settlement in January, 1934, ran under Tugman's own by-line in a story from Portland. Terms, as recommended by the AAUP, included the State Board's agreeing to name acting presidents of both schools (Professor George W. Peavy, forestry, as president in Corvallis) and to abandon the Morse insubordination inquiry. The Board, agreeing with the AAUP, said that pushing the Morse case was "not conducive of harmony." As for the presidency appointments, Kerr in 1934 was on record in favor of them, a sharp change from his previous views. Tugman reported also that there was agreement with another AAUP recommendation that the two presidents sit in on Board of Higher Education meetings and present faculty views—an arrangement that continues to the present.

Finally, one Board member, B.F. Irvine, was quoted:

> "My God, give us peace for the sake of the young people of Oregon." [27]

Editorially, the *Register-Guard* said:

> "The main point is that a setup has been established which has in it the means of removing the distrust which on all sides has made harmony impossible. In Acting President Boyer the University has a spokesman once more. And he is a man whose splendid scholarship, judicial tempera-

ment, and unquestioned idealism and courage will command confidence everywhere. . . . The chancellor is not shorn of either dignity or rank but he has relief from proceeding alone with many situations which could not help but be embarrassing. Success of the new arrangement is more dependent on GOOD FAITH than on any other factor."[28]

Three months later Kerr's agreement to retire brought from the *Register-Guard* its first kind words for the chancellor in two years. The paper praised him for making good on his promise to depart as soon as a new chancellor could be found, and it added that he would leave with "dignity and honor." Admitting its strong past opposition, the *Register-Guard* yet said it recognized Kerr's quarter-century of service to education. Nevertheless, the paper could not resist a slight criticism when it said that changes in Oregon higher education were mostly in mechanics, that what Oregon still needed was "a man to visualize and vitalize scholarship and research. Faith in these Oregon institutions can be restored completely by leadership and service."[29]

Out of the Board's sessions in 1934 the University of Oregon obtained a 4.25 per cent increase in its next appropriations, $660,803 to $688,850, as against .26 of one per cent for Oregon State College, $953,403 to $955,843. Corvallis was still far ahead in funds, but the feeling of unfairness was lessened. The Music Department in Eugene regained status as a full school, and Fine Arts became a department in the School of Architecture and Fine Arts.[30]

No formal report of the AAUP survey into the Oregon situation was published and Tugman noted editorially that "it is considered likely [results of the inquiry] will lie in the files of the organization."[31] This was essentially accurate, although in May the AAUP Committee on Academic Freedom and Tenure did issue a three-paragraph statement that it believed the way was "now clear in Oregon for the steady development of higher education in the state."[32]

A year later Kerr was succeeded by Frederick M. Hunter, chancellor of the University of Denver. Hunter was elected May 25, 1935, and took up residence in Eugene in September, 1935. Kerr retired to a part-time position as director of marketing in the State System of Higher Education.[33] One can only draw the inference that, for a proud, stubborn man, this must have been a bitter personal defeat.

Boyer's presidency was only partially successful and he resigned in 1937 because of academic and administrative pressures and ill health. His successor was Donald M. Erb, a former University of Oregon economics professor who was then at Stanford. Erb became president March 1, 1938. Under Hunter and Erb the higher education quarrels subsided. Erb among other accomplishments brought back the sciences as major fields of study at the University. He served only five and a half years, dying in office unexpectedly December 23, 1943.

The *Register-Guard* in the years following 1934 recognized the changes for the better that had come on the Eugene campus and it gradually forgot—at least played down—the memories of the past. The paper was particularly fond of Erb, for it saw in him a courage to fight for principles, especially his stand in 1938 that, no matter what the merits of the administrative concept of allocation of fields of specialization between the two major colleges, no true university could exist in Eugene without the restoration of major study in the sciences.

In 1950, when the new University of Oregon Union was opened it was named the Donald M. Erb Memorial Student Union.

How Much Did the Register-Guard Help?

The Zorn-MacPherson conflict, the ensuing Kerr-Nelson-Morse imbroglio, and the long struggle upward after 1934 are in actuality more educational history than newspaper history. But this was *local news* to the *Register-Guard*, news that in impact determined the future of Eugene and all Oregon higher education. The paper's principles demanded that the *R-G* become emotionally involved. One may question the technical merits of Bill Tugman's covering many of the very news stories in which he himself was participating. That, however, was his way. And as Wayne Morse said, the University might not have won without the newspaper's help.

Much has been told and retold orally about the battle, but little has heretofore been published about it. Biased as they are in the University of Oregon's favor, the *Register-Guard* files are still the most readily available source on the story. The 35-year-old columns have their own flavor, something no documented centennial history of the University of Oregon, which may be published in the 1970s, is likely to give.

Newspapers may not always review facts accurately, but they do reveal what things were stirring over a given period. And higher education was stirred in Eugene in the depression 1930s—at least emotionally—as it has never been stirred since, despite the University's and the College's (now Oregon State University's) rise to stature in 1967. It is possible that the Eugene *Register-Guard* never fought that hard again, even in the 1950s when it broke with Wayne Morse, then junior senator, over Morse's change in political parties.

---

1. *Register-Guard*, "Dr. Kerr Takes Over New Duties," September 7, 1932.
2. *Register-Guard*, "Hall Out, Kerr Goes In," September 7, 1932.
3. Henry D. Sheldon, *History of the University of Oregon*. Portland, Oregon: Binfords & Mort, 1940, pp. 268-270.
4. Wayne L. Morse, since 1945 U.S. Senator from Oregon, recalls the leaders on the faculty in opposition to Kerr as Dean Gilbert, John T. Ganoe, history; Arthur B. Stillman, b.a.; Harvey Townsent, philosophy; E.C.A. Lesch, English; Harold R. Crosland, psychology; Charles G. Howard and Orlando Hollis, law, and Henry Sheldon, educator. (Morse interview, February 23, 1967.)
5. Interview with Wayne Morse, Washington, D.C., February 23, 1967.
6. Interview with Morse, February 23, 1967.
7. *Register-Guard*, "Nelson Says Schools Must Have Harmony," November 2, 1933, p. 1.
8. *Ibid.*
9. *Register-Guard*, "Nelson Regales OSC Crowd With Story of Eugene Talk," November 3, 1933, p. 1.
10. A. Robert Smith, *The Tiger in the Senate: A Biography of Wayne Morse*. Garden City: Doubleday & Co., 1962.

11. *Register-Guard*, "Dean Morse Scores Nelson, Kerr: A Challenge to the Faculty," November 4, 1933.
12. *Ibid.*
13. *Register-Guard*, "UO Faculty Approves Ungraded Courses," May 4, 1967, p. 1B.
14. *Register-Guard*, "UO Faculty Asks Nelson To Quit Post," November 6, 1933, p. 1.
15. *Register-Guard*, "A Challenge Is Accepted," November 5, 1933.
16. *Register-Guard*, "The Eugene Situation," November 8, 1933, p. 1.
17. *Register-Guard*, "Nelson Resigns Education Post," November 8, 1933, p. 1.
18. *Register-Guard*, "New Man and New Deal," November 9, 1933.
19. *Register-Guard*, "What Is Academic Freedom?" November 9, 1933.
20. *Register-Guard*, "Kerr Must Go for Good of Schools, Say Editors," November 9, 1933, p. 1.
Register-Guard from Corvallis *Gazette-Times,* "Has the Swell Head," November 8, 1933.
21. Interview with Wayne Morse, Washington, D.C. February 23, 1967.
22. *Ibid.*
23. Interview with Orlando John Hollis, January 18, 1967.
24. Sheldon, *op. cit.*, p. 270.
25. Interview, Morse, February 23, 1967.
26. Interview with James H. Gilbert, March 27, 1967.
27. *Register-Guard*, "First Moves Made Toward School Peace," January 16, 1934, p. 1.
28. *Register-Guard*, "Moving Toward Harmony," January 16, 1934.
29. *Register-Guard*, "Kerr Withdraws With Honor," April 17, 1934.
30. *Register-Guard*, "Higher Education Board Approves Budgets," April 16, 1934, p. 1.
31. *Ibid.*
32. *Bulletin of the AAUP*, "State Institutions of Oregon, a Statement," Vol. 20, (May, 1934), p. 303.
33. Sheldon, *op. cit.*, p. 271.

CHAPTER 18

The Register-Guard And Civic Improvement

As early as June 22, 1929, nearly a year and a half before the *Guard* bought the *Register*, Bill Tugman wrote an editorial on city planning in which he looked ahead to the Eugene of the future. The editorial has several times been republished, and it bears repeating here, for it has meaning nearly 40 years later. It read, in part:

> "A great many now living will see the day when the business district of Eugene will cover twice its present area, but these occasional flurries in development emphasize repeatedly the need for systematic city planning. . . .
>
> "Nothing can stop a good town, but some expensive mistakes such as have penalized other cities can be avoided if we ever get down to business on planning. We talk about pulp mills and rayon industries. Just where would be put a rayon plant so that the destruction of property by its sulphur fumes would not offset its value to the community? A plan prepares a city for these contingencies. Without a plan Eugene is apt to find itself with all kinds of marginal developments plunked down without regard to community considerations." [1]

The changes the *Guard* foresaw in 1929 have come. The downtown area has doubled, as Tugman foresaw, and while all the developments proposed for the city did not always come to pass, Eugene has continued to be a good city to live in, whatever its quadrupling of population and developing industry have brought in problems. It didn't get a rayon plant, but its suburb, Springfield, got a pulp mill of the Weyerhaeuser Timber Company that turns out paper products and releases an effluvia of sulphide stench akin to rotten cabbage. Today's *Register-Guard* covers complaints relating to this relatively mild form of pollution, which is chiefly an aesthetic offense. Readers are kept informed of progress in solving the pollution crisis by a newspaper that has always kept in mind the needs of its area as a unit. This includes city and county and an undefined geographical region that the paper calls the "Emerald Empire."

In the course of 40 years the *Register-Guard* has handled important regional news, frequently with depth analyses, pictures and charts, and, as occasions demanded, with editorial crusades. It has dealt with: airport development, Community Chest, the Red Cross, United Appeal, conservation, drainage, flood control, governmental reform, housing, state highway development, law enforcement, public parks and recreation, milk control, vocational education and community college development, basic school support, taxes and finance, cultural activities, and as far back as the early 1940s postwar planning. It has even emphasized the need for neighborliness to make Eugene a better city.

Rarely is an issue of the *Register-Guard* published that does not cover some news of municipal improvement. At random, on the day the author wrote this chapter, we could find this news of Eugene's area changes and developments:

1. Decision to abandon Wilson Junior High School after 52 years service and to plan for a new building by 1969, along with a recommendation for a new Springfield High School at a cost of $2,500,000.
2. Options to be taken on a half-block of land south of the City Hall in the Civic Center for a future Eugene Water and Electric Board Building.
3. Organization in the Willakenzie area across the Willamette River in North Eugene of a "grass roots" group to fight for preservation of the residential nature of the section.

High Street and Tenth Avenue
The Register-Guard began publishing here in 1952

Inset:
1037-1041 Willamette Street about 1940

4. A plan for a drive to raise $250,000 to expand the McKenzie-Willamette Hospital in Springfield.

5. A recommendation for annexation of a 1,000-acre area in South Springfield as a means of providing fire protection.

The first two entries above filled much of page one and the last three were carried in depth on an open page one section-page in Part 2.[2]

The direction of the *Register-Guard* along these lines was set by Alton Baker and Bill Tugman in their first years in Eugene. Tugman led the paper's public course during his tenure, while Baker directed its private course down more personal avenues. Since their deaths there has been no change in policy.

In 1967, six years after the passing of both publisher and editor, the service of each is memorialized in Oregon in a Boy Scout camp and in a state park. In Baker's memory, the Boy Scouts of America on July 21, 1962, dedicated Camp Alton F. Baker, 170 acress on a wooded peninsula extending into Siltcoos Lake on the Oregon Coast south of Florence in Lane County. In Tugman's memory, on June 6, 1963, the Oregon State Highway Commission dedicated William M. Tugman State Park, a 720-acre tract along Eel Lake adjacent to United States Highway 101 nine miles south of Reedsport on the Douglas-Coos County line.[3]

The *Register-Guard's* dedication to planning and public improvement and welfare has brought it and Eugene into national magazine prominence from time to time. In 1944, a survey of what American cities were offering to returning soldiers after World War II, a reporter for the *Woman's Home Companion* singled out Eugene as "doing a bang-up job" in planning for its future. Quoting a comment in the military service paper *Yank*, the reporter said Eugene was "remarkably short on sweet talk and long on down-to-earth action." Direct credit for the city's foresight went to William M. Tugman of the *Register-Guard*. The *Companion* reported that he, with the Lane County Planning Council, was carrying the responsibility for making the city and county ready to welcome 7,500 returning veterans.[4] The Planning Council, originating as a promotion of the *Register-Guard*, was one of the first of its kind, *Guard* editors say, with many American counties today still not having any centralized plan.

In the tribute to Eugene, the *Companion* writer said:

> "Most of Eugene usually finds an excuse during the week to drop in at the newspaper office and gossip with Bill Tugman. . . . It was he through the *Register-Guard* who was behind a group of 100 small businessmen, farmers, labor leaders, lumbermen, merchants and housewives who were working up a roster of people in service. To them letters were going out inviting them home, asking them what jobs they needed, and suggesting further education at the Eugene Vocational School or the University of Oregon."[5]

Meanwhile, Alton Baker as publisher ran the campaign for subscriptions to erect Eugene's Veterans' Memorial Building at Sixteenth and Willamette Streets, an attractive colonial-type structure that was opened shortly after the war.[6] The *Register-Guard* also supported a Committee for Industrial Mobilization that sought to find out how much local businesses would expand after the war and to learn what local opportunities there would be for employes' individual advancement.[7]

"Lane County is doing its share to build a new and better world," the *Companion* concluded.

The Century Progress Fund:
"To Benefit Eugene and Springfield"

More to the point than this national magazine tribute to the *Register-Guard* was the news on page one, December 26, 1943, of the organization of a non-profit Century Progress Fund, "a perpetual fund" whose purpose was to receive gifts from any person, organization, or corporation for the benefit of the Eugene-Springfield community. The immediate goals at the time of founding were to provide adequate playgrounds and parks and "to clean up the Odd Fellows Cemetery." (The cemetery was a tract of pioneer land about three blocks square that had long been hedged in on three sides by the University of Oregon campus and, on the south, by the busy crosstown East 18th Avenue. The University has for years sought to have the cemetery abandoned and it has frequently been subject to suits to quiet title. Relatives of the deceased, however, have so far succeeded in having the University avoid removal of the graves.) For the most part, sporadic maintenance of the cemetery has been kept up by volunteer workers and other cemetery associations.

The five incorporators of the Century Progress Fund included Alton Baker and William M. Tugman of the *Register-Guard*; Loy W. Rowling, vice president of the First National Bank; Donald R. Husband, prominent Lane County legislator; and Donald M. Erb, president of the University of Oregon. Erb, however, had died December 23, 1943, and his place was taken by Dean Orlando John Hollis, acting president. A motivating force behind this planning fund, apart from civic improvement, was the fact that 1943 closed out a century since wagon trains had come to Oregon and that Eugene and Springfield both would reach a century of settlement between 1946 and 1948.[8]

The *Register-Guard* reported that the Fund was tied in closely with Eugene's post-war planning efforts and that it could be used to bring about many city improvements—"things which elude ordinary county, city, and school district action. At the time the Fund was established, a sergeant reporting for *Yank* was shown its prospectus. He commented: "This is the doggondest community." The *Register-Guard* accepted this as a compliment.[9]

Another of the paper's promotional arguments for the Fund was that it provided an outlet for the man or woman wanting to leave something to the community in which he worked and lived. It was also an outlet for the heavy taxpayer "wanting to keep his money in Eugene," for limited givers having only a few dollars to spare, and (with a typical *Register-Guard* lilt) for the "conscience giver—the gambler who has won." [10]

Brought into the support of the Century Progress Fund were more than a dozen Eugene area institutions: officially the Cities of Eugene and Springfield and the County of Lane; the University of Oregon, the Lane County Bar Association, Lane County Medical Association, Eugene Central Labor Council, both the First National Bank and the United States National Bank, the Eugene Chamber of Commerce, the Eugene School District and the Springfield School District, the Business and Professional Women's Club, and the Fortnightly Club and the Commanders' Council. Interestingly, the Eugene *Register-Guard*, the Fund's motivator, is not on the sponsors' list. [11]

The Fund's Achievement: Eugene's Amazon Park

The Fund's greatest success has been the help it gave in acquiring land and in pushing through the Amazon Park and Playground area. "Without Bill Tugman and the *Register-Guard* as the driving force, this development could not have been accomplished," said Virgil M. Cameron, present treasurer of the Fund and a retired executive of the First National Bank.[12] Amazon Park is a huge tract in South Eugene, once a flood-prone region extending from Pearl Street to Hilyard Street (five blocks) and from East 19th to East 30th Avenues. Bordered today on west and south by Amazon Parkway (Pearl) and a new East 30th artery, it contains within it the grounds of South Eugene High School and Roosevelt Junior High School, a public swimming pool, and extensive still-to-be-developed land.

In addition, the Fund has worked for the new Eugene Public Library at West 13th Avenue and Oliver Street, "Gateway Betterment," and a new auditorium (still unrealized). Eugene's east entrance at Judkin's Point and the north approach to downtown at the Ferry Street Bridge (near the point at which Eugene Skinner's city started in the 1840s) both have been made more attractive through Fund support.

The Century Progress Fund never has held a big cash balance, although much "dedicated money" has flowed through its accounts in more than 23 years. It is not today as active as it once was, for, having supplied momentum, its reward has come in seeing Eugene, Springfield, and the county carry on with their own greater financial resources. But it continues to be an outlet into which any well-motivated Eugenean can direct his money and his energies toward making a better place to live.[13]

Carrying the Message Beyond Eugene

Tugman in these years was frequently carrying the newspaper's community message beyond Eugene. In 1944 he wrote two articles for the *National Municipal Review* on Lane County's activities in preparing for the post-war period and in seeking to meet development problems without outside aid. The *Register-Guard* was always squeamish about relying upon Federal help for what it regarded as purely local activity and responsibility.

The editor's pieces in the municipal affairs magazine were somewhat chauvinistic, being filled with phrases like "Eugene and Lane County are proud of. . . ." That aside, however, Tugman talked about post-war adjustment for men and women in service, of integration of the urban area after the war, of Eugene's advantages in having indistinct social lines ("putting on the dog is not done"), and of Lane County's keeping itself debt-free without big Federal grants.

The *Register-Guard* was proud that—still in depression 1938—Eugene voters had taxed themselves to buy Spencer Butte, when it was being threatened by loggers. The Butte is a 2,000-foot elevation five miles south of downtown and east of Willamette Street. Tugman mentioned the city's voting, also in 1937, of a half-mill levy to cover Eugene's share in a civic stadium; of voting $75,000 in 1939 for a new airport (today's more recently developed Mahlon Sweet Field, capable of jet service, is one of the finest in a city Eugene's size); of providing $25,000 for a swimming pool; and of supporting a surcharge on water bills for sewage disposal. By 1943, Tugman wrote, the city had provided $1,500,000 toward a new high school (delayed, however, for more than 10 years); and in 1944 it followed with $375,000 for sewers.

Then, on May 19, 1944, came Eugene's adoption of the city manager form of government, effective January 1, 1945. A manager form of government was one of the editor's long-time desires although, as we shall see, he failed to gain it for Lane County.

The essence of the editor's two articles praising Eugene's and Lane County's projects lay in these words:

> "In Lane County we are doing exactly what is proposed by the great economists, but with cash, and at home-town level, where the control is or can be largely in the hands of those who pay and, despite the obvious limitations, it might be that Lane County 'has something.' We can only say that this much has been done." [14]

In the second article Tugman continued:

> "Sheer ignorance and inefficiency have probably cost the urban taxpayer of the United States much more than all the political manipulation and graft." (Eugene and Lane County, he noted, fortunately had little of this.) "Many times the question is asked: 'How are you going to get the masses of voters interested in . . . [these] complex facts?' It can be done—by honest and competent public officials and by research bureaus which will dig for facts and by intelligent newspaper reporting. But the presentation must be bold and graphic, visual, down to earth. Too much city hall reporting emphasizes inconsequential sensation or bickering." [15]

For the most part Tugman in the *Register-Guard* had reporters follow this steady course of "intelligent newspaper reporting." However, since in these years the *Guard* was still a small paper, the managing editor had to continue being his own star reporter—and always his own editorial writer. Other than Tugman's editorials few appeared in the *Guard* other than syndicated non-local editorials. These were few, except on occasions when Tugman was out of the city. That the managing editor could be editorial writer, reporter, and participant in civic affairs all at the same time was a mark of his intense ability to concentrate. It is true, of course, that many of the *Register-Guard's* editorials were wordy, but there was seldom time for copy-editing.

On occasion Tugman would become so involved in the editorial direction of the paper that—to opponents of his policies at least—he seemed unfair. While in the news columns or in "The Mailbag" the opposition would get its hearings, Tugman did not hesitate to strike back on the editorial page. Readers frequently could not recognize the difference between news and opinion, however objective Tugman could keep the news columns. As a result, since the *Guard* was "bold and graphic, visual, down to earth" and would not flinch, heated arguments arose. We shall shortly take up a number of these.

Tugman Receives the Amos E. Voorhies Plaque

The *Register-Guard's* city and county programs resulted in 1944 in Bill Tugman's gaining the first of many awards he was to receive—the Amos E. Voorhies plaque presented by the Oregon Newspaper Publishers Association "to honor Oregon editors who have given the most outstanding service to their communities." The award, named in honor of Amos E. Voorhies, for 50 years publisher of the Grants Pass *Courier*, was presented at the annual Press Conference of the University of Oregon School of Journalism. Although Tugman was the seventh recipient of the award, he was for practical purposes the third; the first three honored were historical figures in Oregon journalism, while the fourth was Amos Voorhies himself.[16]

Tugman was the first managing editor to be honored, and the honor to him preceded the Voorhies award to Alton Baker, Sr., who received it in 1955.

The account of the citation recited almost chapter and verse Tugman's municipal affairs activities from the school election editorial in 1927 to his programs for post-war development in 1943. In writing for the *Oregon Historical Quarterly* in 1944 two Oregon journalism professors even included among the managing editor's merits his literary talents as expressed in commentaries of his three hypothetical characters whose observations on Eugene life lightened otherwise heavy news and editorial subject matter. These were the philosopher "Ajax McGurk" and the frequently distraught "Mortgage Ridge" couple, "Adrian and Chrystal Fuddle."[17]

The *Guard's* editorials on improving the community, which in total encompassed all of Oregon, often showed deep, sensitive insights. For years Tugman traveled the state, and while most of the paper's specific campaigns were held to its "Emerald Empire," the editor saw the needs of the whole of Oregon. Here the purview covered conservation and flood control, state parks, highways, protection of wildlife, and restoration of natural beauty spots.

Perhaps nothing shows this overview better than an editorial —really a news report—of nearly 30 years ago. It was written from Hart Mountain, high in the desert country of Lake County, where the state maintains an antelope range. Tugman and more than 100 Oregon conservationists and outdoors lovers frequented the Hart Mountain country annually as members of The Order of the Antelope. Much of the order's annual pilgrimage was devoted to fun, but its real purpose was to assist United States conservation leaders in trying to provide for Oregon what the *Guard* wanted: "the most magnificent wildlife display on the American continent."

On this trip (in 1938) the *Guard* editor was almost poetic. He wrote of the 748-mile trek, round trip, to Hart Mountain, the desert valleys, the bird refuge of Harney and Malheur Lakes (south of Burns in Harney County), and Steens Mountain (also Harney County). The account told of artists and photographers drawing and photographing scenes from "the precipice of Abert Rim, seeing flaming sunsets across 100 miles of ridges and peaks, stalking cinnamon ducks and antelope." Tugman reported how "Professor George Hopkins (University of Oregon School of Music) gave a concert on the starlit mountain top," how "Frederick M. Hunter (chancellor) spent most of the first night trying to pump up the new trick air mattress which declined to comfort his bulk," and how older hands told of pioneer battles with Indians.

And of The Order of the Antelope:

> "A strange brotherhood of men of many sorts who seek annually the sanctuary of wilderness and space. 'No guns, no dogs, no women!' reads its First Law, which wives always debate. . . . We would not reveal secrets, but we like to fancy that this order is something which could not be in any other state." [18]

This appreciation of conservation and natural beauty has deep roots in Oregon, and a quarter of a century later Eugene was publicized in the *New Yorker* for its great support of the "outdoor life," as a place where residents "will choose sleeping bags over beds," and where "camp sites are status symbols," where "no matter how sedentary they [newcomers] appear at first sight, [Eugeneans] put them on skis."

And as the *New Yorker* continued:

> "The people of Eugene are acutely conscious of the never ending struggle between the forces of nature and the forces of free enterprise that, by *their* nature, are incessantly hacking away at the wilderness. . . . We are always

aware for that every tree there is an axe. . . . Every tree that comes down is a part of us and everything we cherish, and unless we keep pounding away at reforestation and re-seeding, pounding away, we'll be finished." [19]

William M. Tugman of the *Register-Guard* had been deceased for two years when this article appeared in the *New Yorker*. He would have been pleased with it, would have felt that the newspaper had a part in making the *New Yorker's* "Notes" newsworthy, and pleased that it was continuing its conservation policies in 1967.

---

1. "Building the City," June 22, 1944, p. 4, quoted in Carl C. Webb and George Turnbull, "The Name of William M. Tugman Added to Honor Roll," *Oregon Historical Quarterly*, Vol. 45 (December, 1944), p. 337.
2. *Register-Guard*, March 28, 1967.
3. *Register-Guard*, July 21, 1962.
Register-Guard, June 6, 1963.
"State Park is Dedicated," *Oregon Publisher*. Vol. 32, (July, 1963), p. 16.
4. Patricia Lochridge, "A Town to Come Home To," *Woman's Home Companion*, Vol. 71, (November, 1944), p. 29.
5. *Ibid.*
6. (Re Veterans' Memorial Building campaign)
7. (Re Committee for Industrial Mobilization)
8. *Register-Guard*, "Century Progress Fund Organized in Eugene and Springfield Area," December 26, 1943.
9. *Register-Guard*, "The Century Progress Fund," December 26, 1943.
10. *Ibid.*
11. *Articles of Incorporation*, Century Progress Fund, from Eugene Chamber of Commerce.
12. Interview with V.M. Cameron, March 30, 1967.
13. Present officers are Vernon Gleaves, Eugene lawyer, president; Virgil Cameron; Kenneth Nielsen, Lane County Commissioner, and Charles Gillilan, U.S. National Bank.
14. William M. Tugman, "By Their Own Boostraps," *National Municipal Review*, Vol. 33, (September, 1944), p. 390.
15. William M. Tugman, "By Their Own Bootstraps," *National Municipal Review*, Vol. 33, (October 1944), p. 460.
16. Harvey W. Scott of the *Oregonian* (1865-1910), named in 1938; Asahel Bush of the Salem *Oregon Statesman* (the pioneer daily of 1851), named in 1939; C.S. Jackson, founder in 1902 of the *Oregon Journal*, named in 1940; Voorhies, in 1941; Dean Eric W. Allen, founder of the U.O. School of Journalism, 1942; and former Governor Charles A. Sprague, *Oregon Statesman*, 1943.

17. Webb, *op. cit.*
18. *Register-Guard*, "Hart Mountain, Malheur Lake," July 27, 1938, p. 4.
19. Philip Hamburger, "Notes for a Gazeteer, XLII—Eugene, Ore." *New Yorker*, Vol. 39, (June 1, 1963), p. 95.

CHAPTER 19

Better Cities Don't Come Easy

Improving Eugene wasn't as easy for the *Register-Guard* as the foregoing recitation of accomplishments makes it appear. Often various interests were hurt by the newspaper's civic proposals—or they thought they would be hurt. Often the *Register-Guard* supported improvements that cost money, and money is something conservative economics groups did not want to spend. Often certain business propositions, economically feasible, would run counter to the paper's sense of overall public interest and it would strongly oppose them.

The result obviously was conflict. And the *Register-Guard* never avoided conflict. Most of the times it met it head-on, sometimes with a vigor that alienated powerful elements among Eugene's "establishment." The one who bore the brunt of the opposition was William M. Tugman. People who did not understand activist newspapers or the publisher-editor relationship seldom vented their opposition to the *Register-Guard* on Alton Baker, little recognizing Baker's implicit support of the *Guard's* editorial policies as Tugman carried them out. To those who opposed the *Guard*, Baker was fine, a responsible publisher; the enemies were Tugman's enemies. The *Register-Guard* in the quarter century after 1927, when it came to the opinions of those who opposed it, was quite opposite most other papers in which blows fell on publishers, while the employed managers were regarded as being "all right."

In its obituary editorial on Tugman in 1961, more than six years after he had left the paper, the *Register-Guard* said:

> "There are so many things that occur to those who knew him and loved him. Not that everybody loved him. He had his foes and he wore them proudly. Among his favorite

> sayings was the simple [one], 'If you haven't got any enemies, you don't deserve any friends.' "[1]

In its many campaigns the *Guard* won some and lost some, and some, as baseball idiom would put it, "were rained out." Nearly 15 years ago Paul E. Bluemle, a University of Oregon graduate student in journalism, made a survey of editorial recommendations of the *Register-Guard* over the years 1928-1952. By the *Register-Guard* the author meant Tugman, although in actuality the managing editor was only the aggressive spokesman of general policy.[2]

The study, while mostly directed toward personal candidacies, took up issues, too. The *Guard* in the quarter century made recommendations in 562 out of 699 contests (80.4 per cent). The paper's recommendations carried the county 453 times (80.6 per cent), and Bluemle concluded that "it is highly improbable any other agency accounted for [this] influence."[3] The paper's effectiveness in supporting or opposing issues decided by initiative or referendum was 3.77 per cent greater than in supporting or opposing candidates; and it was more effective in local than in state and national elections. The student found also that "the discernible part" of the paper's influence had been declining.[4] By 1952, of course, the city had become considerably larger, and the *Register-Guard's* influence in molding opinion conceivably could have fallen off. Or, by 1952, it is possible that the *Register-Guard* had built up a backlog of foes, and their influence would be difficult to put into a statistic.

As to the *Register-Guard's* own attitude toward its views on men and issues, Tugman was quoted as saying:

> "I know that over the years a good many people have told me that they waited for my final front page summary and used it as a voting guide. They say . . . 'I usually vote the way you recommend unless I have some personal reason for doing otherwise.' Some stick them up in the

voting booths. The county clerk has complained. I tell him he just has to tear them down. . . .

"What we try to do is to say, 'Here's a frank, considered judgment on these men and issues. This is a result of our study of these things.' "[5]

That was a lot of recommending in 25 years—and the practice goes on in today's *Register-Guard*, although no statistical study has been made of changes in influence in the years since 1952. Most of the campaigns of long ago are today forgotten anyway, but a few still stand forth, and the longer-resident citizens (many not too old, either) can recall the heat these issues generated. Three detailed accounts will serve to point up the civic-issue battles, while the *Register-Guard vs. Wayne Morse* will point up the personal issue. The issues concerned the Byers zoning controversy of 1948, which the *Guard* won; the county manager conflicts of 1948 and 1952, which it twice lost; and the City Council row over closed meetings (also involving zoning), which it also lost. The struggle with Morse—a love-hate affair covering a generation—can only be called a draw.

The Byers Case

Like so many controversies, the Byers affair arose out of a simple action, in this case the decision of the Eugene City Council (March 22, 1948) to approve a zoning change. By 5 to 3, the Council removed the south side of Franklin Boulevard immediately west of Judkins Point from residential zoning to business. The decision would permit one Henry Byers, a Medford restaurant owner, to construct a drive-in restaurant. His proposition had been pending since January, 1946. Byers had told the Council that 65 per cent of the property owners in the block involved favored his request, and that he had already spent $20,000 in preliminary efforts to get his drive-in. The zoning change would be effective in a month (April 23). If there was to be opposition, then a referendum in November could hold the zoning change in abeyance; 1,200 to 1,500 signatures would be needed for a referendum petition.[6]

The immediate objection was "spot zoning" divorced from general city planning. Previously the Eugene Planning Commission had denied Byers' petition but the Council overruled the commission. More important, however, was that the site for the proposed restaurant lay on Eugene's main exit highway (U.S. 99) at the point where the new freeway was to take off. The question of public interest vs. private interest arose as did that of a traffic hazard.

Even before the Council's vote, the *Register-Guard* had intervened editorially with a big "WHY?" It forecast the granting of Byers' petition, raised the issue of lack of agreement at that time on comprehensive zoning to control traffic safety, and asked,

> "Why is the interest of this individual (or any group in that same area) being put above the interest of all the people?"[7]

The *Guard* noted that "business has rights under zoning, but NOT when they conflict with public safety." It added that Byers had paid a stiff price under a real estate "promise" to get the property zoned for restaurant purposes, and continued:

> "No real estate agent or other individual can make such a pledge. No public body is under any obligation to make good such an outrageous pledge. . . . Great caution is needed in dealing with this problem because what is done now affects long years to come. There is a present traffic count of 20,000 cars per day, 1,750 per hour at peak. And more to come!"[8]

The *Guard* editorial brought a request March 30 for copies of it to all members of the Oregon State Highway Commission, with a comment from the commission's chief counsel that "an abutting property owner has no right, vested or otherwise, in traffic on a highway. . . . This whole thing is a question of private interests as against public welfare, and courts have held that public welfare must come first." [9]

Tugman replied that the editorials were forthcoming, that petitions were in circulation for a referendum on the ordinance, and that, if the referendum carried, "repeal of the Council ordinance will serve as a mandate to the Council and City Planning Commission on all similar problems in the vicnity of a major highway. However, it will be a long hard fight, and we do not want to be over-confident."[10]

The long, hard fight, much of it apart from *Register-Guard* news stories and editorials, followed: A letter from the chairman of the Eugene Chamber of Commerce Highway Committee to the Oregon State Highway Commission to refuse curb cuts to Byers pending the outcome of the referendum;[11] a letter on court procedures to enjoin Eugene from issuing a building permit for the restaurant because of "arbitrary and unreasonable exercise of police power by the City Council"; [12] and, on the other side, ads supporting the zoning for Byers. The Sunday before the referendum the Byers supporters ran a 3-column by 9-inch ad on the issue: "To the Voters of Eugene—The Byers' Story." [13] The ad was paid by Hale G. Thompson, chairman of the "Approve Ordinance No. 9125 [Byers property] Committee."

In the same section, on Page 12, appeared the editorial asking for Eugene to overrule the Council. [14] The *Register-Guard* repeated the charge of "SPECIAL PRIVILEGE" in the zoning, cited again the danger factor, and emphasized how the forthcoming freeway would enhance this, stressed how sharp turns by motorists to enter the drive-in would cause fast-moving drivers heading out of the city to brake too suddenly—with peril of collision; and noted that the U.S. and State Highway Commissions had already put $3,000,000 into improvement on the assumption that there would be a free flow of traffic. The paper retraced three years of negotiations over the highway matter and once more called the Council to account for its "great rush" to accommodate Byers. The editorial concluded:

> "[This] is a fight which concerns all of us, everybody who will ever drive on that place of the highway or any other major arterial in this city."

The editorial emphasized that the issue was "not Mr. Byers," but that of the public welfare.[15]

The final city vote was 4,730 to 3,707 to overrule the Council.[16] The property 19 years later continues to offer no impediment to outbound traffic on the freeway to Roseburg and California, now Interstate 5, with the interchange only a few thousand feet beyond the disputed point of 1948.

Interestingly, the *Register-Guard* found time and space for what in retrospect might appear a side issue in an election that saw Harry Truman defeat Tom Dewey, Senator Guy Cordon reelected to a full Senate term (with *Register-Guard* support) after filling out the late Charles L. McNary's term by appointment; Douglas McKay (later Secretary of Interior) winning the Oregon governorship; Harris Ellsworth of Oregon's Fourth District returning to Congress and a whole slate of minor positions being filled.[17]

The Manager Plan: Lane County Votes 'No'

Lane County today operates under what is known as a Home Rule Charter, a streamlined form of county government. This charter, which was voted November 6, 1962, puts more control into the hands of a board of three elected commissioners, who in turn are responsible to the voters. Except for the county assessor and the sheriff, no other county officials are any longer elected. In effect, the burdensome multiplicity of county offices has been reduced, and thereby much of the pulling and hauling among competing departments has been eliminated. From the point of view of the *Register-Guard*, which supported "home rule," Lane County has now a better method of handling its business than it had for decades under the old system, under which responsibility for county operations was scattered over a dozen offices and where, as the *Guard* saw it, political interests were often paramount.

There are other factors about this election, but they are not consequential at this point in telling the *Register-Guard* story. What the election in 1962 did was to give the paper a measure of victory for a point of view it had expressed 14 and 10 years earlier in different form and which, after two bitter crusades, it had twice lost. Some hard feelings were left as a result of the county campaigns of 1948 and 1952—with Bill Tugman suffering the most. What 1962 seemed to prove, after Tugman's death, was that the paper had been years ahead of the readiness of the voters to follow it.

The circumstances were the *Register Guard's* two efforts to have a county manager form of government established. The paper missed, both times.

The county manager idea of 1948 grew out of long years of philosophical debate in the Oregon Legislature over means of improving antiquated forms of county government. Various charter plans had come up in 1929, 1933, 1939, and 1941, with the Legislature finally submitting one in 1943 for the voters to decide upon in 1944. In that year Oregon passed a provision to permit any county that so wished to set up a charter plan for itself. The *Register-Guard* took up the cause and the issue finally came to a head in 1948.[18]

The *Register-Guard's* view was that county government in Oregon had been unchanged since 1852, that "pull" and not merit marked appointments and operations, that too many departments had grown up without logical grouping of functions, and that "real democracy" was unable to operate. The paper supported creation of a County Board with an elected representative from each of seven Lane districts. The county would have six major departments: finance and assessments, records and elections, public works, health and public welfare, education, and law enforcement. The board would appoint a manager to see that these functions were carried out.[19]

The *Guard's* support of the change drew strong opposition from entrenched political leaders, those who were likely to be displaced, and the paper alienated hundreds of precinct workers in both Democratic and Republican parties who also would be displaced. And as the paper outlined what was wrong it stirred up additional wind. Tugman in editorials pointed out "deplorable conditions" of county roads, with $673,900 scattered in "patch and repair"; charged that assessments were chaotic, that there was no system for proper purchasing in many departments, and that since 1940 some 90,000 acres of county-owned timberland had been sold at a fraction of market value. He attacked the inadequacy of courthouse records, lack of minutes, and "repeated informal meetings," the last an implication of secret sessions.[20]

In the early debate County Judge Clinton Hurd, for years a powerful figure in the county, had agreed that improvements in government could be made. But the *Register-Guard's* arguments angered him, and three days before the vote he came out against the charter proposal. Though the paper had used no names, Hurd said in an open letter that the editorials had become intensely personal, particularly as to "unfair" criticisms on roads, timber sales, and lack of minutes.[21] The judged concluded:

> "The arguments for a County Manager for Lane County have become largely a tirade against things that have been done or supposedly been done by the present County Court. . . . We are still waiting for any definite proof that the change would be any improvement and if the tactics now being used by the proponents [of the charter] are any example of what we can expect under a manager plan, then I have had enough."[22]

The *Register-Guard*, replying to Judge Hurd, granted him his right to his views. It could understand his resentment at articles and editorials displaying county inefficiency; it insisted that the paper was attacking a system, not individuals. The paper emphasized that all who had opposed the manager plan had been given space to state their views. To Hurd, personally, it said:

> "We are proud of the record the *Register-Guard* has made in this campaign, even while regretting that we have had to hurt old friends in the process of giving to the public information to which the public is entitled. We have our job to do, too. We have attacked—and shall continue to attack—a SYSTEM of county government under which it is impossible even for so able a man as Judge Hurd to function as he would like to function, and as he has always functioned in running his own office and his own affairs."[23]

The *Register-Guard* had strong support among many political reform groups in the county, among them the most prominent being Olga (Mrs. V.N.) Freeman, who in later years became county treasurer; William S. Fort, today senior judge of the Lane County Circuit Court; and Stanley Darling, one of Eugene's prominent lawyers. Opponents, however, claimed that arguments for a county manager charter were highly theoretical; that Lane County's government whatever arguments about inefficiency might be, was workable and honest; that the charter plan had not been tried in a sufficient number of places; that the plan would result in political sterility, since "the county is the training ground of politics—a man goes up from county clerk to attorney general, to governor, to United States senator."[24]

The "untried" argument the *Guard* countered by citing seven states in which county manager systems had succeeded (Montana, New York, Tennessee, North Carolina, California, Georgia and Virginia), including such mammoth counties as Los Angeles, Fulton (Atlanta), and Arlington.

Proponents even obliquely dragged Charles A. Sprague, the respected editor of Salem's *Oregon Statesman*, to their side.

Sprague, in most instances, agreed with *Guard* ideas. Their arguments quoted him as saying, "I would not like Marion County to be the guinea pig, but it [the manager plan] might be a good idea." Foes said that "if the plan had any real promise the progressive Sprague would clamor for it in Marion County." [25]

The *Guard* found itself, further, with strange bedfellows, one being Dave Hoover, a farmer of Swisshome (in western Lane County), who was an inveterate letter writer generally opposing whatever William M. Tugman supported and who was ultra-conservative in Republican politics. (Two years later Hoover was to try his hand at defeating Senator Morse, with dismal result.) On the county manager idea, though, Hoover said, "To be painfully honest about it, it hurts me to have to agree with anyone, but I must admit that I am with you on this new County Charter business." To Hoover "good government was not made in a day," Lane County had grown too big for the old system, the old County Court had been too long dominated by Eugene and Springfield, and fears of "dictatorship" made no sense.

How much it hurt Hoover to agree with the *Guard* can be seen in that he still had to bring in extraneous matters not at issue: Tugman was wrong on a sales tax, wrong on support for a new courthouse, wrong on Wayne Morse, and wrong on Harold Stassen—right only on the manager plan. [26]

Lane County voters on May 21 said "No," 9,758 to 5,501 against the charter, or by a 63.9 per cent margin.

Tugman on Sunday asked, "Are We Downhearted?" He answered himself, not quite convincingly, "No-o-o-o!"

The large vote pleased the *Register-Guard*. The short time available to campaign and the lack of general leadership hurt. The charter association that had been formed was urged to hold together to try again in two years. Even those who voted "no" must have admitted county government was unsatisfactory. A great deal of light was thrown in that "there is more interest in county government than in 20 years." Then Tugman rounded up the great battle:

> "Complete home rule in county government is needed. Cities have had it since 1910. The *NON-PARTISAN* election of city officials and judges has long been an accepted blessing. County government remains 'the dark continent of politics.' The people of Lane County have rejected this particular manager plan, but they have not rejected management. On the contrary they are demanding it and must have it. . . ." [27]

As so often happened when Tugman and the *Guard* were crusading, other major news was breaking and fighting for space. During the county charter struggle, Harold Stassen of Minnesota was challenging Thomas E. Dewey for the Republican presidential nomination, with the Oregon primary the battleground. This was the year of the great Dewey-Stassen debate in Portland on the issue of outlawing the Communist Party. Dewey "took" Stassen in the Oregon encounter by standing against coercion of speech and against laws to control the Communists. He went on to win the nomination and the Oregon debate was regarded as one deciding factor.

The *Register-Guard* found enough space to give the Dewey-Stassen debate adequate coverage, though it was too busy on the county scene to send a man to Portland. The paper plumped for Dewey, specifically on the free-speech issue. It found the vigorous Oregon political campaign a healthy one for American political vitality and, though not unkind in its feelings for Stassen, said:

> "We feel that when Harold Stassen let himself be persuaded to depart from his original broad constitutional program for dealing with Communists he revealed 'immaturity.' To our way of thinking, Dewey has the tougher mind, the firmer grasp—and the courage—to lead us through this time of trouble." [28]

Whenever civil liberties became a political issue the *Register-Guard* had its own "tough mind." The free-speech issue was to become bigger in the early 1950s. Joseph R. McCarthy, an unknown in 1948, was never able to frighten this Eugene newspaper. But that is a later story.

Though Tugman had hoped the manager plan would come up again in two years, it wasn't put forward a second time until 1952. In 1950 not enough voters signed petitions to get the issue on the ballot. In retrospect, it appears that the sponsors might have been wiser to have waited longer, for the voters were less ready to accept a county charter in 1952 than in 1948. The defeat on the second round was by more than 2 to 1, or 15,299 "no" to only 6,830 "yes."[29]

Essentially, in organization, the second charter referendum was the same as the first: elected non-partisan board of seven from county geographical districts; the board to have power to hire and discharge the manager; all meetings to be public, with at least one each year in each of the districts; board members to be subject to recall; and centralized purchasing to be established.

Opponents continued to charge that the charter would set up a "dictatorship" and be "un-American." The opposition was led by the Lane County Committee for Democracy, led by Frank Reid, a leading Eugene lawyer and later a circuit judge who on a number of occasions had quarrels with the *Register-Guard.* One of these conflicts, starting in 1956 after Tugman had left the paper, resulted in a libel action, *Reid v. Guard* Publishing Company.

Co-sponsors of the 1952 referendum were a Lane County Charter Citizens Committee headed by George A. Todd, a tax consultant, and the League of Women Voters. Much of the 1952 campaign dealt with the effort to eliminate unecessary elective offices: clerk, treasurer, surveyor, specifically.

The *Guard* was not in the forefront of the charter fight the second time as much as it had been the first. However, it said, in urging passage, "This paper is proud to have supported the plan but hasn't participated as in 1948." Tugman stressed the fact that more leaders were working for it "at the grass roots" and that the movement had got on the ballot again despite obstacles. Then he continued:

> "The trouble in our county government is not in the people who hold these offices, because with a few exceptions most of them are fine men and women who want to do a good job. But they can't do their best under the Mexican army setup." [30]

The record seems to show that even though the *Register-Guard* was not so much in the foreground in 1952, voters seemed to think so. And when it did comment, the "Mexican army" metaphors didn't help its cause. Perhaps Editor Tugman was losing patience with the opposition and resented attacks against himself as a person. Anti-*Guard* feeling was higher in 1952 in any case. One letter to the editor offers a good illustration:

> "Eugene (To the Editor)—In regard to the coming election . . . it is quite evident that the editor (Mr. Tugman) is trying to take over the county as he has everything else. . . . Portland has turned down the city manager plan, and did you note the small editorial the *Register-Guard* had on it? Voters, let's wise up! /S/ C.T. Whitney" [31]

The *Guard's* acceptance of defeat was also less philosophical and Tugman's words more caustic after the second election. Tugman wrote that "the case against bungling and mismanagement and cheap party politics in our county business is NOT closed." He then named Frank Reid and his associates as trying to say reform had been foreclosed. Considering the "screams of dictatorship," the "catchwords," and the fact that "county employes on county time in county vehicles cruised the county to pass out the political appeals," Tugman felt the pro-charter vote to be impressive. Long-time attitudes could not be changed at the last minute, he wrote, and added:

> "Take a lesson from California, [where after] a 30-year struggle only 11 of 58 are charter counties. . . ."
>
> "This paper has been under heavy attack for its advocacy of county reform (and we have always printed these attacks no matter how silly or scurrilous and shall continue to do so.) The only mistake has been in misunderstanding the size of the problem and the cunning of the foe." [32]

Two and a half years later Tugman left the *Register-Guard* to buy his own newspaper in Reedsport, Oregon, and seven years later he died. But, eight and a half years later, the county accepted its home rule charter, different in details from the proposals of 1948 and 1952 but accomplishing under county commissioners and fewer elected officials many of the changes the *Register-Guard* had crusaded for. [33] The charter went into effect January 3, 1963.

In addition to increasing the commissioners' power and reducing elective offices, the home rule charter provided other matters for which Tugman had fought: the regular, open public meetings, and no passage of ordinances without the public being given an opportunity to be heard. Behind it in 1962 were Democrats, Republicans, professional groups, labor leaders, farmers, businessmen and homemakers. [34]

Bill Tugman lost these two big fights. Yet, nine years later his supporter in the county manager fight, William S. Fort, by then a circuit judge, recalled the editor's "courage and conviction" in carrying on for better county government and the "able and inquiring mind" that he brought to bear on the issue. [35] His paper added, "[He] left his mark on everything he touched. And everything he touched was better because he had been there." [36]

1. *Register-Guard*, "William M. Tugman, Man of Parts," May 10, 1961.
2. Paul Edward Bluemle, *The Effect of the Editorial Recommendations of William M. Tugman in the Eugene Guard and Register-Guard on Voting Results in Lane County, Oregon, in Primary and General Elections during the Years 1928-1952.* Unpublished M.A. thesis, University of Oregon School of Journalism, 1953.
3. *Ibid.*, pp. 191-195.
4. *Ibid.*, p. 196.
5. *Ibid.*, pp. 183-184.
6. *Register-Guard*, "Byers Gets Okay on Drive-in Plan," March 23, 1948.
7. *Register-Guard*, "Public Safety Subordinated?" March 19, 1948.
8. *Ibid.*
9. J.M. Devers, chief counsel, Oregon State Highway Commission, to W.M. Tugman, March 30, 1948—Tugman papers, University of Oregon Library.
10. Tugman to Devers, April 1, 1948.
11. J.E. Turnbull to T.H. Banfield, chairman, Oregon State Highway Commission, copy in Tugman correspondence.
12. Ray and Pennington law firm to James Hubbard, 2260 East 15th Avenue. Eugene, an opponent of the ordinance, copy in Tugman files.
13. *Register-Guard*, October 31, 1948.
14. Note: Nearly 20 years later, Hale Thompson, in an interview, December 2, 1966, recalling the *Register-Guard* campaign, said he went to the newspaper and asked—while not disputing the right of the *Guard* to crusade—whether the pro-Byers ad might go in a section other than that of the editorial page. He said he was told it would have to go run-of-the-paper, and that it appeared in the same section as the editorial.
15. *Register-Guard*, "Vote 501 X No! Highway Safety," October 31, 1948, p. 12. "No" on the ballot meant that Byers would be refused his request for zoning change.
16. *Register-Guard*, general election coverage of November 3, 1948.
17. *Ibid.*
18. *Register-Guard*, "County Manager; For and Against—'Yes' Say Proponents of Better Government; 'No,' Say Opponents, It Will Not Work," 4-column major display of Page 1 analyzing all phases of a charter plan before referendum of May 21, 1948.
19. *Register-Guard*, "County Manager Charter," May 19, 1948, and news and editorials May 20, 1948.
20. *Register-Guard*, May 11, 1948—arguments in favor.
21. *Register-Guard*, "County Judge Hurd Changes Sides," May 19, 1948, p. 1
22. *Ibid.*
23. *Register-Guard*, "Our Reply to Judge Hurd," May 20, 1948, p. 10.
24. *Register-Guard*, "Country Manager: For and Against," May 11, 1948.
25. *Ibid.*
26. *Register-Guard*, "Farmer Hoover for County Charter," May 20, 1948, p. 10.
27. *Register-Guard*, "Are We Downhearted?"—May 23, 1948, p. 14.
28. *Register-Guard*, "President—Dewey and Free Speech!" May 17, 1948.
29. *Register-Guard*, May 17, 1952, p. 1.

30. *Register-Guard*, "County Manager Charter—Vote 304 Yes." May 13, 1952, p. 10.

31. *Register-Guard*, letter from C.T. Whitney, May 13, 1952.

32. *Register-Guard*, "County Manager Charter Defeated Again," May 18, 1952, p. 10.

33. *Register-Guard*, "Lane County Voters Accept Home Rule Charter," November 7, 1962, p. 1.

34. *Register-Guard*, "Home Rule Facts and Foolish Figures," November 2, 1962.

State of Oregon Voters' Pamphlet, General Election, Lane County. Compiled by Howell Appling, Jr., November 6, 1962, pp. 53-67.

35. *Register-Guard*, "Words of Tribute Come from Far and Near," May 10, 1961, p. 5A.

36. *Register-Guard*, "William M. Tugman, Man of Parts," May 10, 1961.

CHAPTER 20

The Newspaper And The Senator

From 1933 onward, maybe even before 1933 and the great University of Oregon uproar, the paths of the Eugene *Register-Guard* and Wayne Morse crossed each other. In the beginning the relationship was that of the young dean of law and the newspaper united in joint cause, but after the victory over Chancellor William Jasper Kerr occasional brushes occurred, none serious enough to cause permanent damage. Through Morse's years as dean and, during World War II in government service as public member of the War Labor Board, the future Oregon senator received the *Guard's* praises and its support.

The newspaper supported Morse during his first and second successful campaigns for the Senate, in 1944 and 1950. It must be remembered, of course, for whatever meaning the fact has, that Morse in those races was a Republican. The *Register-Guard's* "blessing," however, faded sharply in 1952, the year Morse broke with the Republicans over the Eisenhower-Stevenson campaign, supported Adlai Stevenson, declared himself an Independent, and later joined the Democrats. After 1952 Morse and the newspaper, if they had not become enemies, had agreed to disagree. In 1956 and 1962 the *Register-Guard* opposed the senator, then a Democrat, even though he faced what many observers regarded as weak Republican opposition. Douglas McKay was no match for Morse in 1956, nor was Sig Unander in 1962.

It is oversimplification, however, to say that the split came in 1952, although one student who studied the whole of the *Guard*-Morse relationship from 1944 to 1959 says that was the year.[1] Before Morse broke with the Republicans in mid-campaign he and the *Register-Guard* had had a bitter quarrel in the spring over the steel crisis of 1952; and off and on for years before the Eisenhower campaign he and the newspaper had had their tense moments. These strains in the first 20 years, before and after Morse became senator, were with William M. Tugman.

The break, though, did come in the last years of Tugman's editorship, and it is Tugman principally whom Morse has not forgiven. Yet, since 1954, with the *Guard* for the most part under Alton Baker, Jr., and the new associate editors, Robert B. Frazier and Albert H. Currey, Morse has not re-established rapport. A sort of "cold war"—polite continuance of agreement to disagree—still remains, though neither *Register-Guard* nor Morse for a long, long time has aired publicly an open difference.

Morse will talk today about the *Register-Guard* without anger. Except for strong feelings against Tugman, which could well be sorrow, and his unwillingness to allow the *Register-Guard's* Washington correspondent, A. Robert Smith, to cover his office, the Senator does not strongly criticize the paper today. His feelings toward it may, perhaps, be more described as general scorn for the press in general than for the *Register-Guard* in particular. As he expressed it early in 1967, "any reporter can come in here at any time—*Register-Guard* included."[2] But he does not mean Smith, and that quarrel with the reporter dates from Smith's book, *The Tiger in the Senate: A Biography of Wayne Morse.*[3] The Smith book was quite apart from the *Register-Guard*, though, as Morse says, Smith leaned on Tugman for much of it, and as Smith says, Morse in many ways cooperated with the *Register-Guard* reporter while he was preparing the book.[4]

So the story of the newspaper and the Senator is a complicated one, of ups and downs, deeply bound in intellectual convictions on both sides in which positive forces collided head-on and in which emotions overflowed. Only a depth analysis of motives and the forces of politics and news could reach far enough down to get at true answers to what happened across 30 years. Nevertheless, the story keeps coming up. No history of the

Guard could ever omit the Morse episodes. Wayne Morse recognized that, and while in reopening the door in 1967 he didn't go into details of the past, the fact is that he does see that the paper has its place in the Eugene scheme of things.

In this newspaper history, the fact that the sources are *Register-Guard* sources may make the account appear unbalanced, but Morse always got his share of space in the paper, though toward the end the editorials were negative. The Senator's critics say he wanted only praise. Yet the *Guard* takes its chances in this history that there is a Morse side.

This, then, is an effort to balance scales.

The Guard (Tugman) and Morse: About the Split

Senator Morse was asked on mid-term election day November 8, 1966, whether in view of the long period of quietude in his relations with the *Register-Guard*—at least no emotional editorial reprimands—his attitudes toward the newspaper had softened. After all, his greatest foe, Tugman, was twelve years departed and the *Register-Guard's* new editors had been more than a decade in service. They didn't support him but, less personal, they didn't bait, either. The Senator paused, said nothing for a good 15 to 30 seconds, and shook his head slowly, side to side. The answer was "No," without the word.

"That's too bad," the interviewer said. "But you're busy today"—(it was the day Republican Governor Mark Hatfield defeated Democrat Robert Duncan for the junior Senate seat vacated by Maurine Neuberger. Hatfield, a dove on the Vietnam issue, had run with Morse's support against the hawkish Duncan, who yielded his House seat to run for the Senate in support of the Johnson administration.) "We can talk about it in Washington in February when you have more time."

Morse then commented, "As far as I am concerned, American journalism can be dispensed with." The Senator, as is frequently the case, couldn't have meant it that literally. He was figuratively attacking press attitudes and policies generally—at the moment Vietnam being the issue in which he and journalism diverged. The *Register-Guard* no longer concerned him. That same night, before a Eugene discussion club, Morse gave a cogent position paper on American constitutional policy, namely, that legally we had no business in Vietnam. He was moderate in tone but firm in argument and hardly mentioned the press—except to use the New York *Times* to buttress part of his points. [5]

Three months later the discussion got down more to the *Register-Guard*, particularly its late editor, Tugman. In this the recollections went back to Zorn-MacPherson. Morse conceded Tugman's great help in the early days, but with the editor's support, he noted, always would come what the Senator regarded as a "needle," sharp innuendo within the praise, never outright support.[6] Evidently this hurt, for the Senator is proud, courageous, blunt, and many have said humorless. There was truth in his observation, however, and *Register-Guard* editorials and Tugman's own correspondence bear this out. Two strong men joined in common purpose in the beginning, worked in uncomfortable harmony for nearly two decades, and then irretrievably broke. Each was sure he was right. Neither yielded anything. The *Guard*, however, could editorially have the last word any time it wanted it, despite the fact that Tugman always permitted Morse his replies in long letters to the editor. Eventually communication ceased. It is restored today only as reported news: when Morse makes headlines in press association reports, when he returns to Eugene, and, of course, when he campaigns. One thing the *Register-Guard* has never done—to refuse him his share of space in its columns. It interviews him, as it did on the occasion of the election in November, 1966. [7]

There is no love. And one who tries to make an intellectual assessment of reasons for what happened treads on perilous ground. But upon Tugman's death, Morse recognized the editor's achievements in his testimonial from Washington: "Oregon has lost a great citizen and the journalistic profession a great leader. I am saddened by Bill Tugman's death."[8] And the *Register-Guard* ran Morse's tribute to Tugman second among more than 25 carried in the side account attached to the obituary. The printed record, one will find, is strangely inconsistent.

Where, then, should the Morse-*Register-Guard* story start, that is, after the University battles were over? As good a point as any to begin is in the pre-primary maneuvering of 1944, when Morse was considering his first race for the Senate. In February a former woman reporter for the *Register-Guard*, then attending the Columbia University School of Journalism, was planning a feature on Morse. She wanted "some facets of his character that an outsider (or an Easterner) wouldn't be able to get, things like his life in Eugene and his horse-raising hobby." [9]

Tugman answered the request March 22, 1944. He suggested that she interview Morse herself, for the "best source would be Wayne L. Morse . . . because he is no blushing violet and I am quite sure that he has kept a complete file of everything that was ever printed anywhere about himself." [10]

This could have been enough, but the editor went further, into rather extensive detail:

> 1. "The *Register-Guard* probably would support Morse for Senator "as preferable to the almost impossible Rufus Holman," but it was not ready to announce this so long before the primary. [Note: Rufus Holman, whom Morse defeated for the nomination in May, was a blundering one-term Senator whom the *Register-Guard* regarded as almost a "total loss."]
>
> 2. "Tugman and Morse were "good friends personally," and the *Register-Guard* had "great respect for his ability," but it had "been necessary" on one or two occasions to cross his path.
>
> 3. Morse built an excellent law school and did a great deal to improve relations between bench and bar.
>
> 4. Tugman referred back more than ten years to the famous "philippic against Kerr" which he called "a brave act," but one marred because Morse went too far by

naming Eugene citizens who would have compromised with Kerr. (We cannot help here but recall Morse's words of 1967 that Tugman's praise always had a "needle.")

5. Morse's work as arbitrator in West Coast shipping conflicts during the war "brought out the best of his legal and judicial talent. . . . His record there and as a member of the War Labor Board is very fine indeed."

6. Tugman also defended Morse against "charges that Wayne is a Communist."

This assessment was a generous one. Yet: "The picture of Wayne L. Morse is not entirely clear. . . . He is human like the rest of us." Then came the editor's doubt about Morse's "emotional" tendencies, criticism of him because "he loses [his] sense of perspective," and a forecast that "he must learn to work patiently with other men [and] then can become a very great senator."[11]

This private judgment of the *Register-Guard's* managing editor, read four of Morse's Senate terms later, reveals insights on Tugman's part, and it shows quite possibly that he hoped Morse in office would fashion a career along Tugman's lines. This was 1944, and as years went on Morse didn't work patiently with other men in the way Tugman had hoped.

By April 18 the *Register-Guard* had decided definitely to support Morse. In a letter to Robert W. Sawyer, publisher of the Bend *Bulletin*, Tugman was less enthusiastic than he had been in writing to the Columbia student. The editor said, "I believe that in the main he is sincere and honest even though lacking in wisdom." Tugman, in summary, seemed more concerned with Holman's ineffectualities than with Morse's possibilities. What cannot be determined, therefore, is what the *Register-Guard* would have done in 1944 if Charles L. McNary (then in his last year as a senior senator—McNary died Feb. 25, 1944) had been running in the primary against Morse.

Morse was nominated over Holman, and in November defeated his weak Democratic opponent, Edgar W. Smith. The question whether the new Senator was honestly a Republican or whether he ran as a Republican only because in 1944 no Democrat could win in Oregon has been debated for a score of years since, but it has no bearing on Morse and the *Register-Guard*. He became the new junior senator, following by a few months Guy Cordon of Roseburg, appointed to fill McNary's vacancy and elected for the short term in the same election as Morse. Cordon and Morse served together for 10 years, with the *Register-Guard* always more conversive with the new senior senator, whose moderate and workmanlike ways in the long run made an easier relationship. Cordon was upset in 1954 by Richard L. Neuberger, by which time Morse and the newspaper had split, Morse was changing parties, and Tugman was himself about to leave his editorship.

But for a long time from 1945 Morse and Tugman were on cordial terms. In 1945, after six months in the Senate, Morse wrote Tugman that he was coming west and "looking forward to chat." The letter was signed "Wayne."[12] In the spring of 1946 the two were exchanging pleasantries on matters as minor as the Senator's receiving the *Register-Guard* regularly in Washington.[13] In the fall, before the election of the famous 80th Congress, Morse was writing Tugman, "I'm still hoping the voters are going to recognize the importance of electing a Republican Congress on November 5." The Senator said he was speaking for William Knowland of California."[14]

The two were working together, too, on vital state and federal matters. Early in 1946 Morse had written Tugman about opposition to flood control as expressed by a group of fish packers. The Senator supported the building of Meridian Dam (on the Willamette River 20 miles above Eugene; since named Lookout Point Dam), for "as between protecting life and property from floods, and running whatever danger may be involved to the fishing industry. . . . I have no hesitancy in saying that I favor the construction of Meridian Dam." Tugman agreed, was sure that engineers could find ways to protect fish life, said fishing interests had been unfair in representation, and praised Morse "for your courageous attitude in this matter."[15]

The editor-Senator correspondence continued to cover a wide range of subjects:

1. Memoranda on Morse's work in aiding grazing service in Oregon.[16]

2. Telegram to Tugman informing the editor of Morse's speech on the budget as it affected Willamette Valley flood control.[17] This was followed by a long wire to the Senator pointing out the vital nature of dam construction immediately and noting some $6,000,000 damage that winter by floods between Eugene and Albany, plus loss of 2,000,000 tons of top soil. This telegram illustrated the gravity with which Tugman and the *Register-Guard* treated flood disaster. Calling on Oregon history, Tugman wired Morse:

> "These floods not like slow-moving floods of Mississippi Valley. Only efficient warning system of Engineers save many lives this time. When and if a Chinook and heavy snow in mountains come together as in 1890 and 1860, crest will be at least six feet higher than this year and loss of life and property will be enormous. Meridian Dam should be built without delay. It will be a race to get Meridian built before major disaster occurs."[18]

The dam was completed in 1954; it now backs up a lake for 10 miles upstream from Lowell toward Oakridge and provides one of Oregon's finest power, recreation, and beauty spots. The *Register-Guard* and the state's volatile Senator each deserved their shares of credit in the achievement.

3. On another matter—humanitarian—the two corresponded, in the *Register-Guard's* effort to get a special Congressional pension for a printer in Bend who had been badly shot up in World War II, was long a prisoner in Germany, and had been unable to get government relief.[19]

4. Their confidences even went so far as for Tugman to write Morse about heavy *Register-Guard* expenses in remodeling its plant and planning for a new building.[20]

The general good-will between newspaper and Senator continued through the 1950 election, when the *Register-Guard* had no difficulty supporting Morse for renomination and re-election. In the 1950 primary, with Morse opposed by the ultra-conservative Dave Hoover, the farmer from western Lane County (Swisshome and Deadwood), the *Register-Guard* in its endorsement said, "It is not Morse who is on trial, but Oregon Republicanism itself." It called him "diligent" and "effective."[21] He was "Our Wayne" in those days—in fact remained "Our Wayne" even after the split. The intimacy of the expression, once the favor implicit in it had faded, perhaps became all the harder for the Senator to stomach. But at the time Morse was "our remarkable junior senator," on his way to "becoming one of Oregon's most memorable political characters," to be compared in the future to William E. Borah of Idaho and Hiram Johnson of California.[22]

It didn't happen. For somehow in all the backing Morse received Tugman had his reservations. He probably expressed them best in a letter in 1947 to a newspaperman in Milwaukie, Oregon, who like the student in 1944 wanted to know more about the Senator. Tugman traced back the friendship for 15 years—again to the University days—but, again, the reservations: Morse's "ability to kid himself . . . especially . . . when he is under the stimulus of his salvation complex"; "Wayne means to stand on dead center . . . upon his judgment and conscience, regardless of reactions to right or left. . . . But he slips into inconsistencies"; the *Register-Guard* would probably support him again in 1950; he would probably continue to be a "gadfly in Congress" since he "won't work with colleagues"; and Morse exercises "a good, healthy, challenging influence on the Republican Party, but, frankly, . . . his efforts to reform that party are rather futile. The New Dealers are probably correct when they insist that Wayne belongs on their side."[23]

Morse sensed this editorial doubt, and the working together couldn't last. As he put it in 1967: He had never had direct disagreements with Alton Baker, the publisher, had worked in harmony with Baker in Rotary and in the First Congregational Church of Eugene and had not been concerned with him on *Register-Guard* policy. But the implication was that Baker gave Tugman too much freedom and might have held a tighter rein on his editor. It is an interesting philosophical point—the publisher being held in higher regard than his employe, unusual in most cases of those who judge newspapers. Would Morse feel that way if the *Register-Guard* had continued to back him after 1952?

The story now changes. However, it wasn't politics but press coverage that set off the division in May, 1952. Morse was still a Republican then.

The split, a violent one that was publicly aired, followed the Senator's criticism of the press nationally for its coverage of the steel strike crisis of April, 1952. President Truman had seized the steel mills on April 8 in order to keep production moving, an action that was subsequently declared unconstitutional by the Supreme Court on June 2. The steel workers then walked out and the nation was subjected to weeks of crisis news on the eve of the 1952 conventions.

Morse took Truman's side in the seizure, on the ground that "there was one question of fact that I considered to be determinative, and that was the question as to whether or not it was true that the peril of the security of our country is such that it is of essential importance to keep steel production flowing."[24] Morse said that Defense Secretary Robert Lovett on the 8th had presented an affidavit of emergency to Truman and that this was the controlling point on which the President acted.

The press, however, didn't satisfy Morse in its limited handling of the Lovett matter, for to the Senator it "failed to present an adequate, fair, and accurate analysis of the economic facts involved in the case, or of the significance of the advice which the military officials, including Secretary Lovett, had given to the President. I waited and waited for the press to live up to what I considered to be its clear journalistic responsibility."[25]

After some six weeks the *Register-Guard* took off on Morse, specifically for his charge that on April 24 the New York *Times*, New York *Herald Tribune*, Washington *Post* and other major newspapers had virtually ignored testimony which Lovett gave that day to the subcommittee of the Senate Labor Committee, of which Morse was a member. The *Register-Guard* said that there was nothing new in Lovett's testimony, since on April 18 he had said essentially the same things before the American Society of Newspaper Editors and been covered thoroughly. "Lovett's committee testimony on April 24 received scant attention . . . simply because it was NOT NEWS," the *Guard* editorial said.

Tugman went to extreme lengths to make the newspaper's point. Morse was having "one of his periodic tantrums"; he was one of the cleverest "special pleaders who ever came down the pike." He had "haunted newspaper offices too many years to be ignorant of the ways of newspaper people and the problems they face in the daily selection of what's newsworthy." The editor questioned the Senator's "intellectual integrity" and said he was stooping to use the weapons of the demagogue. It wasn't that "Wayne loves Truman more but because he loves Taft even less." [Senator Robert A. Taft, Ohio Republican, was at that time a candidate for the GOP presidential nomination.]

Tugman also said:

> "The nation knows that to permit Harry Truman or any other president to declare himself above all law and constitutional safeguards would be an even greater disaster [than a shutdown of steel]. . . .
>
> "We find many who are beginning to wonder if the Morse mind is as open and free as the Senator claims it is.
>
> "This is blunt talk such as we would give the Senator if he sat across the desk. We would tell him that this effort to blame . . . the press is the silliest thing he has ever done, and that's a large statement. . . . Morse has great abilities,

> but he would be a more valuable Senator if he would think more and talk less." [26]

The Senator followed with his long letter of June 20. It was retaliation in kind—"only personal malice could cause you to read such intentions and motivations" into his actions. [The May 26 editorial had been followed by two others on June 9 and 10.] He defended his views on the steel issue and, as noted, cited the press transgressions. He charged that the editor had interpreted his consideration of the Lovett matter as if "you were writing a script in connection with your Very Little Theatre hobby." And he concluded:

> "In view of the bitterness of your editorial attack on this controversy, I think it is best that we just agree to disagree, and on that premise I shall consider the matter a closed incident."

The close was the formal "Very truly yours, Wayne Morse." [27]

The months that followed in summer and fall of 1952 caused the editor-Senator relationship to deteriorate further. Morse was treated unkindly by the Republicans in the convention that chose Dwight Eisenhower—and here the *Register-Guard* agreed that the party had disserved him. But then he jumped to Stevenson, and that didn't help him with the *Register-Guard.* In the fall, when there arose an argument over Morse's motives in first supporting Eisenhower, Tugman on one occasion sent a three-page telegram to A. Robert Smith, the correspondent in Washington, asking whether the reporter's coverage of certain Morse activities was accurate. Smith stood firm. So many years later the details are unimportant.

The old rapport never could return. Morse's dealings in Washington with Smith were rocky, and they culminated in 1962 in his anger over Smith's biography. Smith holds that he always sought only to be a good reporter, and that on one occasion, after having been barred by the Senator because of his handling of the row over Morse's committee assignments while the Senator was an Independent, relations were re-established. Morse, said Smith, didn't require a stenographer, as the reporter had suggested.[28]

In 1956, when Morse as a Democrat ran for his third term, the *Register-Guard* strongly supported Douglas McKay, former governor of Oregon and Dwight Eisenhower's Secretary of the Interior, who made the Senate race because the administration wanted and needed a Republican supporter in the Senate. McKay, despite Eisenhower's backing, never had a chance, though in its circulation area the *Guard* did its best to point to his accomplishments and to Morse's "ego-centric" deficiencies. McKay, it said, was the victim of a "smear campaign," although he had been instrumental as Interior Secretary in improving and expanding national parks and in meeting the recreational demands of the West's expanding population. He had added nine new wildlife refuges, done much as governor to keep Oregon's Rogue River and McKenzie River beautiful, and earlier in his career as mayor of Salem helped to develop his home town. Quoting former Governor Charles Sprague, the *Guard* said, "McKay can't pose."

Of Morse, the paper noted that he had been in "three parties" —as a Republican slamming Democrats, as a Democrat slamming Republicans, and as an Independent slamming both. "We believe he stands for Morse above all else," the *Guard* continued.

Although Tugman was gone in 1956 and the younger editors of the *Register-Guard* were more moderate toward Morse than Tugman had been in 1952 during the split, some of the Tugman force came through. The *Guard* called on Morse's junior colleague, elected in 1954 (Democrat Richard L. Neuberger), for a picture of Morse before the Senator became a Democrat.

> "'This lean man . . . has reduced to an exact science the technique of leading a political double life. No Parisian roue ever dashed more expertly between boudoir and counting house than does Morse between the dinners of the

ADA (Americans for Democratic Action) and the annual banquets of the West Coast Lumbermen's Association.' "[29]

The words, without Tugman's bite, were still strong, but by 1956 Democrat Morse was anathema. Still, the former editor's depth of anger didn't come through. When the 1956 returns were in and Eisenhower had carried Oregon while Morse had defeated McKay, the younger editors could see the irony of Oregon's inconsistency. How could Oregon be so strong for the President and also back one of his most bitter enemies? The paper gave the Senator his due, without Bill Tugman's innuendo: "We assume that the Senator is having himself a good laugh at the Oregon press, this newspaper among them."[30] The old supporter-turned-opponent, Tugman, would probably not have taken it that way.

Six years more passed and in 1962 Morse was up a fourth time, his opponent now being Republican Sig Unander, Oregon state treasurer. Morse won again. This time the *Register-Guard* agreed that Morse was "still the champ" and that he won partly because of "Morse's own dynamic political appeal" and partly "because of the list of candidates Morse has defeated. There hasn't been a first-rate candidate among them. We say this with all respect to Sig Unander, a decent guy who fought a good fight and a clean one."[31]

Then, again with balance, the *Guard* left the Morse issue and asserted that the Republican Party in 1962 was the cause of its own troubles. Where it had run appealing liberal candidates it had won; where it had put up "Old Guard" people, it had lost. Mark Hatfield, for example, had been re-elected governor in Oregon, Nelson Rockefeller re-elected in New York, and George Romney elected in Michigan. The Oregon Republicans "muffed it," the paper said, as they had in 1956 with McKay, while the strong candidates who might have beaten Morse "were starved by the people who hold the GOP purse strings."[32]

By 1962 a full 30 years had passed since the tableaux of *Register-Guard* and Wayne Morse had opened. Trying to judge all the scenes, as we noted in beginning this chapter, is impossible. Perhaps, limiting the case to Tugman as editor and Morse as Senator, one could say that the two were in many ways alike, each convinced of the righteousness of his views, whatever they were at a given time. Over Zorn-MacPherson they were together, and in the Kerr episode, and over flood control, and in other joint enterprises. It is interesting, too, that Tugman became irreconcilable when in 1952 Morse dared—bluntly—to reprove the press. Tugman had been a bulldog, too, in Canton when the press was imperiled by the killing of Don Mellett, and that was long before he knew Morse. As for Morse, a rhetorical question can be asked: How can a political leader expect support when he changes parties? It could be, too, that Morse could not forgive Tugman's ever-present "needle."

The relations between the Senator and the newspapers have extended among the other major dailies of Oregon, and Robert Whipple's study included, besides the *Register-Guard*, the *Oregonian*, *Oregon Journal*, *Oregon Statesman* and Salem *Capital-Journal*. But those with the *Register-Guard* are most significant because Eugene is the Senator's home city. The story, in sum, is one of those out of which journalistic history is etched. There have been many others on wider canvases—Horace Greeley and the New York *Tribune* vs. William H. Seward and Col. R.R. McCormick and the Chicago *Tribune* vs. Franklin D. Roosevelt. On a bigger scale Morse and the *Register-Guard* would make the general histories of journalism.

---

1. Robert Blaine Whipple, *The Change and Development of Editorial Attitudes of Selected Oregon Daily Newspapers Toward Senator Morse*. Unpublished M.S. thesis, University of Oregon School of Journalism, 1959.

Morse and *Register-Guard*, pp. 7-86. Salem *Capital-Journal*, Oregon *Statesman*, *Oregonian*, and Oregon *Daily Journal*.

2. Interview, February 23, 1967, with Senator Morse in Washington, D.C.
3. A. Robert Smith, *The Tiger in the Senate: A Biography of Wayne Morse*, Garden City: Doubleday & Co., 1962.
4. Interview with A. Robert Smith, Washington, D.C., February 24, 1967.
5. Interview with Wayne Morse, November 8, 1966.
6. Interview with Wayne Morse, February 23, 1967.

7. *Register-Guard*, interview by Ron Abell, December 21, 1966.
8. *Register-Guard*, "Words of Tribute to Former Editor Come from Far and Near," May 10, 1961.
9. Letter, writer's name withheld, to W.M. Tugman, February 26, 1944, in Tugman correspondence.
10. Letter, Tugman to correspondent.
11. Letter, Tugman to correspondent, March 22, 1944.
12. Letter, Wayne L. Morse to W.M. Tugman, July 5, 1945.
13. Letter, Tugman to Morse, April 27, 1946.
14. Letter, Morse to Tugman, October 30, 1946.
15. Letter, Tugman to Morse, March 29, 1946.
16. Letter, Morse to Tugman, May 29, 1946.
17. Telegram, Morse to Tugman, February 26, 1947.
18. Telegram, Tugman to Morse, undated, 1947.
19. Letter, Tugman to Morse, November 30, 1947.
20. Letter, Tugman to Morse, February 7, 1948.
21. *Register-Guard*, "For U.S. Senator Wayne Morse," May 14, 1950 and October 22, 1950.
22. *Register-Guard*, "Our Remarkable Junior Senator," December 4, 1949.
23. William M. Tugman, letter to Milwaukie editor, July 16, 1947—name of addressee withheld.
24. *Register-Guard*, "In Answer to Criticism: Morse Points to Record," June 20, 1952, p. 1A.
25. *Ibid.*
26. *Register-Guard*, "Senator Morse Indulges in a 'Tantrum'," May 26, 1952, p. 8.
27. *Register-Guard*, "In Answer to Criticism:" *op. cit.*
28. Interview, February 24, 1967.
29. *Register-Guard*, "Doug McKay Best for Oregon, Nation," November 4, 1956, p. 12 A.
30. *Register-Guard*, "America Likes Eisenhower, But. . ." November 7, 1956, p. 6 A.
31. *Register-Guard*, "With These Friends, Who Needs Enemies," November 8, 1962, p. 10 A.
32. *Ibid.*

CHAPTER 21

Civil Liberties

George Lincoln Rockwell, of Arlington, Va., the American Nazi party fuehrer, appeared on the University of Oregon campus in the winter of 1967. In the same week's sequence of campus speakers was Timothy Leary, a discharged Harvard University professor, who took the affirmative side in a debate with a California psychiatrist on the use of LSD and other psychedelic drugs.

The two programs—one on right-wing political extremism, the other on the emotionally surcharged issue of the "beat set" and its practices—had built-in fuses to set off another liberty of speech furor. How can a university dare to permit youth to listen to such insidious lectures? Pressures welled up against the libertarian administration of the university.

In Eugene, so it appears at times, these things "always happen" when the State Legislature is in biennial session. A Clackamas County legislator from Milwaukie, the Rev. Leo M. Thornton, a minister, took a dim view of the doings in Eugene and said so. Perhaps there was need of better controls on student programming at the University of Oregon. Mr. Thornton introduced legislation. Governor Tom McCall, only a few weeks in office, doubted that any such legislation would stand up and he wanted none of it.

For a few days there was a news-story flurry, letters to the editor increased, as always in affairs like this, and the University Assembly Committee invited Mr. Thornton to come to Eugene and give his own speech, which he did. The matter soon subsided. The *Register-Guard* editorially advised Mr. Thornton to think the situation over. And in the news columns the paper ran in full the schedule of campus speakers—names, identifications, dates, and topics—from Vice President Hubert Humphrey's appearance in September, 1966, through the still forthcoming speeches running through May, 1967.

The story filled six columns. The speakers included "big names" like Humphrey and unknowns with esoteric knowledge of varied topics of interest to a scattered few. The balanced fare offered the student body was apparent at once.

Another hurdle in the civil liberties struggle had been taken, and the *Register-Guard* had done its bit. It was not reported at the time, and perhaps it was not known, that statistically George Lincoln Rockwell is the "least acceptable speaker" on all the campuses of the United States. Only 23 per cent of the colleges would permit him platform space.[1]

Eugene has had its brushes through the years with those who would stifle if not overtly suppress civil liberties. The *Register-Guard* however, has championed an open atmosphere and at any inkling that pressures against freedom are at work it has jumped into action with news and editorial support. Many libertarians have given Bill Tugman and Alton Baker the credit for this healthy state of Eugene thought, but the university, too, has led the fight, and so have many of the churches and other free-minded groups. And yet the fight has gone back before the *Register-Guard.* Its support of civil liberties was made easier because in the 1920s, as we have noted many chapters ahead, Charles Fisher of the *Guard* had the courage to take on the Ku Klux Klan.

Perhaps this oversimplifies. But it is true that Eugene, Oregon, when it comes to freedom of thought, is a town in which all conflicts of ideas can be heard and carried, step by step, to conclusion. This was shown from 1965 to 1967 in the long case of the Christian cross, in which by court order, the city was told to remove a privately owned 50-foot lighted cross from the top of Skinner Butte, a public park in downtown Eugene. Strong conservative emotions were aroused because a liberal minority had dared to test the right of a religious symbol to be placed on public property. Editorially, the *Register-Guard* took sides with the liberal minority.

The cases in which the *Register-Guard* has taken up the freedom fight are many, and some have been, on the surface, both minor and funny. Once the newspaper had to go to bat for the *Oregon Daily Emerald* when the Legislature investigated the *Facets* affair. This arose after the college paper's literary section (*Facets*) had run a student's prize essay about drinking practices in an off-beat expresso joint. The piece did have a strong draught.

On a more significant and more perilous level the *Register-Guard* has come to the aid of Jehovah's Witnesses, who boldly held a convention in Eugene in time of war. It backed the University of Oregon faculty in a teachers' oath fight that led dangerously close to oath legislation in the 1951 Legislature. It took Senator Joseph R. McCarthy sharply to task during the Communist scare of 1953 and 1954, winning for William M. Tugman some well deserved praise for the editor's supporting an inquiry into McCarthy's tactics by the American Society of Newspaper Editors. It despised Communist leader Gus Hall when he came to Eugene in 1962, but it defended the right of Eugene to hear him. Each of these conflicts deserves retelling.

More than 1,000 Jehovah's Witnesses, from Portland to Sacramento, converged on Eugene for a four-day coast meeting August 19-22, 1943. They had rented the 4-H building at the Lane County Fairgounds and had been given oral permission to meet "in accordance with the general custom of letting the building be used for all kinds of organizations." [2]

Nevertheless, with World War II going on, the coming of the pacifist Witnesses stirred rumbles of discontent in Eugene. The Witnesses had not applied in writing for a permit and, in fact, a convention without a formal request was illegal under civilian defense regulations. This request the Witnesses patently would not make, for "Jehovah's Witnesses worship and serve Almighty God . . . rather than man." [3] The situation was menacing, particularly since the Witnesses were planning to carry their message beyond the fairgrounds to Eugene streets and from house to house. They planned to use sound cars and phonographs to "demonstrate their belief in Jehovah by their works."

Eugene tempers were short. Police were alerted to prevent townspeople from interfering with the Witnesses. One downtown merchant punched a Witness who handed him a pamphlet. When the merchant was arrested and fined, local feelings became more tense.

The Eugene *Register-Guard* stepped in. On the opening day it splashed an eight-column page one overline: 'Protest Against Jehovah's Witnesses Draws Warning'; and a readout head: 'Officials Take Stand to Maintain Order.' The lead, in two-column measure, boldface, was the First Amendment to the U.S. Constitution. Then followed the news analysis and a statement by Judge Hurd:

> "According to the Supreme Court the Witnesses have a right to meet anywhere they want to and the right of free speech. People here should do nothing that would start a riot or trouble of any sort. This sect has a right to its own opinions, although townspeople may not agree with all of them."[4]

Sheriff Oral E. Crowe helped, too. One of his sons had been a prisoner since Bataan; another was permanently disabled in the war. Crowe said, "It should not be necessary to explain my feelings [but] my deputies . . . will see that order is preserved impartially."[5]

Strangely, even the Witnesses helped. One representative, Dan Campbell, said they would call off their sound truck and that he personally would announce to the convention that county and defense officials had asked Witnesses to refrain from distributing literature in the streets. Somehow it worked.[6]

The *Register-Guard* carried editorials, but it appears that the news treatment is what kept the situation under control. Civilian defense bent a rule on requiring the Witnesses to get a permit, while Judge Hurd said, in effect, "Go and meet." As far as the paper was concerned:

> "The convention is a test of our Americanism. It is our duty to LET THEM STRICTLY ALONE—no matter how irritating it may be, especially to those of us who have men in service, offering their lives for those precious freedoms which these zealots claim but refuse to help to defend. . . . If the Witnesses violate law in any respect, it is for the state and city police or the sheriff or the FBI to take them in hand."[7]

Fifteen years later Jehovah's Witnesses returned to Eugene, again for four days at the fairgrounds. This time the story gained on opening day a full column: "Sect Finds Answer in Bible Verses; Doctrine Sees End of World." As interesting as this was a side story: "Eugene Once Cool Toward Witnesses; Extra Police Kept Order."[8] No editorial was necessary in 1959.

Teachers' Oath

Senate Bill No. 323, submitted in the Forty-Sixth Oregon Legislative Assembly March 15, 1951, provided, in substance, that:

Any person desiring [a] contract with the governing body of any school district shall file with such body a signed written statement, indicating whether he is "a member or has been affiliated with the Communist Party, or any other organization that believes in, advocates, or teaches the overthrow of the United States Government, or the government of Oregon, by force or unlawful means." The employe was to specify also whether he had contributed time or money to the support of such organizations.

If the answer was "yes," then an additional statement "must contain a detailed explanation of his participation." This statement would be attached and become a part of the teacher's contract. Then: "Failure to state fully, completely and accurately any information required . . . is a misrepresentation sufficient to permit the school district governing body to terminate the teacher's contract without further liability. . . ."[9]

A Senate amendment April 26 relieved from a statement teachers who had been associated with "other organizations," and would apply only to Communist Party membership; a House amendment added the words, "no person *knowingly* shall be employed" and required also a statement of "complete disavowal and repudiation of such activities and beliefs." The House added the words that the teacher employed "contrary to these provisions shall *immediately* be discharged." [Italics added].

The bill, growing out of the McCarthy Communist scare, bore some prominent legislative names as sponsors: seven senators, including Lane County's Angus Gibson and Truman Chase; and four House members, including Mark Hatfield, Republican, in 1959 to become governor, and Robert Y. Thornton, Democrat, later to become attorney general.[10]

Fear permeated Oregon's teaching ranks, as it did in other states in which teachers' oath bills came up and, in some, were passed. Once again the *Register-Guard* acted, principally in three outspoken editorials on April 4, April 10, and May 1; less in news coverage, which dealt with the oath peril in undisplayed context as the issue came up for legislative hearings.

In its first editorial the paper called the bill "little better than an instrument of terrorism." Of Lane County's two supporters of the bill the *Register-Guard* said, "We cannot help wondering if they understand the implications of this measure." Every Oregon teacher, it felt, would be vulnerable to the "assaults . . . of crackpots and professional agitators who work under a cloak of patriotism." The *Guard* noted how a teachers' oath would lead to turmoil in the schools, invasion of personal and academic freedom, and be an affront to dignity. An oath was "absolutely unnecessary as a safeguard against subversives, because such persons can be weeded out without jeopardizing the liberty of the entire profession." Stressed also was the need for teachers who know about communism and Marxian philosophy to be free from fear in discussing such social movements so that "school children of today . . . grow up to face [these issues]."

The *Register-Guard* concluded:

> "This measure should NOT be passed. If it is passed we hope Governor McKay will have the courage to veto it. If it should be enacted, there should be a referendum, because we do not believe the free and intelligent people of Oregon would concur in any such 'fantastic' program as this. . . . This measure is an act of fear, unworthy of Americans who believe."[11]

On April 10 the *Guard* questioned the constitutionality of the bill, and it cited a decision by the Third California Court of Appeals at Sacramento finding a loyalty oath enacted by the Board of Regents of the University of California to be in violation of Article 3, Section 20 of the Constitution of California. The California court held that any test stronger than an affirmative declaration of loyalty could not stand. The *Register-Guard*, cheering the California decision, said, "[California] strikes at what Thomas Jefferson pledged himself to fight upon every occasion—'tyranny over the minds of men.'"[12]

The fight against the Oregon oath was carried on more by parliamentary maneuvering and pressure behind the scenes by opponents of Bill 323 than by any aggressive help from teachers themselves. On May 1, the *Register-Guard* chastised the teachers for not making any "strenuous effort" in their own behalf against the bill. They seemed to be relying on revisions that held the bill's application only to Communists. The *Guard* still objected, for: "Does ownership of a copy of Karl Marx or purchase of a copy of the Daily Worker constitute 'membership, affiliation, contribution, subscription, or advocacy'? Don't think these suppositions are absurd." The *Guard* cited the case of a Eugene merchant who found his name on a list of "known Communists" because he subscribed to the "darn thing" [*Daily Worker*] after he became curious. He was a " 'known Commie' in the report of the dumb bunnies who did the sleuthing but lacked gumption to ask anybody on Willamette Street."

The *Guard* called the bill a vicious measure and adjured the teachers not to be inhibited. It hoped the House would hold open hearings, and it repeated that McKay should veto the bill if it passed.[13]

Meanwhile, the Legislature had been in session 113 days, rush-toward-adjournment business was piling up, members were becoming weary, and—insofar as the oath bill was concerned—the libertarians were operating behind the scenes. Tugman of the *Register-Guard* was busy. So was Charles A. Sprague of the *Oregon Statesman.* So was Professor Charles G. Howard of the University of Oregon Law School. So were others of influence—enough influence to "call up some debts" due from members of the Legislature. In a general maneuver to close out various matters, a legislator sympathetic to opponents of Bill 323 moved on May 3 to return it to the House Committee. Before the sponsors realized what had happened the pigeon-holeing motion had been passed and the oath threat was ended. There was considerable supra-journalistic action in all of this, but, as Tugman would often confess, when great stakes were involved, one didn't just sit back and hope for the best.

On page one, May 4, the *Register-Guard* ran a banner, "Oregon Solons Close Record Session." The Legislature had run 116 days, 19 longer than the previous high of 1949. It had passed 1,215 bills, 153 more than the earlier record. The oath bill was not among them. In the jump portion of the summary of legislative business, under "Education" the news report said: "A bill to make teachers sign statements if they have ever been Communists died in the House on the last day" [May 3].[14]

A historian's candid appraisal would have to classify the handling of the oath crisis as "managed news." Nevertheless, great stakes in the battle for freedom were involved.

Professor Howard on May 7 personally wrote a letter of thanks to the *Register-Guard* for its editorials on Senate Bill 323. Howard added also a word of appreciation of the *Guard's* handling of the "MacArthur Row." (The *Register-Guard* had strongly supported Harry Truman in the President's removal of

General Douglas MacArthur from his Korean command in April after the general had disagreed with Truman and civilian direction of the Korean War.)[15]

A week after adjournment, George N. Belknap, secretary of the University of Oregon faculty, wrote:

> "By unanimous vote of the University of Oregon faculty, at its meeting on Wednesday, May 9, I was instructed to express to you [Tugman] the faculty's gratitude for your vigorous editorial opposition to Senate Bill No. 323 and for your personal assistance in the fight to prevent its enactment." (cc/ Harry K. Newburn, president of the university.)

Tugman replied to Belknap that he was grateful for the faculty motion, "but Charley Sprague, of Salem, did more than anyone else to stop Senate Bill 323 in the closing hours." The *Guard* editor added that the editorial about teacher timidity [Oregon Education Association] and their "being more concerned with appropriations than with principles may have been rash, but I hope that teachers will cease to be timid when these issues arise."[16]

Gus Hall: "Rattlesnake in the Front Yard"?

Some of the *Register-Guard's* older readers, those who remember the vociferous Tugman editorials and appreciated them, sometimes say that the larger, institutionalized *Guard* of the 1960s is less inclined to take stands on issues. Under Alton Baker, Jr., Robert B. Frazier, and Albert H. Currey, it is less volatile than under Tugman, true, and it doesn't use the English language for a weapon, as Tugman did. It still follows the old libertarian principles. Let a conflict be tightly drawn and the *Register-Guard* comes out strong. Mostly the style has changed, and some of Tugman's admirers tend to confuse style with substance.

Take the Gus Hall affair, that of the Communist Party secretary of the United States who invited himself to a number of university campuses early in 1962. Hall was promptly turned down by colleges in Washington and by Oregon State University in Corvallis. Reed College in Portland permitted him to speak, but Reed was small and ultraliberal and to the conservatives "tainted" anyway. Interestingly, the Oregon College of Education in Monmouth let Hall speak, but OCE was to be protected because of the greater uproar over permission given to the Communist to speak at the University of Oregon. President Arthur S. Flemming, still in his first year as head of the university, defended the students' right to hear Hall, the date set being February 12, 1962. Governor Mark Hatfield, when asked about Hall's appearance, said he personally was against use of educational facilities for the spread of Communist propaganda, but that each state school determined its own speaking program. He would not interfere. And Flemming allowed permission to Hall to stand.

The uproar over Hall's coming was, once again, what could be expected. The *Register-Guard's* "Mailbag" received the usual increase in letters. One letter, written by a Springfield resident before Hall arrived, was typical:

> "So we allow a rattlesnake to play in our front yard in order to acquaint our children with snake bite. . . . These Reds hope to whip into fanatical frenzy a few dedicated followers. . . . All they care about is 5 per cent who have devoured their propaganda. I am for shutting their mouths and keeping them on the run, clear out of our country." [17]

Another letter, printed the day Hall spoke, said:

> "Oregon's proud tradition of permitting speakers of all kinds to appear and be heard is outdated. Times have changed. Communism must be defeated." [18]

The tradition wasn't outdated for the *Register-Guard.* From the start of the argument it supported Arthur Flemming and, five days before Hall's speech, it asked, "Who decides what the lecture program at the university will be—the university itself or outside pleaders?" It found no cause for alarm "lest this Communist somehow corrupt American youth, a group which over the years has proved itself both tough and resilient." To point out Hall's futility the *Guard* continued:

> "The tattered lackey of the Kremlin has managed to squirm and twist through all the gyrations of the official 'party line.' His performance as a political organizer has been laughable. If he was unable over the years to form a workable political organization among the ignorant, then how in heaven's name can we fear that he can sweep a rooomful of well-read, sophisticated university students along with him? . . . Now, with other, and lesser, universities turning this man down, the university has a chance to reaffirm its belief in the free exchange of ideas."[19]

In substance this editorial only said things differently from the way Tugman, deceased in 1961, would have put matters. He would have had a compulsive drive to classify the fearful who thought Gus Hall would win converts as "boobs," as, 11 years earlier, he had called the detractors of a Eugene merchant who was curious enough to read the *Daily Worker.*

Hall appeared, and he drew 8,000 to the university's Hayward Field, the football stadium—which could have held more. The day was a rainy one, and that might have cut attendance. As it was, the assignment to Hayward Field to accommodate the crowd wasn't necessary. Hall didn't draw enough to fill the indoor McArthur Court.

As the *Register-Guard* said, Hall would have accomplished less had there been less fanfare. It noted, for what must have been an "umpteenth" time in its recent history, that the "principle of free speech set forth in the very first amendment to our Constitution was threatened by those who opposed Hall's appearance."[20]

The next day the paper appraised the Hall visit, what Hall didn't clear up about communism: The whys of the "rape of Hungary" or the Berlin Wall, or of the resuming of the Soviet Russian atomic testing, or the ways in which he had been able to tread the party line amid all its changes. The *Guard* found good in the visit: that "America will go to some trouble in defense of a principle."[21] "It was a proud afternoon, an afternoon that was worthwhile because we learned that what really counts is not the depth of our hatred but the extent of our own critical faith."[22] The paper generously refrained from noting after that fact that other coast universities wouldn't stand up with Oregon.

Two months later Arthur Flemming received the fifth annual Meiklejohn Award of the American Association of University Professors for his outstanding contribution to academic freedom. The AAUP said, "In a *cause celebre* at the University of Oregon, Dr. Flemming stood firm on principle that students should be free to listen to any speaker they choose." The citation was made in Chicago April 24. The award carries the name of Alexander Meiklejohn, sturdy battler for civil liberties for 50 years, who once was president of Amherst College and whose work on *Free Speech and Its Relation to Self-Government* is a philosophical expression worthy of inclusion in journalistic literature.[23]

---

1. Edmund Griffith Williamson and John L. Cowan, *The American Student's Freedom of Expression: A Research Appraisal.* Minneapolis: University of Minnesota Press, 1966.
2. *Register-Gaurd*, quoting County Judge Clinton Hurd in news story, August 19, 1943.
3. *Register-Guard*, "Witnesses Issue Policy Statement," August 22, 1943, p. 4.
4. *Register-Guard*, August 20, 1943, p. 4.
5. *Ibid.*

6. *Register-Guard*, "Witnesses Meet in Second Day." August 21, 1943.
7. *Register-Guard*, "Eugene's Duty—To Uphold Law," August 20, 1943, p. 4.
8. *Register-Guard*, July 9, 1959, p. 1B.
9. *Senate Bill No. 323*, Forty-sixth Oregon Legislative Assembly, 1951. March 15, 1951; amended April 26, 1951; amended in House of Representatives by Committee on State and Federal Affairs after passage in Senate, 25-5, May 2, 1951; died in committee upon adjournment, May 4, 1951.
10. *Ibid.*
11. *Register-Guard*, "An Instrument of Terror," April 4, 1951, p. 10.
12. *Register-Guard*, "Teacher's Oath Unconstitutional," April 10, 1951, p. 10.
13. *Register-Guard*, "Teachers Should Voice Protest," May 1, 1951, p. 10.
14. *Register-Guard*, May 4, 1951, p. 2.
15. Letter, Charles G. Howard to William M. Tugman, Tugman files, University of Oregon, May 7, 1951.
16. Letters, George N. Belknap to W.M. Tugman and Tugman to Belknap, May 10 and May 14, 1951, Tugman correspondence.
17. *Register-Guard*, "Of Gus Hall," February 11, 1962.
18. *Register-Guard*, "Downhill with Gus," February 12, 1962.
19. *Register-Guard*, "Of Open Forums and Closed Minds," February 7, 1962.
20. *Register-Guard*, "In Review," February 12, 1962.
21. *Register-Guard*, "Not About Communism, About America," February 13, 1962.
22. *Ibid.*
23. Quoted matter from text of citation by Professor David Fellman, chairman of the AAUP Committee on Academic Freedom and Tenure.

CHAPTER 22

The Newspaper And Its Responsibilities

What are the responsibilities of a newspaper publisher and his executives in the matter of policy control? This question has been debated for years, never with answers conclusive and satisfactory to all, and it was one that came up after World War II when the Commission on Freedom of the Press was making its studies that resulted in five major books on all phases of communications media practices. One of the interviews conducted for presentation to the commission was with William M. Tugman, with Professor Ralph D. Casey, then director of the University of Minnesota School of Journalism, as interviewer. Professor Casey early in his career in the 1920s was on the faculty of the University of Oregon School of Journalism. Casey had close observation of the Eugene *Guard* in its first years under Alton Baker's control and has watched its course intently in the past 40 years.

One of the comments Professor Casey made to the commission after interviewing Tugman in 1946 was, "Tugman has complete control of editorial pages and the news columns subject to reasonable consultation with the publisher. 'There has never been a tough proposition where I have established a policy in which the publisher hasn't backed me up,' said Tugman. 'I believe, however, that the ultimate authority rests in the hands of the publisher.' "

Tugman told Casey that advertisers in many cases "raised hell" over news and editorial policies, to no avail. (We have referred to this in commenting on the approach during the Byers zoning fight by a Byers supporter to have an ad far separated from an anti-Byers editorial. Here even a request, as apart from a complaint, had no effect.) And in connection with news of major civic activities—schools, health, roads—Tugman said

City Edition

Eugene Register-Guard

LANE COUNTY'S HOME NEWSPAPER

Clouds, Rain Saturday

99th Year, No. 195 — Eugene, Oregon, Friday, May 6, 1966 — THIRTY-FOUR PAGES — Price 5 Cents

R-G Publisher Says in Missouri

Local Coverage Important Role For Newspapers

Spoke Thursday Night

Market Climbs After Dip

GM Announcement Sparks Recovery In Heavy Trading

Two Navy Planes Lost in North

Most Reported Unde…

Edwin M. Baker
General Manager

Alton F. Baker, Jr.
Editor and Publisher

Scientists Find Growth Hormone

Sukarno Labeled 'Virtual Dictator'

Billed Tonight

Eugene Logger Killed in Mishap

Crow High School Scholar Awarded Four-Year Grant

CAROL ANN DEY

INSIDE TODAY

Baseball

Writing new chapters

consultation on approach was among the managing editor, the city editor, and reporters.

Alton Baker, Sr., though he gave his full attention to the business operations of the *Register-Guard*, had himself professional editorial background in Cleveland, as his father, Elbert Baker, had had. He understood the views Tugman held. But, as Tugman told Professor Casey in 1946, a publisher who was not professionally an editor should employ one and "leave him as free as possible to make policy."[1]

This decision by Baker—to leave Tugman alone—enabled Tugman to succeed as an editor. As Tugman himself agreed, ultimate authority rested with Baker. That the publisher didn't use it is evidence of his confidence in his executive. The owner is under pressure, too, when a newspaper pursues a civic cause that at its start is unpopular and often loses, as we have seen. But without publisher backing the news and editorial division is rudderless—and few publishers can be on both business and editorial sides at once.

Alton Baker, Sr., and William M. Tugman both are deceased, but their relationship continues under Alton, Jr., and Tugman's successors: William L. Wasmann, managing editor, and Robert B. Frazier and A.H. Currey, associate editors. Alton, Jr., upon accepting in 1966 for the *Register-Guard* the University of Missouri award for service in journalism, said:

> "I'm sorry to say this, but I believe the most glaring weakness on too many papers is the abdication of editorial responsibility. The easy way is to sit back and not take sides—not ruffle feathers. There is no anonymity in the smaller community. It is hard to kick hell out of an acquaintance in the paper one day and then hobnob with him at a social function that evening. I know from experience. But then, no one ever told me that journalism was going to be easy.
>
> "I submit that if any publisher who is taking the easy way out would hire a good editorial writer and give him a

free hand to express himself, his newspaper would gain not only more respect and more readers, but would prosper in a business way as well."[2]

The *Register-Guard* story from 1927 on is filled with references to the press; its duties, its conflicts, perils to its liberties, pressures from outside forces (government and other), obligations to readers and need for adequate coverage, and competence of personnel. Since Tugman was managing editor and editor for 27 of these 40 years, the groundwork for editorial responsibility was laid under him. *Heavy* coverage of *all* phases of news, however, is really a development of the past 13 years, after Tugman had left and after the *Register-Guard* had become big enough and prosperous enough to take on such things as blanket coverage of sports and women's news, to add interpretative columnists, to expand the "Mailbag," and to go in for a staff-produced magazine (Emerald Empire). Until well after World War II the paper did not have an editorial page free of ads, let alone space for any commentary beyond eight columns. Seldom did it have an editorial cartoon other than what the syndicates offered. "Open" section pages for sports or women's news were rare. Today, county news gets its section, as does local news in a split-run edition.

Tugman carried alone a burden that is now shared by "two and a half editorial writers" and the managing editor. (Alton Baker, Jr., is the "one-half editorial writer" when necessary for relief, and on occasion the *Register-Guard* calls on its newsroom specialists to share the editorial-writing load.)

In fact, Tugman in the early 1950s did not seem to realize how big the *Register-Guard* had become, and even with his energy and power of concentration, he could no longer "do it all." This is possibly one of the reasons he decided to "retire" to a small paper in Reedsport.

But, to refer back to the *Guard* and its attitudes on press responsibility. We have noted the early insertion of the "newspaper is a citizen of its community" statement and the editorial outlining the *Register-Guard's* obligations after Baker had purchased the *Register.*[3] Even before the consolidation the *Guard* expressed itself strongly on issues of control. In May, 1929, a press association report referred to negotiations then pending for the purchase of Boston dailies and those in some other Eastern cities by Eastern newsprint and power interests. This was far away from Eugene, and the details were hardly news, but a "threat" was evident, and the *Guard* had words to say about the matter. (We can recall here how Elbert Baker was concerned about possible department store ownership of the *Register.*)[4]

Across the continent it was, but to the *Guard* "the control of newspapers by special interests never has been and never will be in the public interest. . . . The history of American journalism, while marked by brilliant exceptions, was not a gratifying sight. . . . By and large, they [newspaper publishers] existed on the subsidies of political factions. Advertising was begged as a favor rather than sold as a commodity of value worth every penny of the cost. It was the exceptional editor who did not toady to his railroad pass.[5] The real reason for the boldness of power interests in stepping into newspaper ownership is that the newspaper business has emerged into a position where it stands on its own feet. The only shortcut to domination of newspaper policies is outright ownership."[6]

The *Guard* rebuked press ownership by the non-press. It urged the development of a loyal reading public. It would have professional associations of the press, possibly meaning here ANPA and ASNE, "refuse to accept as equals those who submit to such ownership." It disregarded and pitied "the $25,000 a year high-powered up-to-date newspaper operator who is merely an office boy for his interests." The *Guard* laid the base of the trouble, not to any particular news or editorial policy, but to the unforgivable sins outside control causes newspapers to commit: "suppression, warping, and shading of news reports."[7]

The presidential election of 1936, with Franklin Roosevelt smothering Governor Alfred M. Landon of Kansas, 523 electoral votes to 8, found anti-press forces strong in their denunciations of newspapers for their broad denunciation of the New Deal. Roosevelt had received a "mandate," many said, and, figuratively, as a result of its defeat, "the press is just waiting for someone to carry it out of the ring."

But the *Register-Guard*, quoting Bruce Bliven, then editor of the liberal *New Republic*, said "the death of the press, like Mark Twain's, is greatly exaggerated." Tugman then, with an ironical twist that seemed to dispute his own extensive editorial page influence in Eugene, said that editorial columns are immaterial, that they had little to do with the campaign of 1936, that it was the news and the events reported that re-elected Roosevelt. If the news reporting of 1936 was fair and accurate then the press had done its job, even if the whole of it had editorially supported Landon. The *Guard* referred to world censorship statistics and continued:

> "What all this boils down to is that America is just about the only great country left in which you can sit down and read your paper without having someone peering over your shoulder and blocking out passages which he thinks would not be good for you."

Tugman regarded the news columns as sacred—they should give facts "so that you can make up your mind for yourself, which as an independent American you are more than likely to do anyhow."[8] Eugeneans did that, and as we have seen, the *Register-Guard* lost its crusades from time to time. Tugman in this editorial, however, was not giving enough credit to the paper's editorial influence over and beyond the news. The paper won—on issues at least—more often than it lost.

Pressure Groups

One of the *Register-Guard's* strongest news principles was resistance to pressure groups. A specific example nearly 30 years ago will illustrate this. One E.U. Lee, representing the "Better Eugene Association," with headquarters listed only as a Eugene bank and with membership somewhat vague, was upset because the *Register-Guard* had printed a minor news story that Lee thought reflected on his group's apparent negative attitude toward labor. He seemed to feel the story made the association out as an "agent of Wall Street." The inference is that the paper shouldn't have covered the meeting. The protest to the *Guard* is not available, but Tugman's answer is.

In a long letter to Lee, the managing editor outlined the *Register-Guard's* reaction to this particular publicity complaint. It wasn't desirous of running anything to hurt anyone and it understood the Better Eugene Association's natural reluctance to incur any publicity which might mean personal embarrassment. But the danger in the publicity to the group was far less real than that [if the meeting had not been reported], "the movement will be interpreted as some sort of secret, fascist, iniquitous undercover scheme."

Then the editor, who could be brutally blunt, let his complainant have it!

> "It is difficult for a newspaperman to make any layman understand what we mean by 'impartial news,' but I'll put it this way: That story about [the] meeting would never have been missed by most of our readers if it had been omitted, and I could have spared myself considerable time and effort by forgetting it. It didn't make us a penny richer to print it. But the cumulative effect of forgetting to print the news can be disastrous to the newspaper and its community. It destroys public confidence, without which there is nothing. . . . We do hope you will understand what makes us tick, so there won't be any misunderstanding." [9]

Eleven years later, in a letter to his friend Ralph Casey at Minnesota, Tugman also digressed about this subject: The *Guard,* he told Casey, had found it wise "never to straddle in dealing with pressure groups," and that "the only time the paper found itself in serious trouble occurred when it tried to be diplomatic." Tugman felt there was always difficulty in dealing with labor matters, and he referred back to instances in the 1930s in which, on one occasion, the Employees Council called the paper and the *Register-Guard* "was told what [it] would say henceforth." Tugman didn't argue, but he told the group:

> "They would have a statement in writing in the morning making it perfectly clear that Alton F. Baker and William M. Tugman . . . exercise . . . direction of news policy."

The editor referred in addition to an effort by a fight promoter who approached leading *Register-Guard* advertisers in an effort at "putting on the squeeze." Some of the largest advertisers told the promoter he was "crazy" to attempt such a thing. In another case, the editor had to tell a priest that the *Register-Guard* would defend the rights of Roman Catholics to their beliefs, but where the Church "appears in the field of temporal power it will be judged on the same footing as any other temporal government." This instance arose over the priest's objection to an editorial in 1948 opposing United States recognition of the Franco government of Spain. And that long ago—1949—Tugman referred to the rising discussions of race issues, and the *Register-Guard's* readiness to cover them, despite pressures.

Then the matter of quotations, people trying to push the paper into support of or opposition to someone who said something about a controversial matter:

> "One of the hardest things . . . is to make people understand that when we quote X and Y in controversy, it is no part of our job to vouch for the truth of either one. The truth, so far as we are concerned, is that X said this and Y said that. We cannot look into their souls, nor can we exercise a censorship beyond the rules of libel and decency."

In all these remarks to Professor Casey, Tugman said, "Use them as you see fit and if you want to use my name, you may do so, because at my age I have very few inhibitions." He was 55.[10]

When Professor Casey interviewed Tugman in 1946 for the Commission on Freedom of the Press the editor in seven pages of single-spaced copy went over numerous phases of newspaper problems: perils of government restrictions, cynicism toward the press both among "stupid publishers" and an unconcerned public, determination of newspaper content, self-regulation and codes of ethics, competence of personnel, and schools of journalism.

At the time, Tugman had no immediate fear of governmental restrictions, but he felt it unfortunate that publishers, editors and reporters were never able "as one group to maintain a *professional organization*" [ital. orig.]. He was neutral to negative about unionization of newspaper reporters, who would be under threat of union discipline in coverage of labor matters; but he likewise felt that publishers failed years ago to encourage sympathetic support of . . . an organization to improve hours and wages without union ties. "If reporters and other staff men are paid professionally and if their professional standing . . . is recognized by the publisher, fine," he said. "If publishers treat their men as so much 'paid help,' they will inevitably drive them into unions."[11]

As it happened, 20 years ago an American Newspaper Guild chapter was organized at the *Register-Guard*. But Alton Baker, Sr., who did not look happily on the development, nevertheless was a publisher who, agreeing that standards of professionalism should be maintained, was able to work successfully with the *Guard* chapter. No critical struggles between news staff and management have marred the paper's Guild relations.

The *Register-Guard* has always recognized the difficulty in a moderate-size city of getting balance among local, national, world and specialized news. It has followed in general, as the previous chapters of this book show, a policy that it is the editor's job "to educate his readers." Tugman was on record as being willing to give up comics for news, although the *Register-*

Guard has always had its complement of comic strips. Today, of course, the paper has news hole sufficient to give sports and women's news and big segments of service news a wide play, but, in concept, it is not an entertainment paper. Tugman felt personally that the power to make newspapers better balanced lay within the reading public itself. In his interview with Casey he referred on one occasion to the newspaper troubles in Cleveland after World War I, when the *Plain Dealer* was working toward more responsible coverage. "The public turned against serious and significant information," he said. "Readers wanted sex, murder, sensation. Unless you were willing to see your circulation go to hell in a basket, you had to give the public this type of news."[12] Tugman looked forward to the day "when there will be such a body of enlightened opinion that people will stop reading the Chicago *Tribune.*"

To the *Register-Guard*, the schools of journalism have always been a hope—a concept that for the paper goes back 55 years to Charles Fisher and Eric Allen's arrival in 1912.[13] The *Guard* accepts the schools' competence in vocational training, and then looks into a prospective employe's record in college in history, political science, and economics, plus pure science and mathematics. These are educational goals that better schools of journalism have set forth for years, yet which some "old guard" editors have continued to believe were neglected.

Tugman expressed a somewhat different approach to these ideals in February, 1955, after he had bought the *Port Umpqua Courier* in Reedsport and, at nearly 62, was starting out once more as a community editor. Just having left the *Register-Guard* after 27 years, he chose an ideal time, at the annual Oregon Press Conference of the School of Journalism, to review "The Thirty Years' War." His title was a reference to the European conflict of 1618-48, which Tugman, somewhat inaccurately, called "the most inconclusive struggle in history." He was wondering whether newspaper struggles, too, were inconclusive.

Yet, the editor's words reflected challenge—in 1955 it would be in Reedsport as in 1927 it had been in Eugene:

> "Our problem as editors and publishers does not stop with defending the people's *Right to Know;* nor is the obligation satisfied by giving them only what they *Want to Know;* it must include what they *Ought to Know.*"

Then he reflected back to recall the advice of a small-town Ohio publisher who knew the young Tugman in 1927 and had heard he was going to be Alton Baker's managing editor in Oregon. The old publisher had said:

> " 'Give 'em a good clean print job, so's they can read what's in your goddam sheet; in your news-colyums give 'em all sides of every question; and in your editorials you better say just what you damn well think and mean, because nobody loves a straddler and those who don't like what you said will buy the paper just to see what the sonofabitch is going to say next.' "

Tugman said in his 1955 speech that he had learned some things in his 30 years, but that was probably wishful thinking. He pointed to the merits of "deference" and "good timing," and of editors "keeping low"—being heard and not seen. And he warned of "overconfidence." These qualities were never part of the editor of the *Register-Guard.* On the county-manager issue the timing was wrong, the paper was too confident, it did not defer, and the editor did not keep low. Had he done all these things, Tugman would have violated the still greater precept which he always had to adhere to, "Be yourself." [14]

The McCarthy Affair

Eventually, the *Register-Guard's* reputation spread beyond Oregon, and journalistic organizations around the country began noticing this strong-minded Eugene newspaper. After

Tugman had been promoted to editor in 1950 and Alton Baker, Jr., became managing editor, Tugman was elected to membership in the prestigious American Society of Newspaper Editors, which only occasionally names representatives of papers as small as the *Guard.*[15]

New members of the ASNE, several hundred strong and including big names of the American press, don't usually gain any immediate recognition. Not so with Tugman, however. The question of press integrity of coverage of the 1952 presidential campaign and Joseph R. McCarthy's criticisms of some liberals in the Communists-in-government fight of the time were high-tension issues in 1952 and 1953. At the 1953 ASNE convention, Irving Dilliard, chief editorial writer for the powerful St. Louis *Post-Dispatch*, wanted the ASNE to give some attention to these press matters. Dilliard prepared this resolution for the 1953 ASNE meeting:

> "In view of the serious criticisms of aspects of the newspaper coverage of the 1952 presidential campaign, from within our profession as well as without, and further in view of the grave charges made against our profession by Senator Robert A. Taft of Ohio and Wayne Morse of Oregon,[16] be it resolved that this society request its incoming president to appoint a committee to study these criticisms and charges, this committee to report by the 1954 convention its conclusions and the facts upon which these conclusions, as a demonstration of the full belief of the American Society of Newspaper Editors in the people's right to know."[17]

Dilliard felt the society would not be eager for this bombshell, so he had a second to his motion, an editor from Ohio, primed to get the matter to the floor for debate. When he offered his resolution, however, the Ohio editor had no chance to respond; out popped a second from the floor, and Dilliard was "both surprised and pleased." The St. Louis editor had never met this supporter of his point of view. He was William M. Tugman of the Eugene *Register-Guard.*

However, the debate over coverage of the campaign, said Dilliard, really never had a chance. Before discussion could begin, Walter M. Harrison of Oklahoma City, former managing editor of the *Daily Oklahoman* and once president of ASNE, moved to table. The tabling passed "after a chorus of seconds." Harrison's reasons were that at the time of offering resolutions only 150 of 400 editors were still at the convention—not a fair cross-section to express a view. Further, as Dilliard quoted Harrison, "the charge of press bias is ancient history that has been made for years." In effect, why go over it again?[18]

Dilliard later challenged "this arbitrary procedure," asserting, "The people's right to know will not be denied, not even by the ASNE."[19]

Dilliard's action failed in the convention, but later news developments did bring forth an ASNE committee, on which Tugman served, but for different reasons. On April 24 and May 5, 1953, Joseph R. McCarthy's subcommittee on Investigations and Government Operations (the McCarthy Committee) had James A. Wechsler, editor of the New York *Post*, under fire in a closed-door hearing, without news coverage. Wechsler was questioned about his long-past Communist membership and sympathies—to 1934 and 1937—even though he had broken with the Communists in 1940. He was grilled on books he had written, books used in the government's overseas information program. Wechsler regarded the questioning as actually dealing with his policies as an editor, since in the *Post* he had strongly criticized McCarthy's investigations and had criticized the FBI.

To call a newspaper editor by telephone, tell him to appear before a Senate committee "under penalty of failure to comply" (Wechsler appeared "voluntarily," it was said), brings up grave questions of threats against newspapers.

This sequence of events did result in an ASNE committee being appointed to look into the McCarthy matter. Wechsler, after his appearance, appealed to the society, on the ground that McCarthy was trying to intimidate him and the press, generally. On the committee were: J. Russell Wiggins, managing editor of the Washington *Post*, as chairman; Herbert Brucker, editor of the Hartford *Courant;* Eugene Pulliam, managing editor of the Indianapolis *News;* William M. Tugman, the editor representing the smallest paper among 11; and seven others from metropolitan newspapers. Only the appointee from the Topeka *State Journal* represented a newspaper as small as the *Register-Guard.* (Note: Also—Paul Block, co-publisher, Toledo *Blade;* Raymond L. Crowley, managing editor, St. Louis *Post-Dispatch;* W.H. Fitzpatrick, associate editor, *Wall Street Journal;* George W. Healy, Jr., editor, New Orleans *Times-Picayune;* L.D. Hotchkiss, editor, Los Angeles *Times;* Joseph W. Lee, editorial director, Topeka *State Journal*, and James S. Pope, executive editor, Louisville *Courier-Journal*.)[20]

The ASNE committee worked for more than two months trying to decide whether McCarthy's calling of Wechsler in a closed-door session was a peril to liberty of the press. It came up with an indecisive answer. Seven of the 11 would not say definitely there was a threat. A minority of four said there was. Bill Tugman was among the four. The other three were Wiggins, Brucker, and Pulliam, the last named a political conservative who yet believed that newspapers should resist any efforts to push them around.

The majority of the ASNE reported that the society could not speak collectively, that each member was free to differ with other members, and that among the 11 there was disagreement as to the extent to which Wechsler was intimidated. At least one of the majority felt no damage to freedom of the press was done at all.

Not so for Wiggins, Tugman, Brucker and Pulliam. As Wiggins wrote in a minority report: The McCarthy Committee did impinge; he doubted Wechsler's sincerity in being anti-Communistic after 1940; the hearings should have been open and a record made public, as Wechsler requested; Wechsler was "under the necessity either to answer whatever inquiries were expounded or face prosecution for failure to do so."

The minority report to which Tugman subscribed went into detail in citing Supreme Court decisions relating to the First Amendment and limiting governmental power of investigation and "power to apply sanctions by way of censorship before publication or by way of punishment after publication. . . . Through the harassment of hearings, investigations, reports, and subpoena, government will hold a club over speech and over the press."[21]

The Washington *Post* on August 13 followed up the ASNE committee report with an editorial, "Intimidating the Press," which the *Register-Guard* republished August 19, the essence of which was, "Unless the newspapers recognize the threat to their own freedom, they can scarcely expect successfully to defend freedom for others."[22]

McCarthy, meanwhile, asked for an investigation of the Washington *Post's* Wiggins by the seven majority members of the ASNE committee and tried to make it appear that the seven approved his handling of the Wechsler affair. The Senator failed to understand that the 7-4 vote was only a division on "threat" to the press on the issue, not on the wisdom of McCarthy's interrogating Wechsler. This brought both a news story and a three-column editorial in the *Register-Guard.* Tugman was interviewed August 17 on McCarthy's demand for the probe of Wiggins:

> "I am proud to stand with Wiggins. McCarthy has distorted the facts of the situation, as might be expected, but the attack on Wiggins verifies our conclusions as to McCarthy's methods and purposes. Russ Wiggins needs no defense. I hate to dignify the antics of a demagogue."[23]

In its three-column editorial August 19 the *Register-Guard* went into full detail about the McCarthy-Wechsler battle and quoted copiously from the ASNE minority report. Specifically:

> "Can congressional authority to inquire into public problems be used as a pretext to summon any newspaperman from his work and browbeat him because of his news and editorial policies?"[24]

It wasn't William M. Tugman alone who said "No" to questions like the above. The *Guard* history offers many examples, from George Buys' futile battle against the Hayes elector in 1876 on through the years. And as Alton Baker, Jr., said in 1966: "I am strongly convinced that our 'Great Society,' if you will, needs an alert, a probing and a responsible press. In my state, we are blessed with a number of good newspapers and a journalistic tradition that has been alert to the public interest for many years."[25]

---

1. Ralph D. Casey, interview with William M. Tugman, managing editor, Eugene *Register-Guard*, for Committee on Freedom of the Press, summer, 1946.
2. Alton F. Baker, Jr., *The Newspaper as a Citizen*, address, University of Missouri, Columbia, Mo., May 5, 1966.
3. *Supra.*
4. *Supra.*
5. See pp. 80-88 on Ira Campbell.
6. *Guard*, "Controlled Newspapers," May 13, 1929, p. 4.
7. *Ibid.*
8. *Register-Guard*, "Greatly Exaggerated," January 16, 1937, p. 2.
9. Letter, W.M. Tugman to E.U. Lee, Tugman correspondence, March 2, 1938.
10. W.M. Tugman to Ralph D. Casey, University of Minn. School of Journalism, March 8, 1949.
11. Interview, W.M. Tugman.
12. Interview, *Ibid.*
13. *Supra.*
14. William M. Tugman, *The Thirty Years' War.* Address Oregon Press Conference, Eugene, February 18, 1955.
15. *Register-Guard*, "Editors' Group Admits Tugman," April 17, 1952. *Proceedings*, American Society of Newspaper Editors, 1952.
16. *Supra.*
17. Irving Dilliard, "The Press and the Bill of Rights," second Elijah Lovejoy Memorial Lecture, Colby College, Waterville, Me., November 5, 1953, in *Nieman Reports*, Vol. 8, (January, 1954), p. 13.
18. *Ibid.*

19. "Problems of Journalism," *Proceedings of the 1953 Convention American Society of Newspaper Editors*. Columbia University Press, 1953, pp. 184-185.

20. "The ASNE Report on the Wechsler Case," (text of report addressed to Basil Walters, Chicago *Daily News*, president of ASNE). *Nieman Reports*, Vol. 7, (October, 1953), p. 25.

21. *Ibid.*

22. *Register-Guard*, August 19, 1953.

23. *Register-Guard*, "Editor Protests Wiggins Probe; Intimidation Charge Voiced by Tugman," August 17, 1953, p. 6 A.

24. *Register-Guard*, "Senator McCarthy Wants His Critic Investigated," August 19, 1953, p. 8A.

25. Baker, *op. cit.*

APPENDIX A

REGISTER-GUARD 20-YEAR CLUB

1901
Horace Burnett
Vance Howe

1910
Cora L. Kreamer

1911
A.F. Bremer

1919
R.B. Hill

1923
Sam Bronaugh
J.E. Wells

1924
Marian Fischer
Jennie Garrett
Harry F. Garrett
Frank Hassad
Reuben Radabaugh

1925
Robert K. Bertsch
Edward V. Duke
Howard Hults

1927
Alton F. Baker, Sr.
Margaret Benston
William M. Tugman

1928
Mike Hughes

1929
Dick Cahoon
Lois Ruark

1930
R.M. Fischer

1931
H.T. Wiltshire

1934
Arne Strommer

1935
June Porterfield

1936
Irene McCants
Charlie Rolens

1937
Dave Bauer

1938
Dick Strite
Ralph Thomson

1939
S.A. McDonald

1942
John Courtney

1943
Ann Connell

1944
Floyd Blaser

1945
Tommy Christiana
Doris Christiana
Al Currey
Jerry Fugle
Jim Mallery

1946
Glen Hammaker
Carl Johnson
Dick Lane
W.W. Malkowski
Mel Phelps
Dan Sellard

1947
Alton F. Baker, Jr.
Keith Brunig
Betty Holeman
W.B. Johnston, Jr.
Grace Leavitt
Frank Peterson

1948
Edwin M. Baker
R.S. Courson
C.F. Dobes
Bob Frazier
O.E. Hawes
Lyle Swetland
Marvin Tims
Dan Wyant
Glenn Watson

1949
Ed Coursey
Dean Crocker
Fred Haase
G.K. Stiggins
Robert Shelley
H.A. Thoenig
Bill Wasmann

1950
Al Adams
Harry Eckel
Mary L. Holmer
William Morris
William Morrow
Joe Strub

1951
Pete Cornacchia
Phil Grenon
Elgin Johnson
Roy Moore
Joe Roberts
Frank Willer
Marlin Withrow
Robert Wiltshire

1952
Ray Bascue
Jess Gorham
Tom Jaques
H.F. Johnson
Ralph Klopp
Walter Moss
William Queener
Harland Wilhelm

1954
Mert Heaton
Ross Johnson
Marjorie Mulligan
J.R. Stults

1955
Yvonne Dugan
James Mulkay
Charles McDonald
Richard Sieverts
Jack Young

APPENDIX B

NEWSPAPERS OF EUGENE, OREGON . . . CHRONOLOGY
(In Order of Establishment)

1. PACIFIC JOURNAL— Founded June 17, 1858 (date uncertain); J.F. Wilson and Co., publishers; J.H. Rodgers, editor; expiration date uncertain (about six months).

2. PEOPLE'S PRESS— Founded January 1859 (date uncertain); B.J. Pengra, Republican political leader, engineer, and surveyor publisher; succeeded, 1860, by Joel Ware, bookseller, printer, and Republican political leader. Expiration date uncertain, some time in 1861; length of publication, about two and a half years.

3. DEMOCRATIC HERALD— Founded March 1859 (date uncertain); Alexander Blakely, Democratic political leader, publisher; succeeded by Alexander Noltner, Democratic political leader and printer. Suppressed, 1861, by military order, date uncertain; length of publication, about two years.

4. STATE REPUBLICAN— Founded January 1, 1862; Hilyard Shaw, Republican leader, landowner, and builder, publisher; James Newton Gale, printer; Harrison R. Kincaid, editor. Consolidated with *Oregon Argus*, Salem, May 1863. Length of publication, 14 to 15 months.

5. DEMOCRATIC REGISTER— Founded March 15, 1862; Alexander Noltner, Democratic political leader and printer, publisher; financial interest held by C.H. (Joaquin) Miller, lawyer, literary figure, and editor. Suppressed September 20, 1862, by military order. Length of publication, six months and five days.

6. EUGENE CITY REVIEW— Founded November 1, 1862; Alexander Noltner (see No. 5 above) publisher; C.H. (Joaquin) Miller (see No. 5 above), editor

to February 14, 1863; James O'Meara, editor after Miller. Transferred to Salem as *Weekly Democratic Review,* October 16, 1865. Length of publication, two years, 11-1/2 months.

7. HERALD OF REFORM— Founded January, 1863; the Rev. A.C. Edmunds, Universalist clergyman, publisher.

8. UNION CRUSADER— Founded about November 1, 1863; the Rev. A.C. Edmunds, publisher; Harrison R. Kincaid, contributor; sold on March 7, 1864 to Kincaid.

9. OREGON STATE JOURNAL— Founded March 12, 1864; Harrison R. Kincaid, writer and printer, later Republican political leader, publisher and editor; no changes in name or ownership. Liquidated May 29, 1909, after union disagreement and fire. Length of publication, 45 years 2-1/2 months.

10. EUGENE CITY NEWS— Founded March 10, 1866, date uncertain; John B. Alexander, Democratic political leader and printer, publisher; failed, June 9, 1866. Length of publication, three months.

11. EUGENE CITY GUARD— Founded October 24, 1867 (most likely date); John B. Alexander (see No. 10), publisher; sold to

J.W. Skaggs, Democratic political leader; date of sale uncertain, probably early October 1868; sold again, November 28, 1868, to

William Thompson and William Victor; co-publishers; Thompson, printer, Democratic political leader, and military colonel; Victor, printer (Cherokee Indian). Sold, December 25, 1869, to

George J. Buys and A. Eltzroth, co-publishers; Buys, Democratic political leader; Eltzroth, printer; Buys (1870) purchases Eltzroth's interest and publishes *Guard* alone.

Eugene *Daily Guard*—	False start on a daily, week of May 11-16, 1874; date of suspension of the daily uncertain. George J. Buys sold *City Guard*, May 12, 1877, to
	F.R. Alexander and W.H. Alexander, brothers, also sons of John B. Alexander (see above), co-publishers, Sold, November 2, 1878, to
	Ira L. Campbell and John R. Campbell, brothers, printers and businessmen and Democratic Party supporters.
Eugene *Daily Guard*—	Founded June 8, 1891, by Ira L. Campbell; weekly edition of *City Guard* name changed to Eugene *Weekly Guard*.
	Ira L. Campbell, deceased, October 15, 1904; John R. Campbell and brother Edward L. Campbell continue *Daily* and *Weekly Guard*. Subsequently,
Guard Printing Company—	corporation formed, April 30, 1906; incorporators, John R. Campbell, Edward L. Campbell, and Charles H. Fisher. Subsequently, March 2, 1907, Fisher becomes sole owner; Fisher: entrepreneur of small newspapers and small-city editor.
12. EUGENE DAILY NEWS—	Established under the title of the *EUGENE MORNING NEWS* in 1931; title later changed to *EUGENE DAILY NEWS* which continued until the suspension of publication on May 22, 1942.

BIBLIOGRAPHY

Adams, Roy W. *The Oregon Style.* Unpublished M.A. thesis. University of Oregon School of Journalism. 1958.

Allen, Eric W. "Oregon Journalism in 1887," *Oregon Historical Quarterly.* Vol. 38, (September, 1937), pp. 251-264.

Andrews, J. Cutler. *The North Reports the Civil War.* Pittsburgh: University of Pittsburgh Press, 1955. 813 p.

Ayer Directory of Publications. Philadelphia, Pa.: Ayer Press. Published annually under varying titles since 1869.

Bancroft, Hubert Howe. *The Works of Hubert Howe Bancroft.* San Francisco: The History Company, 1888. Vol. 30, 808 p.

"The Beginnings of Oregon Journalism: an Interview with Harrison R. Kincaid," *Oregon Exchanges.* Vol. 2, (April, 1919), p. 11.

Bluemle, Paul Edward. *The Effect of the Editorial Recommendations of William M. Tugman in the Eugene Guard and Register-Guard on Voting Results in Lane County, Oregon, in Primary and General Elections during the Years of 1928-1952.* Unpublished M.A. thesis. University of Oregon School of Journalism. 1953.

Carey, Charles Henry. *General History of Oregon.* Portland, Oregon: Binfords & Mort, Publishers. 1971.

Dictionary of American Biography, under the auspices of the American Council of Learned Societies. New York: C. Scribner's Sons, 1936. Vol. 18, 657 p.

"Don Mellett's Victory," *Editor & Publisher.* Vol. 59, (January 1, 1927), p. 30.

Eliot, William G., Jr. "Thomas Starr King in Oregon, 1862," *Oregon Historical Quarterly.* Vol. 32, (June, 1931), pp. 105-113.

Eugene City, Oregon *Council Records,* (Ordinance No. 64), 1889.

Eugene City and Lane County Directory. Portland, Oregon: R.L. Polk & Company, 1910, 1918.

Eugene City and Lane County Directory. Portland, Eugene and Albany, Oregon: W.G. Obenauer & Co., 1892.

Eugene, City of, *Council Records,* (Ordinance No. 65,) 1889.

"Eugene *Register* Building New Home," *Oregon Exchanges.* Vol. 9, (April, 1926), p. 1.

"Eugene *Register* Enters Evening Field," *Oregon Exchanges.* Vol. 13, (October, 1929), p. 16.

Gaston, Joseph, *Centennial History of Oregon, 1811-1912,* illustrated. Chicago: S.J. Clarke Publishing Co., 1912. Vol. 2, 1060 p.

Gilbert, James H. *The Crisis of 1932: The Zorn MacPherson Bill.* Unpublished, undated address to Eugene Knights of the Round Table, University of Oregon Special Collections.

Gregory, Winifred. *American Newspapers, 1821-1936, a Union List of Files,* under the auspices of the Biographical Society of America. New York: H.W. Wilson Company, 1937. 791 p.

Hamburger, Philip. "Notes for a Gazeteer, XLII—Eugene, Ore.," *New Yorker.* Vol. 39, (June 1, 1963), p. 95.

Harvey, Paul W. *Tacoma Headlines: An Account of Tacoma News and Newspapers from 1873-1962,* illustrated. Tacoma, Washington: The Tacoma News-Tribune, 1962. 134 p.

Hohenberg, John, ed. *The Pulitzer Prize Story,* illustrated. New York: Columbia University Press, 1959. 375 p.

Jenkins, Frank. "Covering the Morning Field," *Oregon Exchanges.* Vol. 1, (June, 1917) p. 3.

Kincaid, Harrison R. "Excerpts from the Unpublished Reminiscenses of H.R. Kincaid," *Oregon Historical Quarterly.* Vol. 17, (June, 1916), pp. 77-106.

"Pioneer Press Toast," *Lane County Historian.* Vol. 6, (September, 1961), pp. 57-60.

Sunshine and Shadow: The Autobiography of H.R. Kincaid. Microfilm, Oregon State Historical Society. Portland, Oregon 1917.

Lane County, Oregon. *In the Matter of the Estate of Ira L. Campbell, Deceased.* (Probate Record Number 1677), October 15, 1904.

Lee, Alfred McClung. *The Daily Newspaper in America.* New York: The Macmillan Company, 1937. 797 p.

Lochridge, Patricia. "A Town to Come Home To," *Woman's Home Companion.* Vol. 71, (November, 1944), p. 29.

Lockley, Fred. *Oregon's Yesterdays.* New York: Knickerbocker Press, 1928. 350 p.

Ludington, Flora Belle. *The Newspapers of Oregon 1846-1870.* Eugene, Oregon: Koke-Tiffany Co., 1925. 34 p.

McArthur, Lewis A. *Oregon Geographic Names,* 3rd ed. Portland, Oregon: Binfords & Mort, 1952.

McKechnie, F.W. "Leaders of the Oregon Press: Paul R. Kelty," *Oregon Exchanges.* Vol. 2, (December, 1918), p. 16.

Map of Eugene City, Lane County, Oregon. Eugene, Oregon: W.G. Obenauer Company, 1892.

MacPherson, Hector. *Oregon Taxpayer, a monthly review of Oregon problems.* Albany, Oregon: Vol. 1-3, No. 6; August, 1932-June, 1934.

Marberry, M. Marion. *Splendid Poseur: Joaquin Miller, American Poet.* New York: Crowell, 1953. 310 p.
Mecklin, John Moffatt. *The Ku Klux Klan: A Study of the American Mind.* New York: Harcourt, Brace and Company, 1924. 244 p.
Miller, Joaquin. *Overland in a Covered Wagon: An Autobiography*, edited by Sidney G. Firman. New York: D. Appleton & Company, 1930. 129 p.
Miner, Herve W. "Mellett's Successor Avenged Slain Editor," *Editor & Publisher.* Vol. 59, (January 1, 1927), p. 5
Moore, Lucia W., Nina W. McCornack, and Gladys W. McCready. *The Story of Eugene.* New York: Straford House, 1949. 271 p.
Moore W.A. *Thirty-six Years of Progress: A History of Eugene's Water and Utilities Development*, promotional brochure. Eugene, Oregon: Eugene Water and Electric Board, 1947.
"Morning Field Given Up," *Oregon Exchanges.* Vol. 13, (April, 1930), p. 38.

New Home for *Register,*" *Oregon Exchanges.* Vol. 6, (February, 1923), p. 14.
"Newhouse Pays $50 Million for Cleveland *Plain Dealer,*" *Editor & Publisher.* Vol. 100, (March 4, 1967), p. 11.

"Opportunities Everywhere," *Oregon Exchanges.* Vol. 3, (November, 1919), pp. 3-6.
Oregon Blue Book. Compiled and published by the Secretary of State, 1929, 1955.

Page, Miriam. "Letting in the Laity," *Oregon Exchanges.* Vol. 1, (March, 1918), p. 6
"Paul R. Kelty Dies at McMinnville," *Oregon Publisher.* Vol. 12, (March, 1944), p. 2.
Peterson, Martin Severin. *Joaquin Miller: Literary Frontiersman.* Stanford University, California: Stanford University Press, 1937. 198 p.
Problems of Journalism: Proceedings of the 1953 Convention, American Society of Newspaper Editors. Columbia University Press, 1952, 311 p.; 1953, 224 p.
Portrait and Biographical Record of the Willamette Valley, Oregon, illustrated. Chicago: Chapman Publishing Company, 1903. 1571 p.

Rowell, George P. *Centennial Newspaper Exhibition*, 1876. New York.
Rowell's American Newspaper Directory. New York: G.P. Rowell & Co. 1869-1908.

Scott, Harvey W. *History of the Oregon Country*, compiled by Leslie M. Scott. Cambridge, Massachusetts: Riverside Press, 1924. Vol. 1-6.
Shaw, Archer H. *The Plain Dealer: One Hundred Years in Cleveland.* New York: A.A. Knopf, 1942. 402 p.
Sheldon, Henry D. *History of the University of Oregon.* Portland, Oregon: Binfords & Mort, 1940. 288 p.

Smith, A. Robert, *The Tiger in the Senate: A Biography of Wayne Morse.* Garden City: Doubleday & Co., 1962. 453 p.

"State Institutions of Oregon, A Statement," *Bulletin of the AAUP.* Vol. 20, (May, 1934).

State of Oregon Voters' Pamphlet, General Election, Lane County, compiled by Howell Appling, Jr. November 6, 1962, 117 p.

"State Park is dedicated," *Oregon Publisher.* Vol. 32, (July, 1963), p. 16.

Thompson, William. *Reminiscences of a Pioneer.* San Francisco: 1912. 187 p.

Tout, O.B. *The Eugene Directory,* Eugene, Oregon: Press of W.O. Yoran, 1902. 134 p.

Tugman, William M. "By Their Own Bootstraps," *National Municipal Review.* Vol. 33, (September, 1944), pp. 386-390; Vol. 33, (October, 1944), pp. 458-461.

Turnbull, George S. *An Oregon Crusader.* Portland, Oregon: Binfords & Mort, 1955. 246 p.

—. *History of Oregon Newspapers.* Portland, Oregon: Binfords & Mort, 1939.

—. *Journalists in the Making: A History of the School of Journalism at the University of Oregon.* Eugene, Oregon: School of Journalism, University of Oregon, 1965. 162 p.

U.S. Bureau of the Census. *Eighth Census, 1860.* Washington: G.P.O., 1862

—. *Ninth Census, 1870.* Washington: G.P.O., 1872.

—. *Tenth Census, 1880. Washington:* G.P.O., 1883-1888.

—. *Eleventh Census, 1890.* Washington: G.P.O., 1892-1897.

—. *Fourteenth Census, 1920.* Washington: G.P.O., 1921-1923.

University of Oregon. *Catalogue, 1915-1916; Announcements, 1916-1917.* Salem.

"W.F. Gilstrap Leaves Eugene *Register,*" *Oregon Exchanges.* Vol. 1, (June, 1918), p. 8.

Wagner, Harr. *Joaquin Miller and His Other Self.* San Francisco: Harr Wagner Publishing Co., 1929. 312 p.

Walling, Albert G. *Illustrated History of Lane County, Oregon.* Portland, Oregon: Walling Printing and Lithographing House, 1884. 508 p.

Webb, Carl C. and George Turnbull. "The Name of William M. Tugman added to Honor Roll," *Oregon Historical Quarterly.* Vol. 45, (December, 1944), p. 337.

Whipple, Robert Blaine. *The Change and Development of Editorial Attitudes of Selected Oregon Daily Newspapers Toward Senator Wayne Morse.* Unpublished M.S. thesis. University of Oregon School of Journalism, 1959.

Who's Who in Oregon, 1929-30. Oregon City: Oregon City Enterprises, Vol. 1, 241 p.

Williamson, Edmund Griffith and John L. Cowan. *The American Student's Freedom of Expression; A Research Appraisal.* Minneapolis: University of Minnesota Press, 1966.

WARREN C. PRICE

Warren C. Price was born on July 7, 1908 in Milwaukee, Wisconsin.

Most of his adult life was spent in newsrooms and journalism school classrooms. He taught journalism courses at the University of Oregon from 1942 until the time of his death in 1967. During that 25 years he found time, mainly during summer vacations, to "keep his hand in" by working for papers in his beloved Milwaukee, Washington, D.C., Buffalo, Chicago, Des Moines, Oklahoma City and Eugene. For many years he put out the main news pages of the Sunday *Register-Guard.*

Price prided himself on his prodigious memory. He could recall entire sections of the World Almanac, recite pages of railway schedules or give anyone who cared to listen all the pertinent statistics of the Milwaukee Braves baseball games.

To many students he was an absolute tyrant in the classroom. Battle-tested veterans of two wars dreaded his final exams which at times stretched over two and sometimes three weeks.

Price was recognized as a national authority in the fields of journalism law and journalism history. In addition he was qualified as a mathematician and an American historian; two subjects he also taught at the university during the post-World War II years.

He was graduated from the University of Wisconsin with both a bachelor's and a master's degrees. The University of Minnesota granted him posthumously a doctor of philosophy degree for writing this history of the Eugene *Register-Guard.* He also is the author of *The Literature of Journalism*, a bibliography published in 1959. For this work he won two national journalism awards.